HEGEL'S LOGIC

HEGEL'S LOGIC

BEING PART ONE OF THE
ENCYCLOPAEDIA OF
THE PHILOSOPHICAL SCIENCES (1830)
TRANSLATED BY
WILLIAM WALLACE

WITH FOREWORD BY
J. N. FINDLAY, F.B.A.

OXFORD
AT THE CLARENDON PRESS
1975

Oxford University Press, Ely House, London W. 1

GLASGOW NEW YORK TORONTO MELBOURNE WELLINGTON
CAPE TOWN IBADAN NAIROBI DAR ES SALAAM LUSAKA ADDIS ABABA
DELHI BOMBAY CALCUTTA MADRAS KARACHI LAHORE DACCA
KUALA LUMPUR SINGAPORE HONG KONG TOKYO

Casebound ISBN 824502 5
Paperback ISBN 824512 2

First edition 1873
Second edition 1892
Third edition 1975

Printed in Great Britain
at the University Press, Oxford
by Vivian Ridler
Printer to the University

FOREWORD

THE present volume is a reprint, with one or two minor alterations, of the most masterly and influential of all English translations of Hegel: the *Logic of Hegel* translated from the *Encyclopaedia of the Philosophical Sciences* by William Wallace, Whyte's Professor of Moral Philosophy in the University of Oxford, first published close on a century ago. Wallace, like Edward Caird, came to Oxford from across the Border, and was able, owing to some strange affinity of the then Scotland with an earlier Germany, to enter into the finer shades of Hegel's thought, language, and historical milieu in a manner impossible to his southern-born contemporaries, who might adopt and display Hegelian show-pieces in their heavily written works on Logic, Metaphysics, and Epistemology, but who could never follow, in its odd, wavering integrity, the line of a dialectic that was often most tellingly true when it leapt with what seemed the greatest irresponsibility to view matters from some higher, different point of view. That Wallace's often loose paraphrase of the Hegelian text is at all points beyond improvement will not here be maintained: it is, however, a translation for which one may be devoutly thankful, as one cannot be for the first translations of Hegel's other major works. And while the *Zusätze* to the dense text which Leopold von Henning compiled from his own notes, and from the notes of his valued colleagues Hotho, Michelet, and Geyer—whose gaps he had at times the audacity to fill from his own personal memory of what Hegel had said—may fail to satisfy our new-found passions for documentation and doxography, we may be immeasurably glad that we have them too. Some passages from the *Zusätze* in Wallace's rendering have led whole generations of students to a better understanding of Hegel. That 'a progression to infinity is not the real infinite which consists in being at home with itself in its other', that 'the consummation of the infinite End consists merely in removing the illusion that makes it seem yet unaccomplished' and that 'the Absolute Idea may be compared to the old man who utters the same creed as the child, but for whom it is pregnant with the significance of a lifetime': these are almost scriptural statements, contributing as preciously to our thought and language as some of the passages in the King James Bible. The last of the three passages just cited has a peculiar significance for the present writer, since Wallace's *Logic* was among the first books on philosophy that he ever read, and will probably be among the last.

The importance of Wallace's work depends further on the importance of the *Encyclopaedia*, which Wallace was not wrong in describing as 'the only complete, matured, and authentic statement of Hegel's philosophical system'. First published in 1817, and with many of the points made by Hegel in lectures added by him to the 1827 edition, it represents the endlessly proliferating *fourmillement* of Hegel's thought, reduced at least to a modicum of translucency and settled repose. The *Phenomenology of Spirit* of 1807 was, as Wallace says, the flight of a young Pegasus on which only a kingly soul could soar to the empyrean of the Idea: it might have all the 'diamond purity' of Hegelianism, but only consummate skill and patience could hope to use it with advantage. And, as Hegel himself said in *Encyclopaedia* § 25, the *Phenomenology*, though intended to be the introductory first part of his system, which would show how immediate consciousness must necessarily progress to the philosophical point of view, was in fact forced to take account of numberless concrete 'formations of consciousness', Religion, Morality, Art, etc., which were really the subject-matter of other special branches of philosophy, and which included much that had gone on 'behind consciousness' and now required to be raised into consciousness. The *Phenomenology* accordingly had to drag in much that properly belonged in another context, and as such it had defects which led to its replacement in the *Encyclopaedia* (§§ 1–78) by what amounts to a new Introduction, including a *Vorbegriff* and a study of the three main attitudes of previous philosophical thought to objectivity. The *Phenomenology*, for all its brilliance, is therefore ceremoniously trundled away as an Introduction to the whole system, and when Hegel planned its republication in 1831, he penned the following Note, reproduced by his publisher after his death: 'Characteristic early work not to be revised—relevant to the period in which it was written—the abstract Absolute was dominant at the time of the *Preface*' (*Phenomenology*, Hoffmeister edition, p. 578). Its essential content, the development of Consciousness from a stage where it confronts an uninterpreted, objective presence in sense-certainty, to the stage at which it both recognizes and is recognized by countless other embodiments of the same shared rationality, is presented, freed from brilliant incrustations and additions, in §§ 413–39 of the *Encyclopaedia*.

The other great work that preceded the publication of the *Encyclopaedia*, the *Science of Logic*, first published in three parts in 1812, 1813, and 1816, and in a partially revised form after Hegel's death, can be said, despite its vastly greater richness of content and profounder coverage of certain transitions (e.g. the treatment of Natural Law in Book II, Section II, and also the full-length treatments of the Judgement and the Syllogism), to have been superseded by the *Logic* of the *Encyclopaedia*. Hegel, we know, based the lecture-courses he gave on Logic practically every summer in Berlin on the *Encyclopaedia-Compendium*, and it may be presumed that this treatment, greatly augmented as it was in 1827, reflects the pattern into which his thought on Logic had finally fallen, when he looked back on the unimaginable intricacies of the longer treatment in a more distant perspective. Certainly those who have worked through, and attempted to teach, the hardest sections of the longer work, e.g. Hegel's almost inconceivably obscure treatment of Measure in Book I, Section III, and of Show and Reflection in Book II, Section I, Chapter I, cannot help feeling that the line of Hegel's long argument comes out better in the shorter work, and that many of the intricacies of the longer work are merely an interesting but dispensable, and at times artificially stirred up, foam upon its basic waves. It is the view of the present writer that Hegel is better seen macroscopically than microscopically, even though the latter may be a necessary preliminary to the former: the broad drifts of the dialectic, fixed as to starting-point and goal, do not depend on the minuter eddies than can with some strain be seen in it. One has to let the headaches produced by a continuous Bacchantic riot subside into the calm of a more distant, critical vision if one is to profit fully from the majestic assault of Hegel's genius. The

Science of Logic must indeed be used to fill in the spare outlines of the *Encyclopaedia* treatment, but not a few of its windings can be mercifully blurred. The editorial *Zusätze* previously mentioned are also extremely valuable as filling in the *Encyclopaedia*'s spareness: however much they may require to be disentangled and reprocessed in the scholarly editions of the future, they at least bring us into touch with the *spoken* element which is quite essential in a philosophy like Hegel's, and they invariably illuminate and assist understanding, rather than confuse and complicate it.

We shall delay no more on scholarly minutiae. Wallace's *Bibliographical Notice* on the three editions and three Prefaces of the *Encyclopaedia* has not lost its value, and has the merit of stressing the connection of Hegel's Idea with the Idea of Plato and Aristotle in the second edition Preface, and the connection of Hegel's system with philosophical Christianity as brought out in the third edition Preface. The Notes and Illustrations are also valuable and at times amusing. What we must now try to illuminate are the points made in the *Einleitung* and *Vorbegriff* (§§ 1–25), really a new introduction to the System, the sections (§§ 26–78) dealing with the three historic attitudes of past thought to objectivity, the very important sections (§§ 79–83) dealing with three basic 'moments' of all logical thought, and finally the three systematic chapters on the Doctrine of Being, the Doctrine of Essence, and the Doctrine of the Notion, which are parallel to the systematic treatment of the *Science of Logic*.

In the first chapter of the *Encyclopaedia* Hegel tells us that the Divine Absolute, the goal of philosophy as of religion, can only be approached in philosophy through explicit thought: all other forms of experience, such as feeling, intuition, picture-thought, etc., are only implicitly cogitative, and can at best offer us metaphors of the Absolute as it appears to thought. The Absolute is then said in § 6 to be an existent Reason, which is not only present in our subjective self-consciousness, but is also actual in the world, though not always discernible on the surface. The nature of thinking subjectivity comes out with even more clarity in the second chapter of the *Encyclopaedia*. Here its characteristic achievement is seen as the liberation of the Universal from the singularity of the sensed instance and from the mutual externality of such instances and parts of instances. It is also seen as a liberation of the thinking person from his own singularity. The Ego, Hegel tells us, is the Universal in and for itself, and all Egos, *qua* Egos, are just what I am. The Ego, in fact, for Hegel (§ 20) has only a nuance of difference from the *activity* of universalization which is for Hegel the essential thing in thought: it is that activity conceived as a subject, itself universalized and given to itself, and not merely active in specific materials. The liberating activity of the Universal or the Ego is further said to be one that liberates the essential, intrinsic, or true nature of the object: it may profoundly change the *manner* in which things stand before us in sensation, intuition, or representation, but this change of manner is no subjective distortion as maintained in the Critical Philosophy: it is a bringing out of what the thing in itself truly is. (Wallace, we may note, has slightly veered towards Kantianism in translating the Hegelian sentence in § 22, *Es ist somit nur vermittelst einer Veränderung daß die wahre Natur des Gegenstandes zum Bewußtsein kommt*, by 'Thus, it appears, an alteration of the object must be interposed before its true nature can be discovered.' Wallace's words 'of the object' are wrongly placed: Hegel does not hold that the mind alters its object, but that by altering the manner in which that object is given to it, it penetrates to its true, its universal nature.) Hegel further holds that while thinking universality is undoubtedly self-determined and free, it is also free from any personal wantonness or arbitrariness: its freedom consists in thinking in a manner that all thinking individuals have in common, and in immersing itself in the thing (*Sache*) and its actual determinations. The universals that thought liberates are, moreover, to be found in unliberated, merely objective, sleeping form in Nature, associated with all sorts of irrelevances and externalities, and their rise to subjectivity consists merely in their liberation from such immersion, and their coming to be in and for themselves. It is not necessary for one to observe how much all these dicta hark back to Plato and Aristotle rather than to Kant and Fichte.

In §§ 26–83 Hegel then goes on to deal with three philosophical attitudes to objectivity, with the old, pre-critical, realistic Metaphysics in §§ 26–36, with Empiricism and the Critical Philosophy in §§ 37–60, and with the Intuitionism of certain of Hegel's contemporaries in §§ 61–78. By Hegel the old, pre-critical, realistic Metaphysics is seen as superior to the Critical Philosophy in that 'it took the laws of thought to be the fundamental laws and forms of things' and assumed that to think a thing was the means of finding its very self and nature (§ 28). It is, however, inferior to post-critical thought on the basic ground that it does not trouble to inquire into the sense of assertions made about objects of reason which cover all reality, e.g. God, the Cosmos, the Soul, and assumes that one can talk of them in precisely the same way as one talks of ordinary finite objects, borrowing one's conception of them from popular picture-thought, and imagining also that one can pit one antithetical statement about them against another just as one does in the case of ordinary finite things. But when one leaves the finite things of ordinary discourse, one also leaves the rules that govern discourse about such things. One has to frame new concepts of an embracing, non-antithetical kind, and not attempt to take over ill-formed popular concepts without modification. One has also to be prepared for the fact that it may not be possible to apply ordinary predicates to one's new objects, or that it may be equally suitable or unsuitable to affirm or deny such predicates of them. 'The metaphysic of understanding is dogmatic, because it maintains half-truths in their isolation, whereas the idealism of speculative philosophy carries out the principle of totality and can reach beyond the inadequate formularies of abstract thought. Thus idealism would say: The soul is neither finite only nor infinite only; it is really the one just as much as the other, and that way neither the one nor the other' (§ 32). Hegel is saying what has since been expressed by saying that in a new language-game expressions may be given new senses and rules of usage, and that one must not be surprised if expressions which functioned well in old language-games have no function in the new one. But whereas modern linguistic conservatism tends to think that far-reaching departures from ordinary usage are suspect, despite any general charter to 'say what we like', Hegel believes in a series of philosophical games that will perpetually revise and reconstruct older ones, and will follow a certain deep logic in doing so, and so will in the end construct a new set of what may be called 'iridescent' concepts since they find a use for certain conjunctions and combinations of expressions which in a more ordinary use are thought to involve incompatibility or contradiction. Hegel in fact tries to show that there is a well-formed terminal style of discourse built with difficulty on all the patterns of discourse that precede it, and leaving them with a certain restricted validity, which seems from their point of view to involve self-contradiction, though it alone in fact, of all forms of discourse, completely avoids it. Curiously enough in the remarkable *Zusatz* to § 32, Hegel anticipates even the ring of certain pronouncements of modern linguistic philosophy: where Wittgenstein makes it the task of the linguistic philosopher to cure the bewitchment of the understanding through the instruments of our speech (*Philosophical Investigations*, § 109), Hegel says that 'the battle of reason is the struggle to break up the rigidity to which the understanding has reduced everything', the understanding being the form of thought which continues to apply rigid rules and categories, which apply well in ordinary finite contexts, to the new, fluid, iridescent contexts and objects of Reason. That there is such a sphere of truly transcendental discourse, superseding yet gathering together all the forms of discourse that lead up to it, is of course the crowning thought of Hegel, which the chapter on the pre-critical Metaphysics first brings into the open.

In the next chapter Hegel is at first concerned with Empiricism, which has for him the great merit of recognizing that the Universals or Notions which make the world intelligible are necessarily encountered in and through their experienced instantiation in that world. 'Whatever is true must be in the actual world and present to sense-perception' (§ 38). Its deficiency lies, however, in failing to recognize that the Universality we encounter in sense-perception has features which go far beyond what is given in the encounters in question, and are sometimes so categorial that no set of such encounters can ever adequately body them forth. In the Critical Philosophy of Kant this presence of universal, connective, transcendental features is fully realized, and is rightly connected with the thinking 'I' which can put nothing before itself except as embodying such connective universality (§ 42): Kant's error lies, however, in psychologizing and subjectivizing this subordination of the specific and instantial to such universal, connective unity, so that the latter is not thought of as revealing what things in themselves truly are, but only how they *appear* to the subject. The Thing-in-itself which Kant holds to be unknowable is really the most completely knowable of abstractions: it is what we get when we deliberately leave out all empirical content and every vestige of categorial structure. Hegel may therefore be said to have laid bare the crypto-empiricism which haunts the thought of Kant: while recognizing the non-empirical elements which structure experience and knowledge, he is yet forced to deny them reality or validity, since his secret test of these still lies in imagined sense-encounter with particulars. Hegel shows that such secretly empirical prepossessions vitiate Kant's criticism of the Transcendental Ideas: the Soul, the Cosmos, and God. Instead of seeing it as a defect of our merely empirical acquaintance with ourselves that we do not thereby rise to a full awareness of the structuring properties of thinking subjectivity, Kant rather sees it as a defect of that fuller awareness that it does not present us with a particular soul-thing on a level with the particulars of sense (§ 47). And instead of seeing the cosmological antinomies as proofs of the inherent oppositions involved in finite, cosmic actuality, Kant is forced, out of misplaced tenderness for a reality in or behind the cosmos, to see in such antinomies only the distortions of our perceiving and construing intelligence (§ 48). And instead, lastly, of regarding it as a defect of finite sensible objects like a hundred thalers that in their case real existence, vouched for by sense, falls apart from their pure notion or concept, he rather sees it as a defect of an ultimate Reason-object like God, that in His case Being and Notion cannot be held to fall apart as in the finite, empirical case (§ 51).

Hegel further points out, very interestingly, that the so-called proofs of the Divine Existence are not what they are ordinarily thought to be: purely affirmative reasonings in which what we start from furnishes a fixed, solid basis from which we pass on to something which has the same solidity as its premisses. The action of thought is to *negate* the basis from which it starts, to show it up as not being self-subsistent, and so to have in it a springboard from which it can ascend to what is truly self-subsistent and self-explanatory.

> It is [Hegel says] because they do not, with sufficient prominence, express the negative features implied in the exaltation of the mind from the world to God, that the metaphysical proofs of the being of a God are defective interpretations and descriptions of the process . . . That upward spring of the mind signifies that the being which the world has is only a semblance, no real being, no absolute truth; it signifies that, beyond and above that appearance, truth abides in God, so that true being is another name for God . . . Unless the being of the world is nullified, the *point d'appui* for the exaltation is lost. (§ 50, Wallace, pp. 81 f.)

In this passage Hegel not only explains the argument for a self-explanatory, absolute being, he also explains the whole nature of the dialectic. Nowhere does it merely elicit what some firm basis entails: everywhere does it rather overturn its basis as involving incompleteness or conflict, and then progresses by a leap to something more harmonious and complete. Those who expect all thought-advance to be that of the deduction of conclusions from firmly established premisses are quite incapable of dialectical thinking: in dialectic it is the insufficiency of the premisses that leads to the more sufficient conclusion.

Of Kant's other *Critiques* Hegel gives a briefer criticism. Kant's treatment of Practical Reason as a thinking will, laying down objective laws of freedom which determine what shall happen, and legislating for the world as well as for the subject, is highly praised: it is seen as highly superior to a Eudaemonism which merely aims at satisfying the private appetites, wants, and wishes of particular men. Its defect lies, however, in its empty formalism, its failure to see that it is only as organizing such appetites, wants, and wishes, that it can acquire content and concreteness (§ 54). The *Critique of Judgement*, on the other hand, is held to have risen to the speculative height of the Idea, whether in its notion of a beauty in which thought and sensuous conception have grown into one, or in its postulation of a harmony between natural necessity and free purpose (§ 55). Kant is, however, unable to conceive of this harmony as anything more than what *we* demand, or what merely *ought* to be: he is unable to rise to the notion of a harmony which, in being always in process of being achieved and recognized as such, is also in principle actual beyond every limit. Kant's whole procedure is brilliantly characterized as one of 'unifying at one moment what a moment before had been explained to be independent and therefore incapable of unification. And then, at the very moment after unification has been alleged to be the truth, we suddenly come upon the doctrine that the two elements, which, in their true status of unification, have been refused all independent subsistence, are only true and actual in their state of separation' (Wallace, p. 91). Kant, in short, is in a permanent philosophical muddle, and never knows where he has got to nor where he is going.

The third attitude of thought to objectivity (§§ 61–78) is the immediate or intuitive attitude, the spokesman of which is for Hegel Jacobi, though we should probably put Bergson, with his intuitive understanding of duration, or G. E. Moore, with his unshakeable Commonsense Knowledge, in such a position. Hegel is not disposed to reject the view that we may have an intuitive certainty of many all-important things: of our own existence as thinking beings, of the existence of something ideally perfect which perhaps comes up unsought in our thought, of the existence of external objects which make an impression on our senses, and of various ethical and other principles. What he does dispute is that such intuitive immediacy is an infallible mark of objective validity and truth, and that, where an intuitive conviction is valid, it does not also admit of a mediating justification, which, even if it does not amount to a syllogistic deduction, will at least put our conviction in a whole context of other facts and convictions, so that it becomes mediated on every side and not merely self-attested. Hegel believes in the end in a self-mediation which differentiates itself into a large number of mutually mediating insights, and also 'that it lies in the very nature of thought and subjectivity to be inseparable from being and objectivity' (Wallace, p. 99), and this comprehensive self-mediation in a sense justifies all the immediacies that can be chosen as starting-points within it. Hegel's view of an implicit rationality even in immediacies which seem at odds with reason comes out in his subsequent treatment of mysticism (Wallace, p. 121). Mysticism may seem to be, even to itself, an attitude that quarrels with comprehension and consistency, and which is wholly mysterious and ineffable: it reveals itself, however, on closer examination, as a deeply rational attitude which feels the impossibility of maintaining the hard and fast oppositions and distinctions appropriate to ordinary finite objects in the face of certain ultimate objects of Reason.

Hegel is then led on (§§ 79–82) to the very pregnant distinctions between three logical 'moments', which can, in an inadequate perspective, be held apart, but which in their actual being interpenetrate one another in every notion and every true assertion, as well as in the being of all the things in the world. The first of these moments is *das Verständige*, that of the Understanding, whose *métier* it is to separate off what each thing is, in and by itself, from whatever it is only in connection and collaboration with other things, and whose separate nature, thus cut adrift, becomes free from the change and development which variable contexts bring about. It is Hegel's view that this separative action of the Understanding is necessary both for efficient thought and action, in which he is at one with all analysts and all organizers, things in the world having a distinct self-identity which it would be wrong to ignore or blur. But with this recognition of distinctness and separateness goes the belief that it is something that we have to pretend to and strive after, rather than actually achieve, and that it is in fact logically impossible of achievement. It is here that the Logic of Hegel really takes issue with the Common Logic, and that not by violating the rules and forms of that Logic, but by applying them differently. For to Hegel the notion of a content that can with success be held quite apart from other contents which oppose or complete it, is not anything that can be conceived or even symbolized: there is, in fact, a logical flux, a passing of contents tracelessly into one another, which is even more ineluctable and ultimate than the sensible flux from which it is easy to retreat by an effort of abstraction. This logical passage makes it impossible to achieve the clearness, distinctness, and fixity which the Understanding desiderates, except for a limited purpose and in a limited range or span. Plato, the great predecessor of Hegel, passionately fought this logical flux in his earlier dialogues, but in such more mature dialogues as the *Cratylus* and the *Parmenides* he is arguably not far from admitting it. In a given exercise we both can and should preserve comparative clarity, distinctness, and fixity, but the thought-material we are coercing never fully acquiesces in our fixations, and forces endless revision upon us no matter how we seek to withstand this.

There is, therefore, a second necessary 'moment' in logical thought, always emerging out of the fixing, separative acts of the Understanding, a moment which breaks down and destroys the fixities and separations thus produced, and which, after restoring fluidity, makes the emergence of new fixities and distinctions possible. This second moment in thought is called by Hegel Dialectic Proper: it is not unlike the linguistic 'cramps' mentioned by Wittgenstein in the *Blue Book* which make us wish to depart from the conventions of ordinary speech in various philosophically interesting directions. To the Understanding Dialectic readily appears as a wholly destructive, self-contradictory force, but it is rather to be regarded as a force evoked by the inherent absurdity and self-contradiction of the sort of fixity and separateness which the Understanding strives for. And so far is it from being anything genuinely self-nullifying, and so non-existent, that the perpetual flux of being in the world is no more than an instantial manifestation of the essential logical flux. The world changes, not as the early Plato thought, because it participates in ever differing but unchanging Eide, but because the Eide in which it participates are themselves arranged in a developing series, in which each gets taken up and passes away into its logical successor.

It is not, however, possible to fix and separate the flux of Dialectic Proper, any more than anything else, and it is in fact always being taken up into the third moment of logical thought which Hegel calls Reason. This Reason has some of the reasonableness of ordinary speech, which shuns an utter exactness which it knows it cannot reach, and which is not afraid to hesitate and to refuse to say either Yea or Nay in certain obviously borderline situations. That reasonableness has, however, some of the connotation of the lazy, whereas the Hegelian Reason is one that, with the clearest consciousness of what it is doing, sees things in a round of what there is an inclination to call incompatible lights, but in what for a sufficiently experienced and nimble mind are perfectly reconcilable. Such reasonable concepts have the stability of the Understanding, without unleashing the Dialectic which too great an exactness and exclusiveness would at once arouse. They involve, as noted before, something like the experienced iridescence where slight shifts of vision reveal startlingly new colours, or something like the experienced combination of incompatible viewpoints which occurs in stereoscopic or stroboscopic vision. All our conscious references to things out there, to other people, to what has been or what will be or what ought to be, involve what, from the strict standpoint of the Understanding, is a definite contradiction, and which none the less proves a living, incontestable fact: it is not, therefore, an indefensible strategy, nor one different from what most of us practise, to see in the ardent rigidities of the Understanding the true source of contradiction and absurdity, while the iridescent, multi-dimensional poises of Reason are the correct form of the harmonious and true. This at least is what Hegel prescribes in the four remarkable paragraphs we have mentioned: it is arguable that there is no philosopher of any stature who is not great just because he has swallowed, and in some difficult manner digested, and induced others also to swallow and digest, what is, from the standpoint of clear, one-sided thought, a plain and obvious contradiction.

From all these interesting preliminaries to the System, we now turn to the three dialectically ordered chapters of the Logic Proper: the Doctrine of Being, the Doctrine of Essence, and the Doctrine of the Notion or *Begriff*. On these intricately structured chapters we cannot give a running commentary: we can at best state certain general viewpoints from which they may be studied. The Doctrines of Being and Essence form what Hegel calls the Objective Logic: in them what is ideal and universal has not yet separated itself off from the phenomenal surface of the Existent, nor made the latter merely an outflow of itself. When this last happens, we have the Subjective Logic, or Logic of the Notion, which is not, we may note, subjective in an ordinary sense. The Doctrine of Being is said by Hegel (§ 83) to represent the Notion in its immediacy, the Notion as yet implicit or undeveloped. We may ourselves say that it deals with the merely *Descriptive Categories* of Thought and Being, the Categories in which the mere *being* of things comes to light, and is stereotyped into quality and quantity and suchlike attributions, without ever delving beneath the surface or seeking to explain anything. The Doctrine of

Essence is said by Hegel to study the Notion in its Reflection and Mediation, in its Being-for-self, and its Show. We ourselves may say that it deals with the *Explanatory Categories*, those that postulate a deeper level of the permanently essential beneath the surface layer of mere fact: this is the field in which fixed natures or dispositions, relations of mutual influence or necessitation, subordination to unchanging laws, and rigorous distinctions of natural type, play a pivotal part. The Doctrine of the Notion is said by Hegel to be the Notion in its return to self, and in its developed abiding by self: the Notion in and for itself. We ourselves may say that it deals with the *Self-mediated* or *Self-explanatory Categories*, those that, in explaining themselves, and not requiring external justification, also explain everything. They are the absolutist Categories in which traditional Metaphysics has believed, but with which merely descriptive or relativistic types of thought have thought that they could dispense. The Doctrine of the Notion both preserves and sets aside the difficult dualisms and oppositions that have been developed in the Doctrine of Essence, returning to something remotely like the surface-harmony of the Categories of Being. The sense of these somewhat enigmatic characterizations will become plainer in the survey that follows.

The Doctrine of Being begins with the much too famous triad of Being, Nothing, and Becoming, which does no more than attest the indistinguishable emptiness of categories which are without the internal differentiation of mutually contrasted definites or finites. Hegel's philosophy is a philosophy of the definite, the finite, almost from the start: it can attach no meaning to notions in which all fades out in an Oriental blur. The Understanding therefore enters the stage with *Dasein*, finite determinate being, the being of a something which essentially lives in an indefinitely extensible context of other somethings, each having its own peculiarity, its quality, but only sustaining that peculiarity, that quality, in virtue of the contrasting somethings surrounding it. Hegel makes plain that the enumerative thought which does no more than distinguish this from that is not aware of the thoroughgoing relativity which haunts its proceedings: *we*, the logicians, see the inseparability of the this from the that and their mutual relativity, but such relativity will only become *explicit* when we go on to the reflective Categories of Essence. At present we live in a stage of thought where each limited existent seems to have an absolute independence: many philosophers, who hold the world to be simply the aggregate of all that there is, have never advanced beyond this simple position. Hegel, however, makes plain the wholly absurd character of mere qualitative distinctness: we try to grasp its peculiar distinctiveness, but it wholly eludes us. All we can say and communicate regarding each finite, qualified thing is that it is wholly unique and peculiar, and this character it shares with every other finite, qualified thing. Qualities, as Plato pointed out in the *Theaetetus* and elsewhere, are essentially vanishing, private, incommunicable products: if we are to lay hold of anything with our minds and communicate it to minds in general, it can only be in terms of the pure universalities of number and measure. The distinction of the entities in the world therefore becomes a distinction without a difference: each entity has its own pure Being-for-self in which it is indistinguishable from every other entity. But this lack of true difference forces us on from discrete plurality to continuous quantity. We pass into a logical region where every whole fades indistinguishably into wider wholes or reveals other partial wholes within it. The 'Bad Infinites' of the indefinitely Great and the indefinitely Small loom on either side, for Hegel as for Plato, and seem to remove all meaning from number and quantity.

The reasonable result of this dialectic is, however, the emergence of a concept of Measure (*Maß*), in which *relative* magnitude or Ratio, the sort of magnitude that can stay constant despite indefinite alteration in absolute quantity, takes the place of absolute quantity, and which is now re-associated with a quality which is the outward sign of its presence. Hegel here puts forward a doctrine of infinite interest and great scientific relevance, which few of his interpreters have understood: that the contrast between what are commonly called Primary and Secondary Qualities has something necessary about it. Purely quantitative distinctions, even those expressed in fixed ratios, are quite without content unless documented by emergent differences of quality, while purely qualitative distinctions are likewise without meaningful content unless capable of being connected with a continuously varying scheme of quantities. The notion of those reactionaries, from Aristotle to Husserl, who fear to depart from the qualitative 'life-world', as well as the notion of those radical formalists, from Descartes to Einstein, who would like to reduce everything to quantity, are therefore alike rejected. And Hegel further teaches the doctrine of an interestingly necessary out-of-stepness between the qualitative and quantitative aspects of natural being. While the former necessarily proceeds by discrete leaps, the latter is necessarily quite continuous. This means that quantitative change can proceed for a long time without a change in quality, and then, when an appropriate 'node' is passed, a new quality will emerge to attest new underlying ratios, These doctrines are not interesting if treated as mere 'facts of life' as they have been by some Marxists: Hegel makes them interesting by arguing that they are necessarily true.

The logical transition from the Doctrine of Being to the Doctrine of Essence, though veiled in much obscure verbiage, amounts to no more than our complete inability to understand or believe in a mere set of unexplained surface facts, however much decked out in exact formulae of quality and quantity. Mere facts vanish in our hands: they are incapable of being remembered or predicted. The transition to Essence lies simply in our need to form concepts of permanent nature or disposition, or of inviolable law, which will add to the surface description of what momentarily is the deeper, invariant statement of what can be, or what would be, or what must be, or what must have been, whether absolutely or in given circumstances. These categories, whether called 'modal' or 'dynamic' or 'nomic' or 'explanatory', are what certain types of psychologistic or phenomenalistic or logico-mathematical thought try to dispense with altogether: Hegel, however, sees in them something necessary and logical. A world in which there are no clear permanences of nature, no repeating rubrics of class, no definitely limited generalities of behaviour, is not anything that can be thought of or that can be. 'The ordinary consciousness', it is said in the *Zusatz* to § 110, 'conceives things as being, and studies them in quality, quantity, and measure. These immediate characteristics however soon show themselves to be not fixed but transient, and Essence is the result of their dialectic.' To which the *Zusatz* to § 112 adds the following:

> The problem or aim of philosophy is often represented as the ascertainment of the essence of things: a phrase which only means that things instead of being left in their immediacy, must be shown to be mediated by, or based upon, something else . . . There is a permanent in things, and that permanent is in the first instance their essence . . . Still it should be remembered that the only means by which the Essence and the inner self can be verified is their appearance in outward reality.

The *Encyclopaedia* treatment of Essence spares us the quite agonizing obscurities of three types of reflection distinguished in the *Science of Logic*: it proceeds straight to the three basic Categories of Reflection, namely Identity, Difference, and Ground. These are connected by Hegel with much revised versions of the traditional Logical Laws of Identity, Contradiction, Excluded Middle, Identity of Indiscernibles, and Sufficient Ground. Everywhere in the world we must, according to Hegel, dig down to deep identities of Essence, spanning wide ranges of surface-difference, to which an instinct of reason must guide us. This deep identity is not the trivial identity which every arbitrarily distinguished item has with itself, but an identity of *principle* which can be discerned in quite widely disparate acts and thoughts and existences, as Hegel in the dialectic is constantly showing. But everywhere in the world we must likewise dig down to deep differences of Essence: what is the same generically must also be different specifically, and there is nothing even casually individual in which such essential difference is not also present. And such difference of Essence is always ready to be sharpened into incompatibility or opposition, without prejudice to its deeper identity. It is then characteristic of Hegel to find opposition swinging over into a common groundedness which also makes things reciprocally ground and consequent to one another: in the very exclusion of *A* by *B*, there is an entailment that *B*, and not only *A*, should be, and thereby an inclusion of *B* in *A*'s Essence. It is, to take a modern psychoanalytic example, in the most entrenched opposition of the two sexes that their groundedness in a common Man-Womanhood is most palpably evident, as well as the possibility that each of them should develop the traits of the other.

The universal groundedness of things in things has therefore to be dug down to everywhere, and this leads Hegel on to consider the many obscurities which surround the conception of the propertied Thing—in the more precise sense of 'Thing'—all of whose characteristic properties consist solely in the way in which what the Thing is at any moment gears in with what other Things are or might be. Reflections of this relativistic sort soon dissolve the world of self-existent Things into a network of manifestations, in which, however, the essential and permanent, in shifting from Things, has to transfer its force to the new notion of unchanging Laws. The relation of the changeable phenomenal world to the unchanging Law-world is then gone into somewhat inadequately—the *Science of Logic* is here very much better—and the two orders are more and more brought together in a single structure, in which woulds and coulds become part of what is, just as what is becomes merely a special case of what would or what could be. The dialectic then shifts to various forms of immanent and transient conditioning and causality: to a view of things as a single, self-developing Spinozistic Substance, to a view of things as successive phases each enjoying the unique prerogative of momentary actuality, and transmitting the heritage of their predecessors to their successors, and to the view, finally, of the world as consisting of a vast number of interacting Substances, each of which, in being acted upon by the other, may be said equally to act on the other to act upon itself, and so, by a circuit, to be covertly self-active or free.

This covert self-activity or freedom becomes overt self-activity and freedom with the next turn of the dialectic, which carries us over into the Doctrine of the Notion. The 'truth' of the pattern of mutual necessitation with which Essence terminates is said to be Freedom, in that free self-activity is what mutual necessitation dimly prefigures, and what must be rendered overt for the significant completion of the latter. Free self-activity will soon take the form of organic purpose or teleology, of which conscious thought is the culmination, and Hegel is in fact saying that the blind necessities of inorganic nature, and any other blind necessities, are only possible or intelligible as fitting with, or being capable of being used by, pervasive, organic purposes. And Hegel is not saying this because he *wants* the self-explanatory unity of teleology to dominate indefinitely extending, necessitarian explanation, but because he believes that the latter conception is inferior to the former from an explanatory, logical point of view. If unexplainable fact is impossible, and if the explanations of necessitarianism merely refer us back to further unexplained facts without end, then we obviously require a type of explanation that is in a benign manner circular, bent back upon itself, and this we have in the various teleological categories of the Notion.

The Doctrine of the *Begriff* or Notion starts by explaining the doctrine of concrete universality which was lightly sketched in the introductory chapters of the work. True Universality is as much in-the-world or objective as it is in-the-mind or subjective, it is essentially active and self-realizing rather than inert, and it includes in itself the full round of its mutually exclusive species, and lives and achieves full specification in its individual instances. It is, moreover, not this or that specific universal, but rather the generic principle of all universality, or Universality as Such. It is further not to be identified with any chance conception that men may form, but only with the good, the standard form of everything, by exemplying which each thing becomes truly or actually what it is. This last qualification of the Notion is brought out in the §§ 178–9, devoted to Judgements of the Notion, Judgements in which a thing, e.g. a particular man or a work of art, has a *value*-predicate attributed to it, is said to realize its Notion, to be actually or truly this or that. The Hegelian *Begriff* has therefore many of the properties of a Platonic or an Aristotelian *Eidos*, though brought to a clearer focus: it has little that connects it with a *Begriff* in the thought of Hegel's predecessors. Hegel's whole strategy is to see in his principle of active, concrete Universality, a principle that has no contrast, except in and for itself: it is only by an illusion that it can be opposed to an external realm of objective fact, or to an undigested experience on which it imposes order. It does not, however, lie behind the surface of existence as in the case of the categories of Essence, nor is it merely part of this surface, as in the case of the categories of Being, but remains as a permanent directive force, active and fulfilled in specification and instantiation.

This immanent Atlas first displays itself in a transformed version of the traditional judgement-forms and forms of syllogism. In these, operative in the copula 'is', it unites the individual with the species, the species with the genus, and the genus with the individual, in a round of forms that achieve greater 'truth' according as the distinct 'moments' are more profoundly and necessarily united, and not merely brought together in an external, matter-of-fact manner. That Socrates is great and good is more profoundly true, because expressing a coincidence of notion with instance, than that the wallpaper is green or that Caesar crossed the Rubicon, and a disjunctive syllogism that finally places an individual in a whole round of mutually exclusive species has more of the Notion in it than an extensional syllogism that places an individual in one class because he happens to fall in another class that happens to be ranged under the first. These ideas are more fully developed in the *Science of Logic* than the *Encyclopaedia*, and have been more profoundly studied and used by British thinkers like MacRan, Bradley, and Bosanquet than by anyone else.

The going forth of Universality into the specific and the individual can, however, be seen, by a shift of the dialectic, as an inherent reference of the individual instance to the species and genera present in it. The individual becomes a specimen, a concrete embodiment of organizing universality, and lives together with other similar specimens in a world organized by the same Universal. It is here, after a brief skirmish with Mechanism and Chemism, that Hegel puts forth Teleology as the supreme objective expression of the Notion. This Teleology is not that of external design, but of immanent, Aristotelian purpose, and it is not that of a design which borrows its content from outside, but rather design for the sake of design, which remains orientated towards itself in infinitely numerous finite projects that succeed one another: it is, further, not design which is merely relevant to a pre-existent situation, but which is covertly responsible for the pre-existences that it presupposes, and is in fact the secret *raison d'être* of all its means, projects, procedures, and situational backgrounds. To see the objective world as Ideal Pattern, for ever going through its organizing act in its own programme of self-fulfilment, is to achieve the vision of infinite teleology with which Hegel now presents us, thereby rising to the Idea (see § 212, plus *Zusatz*).

The immediate, purely objective expression of the Idea is Life, the actual act or process of living in which all organs and functions serve merely to secure their own integrated continuance, in which everything external is made to do service to organic self-maintenance, which moreover perpetuates itself in an endless series of individuals. The purpose of life is solely to go on living, in a variety of species and specimens, and, in so far as the inorganic environment has any purpose, that purpose is to serve as a stimulus or an instrument or an untoward provocation to more and more living. The maintenance of Life is therefore the Absolute Purpose which explains everything objective.

We see, however, something essentially incomplete, and forced into the bad infinity of perpetual repetition, in the materialized singularity of Life, and this makes our minds leap upwards to a more complete embodiment of immanent Teleology, the embodiment we know as Conscious Cognition, in which Universality enjoys the free life that it can only have in a mind or spirit which uses it for purposes of understanding and mastering the world. Such Conscious Cognition assumes the two forms of Theory and Practice: Theory, in which the Universal is for ever laying hold on what seem to be external, unorganized data, and coming to see them as wholly pervaded by itself, and Practice, which is only a superior form of thinking, which not only organizes on the plane of the Universal, but also creeps down into the last detail of the individual and transforms it utterly. Theory and Practice, however, both seem to exhibit the Bad Infinite: they press on to a goal of perfected understanding and achievement which they can never reach. But at this point, when all seems in jeopardy, the Absolute Idea makes a saving appearance. The line of development involved in infinite teleology, which is simply the line worked out in Hegel's whole dialectic up to this point, is its own goal. The 'Other' which seems to stand around us in Life, and before us in Theory and Practice, is simply the shadow cast by our own spiritual activity, whose whole function, as a shadow, is to retreat endlessly as that activity progresses. This progress is not, as in Fichte, something that *ought* to be completed: it ought not to be completed, because it is perfect as it is.

All unsatisfied endeavour ceases [we read in § 234] when we recognize that the final purpose of the world is accomplished no less than accomplishing itself. Generally speaking, this is the man's way of looking, while the young imagine that the world is utterly sunk in wickedness, and that the first thing needful is a thorough transformation. The religious mind on the contrary views the world as ruled by Divine Providence, and thereby correspondent with what it ought to be. But this harmony between the is and the ought to be is not torpid and rigidly stationary. Good, the final end of the world, has being only while it constantly produces itself. And the world of spirit and the world of nature continue to have this distinction, that the latter moves only in a recurring cycle, while the former also makes progress.

The outcome of the Logic of Hegel, its Absolute Idea, is thus simply the axiomatic convergence, which can also be viewed as a coincidence, of what is and what ought to be, but which is also the Categorical Imperative that this convergence or coincidence should be unendingly pursued, and the religious blessedness of realizing it to be eternally achieved. If these are not axioms or imperatives usually included in Logic, or even in Ethics or Metaphysics, it is perhaps the great merit of Hegel that he has made them pivotal and explanatory, and not left them peripheral and unexplained.

The present Foreword is no more than an attempt to create a sense of the general drift of Hegel's Logic and to show how it anticipates the whole concrete treatment of Nature and Spirit which follows upon it, and which cannot be understood without it. Logic is, for Hegel, the realm of shadows, of simple essentialities, stripped of all sensuous concretion (*Science of Logic*, Lasson, vol. i, p. 41), but it is equally the realm of truth as it is in and for itself and without veil, the presentation of God, as He was in his eternal essence before the creation of Nature and finite Spirit (ibid., p. 31). Those who are unwilling to see Hegel as an ontologist and First Philosopher, or as a theologian in the sense of Aristotle or Proclus, will never be able to make more than a partial use of his brilliant insights, or become liberated from the sheer arbitrariness and inconsequence of much of his detail, which must be carefully studied only to be put in place and set aside.

The Wallace translation of the *Encyclopaedia Logic*, with its inclusion of the precious remains of Hegel's oral discourse, has made the understanding of Hegel's ontology and theology possible to many Anglo-American philosophers in the past, and may now, it is hoped, continue to do so for some time.

J. N. FINDLAY

Boston University
January 1973

CONTENTS

THE SCIENCE OF LOGIC

NOTES AND ILLUSTRATIONS

BIBLIOGRAPHICAL NOTICE
ON THE THREE EDITIONS AND THREE PREFACES OF THE ENCYCLOPAEDIA

The Encyclopaedia of the Philosophical Sciences in Outline is the third in time of the four works which Hegel published. It was preceded by the *Phenomenology of Spirit*, in 1807, and the *Science of Logic* (in two volumes), in 1812–16, and was followed by the *Outlines of the Philosophy of Law* in 1820. The only other works which came directly from his hand are a few essays, addresses, and reviews. The earliest of these appeared in the *Critical Journal of Philosophy*, issued by his friend Schelling and himself, in 1802—when Hegel was one and thirty, which, as Bacon thought, 'is a great deal of sand in the hour-glass'; and the latest were his contributions to the *Jahrbücher für wissenschaftliche Kritik*, in the year of his death (1831).

This *Encyclopaedia* is the only complete, matured, and authentic statement of Hegel's philosophical system. But, as the title-page bears, it is only an outline; and its primary aim is to supply a manual for the guidance of his students. In its mode of exposition the free flight of speculation is subordinated to the needs of the professorial class-room. Pegasus is put in harness. Paragraphs concise in form and saturated with meaning postulate and presuppose the presiding spirit of the lecturer to fuse them into continuity and raise them to higher lucidity. Yet in two directions the works of Hegel furnish a supplement to the defects of the *Encyclopaedia*.

One of these aids to comprehension is the *Phenomenology of Spirit*, published in his thirty-seventh year. It may be going too far to say with David Strauss that it is the Alpha and Omega of Hegel, and his later writings only extracts from it.[1] Yet here the Pegasus of mind soars free through untrodden fields of air, and tastes the joys of first love and the pride of fresh discovery in the

[1] *Christian Märklin*, cap. 3.

quest for truth. The fire of young enthusiasm has not yet been forced to hide itself and smoulder away in apparent calm. The mood is Olympian—far above the turmoil and bitterness of lower earth, free from the bursts of temper which emerge later, when the thinker has to mingle in the fray and endure the shafts of controversy. But the *Phenomenology*, if not less than the *Encyclopaedia* it contains the diamond purity of Hegelianism, is a key which needs consummate patience and skill to use with advantage. If it commands a larger view, it demands a stronger wing of him who would join its voyage through the atmosphere of thought up to its purest empyrean. It may be the royal road to the Idea, but only a kingly soul can retrace its course.

The other commentary on the *Encyclopaedia* is supplied partly by Hegel's other published writings, and partly by the volumes (ix–xv in the Collected Works) in which his editors have given his Lectures on the Philosophy of History, on Aesthetic, on the Philosophy of Religion, and on the History of Philosophy. All of these lectures, as well as the *Philosophy of Law*, published by himself, deal however only with the third part of the philosophic system. That system (p. 23) includes (i) Logic, (ii) Philosophy of Nature, and (iii) Philosophy of Spirit. It is this third part—or rather it is the last two divisions therein (embracing the great general interests of humanity, such as law and morals, religion and art, as well as the development of philosophy itself) which form the topics of Hegel's most expanded teaching. It is in this region that he has most appealed to the liberal culture of the century, and influenced (directly or by reaction) the progress of that philosophical history and historical philosophy of which our own generation is reaping the fast-accumulating fruit. If one may foist such a category into systematic philosophy, we may say that the study of the 'Objective' and 'Absolute Spirit' is the most *interesting* part of Hegel.

Of the second part of the system there is less to be said. For nearly half a century the study of nature has passed almost completely out of the hands of the philosophers into the care of the specialists of science. There are signs indeed everywhere—and among others Helmholtz has lately reminded us—that the higher order of scientific students are ever and anon driven by the very logic of their subject into the precincts or the borders of philosophy. But the name of a Philosophy of Nature still recalls a time of hasty enthusiasms and over-grasping ambition of thought which, in its eagerness to understand the mystery of the universe, jumped to conclusions on insufficient grounds, trusted to bold but fantastic analogies, and lavished an unwise contempt on the plodding industry of the mere hodman of facts and experiments. Calmer retrospection will perhaps modify this verdict, and sift the various contributions (towards a philosophical unity of the sciences) which are now indiscriminately damned by the title of *Naturphilosophie*. For the present purpose it need only be said that, for the second part of the Hegelian system, we are restricted for explanations to the notes collected by the editors of vol. vii, pt. 1, of the Collected Works—notes derived from the annotations which Hegel himself supplied in the eight or more courses of lectures which he gave on the Philosophy of Nature between 1804 and 1830.

Quite other is the case with the Logic—the first division of the *Encyclopaedia*. There we have the collateral authority of the 'Science of Logic', the larger Logic which appeared while Hegel was schoolmaster at Nürnberg. The idea of a new Logic formed the natural sequel to the publication of the *Phenomenology* in 1807. In that year Hegel was glad to accept, as a stop-gap and pot-boiler, the post of editor of the Bamberg Journal. But his interests lay in other directions, and the circumstances of the time and country helped to determine their special form. 'In Bavaria', he says in a letter,[1] 'it looks as if organization were the current business.' A very mania of reform, says another, prevailed. Hegel's friend and fellow Swabian, Niethammer, held an important position in the Bavarian education office, and wished to employ the philosopher in the work of carrying out his plans of reorganizing the higher education of the Protestant subjects of the crown. He asked if Hegel would write a logic for school use, and if he cared to become rector of a grammar school. Hegel, who was already at work on his larger Logic, was only half-attracted by the suggestion. 'The traditional Logic', he replied,[2] 'is a subject on which there are text-books enough, but at the same time it is one which can by no means remain as it is: it is a thing nobody can

[1] Hegel's *Briefe*, i. 141. [2] Ibid. 172.

8245025

make anything of: 'tis dragged along like an old heirloom, only because a substitute—of which the want is universally felt—is not yet in existence. The whole of its rules, still current, might be written on two pages: every additional detail beyond these two is perfectly fruitless scholastic subtlety; or if this logic is to get a thicker body, its expansion must come from psychological paltrinesses.' Still less did he like the prospect of instructing in theology, as then rationalized. 'To write a logic and to be theological instructor is as bad as to be white-washer and chimney-sweep at once.' 'Shall he, who for many long years built his eyrie on the wild rock beside the eagle and learned to breathe the free air of the mountains, now learn to feed on the carcasses of dead thoughts or the still-born thoughts of the moderns, and vegetate in the leaden air of mere babble?'[1]

At Nürnberg he found the post of rector of the 'gymnasium' by no means a sinecure. The school had to be made amid much lack of funds and general bankruptcy of apparatus—all because of an 'all-powerful and unalterable destiny which is called the course of business'. One of his tasks was 'by graduated exercises' 'to introduce his pupils to speculative thought'—and that in the space of four hours weekly.[2] Of its practicability—and especially with himself as instrument—he had grave doubts. In theory, he held that an intelligent study of the ancient classics was the best introduction to philosophy; and practically he preferred starting his pupils with the principles of law, morality, and religion, and reserving the logic and higher philosophy for the highest class. Meanwhile he continued to work on his great Logic, the first volume of which appeared in two parts, 1812, 1813, and the second in 1816.

This is the work which is the real foundation of the Hegelian philosophy. Its aim is the systematic reorganization of the commonwealth of thought. It gives not a criticism, like Kant; not a principle, like Fichte; not a bird's-eye view of the fields of nature and history, like Schelling; it attempts the hard work of reconstructing, step by step, into totality the fragments of the organism of intelligence. It is scholasticism, if scholasticism means an absolute and all-embracing system; but it is a protest against the old school-system and those who tried to rehabilitate it through

[1] Hegel's *Briefe*, i. 138. [2] Ibid. 339.

their comprehensions of the Kantian theory. Apropos of the logic of his contemporary Fries (whom he did not love), published in 1811, he remarks: 'His paragraphs are mindless, quite shallow, bald, trivial; the explanatory notes are the dirty linen of the professorial chair, utterly slack and unconnected.'[1] Of himself he thus speaks:

> I am a schoolmaster who has to teach philosophy—who, possibly for that reason, believes that philosophy like geometry is teachable, and must no less than geometry have a regular structure. But again, a knowledge of the facts in geometry and philosophy is one thing, and the mathematical or philosophical talent which procreates and discovers is another: my province is to discover that scientific form, or to aid in the formation of it.[2]

So he writes to an old college friend; and in a letter to the rationalist theologian Paulus, in 1814,[3] he professes: 'You know that I have had too much to do not merely with ancient literature, but even with mathematics, latterly with the higher analysis, differential calculus, chemistry, to let myself be taken in by the humbug of Naturphilosophie, philosophizing without knowledge of fact and by mere force of imagination, and treating mere fancies, even imbecile fancies, as Ideas.'

In the autumn of 1816 Hegel became professor of philosophy at Heidelberg. In the following year appeared the first edition of his *Encyclopaedia*: two others appeared in his lifetime (in 1827 and 1830). The first edition is a thin octavo volume of pp. xvi+288, published (like the others) at Heidelberg. The Logic in it occupies pp. 1–126 (of which 12 pp. are Einleitung and 18 pp. Vorbegriff); the Philosophy of Nature, pp. 127–204; and the Philosophy of Mind (Spirit), pp. 205–88.

In the Preface the book is described (p. iv) as setting forth 'a new treatment of philosophy on a method which will, as I hope, yet be recognized as the only genuine method identical with the content'. Contrasting his own procedure with a mannerism of the day which used an assumed set of formulae to produce in the facts a show of symmetry even more arbitrary and mechanical than the arrangements imposed *ab extra* in the sciences, he goes on:

> This wilfulness we saw also take possession of the contents of philosophy and ride out on an intellectual knight-errantry—for a while

[1] Ibid. 328. [2] Ibid. 273. [3] Ibid. 373.

imposing on honest true-hearted workers, though elsewhere it was only counted grotesque, and grotesque even to the pitch of madness. But oftener and more properly its teachings—far from seeming imposing or mad—were found out to be familiar trivialities, and its form seen to be a mere trick of wit, easily acquired, methodical, and premeditated, with its quaint combinations and strained eccentricities—the mien of earnestness only covering self-deception and fraud upon the public. On the other side, again, we saw shallowness and unintelligence assume the character of a scepticism wise in its own eyes and of a criticism modest in its claims for reason, enhancing their vanity and conceit in proportion as their ideas grew more vacuous. For a space of time these two intellectual tendencies have befooled German earnestness, have tired out its profound craving for philosophy, and have been succeeded by an indifference and even a contempt for philosophic science, till at length a self-styled modesty has the audacity to let its voice be heard in controversies touching the deepest philosophical problems, and to deny philosophy its right to that cognition by reason, the form of which was what formerly was called *demonstration*.

The first of these phenomena may be in part explained as the youthful exuberance of the new age which has risen in the realm of science no less than in the world of politics. If this exuberance greeted with rapture the dawn of the intellectual renaissance, and without profounder labour at once set about enjoying the Idea and revelling for a while in the hopes and prospects which it offered, one can more readily forgive its excesses; because it is sound at heart, and the surface vapours which it had suffused around its solid worth must spontaneously clear off. But the other spectacle is more repulsive; because it betrays exhaustion and impotence, and tries to conceal them under a hectoring conceit which acts the censor over the philosophical intellects of all the centuries, mistaking them, but most of all mistaking itself.

So much the more gratifying is another spectacle yet to be noted; the interest in philosophy and the earnest love of higher knowledge which in the presence of both tendencies has kept itself single-hearted and without affectation. Occasionally this interest may have taken too much to the language of intuition and feeling; yet its appearance proves the existence of that inward and deeper-reaching impulse of reasonable intelligence which alone gives man his dignity—proves it above all, because that standpoint can only be gained as a *result* of philosophical consciousness; so that what it seems to disdain is at least admitted and recognized as a condition. To this interest in ascertaining the truth I dedicate this attempt to supply an introduction and a contribution towards its satisfaction.

The second edition appeared in 1827. Since the autumn of 1818 Hegel had been professor at Berlin: and the manuscript was sent thence (from August 1826 onwards) to Heidelberg, where Draub, his friend—himself a master in philosophical theology—attended to the revision of the proofs.

To the Introduction [writes Hegel[1]] I have given perhaps too great an amplitude: but it, above all, would have cost me time and trouble to bring within narrower compass. Tied down and distracted by lectures, and sometimes here in Berlin by other things too, I have—without a general survey—allowed myself so large a swing that the work has grown upon me, and there was a danger of its turning into a book. I have gone through it several times. The treatment of the attitudes [of thought] which I have distinguished in it was to meet an interest of the day. The rest I have sought to make more definite, and so far as may be clearer; but the main fault is not mended—to do which would require me to limit the detail more, and on the other hand make the whole more surveyable, so that the contents should better answer the title of an Encyclopaedia.

Again, in Dec. 1826 he writes:[2] 'In the Naturphilosophie I have made essential changes, but could not help here and there going too far into a detail which is hardly in keeping with the tone of the whole. The second half of the Geistesphilosophie I shall have to modify entirely.' In May 1827 Hegel offers his explanation of delay in the Preface, which, like the concluding paragraphs, touches largely on contemporary theology. By August of that year the book was finished, and Hegel off to Paris for a holiday.

In the second edition, which substantially fixed the form of the *Encyclopaedia*, the pages amount to xlii + 534—nearly twice as many as the first, which, however, as Professor Caird remarks, 'has a compactness, a brief energy and conclusiveness of expression, which he never surpassed'. The Logic now occupies pp. 1–214, Philosophy of Nature 215–354, and Philosophy of Spirit 355–534. The second part therefore has gained least; and in the third part the chief single expansions occur towards the close and deal with the relations of philosophy, art, and religion in the State; viz. § 563 (which in the third edition is transposed to § 552), and § 573 (where two pages are enlarged to 18). In the first part, or the Logic, the main increase and alteration falls within the introductory chapters, where 96 pages take the place of 30. The Vorbegriff (preliminary notion) of the first edition had contained the distinction of the three logical 'moments' (see p. 113), with a few remarks on the methods, first of metaphysic, and then (after a brief section

[1] Hegel's *Briefe*, ii. 204. [2] Ibid. 230.

on empiricism) of the 'Critical Philosophy through which philosophy has reached its close'. Instead of this the second edition deals at length, under this head, with the three 'attitudes (or positions) of thought to objectivity'; where, besides a more lengthy criticism of the Critical philosophy, there is a discussion of the doctrines of Jacobi and other Intuitivists.

The Preface, like much else in this second edition, is an assertion of the right and the duty of philosophy to treat independently of the things of God, and an emphatic declaration that the result of scientific investigation of the truth is, not the subversion of the faith, but 'the restoration of that sum of absolute doctrine which thought at first would have put behind and beneath itself—a restoration of it however in the most characteristic and the freest element of the mind'. Any opposition that may be raised against philosophy on religious grounds proceeds, according to Hegel, from a religion which has abandoned its true basis and entrenched itself in formulae and categories that pervert its real nature.

> Yet [he adds (p. vii)] especially where religious subjects are under discussion, philosophy is expressly set aside, as if in that way all mischief were banished and security against error and illusion attained . . . as if philosophy—the mischief thus kept at a distance—were anything but the investigation of Truth, but with a full sense of the nature and value of the intellectual links which give unity and form to all fact whatever. . . . Lessing [he continues (p. xvi)] said in his time that people treat Spinoza like a dead dog.[1] It cannot be said that in recent times Spinozism and speculative philosophy in general have been better treated.

The time was one of feverish unrest and unwholesome irritability. Ever since the so-called Carlsbad decrees of 1819 all the agencies of the higher literature and education had been subjected to an inquisitorial supervision which everywhere surmised political insubordination and religious heresy. A petty provincialism pervaded what was then still the small Residenz-Stadt Berlin; and the King, Frederick William III, cherished to the full that paternal conception of his position which has not been unusual in the royal house of Prussia. Champions of orthodoxy warned him that Hegelianism was un-Christian, if not even anti-Christian. Franz von Baader, the Bavarian religious philosopher (who had spent some

[1] Jacobi's *Werke*, iv. A, p. 63.

months at Berlin during the winter of 1823–4, studying the religious and philosophical teaching of the universities in connection with the revolutionary doctrines which he saw fermenting throughout Europe), addressed the king in a communication which described the prevalent Protestant theology as infidel in its very source, and as tending directly to annihilate the foundations of the faith. Hegel himself had to remind the censor of heresy that 'all speculative philosophy on religion may be carried to atheism: all depends on who carries it; the peculiar piety of our times and the malevolence of demagogues will not let us want carriers'.[1] His own theology was suspected both by the Rationalists and by the Evangelicals. He writes to his wife (in 1827) that he had looked at the university buildings in Louvain and Liège with the feeling that they might one day afford him a resting-place 'when the parsons in Berlin make the Kupfergraben completely intolerable for him'.[2] 'The Roman Curia', he adds, 'would be a more honourable opponent than the miserable cabals of a miserable boiling of parsons in Berlin.' Hence the tone in which the Preface proceeds (p. xviii).

Religion is the kind and mode of consciousness in which the Truth appeals to all men, to men of every degree of education; but the scientific ascertainment of the Truth is a special kind of this consciousness, involving a labour which not all but only a few undertake. The substance of the two is the same; but as Homer says of some stars that they have two names—the one in the language of the gods, the other in the language of ephemeral men—so for that substance there are two languages—the one of feeling, of pictorial thought, and of the limited intellect that makes its home in finite categories and inadequate abstractions, the other the language of the concrete notion. If we propose then to talk of and to criticize philosophy from the religious point of view, there is more requisite than to possess a familiarity with the language of the ephemeral consciousness. The foundation of scientific cognition is the substantiality at its core, the indwelling idea with its stirring intellectual life; just as the essentials of religion are a heart fully disciplined, a mind awake to self-collectedness, a wrought and refined substantiality. In modern times religion has more and more contracted the intelligent expansion of its contents and withdrawn into the intensiveness of piety, or even of feeling—a feeling which betrays its own scantiness and emptiness. So long however as it still has a creed, a doctrine, a system of dogma, it has what philosophy can occupy itself

[1] Hegel's *Briefe*, ii. 54. [2] Ibid. 276.

with and where it can find for itself a point of union with religion. This however is not to be taken in the wrong separatist sense (so dominant in our modern religiosity) representing the two as mutually exclusive, or as at bottom so capable of separation that their union is only imposed from without. Rather, even in what has gone before, it is implied that religion may well exist without philosophy, but philosophy not without religion—which it rather includes. True religion—intellectual and spiritual religion—must have body and substance, for spirit and intellect are above all consciousness, and consciousness implies an *objective* body and substance.

The contracted religiosity which narrows itself to a point in the heart must make that heart's softening and contrition the essential factor of its new birth; but it must at the same time recollect that it has to do with the heart of a spirit, that the spirit is the appointed authority over the heart, and that it can only have such authority so far as it is itself born again. This new birth of the spirit out of natural ignorance and natural error takes place through instruction and through that faith in objective truth and substance which is due to the witness of the spirit. This new birth of the spirit is besides *ipso facto* a new birth of the heart out of that vanity of the one-sided intellect (on which it sets so much) and its discoveries that finite is different from infinite, that philosophy must either be polytheism, or, in acuter minds, pantheism, etc. It is, in short, a new birth out of the wretched discoveries on the strength of which pious humility holds its head so high against philosophy and theological science. If religiosity persists in clinging to its unexpanded and therefore unintelligent intensity, then it can be sensible only of the contrast which divides this narrow and narrowing form from the intelligent expansion of doctrine as such, religious not less than philosophical.

After an appreciative quotation from Franz von Baader, and noting his reference to the theosophy of Böhme, as a work of the past from which the present generation might learn the speculative interpretation of Christian doctrines, he reverts to the position that the only mode in which thought will admit a reconciliation with religious doctrines is when these doctrines have learned to 'assume their worthiest phase—the phase of the notion, of necessity, which binds, and thus also makes free everything, fact no less than thought'. But it is not from Böhme or his kindred that we are likely to get the example of a philosophy equal to the highest theme—to the comprehension of divine things.

If old things are to be revived—an old phase, that is; for the burden of the theme is ever young—the phase of the Idea such as Plato and, still better, as Aristotle conceived it is far more deserving of being recalled—and for the further reason that the disclosure of it, by assimilating it into our system of ideas, is, *ipso facto*, not merely an interpretation of it, but a progress of the science itself. But to interpret such forms of the Idea by no means lies so much on the surface as to get hold of Gnostic and Cabbalistic phantasmagorias; and to develop Plato and Aristotle is by no means the sinecure that it is to note or to hint at echoes of the Idea in the medievalists.

The third edition of the *Encyclopaedia*, which appeared in 1830, consists of pp. lviii+600—a slight additional increase. The increase is in the Logic, eight pages; in the Philosophy of Nature, twenty-three pages; and in the Philosophy of Spirit, thirty-four pages. The concrete topics, in short, gain most.

The Preface begins by alluding to several criticisms of his philosophy—'which for the most part have shown little vocation for the business'—and to his discussion of them in the *Jahrbücher* of 1829 (*Vermischte Schriften*, ii. 149). There is also a paragraph devoted to the quarrel originated by the attack in Hengstenberg's Evangelical Journal on the rationalism of certain professors at Halle (notably Gesenius and Wegscheider)—an attack based on the evidence of students' note-books—and by the protest of students and professors against the insinuations.

It seemed a little while ago [says Hegel (p. xli)] as if there was an initiation, in a scientific spirit and on a wider range, of a more serious inquiry, from the region of theology and even of religiosity, touching God, divine things, and reason. But the very beginning of the movement checked these hopes; the issue turned on personalities, and neither the pretensions of the accusing pietists nor the pretensions of the free reason they accused, rose to the real subject, still less to a sense that the subject could only be discussed on philosophic soil. This personal attack, on the basis of very special externalities of religion, displayed the monstrous assumption of seeking to decide by arbitrary decree as to the Christianity of individuals, and to stamp them accordingly with the seal of temporal and eternal reprobation. Dante, in virtue of the enthusiasm of divine poesy, has dared to handle the keys of Peter, and to condemn by name to the perdition of hell many—already deceased however—of his contemporaries, even Popes and Emperors. A modern philosophy has been made the subject of the infamous charge that in it human individuals usurp the rank of God; but such a fictitious charge—reached by a false logic—pales before the actual assumption of behaving like judges of the world, prejudging the Christianity of individuals, and announcing their utter reprobation. The Shibboleth of this absolute authority is the name of the Lord Christ, and the assertion that the Lord dwells in the hearts of these judges.

But the assertion is ill supported by the fruits they exhibit—the monstrous insolence with which they reprobate and condemn.

But the evangelicals are not alone to blame for the bald and undeveloped nature of their religious life; the same want of free and living growth in religion characterizes their opponents.

By their formal, abstract, nerveless reasoning, the rationalists have emptied religion of all power and substance, no less than the pietists by the reduction of all faith to the Shibboleth of Lord! Lord! One is no whit better than the other: and when they meet in conflict there is no material on which they could come into contact, no common ground, and no possibility of carrying on an inquiry which would lead to knowledge and truth. "Liberal" theology on its side has not got beyond the formalism of appeals to liberty of conscience, liberty of thought, liberty of teaching, to reason itself and to science. Such liberty no doubt describes the *infinite right* of the spirit, and the second special condition of truth, supplementary to the first, faith. But the rationalists steer clear of the material point: they do not tell us the reasonable principles and laws involved in a free and genuine conscience, nor the import and teaching of free faith and free thought; they do not get beyond a bare negative formalism and the liberty to embody their liberty at their fancy and pleasure—whereby in the end it matters not how it is embodied. There is a further reason for their failure to reach a solid doctrine. The Christian community must be, and ought always to be, unified by the tie of a doctrinal idea, a confession of faith; but the generalities and abstractions of the stale, not living, waters of rationalism forbid the specificality of an inherently definite and fully developed body of Christian doctrine. Their opponents, again, proud of the name Lord! Lord! frankly and openly disdain carrying out the faith into the fullness of spirit, reality, and truth.

In ordinary moods of mind there is a long way from logic to religion. But almost every page of what Hegel has called Logic is witness to the belief in their ultimate identity. It was no new principle of later years for him. He had written in post-student days to his friend Schelling: 'Reason and freedom remain our watchword, and our point of union the invisible church.'[1] His parting token of faith with another youthful comrade, the poet Hölderlin, had been 'God's kingdom'.[2] But after 1827 this religious appropriation of philosophy becomes more apparent, and in 1829 Hegel seemed deliberately to accept the position of a Christian philosopher which Göschel had marked out for him.

[1] Hegel's *Briefe*, i. 13. [2] Hölderlin's *Leben* (Litzmann), p. 183.

A philosophy without heart and a faith without intellect [he remarks[1]] are abstractions from the true life of knowledge and faith. The man whom philosophy leaves cold, and the man whom real faith does not illuminate, may be assured that the fault lies in them, not in knowledge and faith. The former is still an alien to philosophy, the latter an alien to faith.

This is not the place—in a philological chapter—to discuss the issues involved in the announcement that the truth awaits us ready to hand[2] 'in all genuine consciousness, in all religions and philosophies'. Yet one remark may be offered against hasty interpretations of a 'speculative' identity. If there is a double edge to the proposition that the actual is the reasonable, there is no less caution necessary in approaching and studying from both sides the far-reaching import of that equation to which Joannes Scotus Erigena gave expression ten centuries ago: *Non alia est philosophia, i.e. sapientiae studium, et alia religio. Quid est aliud de philosophia tractare nisi verae religionis regulas exponere?*

[1] *Verm. Schr.* ii. 144.

[2] Hegel's *Briefe*, ii. 80.

The following Errata in the Edition of the Logic as given in the Collected Works (vol. vi) are corrected in the translation. The references in brackets are to the German text.

Page 74, line 20. Und Objektivität has dropped out after der Subjektivität. [vi, p. 98, l. 10 from bottom.]

P. 76, l. 11. The 2nd ed. reads (die Gedanken) nicht in Solchem, instead of nicht als in Solchem (3rd ed.). [vi, p. 100, l. 3 from bottom.]

P. 133, l. 14 from bottom. Instead of the reading of the *Werke* and of the 3rd ed. read as in ed. II. Also ist dieser Gegenstand nichts. [vi, p. 178, l. 11.]

P. 140, ll. 2–3. Verstandes-Gegenstandes is a mistake for Verstandes-Gegensatzes, as in edd. II and III. [vi, p. 188, l. 2.]

P. 180, l. 29. weiten should be weitern. [vi, p. 251, l. 3 from bottom.]

P. 246, l. 6. Dinglichkeit is a misprint for Dingheit, as in Hegel's own editions. [vi, p. 347, l. 1.]

P. 275, l. 2. For seine Idealität read seiner Idealität. [vi, p. 385, l. 8.]

THE SCIENCE OF LOGIC

(THE FIRST PART OF THE ENCYCLOPAEDIA OF THE PHILOSOPHICAL SCIENCES IN OUTLINE)

BY

G. W. F. HEGEL

I

INTRODUCTION

§ 1

Philosophy misses an advantage enjoyed by the other sciences. It cannot like them rest the existence of its objects on the natural admissions of consciousness, nor can it assume that its method of cognition, either for starting or for continuing, is one already accepted. The objects of philosophy, it is true, are upon the whole the same as those of religion. In both the object is Truth, in that supreme sense in which God and God only is the Truth. Both in like manner go on to treat of the finite worlds of Nature and the human Mind, with their relation to each other and to their truth in God. Some *acquaintance* with its objects, therefore, philosophy may and even must presume, that and a certain interest in them to boot, were it for no other reason than this: that in point of time the mind makes general *images* of objects, long before it makes *notions* of them, and that it is only through these mental images, and by recourse to them, that the thinking mind rises to know and comprehend *thinkingly*.

But with the rise of this thinking study of things, it soon becomes evident that thought will be satisfied with nothing short of showing the *necessity* of its facts, of demonstrating the existence of its objects, as well as their nature and qualities. Our original acquaintance with them is thus discovered to be inadequate. We can assume nothing and assert nothing dogmatically; nor can we accept the assertions and assumptions of others. And yet we must make a beginning: and a beginning, as primary and underived, makes an assumption, or rather is an assumption. It seems as if it were impossible to make a beginning at all.

§ 2

This *thinking study of things* may serve, in a general way, as a description of philosophy. But the description is too wide. If it be correct to say, that thought makes the distinction between man and the lower animals, then everything human is human, for the sole and simple reason that it is due to the operation of thought. Philosophy, on the other hand, is a peculiar mode of thinking—a mode in which thinking becomes knowledge, and knowledge through notions. However great therefore may be the identity and essential unity of the two modes of thought, the philosophic mode gets to be different from the more general thought which acts in all that is human, in all that gives humanity its distinctive character. And this difference connects itself with the fact that the strictly human and thought-induced phenomena of consciousness do not originally appear in the form of a thought, but as a feeling, a perception, or mental image—all of which aspects must be distinguished from the form of thought proper.

According to an old preconceived idea, which has passed into a trivial proposition, it is thought which marks the man off from the animals. Yet trivial as this old belief may seem, it must, strangely enough, be recalled to mind in presence of certain preconceived ideas of the present day. These ideas would put feeling and thought so far apart as to make them opposites, and would represent them as so antagonistic, that feeling, particularly religious feeling, is supposed to be contaminated, perverted, and even annihilated by thought. They also emphatically hold that religion and piety grow out of, and rest upon something else, and not on thought. But those who make this separation forget meanwhile that only man has the capacity for religion, and that animals no more have religion than they have law and morality.

Those who insist on this separation of religion from thinking usually have before their minds the sort of thought that may be styled *after-thought*. They mean 'reflective' thinking, which has to deal with thoughts as thoughts, and brings them into consciousness. Slackness to perceive and keep in view this distinction which philosophy definitely draws in respect of thinking is the source of the crudest objections and reproaches against philosophy. Man—

and that just because it is his nature to think—is the only being that possesses law, religion, and morality. In these spheres of human life, therefore, thinking, under the guise of feeling, faith, or generalized image, has not been inactive: its action and its productions are there present and therein contained. But it is one thing to have such feelings and generalized images that have been moulded and permeated by thought, and another thing to have thoughts about them. The thoughts, to which after-thought upon those modes of consciousness gives rise, are what is comprised under reflection, general reasoning, and the like, as well as under philosophy itself.

The neglect of this distinction between thought in general and the reflective thought of philosophy has also led to another and more frequent misunderstanding. Reflection of this kind has been often maintained to be the condition, or even the only way, of attaining a consciousness and certitude of the Eternal and True. The (now somewhat antiquated) metaphysical proofs of God's existence, for example, have been treated, as if a knowledge of them and a conviction of their truth were the only and essential means of producing a belief and conviction that there is a God. Such a doctrine would find its parallel, if we said that eating was impossible before we had acquired a knowledge of the chemical, botanical, and zoological characters of our food; and that we must delay digestion till we had finished the study of anatomy and physiology. Were it so, these sciences in their field, like philosophy in its, would gain greatly in point of utility; in fact, their utility would rise to the height of absolute and universal indispensableness. Or rather, instead of being indispensable, they would not exist at all.

§ 3

The *Content*, of whatever kind it be, with which our consciousness is taken up, is what constitutes the qualitative character of our feelings, perceptions, fancies, and ideas; of our aims and duties; and of our thoughts and notions. From this point of view, feeling, perception, etc., are the *forms* assumed by these contents. The contents remain one and the same, whether they are felt, seen, represented, or willed, and whether they are merely felt, or felt with an admixture of thoughts, or merely and simply thought. In any one of these forms, or in the admixture of several, the contents confront consciousness, or are its *object*. But when they are thus objects of consciousness, the modes of the several forms ally themselves with the contents; and each form of them appears in consequence to give rise to a special object. Thus what is the same at bottom may look like a different sort of fact.

The several modes of feeling, perception, desire, and will, so far as we are *aware* of them, are in general called ideas (mental representations): and it may be roughly said that philosophy puts thoughts, categories, or, in more precise language, adequate *notions*, in the place of the generalized images we ordinarily call ideas. Mental impressions such as these may be regarded as the metaphors of thoughts and notions. But to have these figurate conceptions does not imply that we appreciate their intellectual significance, the thoughts and rational notions to which they correspond. Conversely, it is one thing to have thoughts and intelligent notions, and another to know what impressions, perceptions, and feelings correspond to them.

This difference will to some extent explain what people call the unintelligibility of philosophy. Their difficulty lies partly in an incapacity—which in itself is nothing but want of habit—for abstract thinking; i.e. in an inability to get hold of pure thoughts and move about in them. In our ordinary state of mind, the thoughts are clothed upon and made one with the sensuous or spiritual material of the hour; and in reflection, meditation, and general reasoning, we introduce a blend of thoughts into feelings, percepts, and mental images. (Thus, in propositions where the subject-matter is due to the senses—e.g. 'This leaf is green'—we have such categories introduced, as being and individuality.) But it is a very different thing to make the thoughts pure and simple our object.

But their complaint that philosophy is unintelligible is as much due to another reason; and that is an impatient wish to have before them as a mental picture that which is in the mind as a thought or notion. When people are asked to apprehend some notion, they often complain that they do not know what they have to think. But the fact is that in a notion there is nothing further to be thought than the notion itself. What the phrase reveals is a hankering after an image with which we are already familiar. The mind, denied the use of its familiar ideas, feels the ground where it once stood firm and at home taken away from beneath it, and, when transported into the region of pure thought, cannot tell where in the world it is.

One consequence of this weakness is that authors, preachers, and orators are found most intelligible, when they speak of things which their readers or hearers already know by rote—things which the latter are conversant with, and which require no explanation.

§ 4

The philosopher then has to reckon with popular modes of thought, and with the objects of religion. In dealing with the ordinary modes of mind, he will first of all, as we saw, have to prove and almost to awaken the need for his peculiar method of knowledge. In dealing with the objects of religion, and with truth as a whole, he will have to show that philosophy is capable of apprehending them from its own resources; and should a difference from religious conceptions come to light, he will have to justify the points in which it diverges.

§ 5

To give the reader a preliminary explanation of the distinction thus made, and to let him see at the same moment that the real import of our consciousness is retained, and even for the first time put in its proper light, when translated into the form of thought and the notion of reason, it may be well to recall another of these old unreasoned beliefs. And that is the conviction that to get at the truth of any object or event, even of feelings, perceptions, opinions, and mental ideas, we must think it over. Now in any case to think things over is at least to transform feelings, ordinary ideas, etc. into thoughts.

Nature has given every one a faculty of thought. But thought is all that philosophy claims as the form proper to her business: and thus the inadequate view which ignores the distinction stated in § 3 leads to a new delusion, the reverse of the complaint previously mentioned about the unintelligibility of philosophy. In other words, this science must often submit to the slight of hearing even people who have never taken any trouble with it talking as if they thoroughly understood all about it. With no preparation beyond an ordinary education they do not hesitate, especially under the influence of religious sentiment, to philosophize and to criticize philosophy. Everybody allows that to know any other science you must have first studied it, and that you can only claim to express a judgement upon it in virtue of such knowledge. Everybody allows that to make a shoe you must have learned and practised the craft of the shoemaker, though every man has a model in his own foot, and possesses in his hands the natural endowments for the operations required. For philosophy alone, it seems to be imagined, such study, care, and application are not in the least requisite.

This comfortable view of what is required for a philosopher has recently received corroboration through the theory of immediate or intuitive knowledge.

§ 6

So much for the form of philosophical knowledge. It is no less desirable, on the other hand, that philosophy should understand that its content is no other than *actuality*, that core of truth which, originally produced and producing itself within the precincts of the mental life, has become the *world*, the inward and outward world, of consciousness. At first we become aware of these contents in what we call Experience. But even Experience, as it surveys the wide range of inward and outward existence, has sense enough to distinguish the mere appearance, which is transient and meaningless, from what in itself really deserves the name of actuality. As it is only in form that philosophy is distinguished from other modes of attaining an acquaintance with this same sum of being, it must necessarily be in harmony with actuality and experience. In fact, this harmony may be viewed as at least an extrinsic means of testing the truth of a philosophy. Similarly it may be held the highest and final aim of philosophic science to bring about, through the ascertainment of this harmony, a reconciliation of the self-conscious reason with the reason which *is* in the world—in other words, with actuality.

In the Preface to my *Philosophy of Law*, p. xix, are found the propositions:

What is reasonable is actual

and

What is actual is reasonable.

These simple statements have given rise to expressions of surprise and hostility, even in quarters where it would be reckoned an insult to presume absence of philosophy, and still more of religion. Religion at least need not be brought in evidence; its doctrines of the divine governments of the world affirm these propositions too decidedly. For their philosophic sense, we must presuppose intelligence enough to know, not only that God is actual, that He is the supreme actuality, that He alone is truly actual; but also, as regards the logical bearings of the question, that existence is in part mere appearance, and only in part actuality. In common life, any freak of fancy, any error, evil and everything of the nature of evil, as well as every degenerate and transitory existence whatever, gets in a casual way the name of actuality. But even our ordinary feelings are enough to forbid a casual (fortuitous) existence getting the emphatic name of an actual; for by fortuitous we mean an existence which has no greater value than that of something possible, which may as well not be as be. As for the term Actuality, these critics would have done well to consider the sense in which I employ it. In a detailed Logic I had treated among other things of actuality, and accurately distinguished it not only from the fortuitous, which, after all, has existence, but even from the cognate categories of existence and the other modifications of being.

The actuality of the rational stands opposed by the popular fancy that Ideas and ideals are nothing but chimeras, and philosophy a mere system of such phantasms. It is also opposed by the very different fancy that Ideas and ideals are something far too excellent to have actuality, or something too impotent to procure it for themselves. This divorce between idea and reality is especially dear to the analytic understanding which looks upon its own abstractions, dreams though they are, as something true and real, and prides itself on the imperative 'ought', which it takes especial pleasure in prescribing even on the field of politics. As if the world had waited on it to learn how it ought to be, and was not! For, if it were as it ought to be, what would come of the precocious wisdom of that 'ought'? When understanding turns this 'ought' against trivial external and transitory objects, against social regulations or conditions, which very likely possess a great relative importance for a certain time and special circles, it may often be right. In such a case the intelligent observer may meet much that fails to satisfy the general requirements of right; for who is not acute enough to see a great deal in his own surroundings which is really far from being as it ought to be? But such acuteness is mistaken in the conceit that, when it examines these objects and pronounces what they ought to be, it is dealing with questions of philosophic science. The object of philosophy is the Idea: and the Idea is not so impotent as merely to have a right or an obligation to exist without actually existing. The object of philosophy is an actuality of which those objects, social regulations and conditions, are only the superficial outside.

§ 7

Thus reflection—thinking things over—in a general way involves the principle (which also means the beginning) of philosophy. And when the reflective spirit arose again in its independence in modern times, after the epoch of the Lutheran Reformation, it did not, as in its beginnings among the Greeks, stand merely aloof, in a world of its own, but at once turned its energies also upon the apparently illimitable material of the phenomenal world. In this way the name philosophy came to be applied to all those branches of knowledge, which are engaged in ascertaining the standard and Universal in the ocean of empirical individualities, as well as in ascertaining the Necessary element, or Laws, to be found in the apparent disorder of the endless masses of the fortuitous. It thus appears that modern philosophy derives its materials from our own personal observations and perceptions of the external and internal world, from nature as well as from the mind and heart of man, when both stand in the immediate presence of the observer.

This principle of Experience carries with it the unspeakably important condition that, in order to accept and believe any fact, we must be in contact with it; or, in more exact terms, that we must find the fact united and combined with the certainty of our own selves. We must be in touch with our subject-matter, whether it be by means of our external senses, or, else, by our profounder mind and our intimate self-consciousness. This principle is the same as that which has in the present day been termed faith, immediate knowledge, the revelation in the outward world, and, above all, in our own heart.

Those sciences, which thus got the name of philosophy, we call *empirical* sciences, for the reason that they take their departure from experience. Still the essential results which they aim at and provide are laws, general propositions, a theory—the thoughts of what is found existing. On this ground the Newtonian physics was called Natural Philosophy. Hugo Grotius, again, by putting together and comparing the behaviour of states towards each other as recorded in history, succeeded, with the help of the ordinary methods of general reasoning, in laying down certain general principles, and establishing a theory which may be termed the Philosophy of International Law. In England this is still the usual signification of the term philosophy. Newton continues to be celebrated as the greatest of philosophers: and the name goes down as far as the price-lists of instrument-makers. All instruments, such as the thermometer and barometer, which do not come under the special head of magnetic or electric apparatus, are styled philosophical instruments.[1] Surely thought, and not a mere combination of wood, iron, etc., ought to be called the instrument of philosophy! The recent science of Political Economy in particular, which in Germany is known as Rational Economy of the State, or intelligent national economy, has in England especially appropriated the name of philosophy.[2]

[1] The journal too, edited by Thomson, is called 'Annals of Philosophy; or, Magazine of Chemistry, Mineralogy, Mechanics, Natural History, Agriculture, and Arts'. We can easily guess from the title what sort of subjects are here to be understood under the term 'philosophy'. Among the advertisements of books just published, I lately found the following notice in an English newspaper: 'The Art of Preserving the Hair, on Philosophical Principles, neatly printed in post 8vo, price seven shillings'. By philosophical principles for the preservation of the hair are probably meant chemical or physiological principles.

[2] In connection with the general principles of Political Economy, the term 'philosophical' is frequently heard from the lips of English statesmen, even in

§ 8

In its own field this empirical knowledge may at first give satisfaction; but in two ways it is seen to come short. In the first place there is another circle of objects which it does not embrace. These are Freedom, Spirit, and God. They belong to a different sphere, not because it can be said that they have nothing to do with experience; for though they are certainly not experiences of the senses, it is quite an identical proposition to say that whatever is in consciousness is experienced. The real ground for assigning them to another field of cognition is that in their scope and *content* these objects evidently show themselves as infinite.

There is an old phrase often wrongly attributed to Aristotle, and supposed to express the general tenor of his philosophy. *Nihil est in intellectu quod non fuerit in sensu*: there is nothing in thought which has not been in sense and experience. If speculative philosophy refused to admit this maxim, it can only have done so from a misunderstanding. It will, however, on the converse side no less assert: *Nihil est in sensu quod non fuerit in intellectu.* And this may be taken in two senses. In the general sense it means that *νοῦς* or spirit (the more profound idea of *νοῦς* in modern thought) is the cause of the world. In its special meaning (see § 2) it asserts that the sentiment of right, morals, and religion is a sentiment (and in that way an experience) of such scope and such character that it can spring from and rest upon thought alone.

their public speeches. In the House of Commons, on 2 Feb. 1825, Brougham, speaking on the address in reply to the speech from the throne, talked of 'the statesman-like and philosophical principles of Free-trade—for philosophical they undoubtedly are—upon the acceptance of which his majesty this day congratulated the House'. Nor is this language confined to members of the Opposition. At the shipowners' yearly dinner in the same month, under the chairmanship of the Premier Lord Liverpool, supported by Canning the Secretary of State, and Sir C. Long the Paymaster-General of the Army, Canning in reply to the toast which had been proposed said: 'A period has just begun, in which ministers have it in their power to apply to the administration of this country the sound maxims of a profound philosophy.' Differences there may be between English and German philosophy: still, considering that elsewhere the name of philosophy is used only as a nickname and insult, or as something odious, it is a matter of rejoicing to see it still honoured in the mouth of the English Government.

§ 9

But in the second place in point of *form* the subjective reason desires a further satisfaction than empirical knowledge gives; and this form is, in the widest sense of the term, Necessity (§ 1). The method of empirical science exhibits two defects. The first is that the Universal or general principle contained in it, the genus, or kind, etc., is, on its own account, indeterminate and vague, and therefore not on its own account connected with the Particulars or the details. Either is external and accidental to the other; and it is the same with the particular facts which are brought into union: each is external and accidental to the others. The second defect is that the beginnings are in every case data and postulates, neither accounted for nor deduced. In both these points the form of necessity fails to get its due. Hence reflection, whenever it sets itself to remedy these defects, becomes speculative thinking, the thinking proper to philosophy. As a species of reflection, therefore, which, though it has a certain community of nature with the reflection already mentioned, is nevertheless different from it, philosophic thought thus possesses, in addition to the common forms, some forms of its own, of which the Notion may be taken as the type.

The relation of speculative science to the other sciences may be stated in the following terms. It does not in the least neglect the empirical facts contained in the several sciences, but recognizes and adopts them: it appreciates and applies towards its own structure the universal element in these sciences, their laws and classifications: but besides all this, into the categories of science it introduces, and gives currency to, other categories. The difference, looked at in this way, is only a change of categories. Speculative Logic contains all previous Logic and Metaphysics: it preserves the same forms of thought, the same laws and objects—while at the same time remodelling and expanding them with wider categories.

From *notion* in the speculative sense we should distinguish what is ordinarily called a notion. The phrase, that no notion can ever comprehend the Infinite, a phrase which has been repeated over and over again till it has grown axiomatic, is based upon this narrow estimate of what is meant by notions.

§ 10

This thought, which is proposed as the instrument of philosophic knowledge, itself calls for further explanation. We must understand in what way it possesses necessity or cogency: and when it claims to be equal to the task of apprehending the absolute objects (God, Spirit, Freedom), that claim must be substantiated. Such an explanation, however, is itself a lesson in philosophy, and properly falls within the scope of the science itself. A preliminary attempt to make matters plain would only be unphilosophical, and consist of a tissue of assumptions, assertions, and inferential pros and cons, i.e. of dogmatism without cogency, as against which there would be an equal right of counter-dogmatism.

A main line of argument in the Critical Philosophy bids us pause before proceeding to inquire into God or into the true being of things, and tells us first of all to examine the faculty of cognition and see whether it is equal to such an effort. We ought, says Kant, to become acquainted with the instrument, before we undertake the work for which it is to be employed; for if the instrument be insufficient, all our trouble will be spent in vain. The plausibility of this suggestion has won for it general assent and admiration; the result of which has been to withdraw cognition from an interest in its objects and absorption in the study of them, and to direct it back upon itself; and so turn it to a question of form. Unless we wish to be deceived by words, it is easy to see what this amounts to. In the case of other instruments, we can try and criticize them in other ways than by setting about the special work for which they are destined. But the examination of knowledge can only be carried out by an act of knowledge. To examine this so-called instrument is the same thing as to know it. But to seek to know before we know is as absurd as the wise resolution of Scholasticus, not to venture into the water until he had learned to swim.

Reinhold saw the confusion with which this style of commencement is chargeable, and tried to get out of the difficulty by starting with a hypothetical and problematical stage of philosophizing. In this way he supposed that it would be possible, nobody can tell how, to get along, until we found ourselves, further on, arrived at the primary truth of truths. His method, when closely looked into, will be seen to be identical with a very common practice. It starts from a substratum of experiential fact, or from a provisional assumption which has been brought into a definition; and then proceeds to analyse this starting-point. We can detect in Reinhold's argument a perception of the truth, that the usual course which proceeds by assumptions and anticipations is no better than a hypothetical and problematical mode of procedure. But his perceiving this does not alter the character of this method; it only makes clear its imperfections.

§ 11

The special conditions which call for the existence of philosophy may be thus described. The mind or spirit, when it is sentient or perceptive, finds its object in something sensuous; when it imagines, in a picture or image; when it wills, in an aim or end. But in contrast to, or it may be only in distinction from, these forms of its existence and of its objects, the mind has also to gratify the cravings of its highest and most inward life. That innermost self is thought. Thus the mind renders thought its object. In the best meaning of the phrase, it comes to itself; for thought is its principle, and its very unadulterated self. But while thus occupied, thought entangles itself in contradictions, i.e. loses itself in the hard-and-fast non-identity of its thoughts, and so, instead of reaching itself, is caught and held in its counterpart. This result, to which honest but narrow thinking leads the mere understanding, is resisted by the loftier craving of which we have spoken. That craving expresses the perseverance of thought, which continues true to itself, even in this conscious loss of its native rest and independence, 'that it may overcome' and work out in itself the solution of its own contradictions.

To see that thought in its very nature is dialectical, and that, as understanding, it must fall into contradiction—the negative of itself—will form one of the main lessons of logic. When thought grows hopeless of ever achieving, by its own means, the solution of the contradiction which it has by its own action brought upon itself, it turns back to those solutions of the question with which the mind had learned to pacify itself in some of its other modes and forms. Unfortunately, however, the retreat of thought has led it, as Plato noticed even in his time, to a very uncalled-for hatred of reason (misology); and it then takes up against its own endeavours that hostile attitude of which an example is seen in the doctrine that 'immediate' knowledge, as it is called, is the exclusive form in which we become cognizant of truth.

§ 12

The rise of philosophy is due to these cravings of thought. Its point of departure is Experience; including under that name both our immediate consciousness and the inductions from it. Awakened, as it were, by this stimulus, thought is vitally characterized by raising itself above the natural state of mind, above the senses and inferences from the senses into its own unadulterated element, and by assuming, accordingly, at first a stand-aloof and negative attitude towards the point from which it started. Through this state of antagonism to the phenomena of sense its first satisfaction is found in itself, in the Idea of the universal essence of these phenomena: an Idea (the Absolute, or God) which may be more or less abstract. Meanwhile, on the other hand, the sciences, based on experience, exert upon the mind a stimulus to overcome the form in which their varied contents are presented, and to elevate these contents to the rank of necessary truth. For the facts of science have the aspect of a vast conglomerate, one thing coming side by side with another, as if they were merely given and presented—as in short devoid of all essential or necessary connection. In consequence of this stimulus thought is dragged out of its unrealized universality and its fancied or merely possible satisfaction, and impelled onwards to a development from itself. On one hand this development only means that thought incorporates the contents of science, in all their speciality of detail as submitted. On the other it makes these contents imitate the action of the original creative thought, and present the aspect of a free evolution determined by the logic of the fact alone.

On the relation between 'immediacy' and 'mediation' in consciousness we shall speak later, expressly and with more detail. Here it may be sufficient to premise that, though the two 'moments' or factors present themselves as distinct, still neither of them can be absent, nor can one exist apart from the other. Thus the knowledge of God, as of every supersensible reality, is in its true character an exaltation above sensations or perceptions: it consequently involves a negative attitude to the initial data of sense, and to that extent implies mediation. For to mediate is to take something as a beginning and to go onward to a second thing; so that the existence of this second thing depends on our having reached it from something else contradistinguished from it. In spite of this, the knowledge of God is no mere sequel, dependent on the empirical phase of consciousness: in fact, its independence is essentially secured through this negation and exaltation. No doubt, if we attach an unfair prominence to the fact of mediation, and represent it as implying a state of conditionedness, it may be said—not that the remark would mean much—that philosophy is the child of experience, and owes its rise to *a posteriori* fact. (As a matter of fact, thinking is always the negation of what we have immediately before us.) With as much truth however we may be said to owe eating to the means of nourishment, so long as we can have no eating without them. If we take this view, eating is certainly represented as ungrateful: it devours that to which it owes itself. Thinking, upon this view of its action, is equally ungrateful.

But there is also an *a priori* aspect of thought, where by a mediation, not made by anything external but by a reflection into self, we have that immediacy which is universality, the self-complacency of thought which is so much at home with itself that it feels an innate indifference to descend to particulars, and in that way to the development of its own nature. It is thus also with religion, which whether it be rude or elaborate, whether it be invested with scientific precision of detail or confined to the simple faith of the heart, possesses, throughout, the same intensive nature of contentment and felicity. But if thought never gets further than the universality of the Ideas, as was perforce the case in the first philosophies (when the Eleatics never got beyond Being, or Heraclitus beyond Becoming), it is justly open to the charge of formalism. Even in a more advanced phase of philosophy, we may often find a doctrine which has mastered merely certain abstract propositions or formulae, such as, 'In the absolute all is one',

'Subject and object are identical'—and only repeating the same thing when it comes to particulars. Bearing in mind this first period of thought, the period of mere generality, we may safely say that experience is the real author of *growth* and *advance* in philosophy. For, firstly, the empirical sciences do not stop short at the mere observation of the individual features of a phenomenon. By the aid of thought, they are able to meet philosophy with materials prepared for it, in the shape of general uniformities, i.e. laws, and classifications of the phenomena. When this is done, the particular facts which they contain are ready to be received into philosophy. This, secondly, implies a certain compulsion on thought itself to proceed to these concrete specific truths. The reception into philosophy of these scientific materials, now that thought has removed their immediacy and made them cease to be mere data, forms at the same time a development of thought out of itself. Philosophy, then, owes its development to the empirical sciences. In return it gives their contents what is so vital to them, the freedom of thought—gives them, in short, an *a priori* character. These contents are now warranted necessary, and no longer depend on the evidence of facts merely, that they were so found and so experienced. The fact as experienced thus becomes an illustration and a copy of the original and completely self-supporting activity of thought.

§ 13

Stated in exact terms, such is the origin and development of philosophy. But the History of Philosophy gives us the same process from a historical and external point of view. The stages in the evolution of the Idea there seem to follow each other by accident, and to present merely a number of different and unconnected principles, which the several systems of philosophy carry out in their own way. But it is not so. For these thousands of years the same Architect has directed the work: and that Architect is the one living Mind whose nature is to think, to bring to self-consciousness what it is, and, with its being thus set as object before it, to be at the same time raised above it, and so to reach a higher stage of its own being. The different systems which the history of philosophy presents are therefore not irreconcilable with unity.

We may either say, that it is one philosophy at different degrees of maturity: or that the particular principle, which is the groundwork of each system, is but a branch of one and the same universe of thought. In philosophy the latest birth of time is the result of all the systems that have preceded it, and must include their principles; and so, if, on other grounds, it deserve the title of philosophy, will be the fullest, most comprehensive, and most adequate system of all.

The spectacle of so many and so various systems of philosophy suggests the necessity of defining more exactly the relation of Universal to Particular. When the universal is made a mere form and co-ordinated with the particular, as if it were on the same level, it sinks into a particular itself. Even common sense in everyday matters is above the absurdity of setting a universal *beside* the particulars. Would any one, who wished for fruit, reject cherries, pears, and grapes, on the ground that they were cherries, pears, or grapes, and not fruit? But when philosophy is in question, the excuse of many is that philosophies are so different, and none of them is *the* philosophy—that each is only *a* philosophy. Such a plea is assumed to justify any amount of contempt for philosophy. And yet cherries too are fruit. Often, too, a system, of which the principle is the universal, is put on a level with another of which the principle is a particular, and with theories which deny the existence of philosophy altogether. Such systems are said to be only different views of philosophy. With equal justice, light and darkness might be styled different kinds of light.

§ 14

The same evolution of thought which is exhibited in the history of philosophy is presented in the System of Philosophy itself. Here, instead of surveying the process, as we do in history, from the outside, we see the movement of thought clearly defined in its native medium. The thought, which is genuine and self-supporting, must be intrinsically concrete; it must be an Idea; and when it is viewed in the whole of its universality, it is the Idea, or the Absolute. The science of this Idea must form a system. For the truth is concrete; that is, while it gives a bond and principle of unity, it also possesses an internal source of development. Truth, then, is only possible as a universe or totality of thought; and the freedom of the whole, as well as the necessity of the several subdivisions, which it implies, are only possible when these are discriminated and defined.

Unless it is a system, a philosophy is not a scientific production. Unsystematic philosophizing can only be expected to give expression to personal peculiarities of mind, and has no principle for the regulation of its contents. Apart from their interdependence and organic union, the truths of philosophy are valueless, and must then be treated as baseless hypotheses, or personal convictions. Yet many philosophical treatises confine themselves to such an exposition of the opinions and sentiments of the author.

The term *system* is often misunderstood. It does not denote a philosophy, the principle of which is narrow and to be distinguished from others. On the contrary, a genuine philosophy makes it a principle to include every particular principle.

§ 15

Each of the parts of philosophy is a philosophical whole, a circle rounded and complete in itself. In each of these parts, however, the philosophical Idea is found in a particular specificality or medium. The single circle, because it is a real totality, bursts through the limits imposed by its special medium, and gives rise to a wider circle. The whole of philosophy in this way resembles a circle of circles. The Idea appears in each single circle, but, at the same time, the whole Idea is constituted by the system of these peculiar phases, and each is a necessary member of the organization.

§ 16

In the form of an Encyclopaedia, the science has no room for a detailed exposition of particulars, and must be limited to setting forth the commencement of the special sciences and the notions of cardinal importance in them.

How much of the particular parts is requisite to constitute a particular branch of knowledge is so far indeterminate, that the part, if it is to be something true, must be not an isolated member merely, but itself an organic whole. The entire field of philosophy therefore really forms a single science; but it may also be viewed as a total, composed of several particular sciences.

The encylopaedia of philosophy must not be confounded with ordinary encyclopaedias. An ordinary encyclopaedia does not pretend to be more than an aggregation of sciences, regulated by no principle, and merely as experience offers them. Sometimes it even includes what merely bear the name of sciences, while they are nothing more than a collection of bits of information. In an aggregate like this, the several branches of knowledge owe their place in the encyclopaedia to extrinsic reasons, and their unity is therefore artificial: they are *arranged*, but we cannot say they form a *system*. For the same reason, especially as the materials to be combined also depend upon no one rule or principle, the arrangement is at best an experiment, and will always exhibit inequalities.

An encyclopaedia of philosophy excludes three kinds of partial science. I. It excludes mere aggregates of bits of information. Philology in its prima facie aspect belongs to this class. II. It rejects the quasi-sciences, which are founded on an act of arbitrary will alone, such as Heraldry. Sciences of this class are positive from beginning to end. III. In another class of sciences, also styled positive, but which have a rational basis and a rational beginning, philosophy claims that constituent as its own. The positive features remain the property of the sciences themselves.

The positive element in the last class of sciences is of different sorts. (i) Their commencement, though rational at bottom, yields to the influence of fortuitousness, when they have to bring their universal truth into contact with actual facts and the single phenomena of experience. In this region of chance and change, the adequate notion of science must yield its place to reasons or grounds of explanation. Thus, e.g. in the science of jurisprudence, or in the system of direct and indirect taxation, it is necessary to have certain points precisely and definitively settled which lie beyond the competence of the absolute lines laid down by the pure notion. A certain latitude of settlement accordingly is left; and each point may be determined in one way on one principle, in another way on another, and admits of no definitive certainty. Similarly the Idea of Nature, when parcelled out in detail, is dissipated into contingencies. Natural history, geography, and medicine stumble upon descriptions of existence, upon kinds and distinctions, which are not determined by reason, but by sport and adventitious incidents. Even history comes under the same category. The Idea is its essence and inner nature; but, as it appears, everything is under contingency and in the field of voluntary action. (ii) These sciences are positive also in failing to recognize the finite nature of what they predicate, and to point out how these categories and their whole sphere pass into a higher. They assume their statements to possess an authority beyond appeal. Here the fault lies in the finitude of the form, as in the previous instance it lay in the matter. (iii) In close sequel to this, sciences are positive in consequence of the inadequate grounds on which their conclusions rest: based as these are on detached and casual inference, upon feeling, faith, and authority, and, generally speaking, upon the deliverances of inward and outward perception. Under this head we must also class the philosophy which proposes to build upon 'anthropology', facts of consciousness, inward sense, or outward experience. It may happen, however, that empirical is an epithet applicable only to the form of scientific exposition, while intuitive sagacity has arranged what are mere phenomena, according to the essential sequence of the notion. In such a case the contrasts between the varied and numerous phenomena brought together serve to eliminate the external and accidental circumstances of their conditions, and the universal thus comes clearly into view. Guided by such an intuition, experimental physics will present the rational science of Nature—as history will present the science of human affairs and actions—in an external picture, which mirrors the philosophic notion.

§ 17

It may seem as if philosophy, in order to start on its course, had, like the rest of the sciences, to begin with a subjective presupposition. The sciences postulate their respective objects, such as space, number, or whatever it be; and it might be supposed that philosophy had also to postulate the existence of thought. But the two cases are not exactly parallel. It is by the free act of thought that it occupies a point of view, in which it is for its own self, and thus gives itself an object of its own production. Nor is this all. The very point of view, which originally is taken on its own evidence only, must in the course of the science be converted to a result—the ultimate result in which philosophy returns into itself and reaches the point with which it began. In this manner philosophy exhibits the appearance of a circle which closes with itself, and has no beginning in the same way as the other sciences have. To speak of a beginning of philosophy has a meaning only in relation to a person who proposes to commence the study, and not in relation to the science as science. The same thing may be thus expressed. The notion of science—the notion therefore with which we start—which, for the very reason that it is initial, implies a separation between the thought which is our object, and the subject philosophizing which is, as it were, external to the former, must be grasped and comprehended by the science itself. This is in short, the one single aim, action, and goal of philosophy—to arrive at the notion of its notion, and thus secure its return and its satisfaction.

§ 18

As the whole science, and only the whole, can exhibit what the Idea or system of reason is, it is impossible to give in a preliminary way a general impression of a philosophy. Nor can a division of philosophy into its parts be intelligible, except in connection with the system. A preliminary division, like the limited conception from which it comes, can only be an anticipation. Here however it is premised that the Idea turns out to be the thought which is completely identical with itself, and not identical simply in the abstract, but also in its action of setting itself over against itself, so as to gain a being of its own, and yet of being in full possession of itself while it is in this other. Thus philosophy is subdivided into three parts:

I. Logic: the science of the Idea in and for itself.

II. The Philosophy of Nature: the science of the Idea in its otherness.

III. The Philosophy of Mind: the science of the Idea come back to itself out of that otherness.

As observed in § 15, the differences between the several philosophical sciences are only aspects or specializations of the one Idea or system of reason, which and which alone is alike exhibited in these different media. In Nature nothing else would have to be discerned, except the Idea; but the Idea has here divested itself of its proper being. In Mind, again, the Idea has asserted a being of its own, and is on the way to become absolute. Every such form in which the Idea is expressed is at the same time a passing or fleeting stage; and hence each of these subdivisions has not only to know its contents as an object which has being for the time, but also in the same act to expound how these contents pass into their higher circle. To represent the relation between them as a division, therefore, leads to misconception; for it co-ordinates the several parts or sciences one beside another, as if they had no innate development, but were, like so many species, really and radically distinct.

II

PRELIMINARY NOTION

§ 19

Logic is the science of the pure Idea; pure, that is, because the Idea is in the abstract medium of Thought.

This definition, and the others which occur in these introductory outlines, are derived from a survey of the whole system, to which accordingly they are subsequent. The same remark applies to all prefatory notions whatever about philosophy.

Logic might have been defined as the science of thought, and of its laws and characteristic forms. But thought, as thought, constitutes only the general medium, or qualifying circumstance, which renders the Idea distinctively logical. If we identify the Idea with thought, thought must not be taken in the sense of a method or form, but in the sense of the self-developing totality of its laws and peculiar terms. These laws are the work of thought itself, and not a fact which it finds and must submit to.

From different points of view, Logic is either the hardest or the easiest of the sciences. Logic is hard, because it has to deal not with perceptions, nor, like geometry, with abstract representations of the senses, but with the pure abstractions; and because it demands a force and facility of withdrawing into pure thought, of keeping firm hold on it, and of moving in such an element. Logic is easy, because its facts are nothing but our own thought and its familiar forms or terms: and these are the acme of simplicity, the ABC of everything else. They are also what we are best acquainted with: such as 'is' and 'is not'; quality and magnitude; being potential and being actual; one, many, and so on. But such an acquaintance only adds to the difficulties of the study; for while, on the one hand, we naturally think it is not worth our trouble to occupy ourselves any longer with things so familiar, on the other hand, the problem is to become acquainted with them in a new way, quite opposite to that in which we know them already.

The utility of Logic is a matter which concerns its bearings upon the student, and the training it may give for other purposes. This logical training consists in the exercise in thinking which the student has to go through (this science is the thinking of thinking): and in the fact that he stores his head with thoughts, in their native unalloyed character. It is true that Logic, being the absolute form of truth, and another name for the very truth itself, is something more than merely useful. Yet if what is noblest, most liberal, and most independent is also most useful, Logic has some claim to the latter character. Its utility must then be estimated at another rate than exercise in thought for the sake of the exercise.

(1) The first question is: What is the object of our science? The simplest and most intelligible answer to this question is that Truth is the object of Logic. Truth is a noble word, and the thing is nobler still. So long as man is sound at heart and in spirit, the search for truth must awake all the enthusiasm of his nature. But immediately there steps in the objection—are *we* able to know truth? There seems to be a disproportion between finite beings like ourselves and the truth which is absolute: and doubts suggest themselves whether there is any bridge between the finite and the infinite. God is truth: how shall we know Him? Such an undertaking appears to stand in contradiction with the graces of lowliness and humility. Others who ask whether we can know the truth have a different purpose. They want to justify themselves in living on contented with their petty, finite aims. And humility of this stamp is a poor thing.

But the time is past when people asked: How shall I, a poor worm of the dust, be able to know the truth? And in its stead we find vanity and conceit: people claim, without any trouble on their part, to breathe the very atmosphere of truth. The young have been flattered into the belief that they possess a natural birthright of moral and religious truth. And in the same strain, those of riper years are declared to be sunk, petrified, ossified in falsehood. Youth, say these teachers, sees the bright light of dawn: but the older generation lies in the slough and mire of the common day. They admit that the special sciences are something that certainly ought to be cultivated, but merely as the means to satisfy the needs of outer life. In all this it is not humility which holds back from the knowledge and study of the truth, but a conviction that we are already in full possession of it. And no doubt the young carry with them the hopes of their elder compeers; on them rests the advance of the world and science. But these hopes are set upon the young, only on the condition that, instead of remaining as they are, they undertake the stern labour of mind.

This modesty in truth-seeking has still another phase: and that is the genteel indifference to truth, as we see it in Pilate's conversation with Christ. Pilate asked 'What is truth?' with the air of a man who had settled accounts with everything long ago, and concluded that nothing particularly matters—he meant much the same as Solomon when he says: 'All is vanity'. When it comes to this, nothing is left but self-conceit.

The knowledge of the truth meets an additional obstacle in timidity. A slothful mind finds it natural to say: 'Don't let it be supposed that we mean to be in earnest with our philosophy. We shall be glad *inter alia* to study Logic: but Logic must be sure to leave us as we were before.' People have a feeling that, if thinking passes the ordinary range of our ideas and impressions, it cannot but be on the evil road. They seem to be trusting themselves to a sea on which they will be tossed to and fro by the waves of thought, till at length they again reach the sandbank of this temporal scene, as utterly poor as when they left it. What comes of such a view, we see in the world. It is possible within these limits to gain varied information and many accomplishments, to become a master of official routine, and to be trained for special purposes. But it is quite another thing to educate the spirit for the higher life and to devote our energies to its service. In our own day it may be hoped a longing for something better has sprung up among the young, so that they will not be contented with the mere straw of outer knowledge.

(2) It is universally agreed that thought is the object of Logic. But of thought our estimate may be very mean, or it may be very high. On one hand, people say: 'It is *only* a thought.' In their view thought is subjective, arbitrary and accidental—distinguished from the thing itself, from the true and the real. On the other hand, a very high estimate may be formed of thought; when thought alone is held adequate to attain the highest of all things, the nature of God, of which the senses can tell us nothing. God is a spirit, it is said, and must be worshipped in spirit and in truth. But the merely felt and sensible, we admit, is not the spiritual; its heart of hearts is in thought; and only spirit can know spirit. And though it is true that spirit can demean itself as feeling and sense—as is the case in religion, the mere feeling, as a mode of consciousness, is one thing, and its contents another. Feeling, as feeling, is the general form of the sensuous nature which we have in common with the brutes. This form, viz. feeling, may possibly seize and appropriate the full organic truth: but the form has no real congruity with its contents. The form of feeling is the lowest in which spiritual truth can be expressed. The world of spiritual existences, God himself, exists in proper truth, only in thought and as thought. If this be so, therefore, thought, far from being a mere thought, is the highest and, in strict accuracy, the sole mode of apprehending the eternal and absolute.

As of thought, so also of the science of thought, a very high or a very low opinion may be formed. Any man, it is supposed, can think without Logic, as he can digest without studying physiology. If he have studied

Logic, he thinks afterwards as he did before, perhaps more methodically, but with little alteration. If this were all, and if Logic did no more than make men acquainted with the action of thought as the faculty of comparison and classification, it would produce nothing which had not been done quite as well before. And in point of fact Logic hitherto had no other idea of its duty than this. Yet to be well informed about thought, even as a mere activity of the subject-mind, is honourable and interesting for man. It is in knowing what he is and what he does that man is distinguished from the brutes. But we may take the higher estimate of thought—as what alone can get really in touch with the supreme and true. In that case, Logic as the science of thought occupies a high ground. If the science of Logic then considers thought in its action and its productions (and thought being no resultless energy produces thoughts and the particular thought required), the theme of Logic is in general the supersensible world, and to deal with that theme is to dwell for a while in that world. Mathematics is concerned with the abstractions of time and space. But these are still the object of sense, although the sensible is abstract and idealized. Thought bids adieu even to this last and abstract sensible: it asserts its own native independence, renounces the field of the external and internal sense, and puts away the interests and inclinations of the individual. When Logic takes this ground, it is a higher science than we are in the habit of supposing.

(3) The necessity of understanding Logic in a deeper sense than as the science of the mere form of thought is enforced by the interests of religion and politics, of law and morality. In earlier days men meant no harm by thinking: they thought away freely and fearlessly. They thought about God, about Nature, and the State; and they felt sure that a knowledge of the truth was obtainable through thought only, and not through the senses or any random ideas or opinions. But while they so thought, the principal ordinances of life began to be seriously affected by their conclusions. Thought deprived existing institutions of their force. Constitutions fell a victim to thought: religion was assailed by thought: firm religious beliefs which had been always looked upon as revelations were undermined, and in many minds the old faith was upset. The Greek philosophers, for example, became antagonists of the old religion, and destroyed its beliefs. Philosophers were accordingly banished or put to death, as revolutionists who had subverted religion and the state, two things which were inseparable. Thought, in short, made itself a power in the real world, and exercised enormous influence. The matter ended by drawing attention to the influence of thought, and its claims were submitted to a more rigorous scrutiny, by which the world professed to find that thought arrogated too much and was unable to perform what it had undertaken. It had not—people said—learned the real being of God, of Nature and Mind. It had not learned what the truth was. What it had done was to overthrow religion and the state. It became urgent therefore

to justify thought, with reference to the results it had produced: and it is this examination into the nature of thought and this justification which in recent times has constituted one of the main problems of philosophy.

§ 20

If we take our prima facie impression of thought, we find on examination first (a) that, in its usual subjective acceptation, thought is one out of many activities or faculties of the mind, co-ordinate with such others as sensation, perception, imagination, desire, volition, and the like. The product of this activity, the form or character peculiar to thought, is the UNIVERSAL, or, in general, the abstract. Thought, regarded as an *activity*, may be accordingly described as the *active* universal, and, since the deed, its product, is the universal once more, may be called a self-actualizing universal. Thought conceived as a *subject* (agent) is a thinker, and the subject existing as a thinker is simply denoted by the term 'I'.

The propositions giving an account of thought in this and the following sections are not offered as assertions or opinions of mine on the matter. But in these preliminary chapters any deduction or proof would be impossible, and the statements may be taken as matters in evidence. In other words, every man, when he thinks and considers his thoughts, will discover by the experience of his consciousness that they possess the character of universality as well as the other aspects of thought to be afterwards enumerated. We assume of course that his powers of attention and abstraction have undergone a previous training, enabling him to observe correctly the evidence of his consciousness and his conceptions.

This introductory exposition has already alluded to the distinction between Sense, Conception, and Thought. As the distinction is of capital importance for understanding the nature and kinds of knowledge, it will help to explain matters if we here call attention to it. For the explanation of *Sense*, the readiest method certainly is to refer to its external source—the organs of sense. But to name the organ does not help much to explain what is apprehended by it. The real distinction between sense and thought lies in this—that the essential feature of the sensible is individuality, and as the individual (which, reduced to its simplest terms, is the atom) is also a member of a group, sensible existence presents a number of mutually exclusive units—of units, to speak in more definite and abstract formulae, which exist side by side with, and after, one another. *Conception* or picture-thinking works with materials from the same sensuous source. But these materials when *conceived* are expressly characterized as in me and therefore mine; and secondly, as universal, or simple, because only referred to self. Nor is sense the only source of materialized conception. There are conceptions constituted by materials emanating from self-conscious thought, such as those of law, morality, religion, and even of thought itself, and it requires some effort to detect wherein lies the difference between such conceptions and thoughts having the same import. For it is a thought of which such conception is the vehicle, and there is no want of the form of universality, without which no content could be in me, or be a conception at all. Yet here also the peculiarity of conception is, generally speaking, to be sought in the individualism or isolation of its contents. True it is that, for example, law and legal provisions do not exist in a sensible space, mutually excluding one another. Nor as regards time, though they appear to some extent in succession, are their contents themselves conceived as affected by time, or as transient and changeable in it. The fault in conception lies deeper. These ideas, though implicitly possessing the organic unity of mind, stand isolated here and there on the broad ground of conception, with its inward and abstract generality. Thus cut adrift, each is simple, unrelated: Right, Duty, God. Conception in these circumstances either rests satisfied with declaring that Right is Right, God is God; or in a higher grade of culture it proceeds to enunciate the attributes: as, for instance, God is the Creator of the world, omniscent, almighty, etc. In this way several isolated, simple predicates are strung together: but in spite of the link supplied by their subject, the predicates never get beyond mere contiguity. In this point Conception coincides with Understanding: the only distinction being that the latter introduces relations of universal and particular, of cause and effect, etc., and in this way supplies a necessary connection to the isolated ideas of conception; which last has left them side by side in its vague mental spaces, connected only by a bare 'and'.

The difference between conception and thought is of special

importance: because philosophy may be said to do nothing but transform conceptions into thoughts—though it works the further transformation of a mere thought into a notion.

Sensible existence has been characterized by the attributes of individuality and mutual exclusion of the members. It is well to remember that these very attributes of sense are thoughts and general terms. It will be shown in the Logic that thought (and the universal) is not a mere opposite of sense: it lets nothing escape it, but, outflanking its other, is at once that other and itself. Now language is the work of thought: and hence all that is expressed in language must be universal. What I only mean or suppose is mine: it belongs to me—this particular individual. But language expresses nothing but universality; and so I cannot say what I merely *mean*. And the unutterable—feeling or sensation—far from being the highest truth, is the most unimportant and untrue. If I say 'the individual', 'this individual', 'here', 'now', all these are universal terms. Everything and anything is an individual, a 'this', and if it be sensible, is here and now. Similarly when I say 'I', I *mean* my single self to the exclusion of all others; but what I *say*, viz. 'I', is just every 'I', which in like manner excludes all others from itself. In an awkward expression which Kant used, he said that I *accompany* all my conceptions—sensations, too, desires, actions, etc. 'I' is in essence and act the universal: and such partnership is a form, though an external form, of universality. All other men have it in common with me to be 'I'; just as it is common to all my sensations and conceptions to be mine. But 'I', in the abstract, as such, is the mere act of self-concentration or self-relation, in which we make abstraction from all conception and feeling, from every state of mind and every peculiarity of nature, talent, and experience. To this extent, 'I' is the existence of a wholly *abstract* universality, a principle of abstract freedom. Hence thought, viewed as a subject, is what is expressed by the word 'I'; and since I am at the same time in all my sensations, conceptions, and states of consciousness, thought is everywhere present, and is a category that runs through all these modifications.

Our first impression when we use the term 'thought' is of a subjective activity—one among many similar faculties, such as memory, imagination, and will. Were thought merely an activity of the subject-mind and treated under that aspect by Logic, Logic would resemble the other sciences in possessing a well-marked object. It might in that case seem arbitrary to devote a special science to thought, while will, imagination, and the rest were denied the same privilege. The selection of one faculty however might even in this view be very well grounded on a certain authority acknowledged to belong to thought, and on its claim to be regarded as the true nature of man, in which consists his distinction from the brutes. Nor is it unimportant to study thought even as a subjective energy. A detailed analysis of its nature would exhibit rules and laws, a knowledge of which is derived from experience. A treatment of the laws of thought, from this point of view, used once to form the body of logical science. Of that science Aristotle was the founder. He succeeded in assigning to thought what properly belongs to it. Our thought is extremely concrete; but in its composite contents we must distinguish the part that properly belongs to thought, or to the abstract mode of its action. A subtle spiritual bond, consisting in the agency of thought, is what gives unity to all these contents, and it was this bond, the form as form, that Aristotle noted and described. Up to the present day, the logic of Aristotle continues to be the received system. It has indeed been spun out to greater length, especially by the labours of the medieval Schoolmen who, without making any material additions, merely refined in details. The moderns also have left their mark upon this logic, partly by omitting many points of logical doctrine due to Aristotle and the Schoolmen, and partly by foisting in a quantity of psychological matter. The purport of the science is to become acquainted with the procedure of finite thought: and, if it is adapted to its presupposed object, the science is entitled to be styled correct. The study of this formal logic undoubtedly has its uses. It sharpens the wits, as the phrase goes, and teaches us to collect our thoughts and to abstract—whereas in common consciousness we have to deal with sensuous conceptions which cross and perplex one another. Abstraction moreover implies the concentration of the mind on a single point, and thus induces the habit of attending to our inward selves. An acquaintance with the forms of finite thought may be made a means of training the mind for the empirical sciences, since their method is regulated by these forms: and in this sense logic has been designated Instrumental. It is true, we may be still more liberal, and say: Logic is to be studied not for its utility, but for its own sake; the superexcellent is not to be sought for the sake of mere utility. In one sense this is quite correct; but it may be replied that the superexcellent is also the most useful, because it is the all-sustaining principle which, having a subsistence of its own, may therefore serve as the vehicle of special ends which it furthers and secures. And thus, special ends, though they have no right to be set first, are still fostered by the presence of the highest good. Religion, for instance, has an absolute value of its own; yet at the same time other ends flourish and succeed in its train. As Christ says: 'Seek ye first the kingdom of God, and all these things shall be added unto you.' Particular ends can be attained only in the attainment of what absolutely is and exists in its own right.

§ 21

(b) Thought was described as active. We now, in the second place, consider this action in its bearings upon objects, or as reflection upon something. In this case the universal or product of its operation contains the value of the thing—is the essential, inward, and true.

In § 5 the old belief was quoted that the reality in object, circumstance, or event, the intrinsic worth or essence, the thing on which everything depends, is not a self-evident datum of consciousness, or coincident with the first appearance and impression of the object; that, on the contrary, Reflection is required in order to discover the real constitution of the object—and that by such reflection it will be ascertained.

To reflect is a lesson which even the child has to learn. One of his first lessons is to join adjectives with substantives. This obliges him to attend and distinguish: he has to remember a rule and apply it to the particular case. This rule is nothing but a universal: and the child must see that the particular adapts itself to this universal. In life, again, we have ends to attain. And with regard to these we ponder which is the best way to secure them. The end here represents the universal or governing principle and we have means and instruments whose action we regulate in conformity to the end. In the same way reflection is active in questions of conduct. To reflect here means to recollect the right, the duty—the universal which serves as a fixed rule to guide our behaviour in the given case. Our particular act must imply and recognize the universal law. We find the same thing exhibited in our study of natural phenomena. For instance, we observe thunder and lightning. The phenomenon is a familiar one, and we often perceive it. But man is not content with a bare acquaintance, or with the fact as it appears to the senses; he would like to get behind the surface, to know what it is, and to comprehend it. This leads him to reflect: he seeks to find out the cause as something distinct from the mere phenomenon: he tries to know the inside in its distinction from the outside. Hence the phenomenon becomes double, it splits into inside and outside, into force and its manifestation, into cause and effect. Once more we find the inside or the force identified with the universal and permanent: not this or that flash of lightning, this or that plant—but that which continues the same in them all. The sensible appearance is individual and evanescent: the permanent in it is discovered by reflection.

Nature shows us a countless number of individual forms and phenomena. Into this variety we feel a need of introducing unity: we compare, consequently, and try to find the universal of each single case. Individuals are born and perish: the species abides and recurs in them all: and its existence is only visible to reflection. Under the same head fall such laws as those regulating the motion of the heavenly bodies. To-day we see the stars here, and tomorrow there; and our mind finds something incongruous in this chaos—something in which it can put no faith, because it believes in order and in a simple, constant, and universal law. Inspired by this belief, the mind has directed its reflection towards the phenomena, and learnt their laws. In other words, it has established the movement of the heavenly bodies to be in accordance with a universal law from which every change of position may be known and predicted. The case is the same with the influences which make themselves felt in the infinite complexity of human conduct. There, too, man has the belief in the sway of a general principle. From all these examples it may be gathered how reflection is always seeking for something fixed and permanent, definite in itself and governing the particulars. This universal which cannot be apprehended by the senses counts as the true and essential. Thus, duties and rights are all-important in the matter of conduct; and an action is true when it conforms to those universal formulae.

In thus characterizing the universal, we become aware of its antithesis to something else. This something else is the merely immediate, outward, and individual, as opposed to the mediate, inward, and universal. The universal does not exist externally to the outward eye as a universal. The kind as kind cannot be perceived: the laws of the celestial motions are not written on the sky. The universal is neither seen nor heard, its existence is only for the mind. Religion leads us to a universal, which embraces all else within itself, to an Absolute by which all else is brought into being: and this Absolute is an object not of the senses but of the mind and of thought.

§ 22

(c) By the act of reflection something is *altered* in the way in which the fact was originally presented in sensation, perception, or conception. Thus, as it appears, an alteration must be interposed before the true nature of the object can be discovered.

What reflection elicits is a product of our thought. Solon, for instance, produced out of his head the laws he gave to the Athenians. This is half of the truth: but we must not on that account forget that the universal (in Solon's case, the laws) is the very reverse of merely subjective, or fail to note that it is the essential, true, and objective being of things. To discover the truth in things, mere attention is not enough; we must call in the action of our own faculties to transform what is immediately before us. Now, at first sight, this seems an inversion of the natural order, calculated to thwart the very purpose on which knowledge is bent. But the method is not so irrational as it seems. It has been the conviction of every age that the only way of reaching the permanent substratum was to transmute the given phenomenon by means of reflection. In modern times a doubt has for the first time been raised on this point in connection with the difference alleged to exist between the products of our thought and the things in their own nature. This real nature of things, it is said, is very different from what we make out of them. The divorce between thought and thing is mainly the work of the Critical Philosophy, and runs counter to the conviction of all previous ages, that their agreement was a matter of course. The antithesis between them is the hinge on which modern philosophy turns. Meanwhile the natural belief of men gives the lie to it. In common life we reflect, without particularly reminding ourselves that this is the process of arriving at the truth, and we think without hesitation, and in the firm belief that thought coincides with thing. And this belief is of the greatest importance. It marks the diseased state of the age when we see it adopt the despairing creed that our knowledge is only subjective, and that beyond this subjective we cannot go. Whereas, rightly understood, truth is objective, and ought so to regulate the conviction of every one, that the conviction of the individual is stamped as wrong when it does not agree with this rule. Modern views, on the contrary, put great value on the mere fact of conviction, and hold that to be convinced is good for its own sake, whatever be the burden of our conviction—there being no standard by which we can measure its truth.

We said above that, according to the old belief, it was the characteristic right of the mind to know the truth. If this be so, it also implies that everything we know both of outward and inward nature, in one word, the objective world, is in its own self the same as it is in thought, and that to think is to bring out the truth of our object, be it what it may. The business of philosophy is only to bring into explicit consciousness what the world in all ages has believed about thought. Philosophy therefore advances nothing new; and our present discussion has led us to a conclusion which agrees with the natural belief of mankind.

§ 23

(d) The real nature of the object is brought to light in reflection; but it is no less true that this exertion of thought is *my* act. If this be so, the real nature is a *product* of *my* mind, in its character of thinking subject—generated by me in my simple universality, self-collected and removed from extraneous influences—in one word, in my Freedom.

'Think for yourself' is a phrase which people often use as if it had some special significance. The fact is, no man can think for another, any more than he can eat or drink for him and the expression is a pleonasm. To think is in fact *ipso facto* to be free, for thought as the action of the universal is an abstract relating of self to self, where, being at home with ourselves, and as regards our subjectivity utterly blank, our consciousness is, in the matter of its contents, only in the fact and its characteristics. If this be admitted, and if we apply the term humility or modesty to an attitude where our subjectivity is not allowed to interfere by act or quality, it is easy to appreciate the question touching the humility or modesty and pride of philosophy. For in point of contents, thought is only true in proportion as it sinks itself in the facts; and in point of form it is no private or particular state or act of the subject, but rather that attitude of consciousness where the abstract self, freed from all the special limitations to which its ordinary states or qualities are liable, restricts itself to that universal action in which it is identical with all individuals. In these circumstances philosophy may be acquitted of the charge of pride. And when Aristotle summons the mind to rise to the dignity of that attitude, the dignity he seeks is won by letting slip all our individual opinions and prejudices, and submitting to the sway of the fact.

§ 24

With these explanations and qualifications, thoughts may be termed Objective Thoughts—among which are also to be included the forms which are more especially discussed in the common logic, where they are usually treated as forms of conscious thought only. *Logic therefore coincides with Metaphysics, the science of things set and held in thoughts*—thoughts accredited able to express the essential reality of things.

An exposition of the relation in which such forms as notion, judgement, and syllogism stand to others, such as causality, is a matter for the science itself. But this much is evident beforehand. If thought tries to form a notion of things, this notion (as well as its proximate phases, the judgement and syllogism) cannot be composed of articles and relations which are alien and irrelevant to the things. Reflection, it was said above, conducts to the universal of things: which universal is itself one of the constituent factors of a notion. To say that Reason or Understanding is in the world, is equivalent in its import to the phrase 'Objective Thought'. The latter phrase however has the inconvenience that thought is usually confined to express what belongs to the mind or consciousness only, while objective is a term applied, at least primarily, only to the non-mental.

(1) To speak of thought or objective thought as the heart and soul of the world, may seem to be ascribing consciousness to the things of nature. We feel a certain repugnance against making thought the inward function of things, especially as we speak of thought as marking the divergence of man from nature. It would be necessary, therefore, if we use the term thought at all, to speak of nature as the system of unconscious thought, or, to use Schelling's expression, a petrified intelligence. And in order to prevent misconception, 'thought-form' or 'thought-type' should be substituted for the ambiguous term thought.

From what has been said the principles of logic are to be sought in a system of thought-types or fundamental categories, in which the opposition between subjective and objective, in its usual sense, vanishes. The signification thus attached to thought and its characteristic forms may be illustrated by the ancient saying that '*νοῦς* governs the world', or by our own phrase that 'Reason is in the world'; which means that Reason is the soul of the world it inhabits, its immanent principle, its most proper and inward nature, its universal. Another illustration is offered by the circumstance that in speaking of some definite animal we say it is (an) animal. Now, the animal, *qua* animal, cannot be shown; nothing can be pointed out excepting some special animal. Animal, *qua* animal, does not exist: it is merely the universal nature of the individual animals, while each existing animal is a more concretely defined and particularized thing. But to be an animal—the law of kind which is the universal in this case—is the property of the particular animal, and constitutes its definite essence. Take away from the dog its animality, and it becomes impossible to say what it is. All things have a permanent inward nature, as well as an outward existence. They live and die, arise and pass away; but their essential and universal part is the kind; and this means much more than something *common* to them all.

If thought is the constitutive substance of external things, it is also the universal substance of what is spiritual. In all human perception thought is present; so too thought is the universal in all the acts of conception and recollection; in short, in every mental activity, in willing, wishing, and the like. All these faculties are only further specializations of thought. When it is presented in this light, thought has a different part to play from what it has if we speak of a faculty of thought, one among a crowd of other faculties, such as perception, conception, and will, with which it stands on the same level. When it is seen to be the true universal of all that nature and mind contain, it extends its scope far beyond all these, and becomes the basis of everything. From this view of thought, in its objective meaning as *νοῦς*, we may next pass to consider the subjective sense of the term. We say first, Man is a being that thinks; but we also say at the same time, Man is a being that perceives and wills. Man is a thinker, and is universal; but he is a thinker only because he feels his own universality. The animal too is by implication universal, but the universal is not consciously felt by it to be universal: it feels only the individual. The animal sees a singular object, for instance, its food, or a man. For the animal all this never goes beyond an individual thing. Similarly, sensation has to do with nothing but singulars, such as *this* pain or *this* sweet taste. Nature does not bring its *νοῦς* into consciousness: it is man who first makes himself double so as to be a universal for a universal. This first happens when man knows that he is 'I'. By the term 'I' I mean myself, a single and altogether determinate person. And yet I really utter nothing peculiar to myself, for every one else is an 'I' or 'Ego', and when I call myself 'I', though I indubitably mean the single person myself, I express a thorough universal. 'I', therefore, is mere being-for-self, in which everything peculiar or marked is renounced and buried out of sight; it is as it were the ultimate and unanalysable point of consciousness. We may say 'I' and thought are the same, or, more definitely, 'I' is thought as a thinker. What I have in my consciousness is for me. 'I' is the vacuum or receptacle for anything and everything: for which everything is and which stores up everything in itself. Every man is a whole world of conceptions, that lie buried in the night of the 'Ego'. It follows that the 'Ego' is the universal in which we leave aside all that is particular, and in which at the same time all the particulars have a latent existence. In other words, it is not a mere universality and nothing more, but the universality which includes in it everything. Commonly we use the word 'I' without attaching much importance to it, nor is it an object of study except to philosophical analysis. In the 'Ego', we have thought before us in its utter purity. While the brute cannot say 'I', man can, because it is his nature to think. Now in the 'Ego' there are a variety of contents, derived both from within and from without, and according to the nature of these contents our state may be described as perception, or conception, or reminiscence. But in all of them the 'I' is found: or in them all thought is present. Man, therefore, is always thinking, even in his perceptions: if he observes anything, he always observes it as a universal, fixes on a single point which he places in relief, thus withdrawing his attention from other points, and takes it as abstract and universal, even if the universality be only in form.

In the case of our ordinary conceptions, two things may happen. Either the contents are moulded by thought, but not the form; or, the form belongs to thought and not the contents. In using such terms, for instance, as anger, rose, hope, I am speaking of things which I have learnt in the way of sensation, but I express these contents in a universal mode, that is, in the form of thought. I have left out much that is particular and given the contents in their generality: but still the contents remain sense-derived. On the other hand, when I represent God, the content is undeniably a product of pure thought, but the form still retains the sensuous limitations which it has as I find it immediately present in myself. In these generalized images the content is not merely and simply sensible, as it is in a visual inspection; but either the content is sensuous and the form appertains to thought, or vice versa. In the first case the material is given to us, and our thought supplies the form: in the second case the content which has its source in thought is by means of the form turned into a something given, which accordingly reaches the mind from without.

(2) Logic is the study of thought pure and simple, or of the pure thought-forms. In the ordinary sense of the term, by thought we generally represent to ourselves something more than simple and unmixed thought; we mean some thought, the material of which is from experience. Whereas in logic a thought is understood to include nothing else but what depends on thinking and what thinking has brought into existence. It is in these circumstances that thoughts are *pure* thoughts. The mind is then in its own home-element and therefore free; for freedom means that the other thing with which you deal is a second self—so that you never leave your own ground but give the law to yourself. In the impulses or appetites the beginning is from something else, from something which we feel to be external. In this case then we speak of dependence. For freedom it is necessary that we should feel no presence of something else which is not ourselves. The natural man, whose motions follow the rule only of his appetites, is not his own master. Be he as self-willed as he may, the constituents of his will and opinion are not his own, and his freedom is merely formal. But when we *think*, we renounce our selfish and particular being, sink ourselves in the thing, allow thought to follow its own course, and if we add anything of our own, we think ill.

If in pursuance of the foregoing remarks we consider Logic to be the system of the pure types of thought, we find that the other philosophical sciences, the Philosophy of Nature and the Philosophy of Mind, take the place, as it were, of an Applied Logic, and that Logic is the soul which animates them both. Their problem in that case is only to recognize the logical forms under the shapes they assume in Nature and Mind—shapes which are only a particular mode of expression for the forms of pure thought. If for instance we take the syllogism (not as it was understood in the old formal logic, but as its real value), we shall find it gives expression to the law that the particular is the middle term which fuses together the extremes of the universal and the singular. The syllogistic form is a universal form of all things. Everything that exists is a particular, which couples together the universal and the singular. But Nature is weak and fails to exhibit the logical forms in their purity. Such a feeble exemplification of the syllogism may be seen in the magnet. In the middle or point of indifference of a magnet, its two poles, however they may be distinguished, are brought into one. Physics also teaches us to see the universal or essence in Nature: and the only difference between it and the Philosophy of Nature is that the latter brings before our mind the adequate forms of the notion in the physical world.

It will now be understood that Logic is the all-animating spirit of all the sciences, and its categories the spiritual hierarchy. They are the heart and centre of things: and yet at the same time they are always on our lips, and, apparently at least, perfectly familiar objects. But things thus familiar are usually the greatest strangers. Being, for example, is a category of pure thought: but to make 'is' an object of investigation never occurs to us. Common fancy puts the Absolute far away in a world beyond. The Absolute is rather directly before us, so present that so long as we think, we must, though without express consciousness of it, always carry it with us and always use it. Language is the main depository of these types of thought; and one use of the grammatical instruction which children receive is unconsciously to turn their attention to distinctions of thought.

Logic is usually said to be concerned with forms *only* and to derive the material for them from elsewhere. But this 'only', which assumes that the logical thoughts are nothing in comparison with the rest of the contents, is not the word to use about forms which are the absolutely real ground of everything. Everything else rather is an 'only' compared with these thoughts. To make such abstract forms a problem presupposes in the inquirer a higher level of culture than ordinary; and to study them in themselves and for their own sake signifies in addition that these thought-types must be deduced out of thought itself, and their truth or reality examined by the light of their own laws. We do not assume them as data from without, and then define them or exhibit their value and authority by comparing them with the shape they take in our minds. If we thus acted, we should proceed from observation and experience, and should, for instance, say we habitually employ the term 'force' in such a case, and such a meaning. A definition like that would be called correct, if it agreed with the conception of its object present in our ordinary state of mind. The defect of this empirical method is that a notion is not defined as it is in and for itself, but in terms of something assumed, which is then used as a criterion and standard of correctness. No such test need be applied: we have merely to let the thought-forms follow the impulse of their own organic life.

To ask if a category is true or not, must sound strange to the ordinary mind: for a category apparently becomes true only when it is applied to a given object, and apart from this application it would seem meaningless to inquire into the truth. But this is the very question on which everything turns. We must however in the first place understand clearly what we mean by Truth. In common life truth means the agreement of an object with our conception of it. We thus presuppose an object to which our conception must conform. In the philosophical sense of the word, on the other hand, truth may be described, in general abstract terms, as the agreement of a thought-content with itself. This meaning is quite different from the one given above. At the same time the deeper and philosophical meaning of truth can be partially traced even in the ordinary usage of language. Thus we speak of a true friend; by which we mean a friend whose manner of conduct accords with the notion of friendship. In the same way we speak of a true work of Art. Untrue in this sense means the same as bad, or self-discordant. In this sense a bad state is an untrue state; and evil and untruth may be said to consist in the contradiction subsisting between the function or notion and the existence of the object. Of such a bad object we may form a correct representation, but the import of such representation is inherently false. Of these correctnesses, which are at the same time untruths, we may have many in our heads. God alone is the thorough harmony of notion and reality. All finite things involve an untruth: they have a notion and an existence, but their existence does not meet the requirements of the notion. For this reason they must perish, and then the incompatibility between their notion and their existence becomes manifest. It is in the kind that the individual animal has its notion; and the kind liberates itself from this individuality by death.

The study of truth, or, as it is here explained to mean, consistency, constitutes the proper problem of logic. In our everyday mind we are never troubled with questions about the truth of the forms of thought. We may also express the problem of logic by saying that it examines the forms of thought touching their capability to hold truth. And the question comes to this: What are the forms of the infinite, and what are the forms of the finite? Usually no suspicion attaches to the finite forms of thought; they are allowed to pass unquestioned. But it is from conforming to finite categories in thought and action that all deception originates.

(3) Truth may be ascertained by several methods, each of which however is no more than a form. Experience is the first of these methods. But the method is only a form: it has no intrinsic value of its own. For in experience everything depends upon the mind we bring to bear upon actuality. A great mind is great in its experience; and in the motley play of phenomena at once perceives the point of real significance. The idea is present, in actual shape, not something, as it were, over the hill and far away. The genius of a Goethe, for example, looking into nature or history, has great experiences, catches sight of the living principle, and gives expression to it. A second method of apprehending the truth is Reflection, which defines it by intellectual relations of condition and conditioned. But in these two modes the absolute truth has not yet found its appropriate form. The most perfect method of knowledge proceeds in

the pure form of thought: and here the attitude of man is one of entire freedom.

That the form of thought is the perfect form, and that it presents the truth as it intrinsically and actually is, is the general dogma of all philosophy. To give a proof of the dogma there is, in the first instance, nothing to do but show that these other forms of knowledge are finite. The grand Scepticism of antiquity accomplished this task when it exhibited the contradictions contained in every one of these forms. That Scepticism indeed went further: but when it ventured to assail the forms of reason, it began by insinuating under them something finite upon which it might fasten. All the forms of finite thought will make their appearance in the course of logical development, the order in which they present themselves being determined by necessary laws. Here in the introduction they could only be unscientifically assumed as something given. In the theory of logic itself these forms will be exhibited, not only on their negative, but also on their positive side.

When we compare the different forms of ascertaining truth with one another, the first of them, immediate knowledge, may perhaps seem the finest, noblest, and most appropriate. It includes everything which the moralists term innocence as well as religious feeling, simple trust, love, fidelity, and natural faith. The two other forms, first reflective, and secondly philosophical cognition, must leave that unsought natural harmony behind. And so far as they have this in common, the methods which claim to apprehend the truth by thought may naturally be regarded as part and parcel of the pride which leads man to trust to his own powers for a knowledge of the truth. Such a position involves a thorough-going disruption, and, viewed in that light, might be regarded as the source of all evil and wickedness—the original transgression. Apparently therefore the only way of being reconciled and restored to peace is to surrender all claims to think or know.

This lapse from natural unity has not escaped notice, and nations from the earliest times have asked the meaning of the wonderful division of the spirit against itself. No such inward disunion is found in nature: natural things do nothing wicked.

The Mosaic legend of the Fall of Man has preserved an ancient picture representing the origin and consequences of this disunion. The incidents of the legend form the basis of an essential article of the creed, the doctrine of original sin in man and his consequent need of succour. It may be well at the commencement of logic to examine the story which treats of the origin and the bearings of the very knowledge which logic has to discuss. For, though philosophy must not allow herself to be overawed by religion, or accept the position of existence on sufferance, she cannot afford to neglect these popular conceptions. The tales and allegories of religion, which have enjoyed for thousands of years the veneration of nations, are not to be set aside as antiquated even now.

Upon a closer inspection of the story of the Fall we find, as was already said, that it exemplifies the universal bearings of knowledge upon the spiritual life. In its instinctive and natural stage, spiritual life wears the garb of innocence and confiding simplicity; but the very essence of spirit implies the absorption of this immediate condition in something higher. The spiritual is distinguished from the natural, and more especially from the animal, life, in the circumstance that it does not continue a mere stream of tendency, but sunders itself to self-realization. But this position of severed life has in its turn to be suppressed, and the spirit has by its own act to win its way to concord again. The final concord then is spiritual; that is, the principle of restoration is found in thought, and thought only. The hand that inflicts the wound is also the hand which heals it.

We are told in our story that Adam and Eve, the first human beings, the types of humanity, were placed in a garden, where grew a tree of life and a tree of the knowledge of good and evil. God, it is said, had forbidden them to eat of the fruit of this latter tree: of the tree of life for the present nothing further is said. These words evidently assume that man is not intended to seek knowledge, and ought to remain in the state of innocence. Other meditative races, it may be remarked, have held the same belief that the primitive state of mankind was one of innocence and harmony. Now all this is to a certain extent correct. The disunion that appears throughout humanity is not a condition to rest in. But it is a mistake to regard the natural and immediate harmony as the right state. The mind is not mere instinct: on the contrary, it essentially involves the tendency to reasoning and meditation. Childlike innocence no doubt has in it something fascinating and attractive: but only because it reminds us of what the spirit must win for itself. The harmoniousness of childhood is a gift from the hand of nature: the second harmony must spring from the labour and culture of the spirit. And so the words of Christ, 'Except ye *become* as little children', etc., are very far from telling us that we must always remain children.

Again, we find in the narrative of Moses that the occasion which led man to leave his natural unity is attributed to solicitation from without. The serpent was the tempter. But the truth is, that the step into opposition, the awakening of consciousness, follows from the very nature of man; and the same history repeats itself in every son of Adam. The serpent represents likeness to God as consisting in the knowledge of good and evil: and it is just this knowledge in which man participates when he breaks with the unity of his instinctive being and eats of the forbidden fruit. The first reflection of awakened consciousness in men told them that they were naked. This is a naïve and profound trait. For the sense of shame bears evidence to the separation of man from his natural and sensuous life. The beasts never get so far as this separation, and they feel no shame. And it is in the human feeling of shame that we are to seek the spiritual and moral origin of dress, compared with which the merely physical need is a secondary matter.

Next comes the Curse, as it is called, which God pronounced upon man. The prominant point in that curse turns chiefly on the contrast between man and nature. Man must work in the sweat of his brow: and woman bring forth in sorrow. As to work, if it is the result of the disunion, it is also the victory over it. The beasts have nothing more to do but to pick up the materials required to satisfy their wants: man on the contrary can only satisfy his wants by himself producing and transforming the necessary means. Thus even in these outside things man is dealing with himself.

The story does not close with the expulsion from Paradise. We are further told, God said, 'Behold Adam is become as one of us, to know good and evil.' Knowledge is now spoken of as divine, and not, as before, as something wrong and forbidden. Such words contain a confutation of the idle talk that philosophy pertains only to the finitude of the mind. Philosophy is knowledge, and it is through knowledge that man first realizes his original vocation, to be the image of God. When the record adds that God drove men out of the garden of Eden to prevent their eating of the tree of life, it only means that on his natural side certainly man is finite and mortal, but in knowledge infinite.

We all know the theological dogma that man's nature is evil, tainted with what is called Original Sin. Now while we accept the dogma, we must give up the setting of incident which represents original sin as consequent upon an accidental act of the first man. For the very notion of spirit is enough to show that man is evil by nature, and it is an error to imagine that he could ever be otherwise. To such extent as man is and acts like a creature of nature, his whole behaviour is what it ought not to be. For the spirit it is a duty to be free, and to realize itself by its own act. Nature is for man only the starting-point which he has to transform. The theological doctrine of original sin is a profound truth; but modern enlightenment prefers to believe that man is naturally good, and that he acts right so long as he continues true to nature.

The hour when man leaves the path of mere natural being marks the difference between him, a self-conscious agent, and the natural world. But this schism, though it forms a necessary element in the very notion of spirit, is not the final goal of man. It is to this state of inward breach that the whole finite action of thought and will belongs. In that finite sphere man pursues ends of his own and draws from himself the material of his conduct. While he pursues these aims to the uttermost, while his knowledge and his will seek himself, his own narrow self apart from the universal, he is evil; and his evil is to be subjective.

We seem at first to have a double evil here: but both are really the same. Man in so far as he is spirit is not the creature of nature: and when he behaves as such, and follows the cravings of appetite, he wills to be so.

The natural wickedness of man is therefore unlike the natural life of animals. A mere natural life may be more exactly defined by saying that the natural man as such is an individual: for nature in every part is in the bonds of individualism. Thus when man wills to be a creature of nature, he wills in the same degree to be an individual simply. Yet against such impulsive and appetitive action, due to the individualism of nature, there also steps in the law or general principle. This law may either be an external force, or have the form of divine authority. So long as he continues in his natural state, man is in bondage to the law. It is true that among the instincts and affections of man, there are social or benevolent inclinations, love, sympathy, and others, reaching beyond his selfish isolation. But so long as these tendencies are instinctive, their virtual universality of scope and purport is vitiated by the subjective form which always allows free play to self-seeking and random action.

§ 25

The term 'Objective Thoughts' indicates the *truth*—the truth which is to be the absolute *object* of philosophy, and not merely the goal at which it aims. But the very expression cannot fail to suggest an opposition, to characterize and appreciate which is the main motive of the philosophical attitude of the present time, and which forms the real problem of the question about truth and our means of ascertaining it. If the thought-forms are vitiated by a fixed antithesis, i.e. if they are only of a finite character, they are unsuitable for the self-centred universe of truth, and truth can find no adequate receptacle in thought. Such thought, which can produce only limited and partial categories and proceed by their means, is what in the stricter sense of the word is termed Understanding. The finitude, further, of these categories lies in two points. Firstly, they are only subjective, and the antithesis of an objective permanently clings to them. Secondly, they are always of restricted content, and so persist in antithesis to one another and still more to the Absolute. In order more fully to explain the position and import here attributed to logic, the attitudes in which thought is supposed to stand to objectivity will next be examined by way of further introduction.

In my Phenomenology of the Spirit, which on that account was at its publication described as the first part of the System of Philosophy, the method adopted was to begin with the first and simplest phase of mind, immediate consciousness, and to show how that stage gradually of necessity worked onward to the philosophical point of view, the necessity of that view being proved by the process. But in these circumstances it was impossible to restrict the quest to the mere form of consciousness. For the stage of philosophical knowledge is the richest in material and organization, and therefore, as it came before us in the shape of a result, it presupposed the existence of the concrete formations of consciousness, such as individual and social morality, art and religion. In the development of consciousness, which at first sight appears limited to the point of form merely, there is thus at the same time included the development of the matter or of the objects discussed in the special branches of philosophy. But the latter process must, so to speak, go on behind consciousness, since those facts are the essential nucleus which is raised into consciousness. The exposition accordingly is rendered more intricate, because so much that properly belongs to the concrete branches is prematurely dragged into the introduction. The survey which follows in the present work has even more the inconvenience of being only historical and inferential in its method. But it tries especially to show how the questions men have proposed, outside the school, on the nature of Knowledge, Faith, and the like—questions which they imagine to have no connection with abstract thoughts—are really reducible to the simple categories, which first get cleared up in Logic.

III

FIRST ATTITUDE OF THOUGHT TO OBJECTIVITY

§ 26

The first of these attitudes of thought is seen in the method which has no doubts and no sense of the contradiction in thought, or of the hostility of thought against itself. It entertains an unquestioning belief that reflection is the means of ascertaining the truth, and of bringing the objects before the mind as they really are. And in this belief it advances straight upon its objects, takes the materials furnished by sense and perception, and reproduces them from itself as facts of thought; and then, believing this result to be the truth, the method is content. Philosophy in its earliest stages, all the sciences, and even the daily action and movement of consciousness, live in this faith.

§ 27

This method of thought has never become aware of the antithesis of subjective and objective: and to that extent there is nothing to prevent its statements from possessing a genuinely philosophical and speculative character, though it is just as possible that they may never get beyond finite categories, or the stage where the antithesis is still unresolved. In the present introduction the main question for us is to observe this attitude of thought in its extreme form; and we shall accordingly first of all examine its second and inferior aspect as a philosophic system. One of the clearest instances of it, and one lying nearest to ourselves, may be found in the Metaphysic of the Past as it subsisted among us previous to the philosophy of Kant. It is however only in reference to the history of philosophy that this Metaphysic can be said to belong to the past: the thing is always and at all places to be found, as the view which the abstract understanding takes of the objects of reason. And it is in this point that the real and immediate good lies of a closer examination of its main scope and its *modus operandi.*

§ 28

This metaphysical system took the laws and forms of thought to be the fundamental laws and forms of things. It assumed that to think a thing was the means of finding its very self and nature: and to that extent it occupied higher ground than the Critical Philosophy which succeeded it. But in the first instance (1) *these terms of thought were cut off from their connection*, their solidarity; each was believed valid by itself and capable of serving as a predicate of the truth. It was the general assumption of this metaphysic that a knowledge of the Absolute was gained by assigning predicates to it. It neither inquired what the terms of the understanding specially meant or what they were worth, nor did it test the method which characterizes the Absolute by the assignment of predicates.

As an example of such predicates may be taken: Existence, in the proposition, 'God has existence'; Finitude or Infinity, as in the question, 'Is the world finite or infinite?'; Simple and Complex, in the proposition, 'The Soul is simple'—or again, 'The thing is a unity, a whole', etc. Nobody asked whether such predicates had any intrinsic and independent truth, or if the propositional form could be a form of truth.

The Metaphysic of the past assumed, as unsophisticated belief always does, that thought apprehends the very self of things, and that things, to become what they truly are, require to be thought. For Nature and the human soul are a very Proteus in their perpetual transformations; and it soon occurs to the observer that the first crude impression of things is not their essential being. This is a point of view the very reverse of the result arrived at by the Critical Philosophy; a result, of which it may be said, that it bade man go and feed on mere husks and chaff.

We must look more closely into the procedure of that old metaphysic. In the first place it never went beyond the province of the analytic understanding. Without preliminary inquiry it adopted the abstract categories of thought and let them rank as predicates of truth. But in using the term thought we must not forget the difference between finite or discursive thinking and the thinking which is infinite and rational. The categories, as they meet us prima facie and in isolation, are finite forms. But truth is always infinite, and cannot be expressed or presented to consciousness in finite terms. The phrase *infinite thought* may excite surprise, if we adhere to the modern conception that thought is always limited. But it is, speaking rightly, the very essence of thought to be infinite. The nominal explanation of calling a thing finite is that it has an end, that it exists up to a certain point only, where it comes into contact with, and is limited by, its other. The finite therefore subsists in reference to its other, which is its negation and presents itself as its limit. Now thought is always in its own sphere; its relations are with itself, and it is its own object. In having a thought for object, I am at home with myself. The thinking power, the 'I', is therefore infinite, because, when it thinks, it is in relation to an object which is itself. Generally speaking, an object means a something else, a negative confronting me. But in the case where thought thinks itself, it has an object which is at the same time no object: in other words, its objectivity is suppressed and transformed into an idea. Thought, as thought, therefore in its unmixed nature involves no limits; it is finite only when it keeps to limited categories, which it believes to be ultimate. Infinite or speculative thought, on the contrary, while it no less defines, does in the very act of limiting and defining make that defect vanish. And so infinity is not, as most frequently happens, to be conceived as an abstract away and away for ever and ever, but in the simple manner previously indicated.

The thinking of the old metaphysical system was finite. Its whole mode of action was regulated by categories, the limits of which it believed to be permanently fixed and not subject to any further negation. Thus, one of its questions was: Has God existence? The question supposes that existence is an altogether positive term, a sort of *ne plus ultra*. We shall see however at a later point that existence is by no means a merely positive term, but one which is too low for the Absolute Idea, and unworthy of God. A second question in these metaphysical systems was: Is the world finite or infinite? The very terms of the question assume that the finite is a permanent contradictory to the infinite: and one can easily see that, when they are so opposed, the infinite, which of course ought to be the whole, only appears as a single aspect and suffers restriction from the finite. But a restricted infinity is itself only a finite. In the same way it was asked whether the soul was simple or composite. Simpleness was, in other words, taken to be an ultimate characteristic, giving expression to a whole truth. Far from being so, simpleness is the expression of a half-truth, as one-sided and abstract as existence—a term of thought, which, as we shall hereafter see, is itself untrue and hence unable to hold truth. If the soul be viewed as merely and abstractly simple, it is characterized in an inadequate and finite way.

It was therefore the main question of the pre-Kantian metaphysic to discover whether predicates of the kind mentioned were to be ascribed to its objects. Now these predicates are after all only limited formulae of the understanding which, instead of expressing the truth, merely impose a limit. More than this, it should be noted that the chief feature of the method lay in 'assigning' or 'attributing' predicates to the object that was to be cognized, for example, to God. But attribution is no more than an external reflection about the object: the predicates by which the object is to be determined are supplied from the resouces of picture-thought, and are applied in a mechanical way. Whereas, if we are to have genuine cognition, the object must characterize its own self and not derive its predicates from without. Even supposing we follow the method of predicating, the mind cannot help feeling that predicates of this sort fail to exhaust the object. From the same point of view the Orientals are quite correct in calling God the many-named or the myriad-named One. One after another of these finite categories leaves the soul unsatisfied, and the Oriental sage is compelled unceasingly to seek for more and more of such predicates. In finite things it is no doubt the case that they have to be characterized through finite predicates: and with these things the understanding finds proper scope for its special action. Itself finite, it knows only the nature of the finite. Thus, when I call some action a theft, I have characterized the action in its essential facts; and such a knowledge is sufficient for the judge. Similarly, finite things stand to each other as cause and effect, force and exercise, and when they are apprehended in these categories, they are known in their finitude. But the objects of reason cannot be defined by these finite predicates. To try to do so was the defect of the old metaphysic.

§ 29

Predicates of this kind, taken individually, have but a limited range of meaning, and no one can fail to perceive how inadequate they are, and how far they fall below the fullness of detail which our imaginative thought gives, in the case, for example, of God, Mind, or Nature. Besides, though the fact of their being all predicates of one subject supplies them with a certain connection, their several meanings keep them apart: and consequently each is brought in as a stranger in relation to the others.

The first of these defects the Orientals sought to remedy, when, for example, they defined God by attributing to Him many names; but still they felt that the number of names would have had to be infinite.

§ 30

(2) In the second place, *the metaphysical systems adopted a wrong criterion.* Their objects were no doubt totalities which in their own

proper selves belong to reason that is, to the organized and systematically developed universe of thought. But these totalities —God, the Soul, the World—were taken by the metaphysician as subjects made and ready, to form the basis for an application of the categories of the understanding. They were assumed from popular conception. Accordingly popular conception was the only canon for settling whether or not the predicates were suitable and sufficient.

§ 31

The common conceptions of God, the Soul, the World, may be supposed to afford thought a firm and fast footing. They do not really do so. Besides having a particular and subjective character clinging to them, and thus leaving room for great variety of interpretation, they themselves first of all require a firm and fast definition by thought. This may be seen in any of these propositions where the predicate, or in philosophy the category, is needed to indicate what the subject, or the conception we start with, is.

In such a sentence as 'God is eternal', we begin with the conception of God, not knowing as yet what he is: to tell us that, is the business of the predicate. In the principles of logic, accordingly, where the terms formulating the subject-matter are those of thought only, it is not merely superfluous to make these categories predicates to propositions in which God, or, still vaguer, the Absolute, is the subject, but it would also have the disadvantage of suggesting another canon than the nature of thought. Besides, the propositional form (and for proposition, it would be more correct to substitute judgement) is not suited to express the concrete—and the true is always concrete—or the speculative. Every judgement is by its form one-sided and, to that extent, false.

This metaphysic was not free or objective thinking. Instead of letting the object freely and spontaneously expound its own characteristics, metaphysic presupposed it ready-made. If anyone wishes to know what free thought means, he must go to Greek philosophy: for Scholasticism, like these metaphysical systems, accepted its facts, and accepted them as a dogma from the authority of the Church. We moderns, too, by our whole upbringing, have been initiated into ideas which it is extremely difficult to overstep, on account of their far-reaching significance. But the ancient philosophers were in a different position. They were men who lived wholly in the perceptions of the senses, and who, after their rejection of mythology and its fancies, presupposed nothing but the heaven above and the earth around. In these material, non-metaphysical surroundings, thought is free and enjoys its own privacy—cleared of everything material, and thoroughly at home. This feeling that we are all our own is characteristic of free thought—of that voyage into the open, where nothing is below us or above us, and we stand in solitude with ourselves alone.

§ 32

(3) In the third place, *this system of metaphysic turned into Dogmatism.* When our thought never ranges beyond narrow and rigid terms, we are forced to assume that of two opposite assertions, such as were the above propositions, the one must be true and the other false.

Dogmatism may be most simply described as the contrary of Scepticism. The ancient Sceptics gave the name of Dogmatism to every philosophy whatever holding a system of definite doctrine. In this large sense Scepticism may apply the name even to philosophy which is properly Speculative. But in the narrower sense, Dogmatism consists in the tenacity which draws a hard and fast line between certain terms and others opposite to them. We may see this clearly in the strict 'either—or': for instance, The world is either finite or infinite; but one of these two it must be. The contrary of this rigidity is the characteristic of all Speculative truth. There no such inadequate formulae are allowed, nor can they possibly exhaust it. These formulae Speculative truth holds in union as a totality, whereas Dogmatism invests them in their isolation with a title to fixity and truth.

It often happens in philosophy that the half-truth takes its place beside the whole truth and assumes on its own account the position of something permanent. But the fact is that the half-truth, instead of being a fixed or self-subsistent principle, is a mere element absolved and included in the whole. The metaphysic of understanding is dogmatic, because it maintains half-truths in their isolation: whereas the idealism of speculative philosophy carries out the principle of totality and shows that it can reach beyond the inadequate formularies of abstract thought. Thus idealism would say: The soul is neither finite only, nor infinite only; it is really the one just as much as the other, and in that way neither the one nor the other. In other words, such formularies in their isolation are inadmissible, and only come into account as formative elements in a larger notion. Such idealism we see even in the ordinary phases of consciousness. Thus we say of sensible things, that they are changeable: that is, they *are*, but it is equally true that they are *not*. We show more obstinacy in dealing with the categories of the understanding. These are terms which we believe to be somewhat firmer—or even absolutely firm and fast. We look upon them as separated from each other by an infinite chasm, so that opposite categories can never get at each other. The battle of reason is the struggle to break up the rigidity to which the understanding has reduced everything.

§ 33

The *first* part of this metaphysic in its systematic form is Ontology, or the doctrine of the abstract characteristics of Being. The multitude of these characteristics, and the limits set to their applicability, are not founded upon any principle. They have in consequence to be enumerated as experience and circumstances direct, and the import ascribed to them is founded only upon common sensualized conceptions, upon assertions that particular words are used in a particular sense, and even perhaps upon etymology. If experience pronounces the list to be complete, and if the usage of language, by its agreement, shows the analysis to be correct, the metaphysician is satisfied; and the intrinsic and independent truth and necessity of such characteristics is never made a matter of investigation at all.

To ask if being, existence, finitude, simplicity, complexity, etc. are notions intrinsically and independently true, must surprise those who believe that a question about truth can only concern propositions (as to whether a notion is or is not with truth to be attributed, as the phrase is, to a subject), and that falsehood lies in the contradiction existing between the subject in our ideas, and the notion to be predicated of it. Now as the notion is concrete, it and every character of it in general is essentially a self-contained unity of distinct characteristics. If truth then were nothing more than the absence of contradiction, it would be first of all necessary in the case of every notion to examine whether it, taken individually, did not contain this sort of intrinsic contradiction.

§ 34

The *second* branch of the metaphysical system was Rational Psychology or Pneumatology. It dealt with the metaphysical nature of the Soul—that is, of the Mind regarded as a thing. It expected to find immortality in a sphere dominated by the laws of composition, time, qualitative change, and quantitative increase or decrease.

The name 'rational', given to this species of psychology, served to contrast it with empirical modes of observing the phenomena of the soul. Rational psychology viewed the soul in its metaphysical nature, and through the categories supplied by abstract thought. The rationalists endeavoured to ascertain the inner nature of the soul as it is in itself and as it is for thought. In philosophy at present we hear little of the soul: the favourite term is now mind (spirit). The two are distinct, soul being as it were the middle term between body and spirit, or the bond between the two. The mind, as soul, is immersed in corporeity, and the soul is the animating principle of the body.

The pre-Kantian metaphysic, we say, viewed the soul as a thing. 'Thing' is a very ambiguous word. By a thing, we mean, firstly, an immediate existence, something we represent in sensuous form: and in this meaning the term has been applied to the soul. Hence the question regarding the seat of the soul. Of course, if the soul have a seat, it is in space and sensuously envisaged. So, too, if the soul be viewed as a thing, we can ask whether the soul is simple or composite. The question is important as bearing on the immortality of the soul, which is supposed to depend on the absence of composition. But the fact is, that in abstract simplicity we have a category, which as little corresponds to the nature of the soul, as that of compositeness.

One word on the relation of rational to empirical psychology. The former, because it sets itself to apply thought to cognize mind and even to demonstrate the result of such thinking, is the higher; whereas empirical psychology starts from perception, and only recounts and describes what perception supplies. But if we propose to think the mind, we must not be quite so shy of its special phenomena. Mind is essentially active in the same sense as the Schoolmen said that God is 'absolute actuosity'. But if the mind is active it must as it were utter itwelf. It is wrong therefore to take the mind for a processless *ens*, as did the old metaphysic which divided the processless inward life of the mind from its outward life. The mind, of all things, must be looked at in its concrete actuality, in its energy; and in such a way that its manifestations are seen to be determined by its inward force.

§ 35

The *third* branch of metaphysics was Cosmology. The topics it embraced were the world, its contingency, necessity, eternity, limitation in time and space: the laws (only formal) of its changes: the freedom of man and the origin of evil.

To these topics it applied what were believed to be thoroughgoing contrasts: such as contingency and necessity; eternal and internal necessity; efficient and final cause, or causality in general and design; essence or substance and phenomenon; form and matter; freedom and necessity; happiness and pain; good and evil.

The object of Cosmology comprised not merely Nature, but Mind too, in its external complication in its phenomenon—in fact, existence in general, or the sum of finite things. This object however it viewed not as a concrete whole, but only under certain abstract points of view. Thus the questions Cosmology attempted to solve were such as these: Is accident or necessity dominant in the world? Is the world eternal or created? It was therefore a chief concern of this study to lay down what were called general cosmological laws: for instance, that Nature does not act by fits and starts. And by fits and starts (*saltus*) they meant a qualitative difference or qualitative alteration showing itself without any antecedent determining mean: whereas, on the contrary, a gradual change (of quantity) is obviously not without intermediation.

In regard to Mind as it makes itself felt in the world, the questions which Cosmology chiefly discussed turned upon the freedom of man and the origin of evil. Nobody can deny that these are questions of the highest importance. But to give them a satisfactory answer, it is above all things necessary not to claim finality for the abstract formulae of understanding, or to suppose that each of the two terms in an antithesis has an independent subsistence or can be treated in its isolation as a complete and self-centred truth. This however is the general position taken by the metaphysicians before Kant, and appears in their cosmological discussions, which for that reason were incapable of compassing their purpose, to understand the phenomena of the world. Observe how they proceed with the distinction between freedom and necessity, in their application of these categories to Nature and Mind. Nature they regard as subject in its workings to necessity; Mind they hold to be free. No doubt there is a real foundation for this distinction in the very core of the Mind itself: but freedom and necessity, when thus abstractly opposed, are terms applicable only in the finite world to which, as such, they belong. A freedom involving no necessity, and mere necessity without freedom, are abstract and in this way untrue formulae of thought. Freedom is no blank indeterminateness: essentially concrete, and unvaryingly self-determinate, it is so far at the same time necessary. Necessity, again, in the ordinary acceptation of the term in popular philosophy, means determination from without only—as in finite mechanics, where a body moves only when it is struck by another body, and moves in the direction communicated to it by the impact. This however is a merely external necessity, not the real inward necessity which is identical with freedom.

The case is similar with the contrast of Good and Evil—the favourite contrast of the introspective modern world. If we regard Evil as possessing a fixity of its own, apart and distinct from Good, we are to a certain extent right: there is an opposition between them; nor do those who maintain the apparent and relative character of the opposition mean that Evil and Good in the Absolute are one, or, in accordance with the modern phrase, that a thing first becomes evil from our way of looking at it. The error arises when we take Evil as a permanent positive, instead of—what it really is—a negative which, though it would fain assert itself, has no real persistence, and is, in fact, only the absolute sham-existence of negativity in itself.

§ 36

The *fourth* branch of metaphysics is Natural or Rational Theology. The notion of God, or God as a possible being, the proofs of his existence, and his properties, formed the study of this branch.

(a) When understanding thus discusses the Deity, its main purpose is to find what predicates correspond or not to the fact we have in our imagination as God. And in doing it assumes the contrast between positive and negative to be absolute; and hence, in the long run, nothing is left for the notion as understanding takes it, but the empty abstraction of indeterminate Being, of mere reality or positivity, the lifeless product of modern 'Deism.'

(b) The method of demonstration employed in finite knowledge must always lead to an inversion of the true order. For it requires the statement of some objective ground for God's being, which thus acquires the appearance of being derived from something else. This mode of proof, guided as it is by the canon of mere analytical identity, is embarrassed by the difficulty of passing from the finite to the infinite. Either the finitude of the existing world, which is left as much a fact as it was before, clings to the notion of Deity, and God has to be defined as the immediate substance of that world—which is Pantheism: or he remains an object set over against the subject, and in this way, finite—which is Dualism.

(c) The attributes of God which ought to be various and precise had, properly speaking, sunk and disappeared in the abstract notion of pure reality, of indeterminate Being. Yet in our material thought, the finite world continues, meanwhile, to have a real being, with God as a sort of antithesis: and thus arises the further picture of different relations of God to the world. These, formulated as properties, must, on the one hand, as relations to finite circumstances, themselves possess a finite character (giving us such properties as just, gracious, mighty, wise, etc.); on the other hand they must be infinite. Now on this level of thought the only means, and a hazy one, of reconciling these opposing requirements was quantitative exaltation of the properties, forming them into indeterminateness—into the *sensus eminentior*. But it was an expedient which really destroyed the property and left a mere name.

The object of the old metaphysical theology was to see how far unassisted reason could go in the knowledge of God. Certainly a reason-derived knowledge of God is the highest problem of philosophy. The earliest teachings of religion are figurate conceptions of God. These conceptions, as the Creed arranges them, are imparted to us in youth. They are the doctrines of our religion, and in so far as the individual rests his faith on these doctrines and feels them to be the truth, he has all he needs as a Christian. Such is faith: and the science of this faith is Theology. But until Theology is something more than a bare enumeration and compilation of these doctrines *ab extra*, it has no right to the title of science. Even the method so much in vogue at present—the purely historical mode of treatment—which for example reports what has been said by this or the other Father of the Church—does not invest theology with a scientific character. To get that, we must go on to comprehend the facts by thought—which is the business of philosophy. Genuine theology is thus at the same time a real philosophy of religion, as it was, we may add, in the Middle Ages.

And now let us examine this rational theology more narrowly. It was a science which approached God not by reason but by understanding, and, in its mode of thought, employed the terms without any sense of their mutual limitations and connections. The notion of God formed the subject of discussion; and yet the criterion of our knowledge was derived from such an extraneous source as the materialized conception of God. Now thought must be free in its movements. It is no doubt to be remembered that the result of independent thought harmonizes with the import of the Christian religion: for the Christian religion is a revelation of reason. But such a harmony surpassed the efforts of rational theology. It proposed to define the figurate conception of God in terms of thought; but it resulted in a notion of God which was what we may call the abstract of positivity or reality, to the exclusion of all negation. God was accordingly defined to be the most real of all beings. Anyone can see however that this most real of beings, in which negation forms no part, is the very opposite of what it ought to be and of what understanding supposes it to be. Instead of being rich and full above all measure, it is so narrowly conceived that it is, on the contrary, extremely poor and altogether empty. It is with reason that the heart craves a concrete body of truth; but without definite feature, that is, without negation, contained in the notion, there can only be an abstraction. When the notion of God is apprehended only as that of the abstract or most real being, God is, as it were, relegated to another world beyond: and to speak of a knowledge of him would be meaningless. Where there is no definite quality, knowledge is impossible. Mere light is mere darkness.

The second problem of rational theology was to prove the existence of God. Now, in this matter, the main point to be noted is that demonstration, as the understanding employs it, means the dependence of one truth on another. In such proofs we have a presupposition—something firm and fast, from which something else follows; we exhibit the dependence of some truth from an assumed starting-point. Hence, if this mode of demonstration is applied to the existence of God, it can only mean that the being of God is to depend on other terms, which will then constitute the ground of his being. It is at once evident that this will lead to some mistake: for God must be simply and solely the ground of everything, and in so far not dependent upon anything else. And a perception of this danger has in modern times led some to say that God's existence is not capable of proof, but must be immediately or intuitively apprehended. Reason, however, and even sound common sense give demonstration a meaning quite different from that of the understanding. The demonstration of reason no doubt starts from something which is not God. But, as it advances, it does not leave the starting-point a mere unexplained fact, which is what it was. On the contrary it exhibits that point as derivative and called into being, and then God is seen to be primary, truly immediate, and self-subsisting, with the means of derivation wrapped up and absorbed in himself. Those who say: 'Consider Nature, and Nature will lead you to God; you will find an absolute final cause' do not mean that God is something derivative: they mean that it is we who proceed to God himself from another; and in this way God, though the consequence, is also the absolute ground of the initial step. The relation of the two things is reversed; and what came as a consequence being shown to be an antecedent, the original antecedent is reduced to a consequence. This is always the way, moreover, whenever reason demonstrates.

If in the light of the present discussion we cast one glance more on the metaphysical method as a whole, we find its main characteristic was to make abstract identity its principle and to try to apprehend the objects of reason by the abstract and finite categories of the understanding. But this infinite of the understanding, this pure essence, is still finite: it has excluded all the variety of particular things, which thus limit and deny it. Instead of winning a concrete, this metaphysic stuck fast on an abstract, identity. Its good point was the perception that thought alone constitutes the essence of all that is. It derived its materials from earlier philosophers, particularly the Schoolmen. In speculative philosophy the understanding undoubtedly forms a stage, but not a stage at which we should keep for ever standing. Plato is no metaphysician of this imperfect type, still less Aristotle, although the contrary is generally believed.

IV

SECOND ATTITUDE OF THOUGHT TO OBJECTIVITY

I. EMPIRICISM

§ 37

Under these circumstances a double want began to be felt. Partly it was the need of a concrete subject-matter, as a counterpoise to the abstract theories of the understanding, which is unable to advance unaided from its generalities to specialization and determination. Partly, too, it was the demand for something fixed and secure, so as to exclude the possibility of proving anything and everything in the sphere, and according to the method, of the finite formulae of thought. Such was the genesis of Empirical philosophy, which abandons the search for truth in thought itself, and goes to fetch it from Experience, the outward and the inward present.

The rise of Empiricism is due to the need thus stated of concrete contents, and a firm footing—needs which the abstract metaphysic of the understanding failed to satisfy. Now by concreteness of contents it is meant that we must know the objects of consciousness as intrinsically determinate and as the unity of distinct characteristics. But, as we have already seen, this is by no means the case with the metaphysic of understanding, if it conform to its principle. With the mere understanding, thinking is limited to the form of an abstract universal, and can never advance to the particularization of this universal. Thus we find the metaphysicians engaged in an attempt to elicit by the instrumentality of thought what was the essence or fundamental attribute of the Soul. The Soul, they said, is simple. The simplicity thus ascribed to the Soul meant a mere and utter simplicity, from which difference is excluded: difference, or in other words composition, being made the fundamental attribute of body, or of matter in general. Clearly, in simplicity of this narrow type we have a very shallow category, quite incapable of embracing the wealth of the soul or of the mind. When it thus appeared that abstract metaphysical thinking was inadequate, it was felt that resource must be had to empirical psychology. The same happened in the case of Rational Physics. The current phrases there were, for instance, that space is infinite, that Nature makes no leap, etc. Evidently this phraseology was wholly unsatisfactory in presence of the plentitude and life of nature.

§ 38

To some extent this source from which Empiricism draws is common to it with metaphysic. It is in our materialized conceptions, i.e. in facts which emanate, in the first instance, from experience, that metaphysic also finds the guarantee for the correctness of its definitions (including both its initial assumptions and its more detailed body of doctrine). But, on the other hand, it must be noted that the single sensation is not the same thing as experience, and that the Empirical School elevates the facts included under sensation, feeling, and perception into the form of general ideas, propositions, or laws. This, however, it does with the reservation that these general principles (such as force) are to have no further import or validity of their own beyond that taken from the sense-impression, and that no connection shall be deemed legitimate except what can be shown to exist in phenomena. And on the subjective side Empirical cognition has its stable footing in the fact that in a sensation consciousness is directly present and certain of itself.

In Empiricism lies the great principle that whatever is true must be in the actual world and present to sensation. This principle contradicts that 'ought to be' on the strength of which 'reflection' is vain enough to treat the actual present with scorn and to point to a scene beyond—a scene which is assumed to have place and being only in the understanding of those who talk of it. No less than Empiricism, philosophy (§ 7) recognizes only what is, and has nothing to do with what merely ought to be and what is thus confessed not to exist. On the subjective side, too, it is right to notice the valuable principle of freedom involved in Empiricism. For the main lesson of Empiricism is that man must see for himself and feel that he is present in every fact of knowledge which he has to accept.

When it is carried out to its legitimate consequences, Empiricism—being in its facts limited to the finite sphere—denies the supersensible in general, or at least any knowledge of it which would define its nature; it leaves thought no powers except abstraction and formal universality and identity. But there is a fundamental delusion in all scientific empiricism. It employs the metaphysical categories of matter, force, those of one, many, generality, infinity, etc.; following the clue given by these categories it proceeds to draw conclusions, and in so doing presupposes and applies the syllogistic form. And all the while it is unaware that it contains metaphysics—in wielding which, it makes use of those categories and their combinations in a style utterly thoughtless and uncritical.

From Empiricism came the cry: 'Stop roaming in empty abstractions, keep your eyes open, lay hold on man and nature as they are here before you, enjoy the present moment.' Nobody can deny that there is a good deal of truth in these words. The everyday world, what is here and now, was a good exchange for the futile other-world—for the mirages and the chimeras of the abstract understanding. And thus was acquired an infinite principle—that solid footing so much missed in the old metaphysic. Finite principles are the most that the understanding can pick out—and these being essentially unstable and tottering, the structure they supported must collapse with a crash. Always the instinct of reason was to find an infinite principle. As yet, the time had not come for finding it in thought. Hence, this instinct seized upon the present, the Here, the This—where doubtless there is implicit infinite form, but not in the genuine existence of that form. The external world is the truth, it if could but know it: for the truth is actual and must exist. The infinite principle, the self-centred truth, therefore, is in the world for reason to discover: though it exists in an individual and sensible shape, and not in its truth.

Besides, this school makes sense-perception the form in which fact is to be apprehended; and in this consists the defect of Empiricism. Sense-perception as such is always individual, always transient: not indeed that the process of knowledge stops short at sensation: on the contrary, it proceeds to find out the universal and permanent element in the individual apprehended by sense. This is the process leading from simple perception to experience.

In order to form experiences, Empiricism makes especial use of the form of Analysis. In the impression of sense we have a concrete of many elements, the several attributes of which we are expected to peel off one by one, like the coats of an onion. In thus dismembering the thing, it is understood that we disintegrate and take to pieces these attributes which have coalesced, and add nothing but our own act of disintegration. Yet analysis is the process from the immediacy of sensation to thought: those attributes, which the object analysed contains in union, acquire the form of universality by being separated. Empiricism therefore labours under a delusion, if it supposes that, while analysing the objects, it leaves them as they were: it really transforms the concrete into an abstract. And as a consequence of this change the living thing is killed: life can exist only in the concrete and one. Not that we can do without this division, if it be our intention to comprehend. Mind itself is an inherent division. The error lies in forgetting that this is only one half of the process, and that the main point is the reunion of what has been parted. And it is where analysis never gets beyond the stage of partition that the words of the poet are true:

> Encheiresin Naturae nennt's die Chemie,
> Spottet ihrer selbst, und weiß nicht, wie:
> Hat die Theile in ihrer Hand,
> Fehlt leider nur das geistige Band.

Analysis starts from the concrete; and the possession of this material gives it a considerable advantage over the abstract thinking of the old metaphysics. It establishes the differences in things, and this is very important; but these very differences are nothing after all but abstract attributes, i.e. thoughts. These thoughts, it is assumed, contain the real essence of the objects; and thus once more we see the axiom of bygone metaphysics reappear, that the truth of things lies in thought.

Let us next compare the empirical theory with that of metaphysics in the matter of their respective contents. We find the latter, as already stated, taking for its theme the universal objects of the reason, viz. God, the Soul, and the World: and these themes, accepted from popular conception, it was the problem of philosophy to reduce into the form of thoughts. Another specimen of the same method was the Scholastic philosophy, the theme presupposed by which was formed by the dogmas of the Christian Church; and it aimed at fixing their meaning and giving them a systematic arrangement through thought. The facts on which Empiricism is based are of entirely different kind. They are the sensible facts of nature and the facts of the finite mind. In other words, Empiricism deals with a finite material, and the old metaphysicians had an infinite—though, let us add, they made this infinite content finite by the finite form of the understanding. The same finitude of form reappears in Empiricism—but here the facts are finite also. To this extent, then, both modes of philosophizing have the same method; both proceed from data or assumptions, which they accept as ultimate. Generally speaking, Empiricism finds the truth in the outward world; and even if it allow a supersensible world, it holds knowledge of that world to be impossible, and would restrict us to the province of sense-perception. This doctrine when systematically carried out produces what has been latterly termed Materialism. Materialism of this stamp looks upon matter, *qua* matter, as the genuine objective world. But with matter we are at once introduced to an abstraction, which as such cannot be perceived, and it may be maintained that there is no matter, because, as it exists, it is always something definite and concrete. Yet the abstraction we term matter is supposed to lie at the basis of the whole world of sense, and expresses the sense-world in its simplest terms as out-and-out individualization, and hence a congeries of points in mutual exclusion. So long then as this sensible sphere is and continues to be for Empiricism a mere datum, we have a doctrine of bondage: for we become free, when we are confronted by no absolutely alien world, but depend upon a fact which we ourselves are. Consistently with the empirical point of view, besides, reason and unreason can only be subjective: in other words, we must take what is given just as it is, and we have no right to ask whether and to what extent it is rational in its own nature.

§ 39

Touching this principle it has been justly observed that in what we call Experience, as distinct from mere single perception of single facts, there are two elements. The one is the matter, infinite in its multiplicity, and as it stands a mere set of singulars: the other is the form, the characteristics of universality and necessity. Mere experience no doubt offers many, perhaps innumerable, cases of similar perceptions: but, after all, no multitude, however great, can be the same thing as universality. Similarly, mere experience affords perceptions of changes succeeding each other and of objects in juxtaposition; but it presents no necessary connection. If perception, therefore, is to maintain its claim to be the sole basis of what men hold for truth, universality and necessity appear something illegitimate: they become an accident of our minds, a mere custom, the content of which might be otherwise constituted than it is.

It is an important corollary of this theory, that on this empirical mode of treatment legal and ethical principles and laws, as well as the truths of religion, are exhibited as the work of chance, and stripped of their objective character and inner truth.

The scepticism of Hume, to which this conclusion was chiefly due, should be clearly marked off from Greek scepticism. Hume assumes the truth of the empirical element, feeling and sensation, and proceeds to challenge universal principles and laws, because they have no warranty from sense-perception. So far was ancient scepticism from making feeling and sensation the canon of truth, that it turned against the deliverances of sense first of all. (On modern scepticism as compared with ancient, see Schelling and Hegel's *Critical Journal of Philosophy*, 1802, Vol. I. i.)

II. THE CRITICAL PHILOSOPHY

§ 40

In common with Empiricism the Critical Philosophy assumes that experience affords the one sole foundation for cognitions; which however it does not allow to rank as truths, but only as knowledge of phenomena.

The Critical theory starts originally from the distinction of elements presented in the analysis of experience, viz. the matter of sense, and its universal relations. Taking into account Hume's criticism on this distinction as given in the preceding section, viz. that sensation does not explicitly apprehend more than an individual or more than a mere event, it insists at the same time on the *fact* that universality and necessity are seen to perform a function equally essential in constituting what is called experience. This element, not being derived from the empirical facts as such, must belong to the spontaneity of thought; in other words, it is *a priori*. The Categories or Notions of the Understanding constitute the *objectivity* of experiential cognitions. In every case they involve a connective reference, and hence through their means are formed synthetic judgements *a priori*, that is, primary and underivative connections of opposites.

Even Hume's scepticism does not deny that the characteristics of universality and necessity are found in cognition. And even in Kant this fact remains a presupposition after all; it may be said, to use the ordinary phraseology of the sciences, that Kant did no more than offer another *explanation* of the fact.

§ 41

The Critical Philosophy proceeds to test the value of the categories employed in metaphysic, as well as in other sciences and in ordinary conception. This scrutiny however is not directed to the content of these categories, nor does it inquire into the exact relation they bear to one another: but simply considers them as affected by the contrast between subjective and objective. The contrast, as we are to understand it here, bears upon the distinction (see preceding §) of the two elements in experience. The name of objectivity is here given to the element of universality and necessity, i.e. to the categories themselves, or what is called the *a priori* constituent. The Critical Philosophy however widened the contrast in such a way, that the subjectivity comes to embrace the *ensemble* of experience, including both of the aforesaid elements; and nothing remains on the other side but the 'thing-in-itself'.

The special forms of the *a priori* element, in other words, of thought, which in spite of its objectivity is looked upon as a purely subjective act, present themselves as follows in a systematic order which, it may be remarked, is solely based upon psychological and historical grounds.

(1) A very important step was undoubtedly made, when the terms of the old metaphysic were subjected to scrutiny. The plain thinker pursued his unsuspecting way in those categories which had offered themselves naturally. It never occurred to him to ask to what extent these categories had a value and authority of their own. If, as has been said, it is characteristic of free thought to allow no assumptions to pass unquestioned, the old metaphysicians were not free thinkers. They accepted their categories as they were, without further trouble, as an *a priori* datum, not yet tested by reflection. The Critical philosophy reversed this. Kant undertook to examine how far the forms of thought were capable of leading to the knowledge of truth. In particular he demanded a criticism of the faculty of cognition as preliminary to its exercise. That is a fair demand, if it mean that even the forms of thought must be made an object of investigation. Unfortunately there soon creeps in the misconception of already knowing before you know—the error of refusing to enter the water until you have learnt to swim. True, indeed, the forms of thought should be subjected to a scrutiny before they are used: yet what is this scrutiny but *ipso facto* a cognition? So that what we want is to combine in our process of inquiry the action of the forms of thought with a criticism of them. The forms of thought must be studied in their essential nature and complete development: they are at once the object of research and the action of that object. Hence they examine themselves: in their own action they must determine their limits, and point out their defects. This is that action of thought, which will hereafter be specially considered under the name of Dialectic, and regarding which we need only at the outset observe that, instead of being brought to bear upon the categories from without, it is immanent in their own action.

We may therefore state the first point in Kant's philosophy as follows: Thought must itself investigate its own capacity of knowledge. People in the present day have got over Kant and his philosophy: everybody wants to get further. But there are two ways of going further—a backward and a forward. The light of criticism soon shows that many of our modern essays in philosophy are mere repetitions of the old metaphysical method, an endless and uncritical thinking in a groove determined by the natural bent of each man's mind.

(2) Kant's examination of the categories suffers from the grave defect of viewing them, not absolutely and for their own sake, but in order to see whether they are *subjective* or *objective*. In the language of common life we mean by objective what exists outside of us and reaches us from without by means of sensation. What Kant did was to deny that the categories, such as cause and effect, were, in this sense of the word, objective, or given in sensation, and to maintain on the contrary that they belonged to our own thought itself, to the spontaneity of thought. To that extent therefore they were subjective. And yet in spite of this, Kant gives the name objective to what is thought, to the universal and necessary, while he describes as subjective whatever is merely felt. This arrangement apparently reverses the first-mentioned use of the word, and has caused Kant to be charged with confusing language. But the charge is unfair if we more narrowly consider the facts of the case. The vulgar believe that the objects of perception which confront them, such as an individual animal, or a single star, are independent and permanent existences, compared with which thoughts are unsubstantial and dependent on something else. In fact however the perceptions of sense are the properly dependent and secondary feature, while the thoughts are really independent and primary. This being so, Kant gave the title objective to the intellectual factor, to the universal and necessary: and he was quite justified in so doing. Our sensations on the other hand are subjective; for sensations lack stability in their own nature, and are no less fleeting and evanescent than thought is permanent and self-subsisting. At the present day, the special line of distinction established by Kant between the subjective and objective is adopted by the phraseology of the educated world. Thus the criticism of a work of art ought, it is said, to be not subjective, but objective; in other words, instead of springing from the particular and accidental feeling or temper of the moment, it should keep its eye on those general points of view which the laws of art establish. In the same acceptation we can distinguish in any scientific pursuit the objective and the subjective interest of the investigation.

But after all, objectivity of thought, in Kant's sense, is again to a certain extent subjective. Thoughts, according to Kant, although universal and necessary categories, are *only our* thoughts—separated by an impassable gulf from the thing, as it exists apart from our knowledge. But the true objectivity of thinking means that the thoughts, far from being merely ours, must at the same time be the real essence of the things, and of whatever is an object to us.

Objective and subjective are convenient expressions in current use, the employment of which may easily lead to confusion. Up to this point, the discussion has shown three meanings of objectivity. First, it means what has external existence, in distinction from which the subjective is what is only supposed, dreamed, &c. Secondly, it has the meaning, attached to it by Kant, of the universal and necessary, as distinguished from the particular, subjective, and occasional element which belongs to our sensations. Thirdly, as has been just explained, it means the thought-apprehended essence of the existing thing, in contradistinction from what is merely *our* thought, and what consequently is still separated from the thing itself, as it exists in independent essence.

§ 42

(a) **The Theoretical Faculty.** Cognition *qua* cognition. The specific ground of the categories is declared by the Critical system to lie in the primary identity of the 'I' in thought—what Kant calls the 'transcendental unity of self-consciousness'. The impressions from feeling and perception are, if we look to their contents, a multiplicity or miscellany of elements: and the multiplicity is equally conspicuous in their form. For sense is marked by a mutual exclusion of members; and that under two aspects, namely space and time, which, being the forms, that is to say, the universal type of perception, are themselves *a priori*. This congeries, afforded by sensation and perception, must however be reduced to an identity or primary synthesis. To accomplish this the 'I' brings it in relation to itself and unites it there in *one* consciousness which Kant calls 'pure apperception'. The specific modes in which the Ego refers to itself the multiplicity of sense are the pure concepts of the understanding, the Categories.

Kant, it is well known, did not put himself to much trouble in discovering the categories. 'I', the unity of self-consciousness, being quite abstract and completely indeterminate, the question arises, how are we to get at the specialized forms of the 'I', the categories? Fortunately, the common logic offers to our hand an empirical classification of the kinds of *judgement*. Now, to judge is the same as to *think* of a determinate object. Hence the various modes of judgement, as enumerated to our hand, provide us with the several categories of thought. To the philosophy of Fichte belongs the great merit of having called attention to the need of exhibiting the *necessity* of these categories and giving a genuine *deduction* of them. Fichte ought to have produced at least one effect on the method of logic. One might have expected that the general laws of thought, the usual stock-in-trade of logicians, or the classification of notions, judgements, and syllogisms, would be no longer taken merely from observation and so only empirically treated, but be deduced from thought itself. If thought is to be capable of proving anything at all, if logic must insist upon the necessity of proofs, and if it proposes to teach the theory of demonstration, its first care should be to give a reason for its own subject-matter, and to see that it is necessary.

(1) Kant therefore holds that the categories have their source in the 'Ego', and that the 'Ego' consequently supplies the characteristics of universality and necessity. If we observe what we have before us primarily, we may describe it as a congeries or diversity: and in the categories we find the simple points or units, to which this congeries is made to converge. The world of sense is a scene of mutual exclusion: its being is outside itself. That is the fundamental feature of the sensible. 'Now' has no meaning except in reference to a before and a hereafter. Red, in the same way, only subsists by being opposed to yellow and blue. Now this other thing is outside the sensible; which latter is, only in so far as it is not the other, and only in so far as that other is. But thought, or the 'Ego', occupies a position the very reverse of the sensible, with its mutual exclusions, and its being outside itself. The 'I' is the primary identity—at one with itself and all at home in itself. The word 'I' expresses the mere act of bringing-to-bear-upon-self: and whatever is placed in this unit or focus is affected by it and transformed into it. The 'I' is as it were the crucible and the fire which consumes the loose plurality of sense and reduces it to unity. This is the process which Kant calls pure apperception in distinction from the common apperception, to which the plurality it receives is a plurality still; whereas pure apperception is rather an act by which the 'I' makes the materials 'mine'.

This view has at least the merit of giving a correct expression to the nature of all consciousness. The tendency of all man's endeavours is to understand the world, to appropriate and subdue it to himself: and to this end the positive reality of the world must be as it were crushed and pounded, in other words, idealized. At the same time we must note that it is not the mere act of *our* personal self-consciousness which introduces an absolute unity into the variety of sense. Rather, this identity is itself the absolute. The absolute is, as it were, so kind as to leave individual things to their own enjoyment, and it again drives them back to the absolute unity.

(2) Expressions like 'transcendental unity of self-consciousness' have an ugly look about them, and suggest a monster in the background: but their meaning is not so abstruse as it looks. Kant's meaning of transcendental may be gathered by the way he distinguishes it from transcendent. The *transcendent* may be said to be what steps out beyond the categories of the understanding: a sense in which the term is first employed in mathematics. Thus in geometry you are told to conceive the circumference of a circle as formed of an infinite number of infinitely small straight lines. In other words, characteristics which the understanding holds to be totally different, the straight line and the curve, are expressly invested with identity. Another transcendent of the same kind is the self-consciousness which is identical with itself and infinite in itself, as distinguished from the ordinary consciousness which derives its form and tone from finite materials. That unity of self-consciousness, however, Kant called *transcendental* only; and he meant thereby that the unity was only in our minds and did not attach to the objects apart from our knowledge of them.

(3) To regard the categories as subjective only, i.e. as a part of ourselves, must seem very odd to the natural mind; and no doubt there is something queer about it. It is quite true however that the categories are not contained in the sensation as it is given us. When, for instance, we look at a piece of sugar, we find it is hard, white, sweet, etc. All these properties we say are united in one object. Now it is this unity that is not found in the sensation. The same thing happens if we conceive two events to stand in the relation of cause and effect. The senses only inform us of the two several occurrences which follow each other in time. But that the one is cause, the other effect—in other words, the causal nexus between the two—is not perceived by sense; it is only evident to thought. Still, though the categories, such as unity, or cause and effect, are strictly the property of thought, it by no means follows that they must be ours merely and not also characteristics of the objects. Kant however confines them to the subject-mind, and his philosophy may be styled subjective idealism: for he holds that both the form and the matter of knowledge are supplied by the Ego—or knowing subject—the form by our intellectual, the matter by our sentient ego.

So far as regards the content of this subjective idealism, not a word need be wasted. It might perhaps at first sight be imagined, that objects would lose their reality when their unity was transferred to the subject. But neither we nor the objects would have anything to gain by the mere fact that they possessed being. The main point is not, that they are, but what they are, and whether or not their content is true. It does no good to the things to say merely that they have being. What has being, will also cease to be when time creeps over it. It might also be alleged that subjective idealism tended to promote self-conceit. But surely if a man's world be the sum of his sensible perceptions, he has no reason to be vain of such a world. Laying aside therefore as unimportant this distinction between subjective and objective, we are chiefly interested in knowing what a thing is: i.e. its content, which is no more objective than it is subjective. If mere existence be enough to make objectivity, even a crime is objective: but it is an existence which is nullity at the core, as is definitely made apparent when the day of punishment comes.

§ 43

The Categories may be viewed in two aspects. On the one hand it is by their instrumentality that the mere perception of sense rises to objectivity and experience. On the other hand these notions are unities in our consciousness merely: they are consequently conditioned by the material given to them, and having nothing of their own they can be applied to use only within the range of experience. But the other constituent of experience, the impressions of feeling and perception, is not one whit less subjective than the categories.

To assert that the categories taken by themselves are empty can scarcely be right, seeing that they have a content, at all events, in the special stamp and significance which they possess. Of course the content of the categories is not perceptible to the senses, nor is it in time and space: but that is rather a merit than a defect. A glimpse of this meaning of *content* may be observed to affect our ordinary thinking. A book or a speech for example is said to have a great deal in it, to be full of content, in proportion to the greater number of thoughts and general results to be found in it: while, on the contrary, we should never say that any book, e.g. a novel, had much in it, because it included a great number of single incidents, situations, and the like. Even the popular voice thus recognizes that something more than the facts of sense is needed to make a work pregnant with matter. And what is this additional desideratum but thoughts, or in the first instance the categories? And yet it is not altogether wrong, it should be added, to call the categories of themselves empty, if it be meant that they and the logical Idea, of which they are the members, do not constitute the whole of philosophy, but necessarily lead onwards in due progress to the real departments of Nature and Mind. Only let the progress not be misunderstood. The logical Idea does not thereby come into possession of a content originally foreign to it: but by its own native action is specialized and developed to Nature and Mind.

§ 44

It follows that the categories are no fit terms to express the Absolute—the Absolute not being given in perception—and Understanding, or knowledge by means of the categories, is consequently incapable of knowing the Things-in-themselves.

The Thing-in-itself (and under 'thing' is embraced even Mind and God) expresses the object when we leave out of sight all that consciousness makes of it, all its emotional aspects, and all specific thoughts of it. It is easy to see what is left—utter abstraction, total emptiness, only described still as an 'other-world'—the negative of every image, feeling, and definite thought. Nor does it require much penetration to see that this *caput mortuum* is still only a product of thought, such as accrues when thought is carried on to abstraction unalloyed: that it is the work of the empty 'Ego', which makes an object out of this empty self-identity of its own. The *negative* characteristic which this abstract identity receives as an *object* is also enumerated among the categories of Kant, and is no less familiar than the empty identity aforesaid. Hence one can only read with surprise the perpetual remark that we do not know the Thing-in-itself. On the contrary there is nothing we can know so easily.

§ 45

It is Reason, the faculty of the Unconditioned, which discovers the conditioned nature of the knowledge comprised in experience. What is thus called the object of Reason, the Infinite or Unconditioned, is nothing but self-sameness, or the primary identity of the 'Ego' in thought (mentioned in § 42). Reason itself is the name given to the abstract 'Ego' or thought, which makes this pure identity its aim or object (cf. note to the preceding §). Now this identity, having no definite attribute at all, can receive no illumination from the truths of experience, for the reason that these refer always to definite facts. Such is the sort of Unconditioned that is supposed to be the absolute truth of Reason—what is termed the *Idea*; while the cognitions of experience are reduced to the level of untruth and declared to be appearances.

Kant was the first definitely to signalize the distinction between Reason and Understanding. The object of the former, as he applied the term, was the infinite and unconditioned, of the latter the finite and conditioned. Kant did valuable service when he enforced the finite character of the cognitions of the understanding founded merely upon experience, and stamped their contents with the name of appearance. But his mistake was to stop at the purely negative point of view, and to limit the unconditionality of Reason to an abstract self-sameness without any shade of distinction. It degrades Reason to a finite and conditioned thing, to identify it with a mere stepping beyond the finite and conditioned range of understanding. The real infinite, far from being a mere transcendence of the finite, always involves the absorption of the finite into its own fuller nature. In the same way Kant restored the Idea to its proper dignity: vindicating it for Reason, as a thing distinct from abstract analytic determinations or from the merely sensible conceptions which usually appropriate to themselves the name of ideas. But as respects the Idea also, he never got beyond its negative aspect, as what ought to be but is not.

The view that the objects of immediate consciousness, which constitute the body of experience, are mere appearances (phenomena) was another important result of the Kantian philosophy. Common Sense, that mixture of sense and understanding, believes the objects of which it has knowledge to be severally independent and self-supporting; and when it becomes evident that they tend towards and limit one another, the interdependence of one upon another is reckoned something foreign to them and to their true nature. The very opposite is the truth. The things immediately known are mere appearances—in other words, the ground of their being is not in themselves but in something else. But then comes the important step of defining what this something else is. According to Kant, the things that we know about are *to us* appearances only, and we can never know their essential nature, which belongs to another world we cannot approach. Plain minds have not unreasonably taken exception to this subjective idealism, with its reduction of the facts of consciousness to a purely personal world, created by ourselves alone. For the true statement of the case is rather as follows. The things of which we have direct consciousness are mere phenomena, not for us only, but in their own nature; and the true and proper case of these things, finite as they are, is to have their existence founded not in themselves but in the universal divine Idea. This view of things, it is true, is as idealist as Kant's; but in contradistinction to the subjective idealism of the Critical philosophy should be termed absolute idealism. Absolute idealism, however, though it is far in advance of vulgar realism, is by no means merely restricted to philosophy. It lies at the root of all religion; for religion too believes the actual world we see, the sum total of existence, to be created and governed by God.

§ 46

But it is not enough simply to indicate the existence of the object of Reason. Curiosity impels us to seek for knowledge of this identity, this empty thing-in-itself. Now *knowledge* means such an acquaintance with the object as apprehends its distinct and special subject-matter. But such subject-matter involves a complex inter-connection in the object itself, and supplies a ground of connection with many other objects. In the present case, to express the nature of the features of the Infinite or Thing-in-itself, Reason would have nothing except the categories: and in any endeavour so to employ them Reason becomes over-soaring or 'transcendent'.

Here begins the second stage of the Criticism of Reason—which, as an independent piece of work, is more valuable than the first. The first part, as has been explained above, teaches that the categories originate in the unity of self-consciousness; that any knowledge which is gained by their means has nothing objective in it, and that the very objectivity claimed for them is only subjective. So far as this goes, the Kantian Criticism presents that 'common' type of idealism known as Subjective Idealism. It asks no questions about the meaning or scope of the categories, but simply considers the abstract form of subjectivity and objectivity, and that even in such a partial way that the former aspect, that of subjectivity, is retained as a final and purely affirmative term of thought. In the second part, however, when Kant examines the *application*, as it is called, which Reason makes of the categories in order to know its objects, the content of the categories, at least in some points of view, comes in for discussion: or, at any rate, an opportunity presented itself for a discussion of the question. It is worth while to see what decision Kant arrives at on the subject of metaphysic, as this application of the categories to the unconditioned is called. His method of procedure we shall here briefly state and criticize.

§ 47

(*a*) The first of the unconditioned entities which Kant examines is the Soul (see above, § 34). 'In my consciousness', he says, 'I always find that I (1) am the determining subject; (2) am singular, or abstractly simple; (3) am identical, or one and the same, in all the variety of what I am conscious of; (4) distinguish myself as thinking from all the things outside me.'

Now the method of the old metaphysic, as Kant correctly states it, consisted in substituting for these statements of experience the corresponding categories or metaphysical terms. Thus arise these four new propositions: (a) the Soul is a substance; (b) it is a simple substance; (c) it is numerically identical at the various periods of existence; (d) it stands in relation to space.

Kant discusses this translation, and draws attention to the Paralogism or mistake of confounding one kind of truth with another. He points out that empirical attributes have here been replaced by categories; and shows that we are not entitled to argue from the former to the latter, or to put the latter in place of the former.

This criticism obviously but repeats the observation of Hume (§ 39) that the categories as a whole—ideas of universality and necessity—are entirely absent from sensation; and that the empirical fact both in form and contents differs from its intellectual formulation.

If the purely empirical fact were held to constitute the credentials of the thought, then no doubt it would be indispensable to be able precisely to identify the 'idea' in the 'impression'.

And in order to make out, in his criticism of the metaphysical psychology, that the soul cannot be described as substantial, simple, self-same, and as maintaining its independence in intercourse with the material world, Kant argues from the single ground that the several attributes of the soul, which consciousness lets us feel in *experience*, are not exactly the same attributes as result from the action of *thought* thereon. But we have seen above that according to Kant all knowledge, even experience, consists in thinking our impressions—in other words, in transforming into intellectual categories the attributes primarily belonging to sensation.

Unquestionably one good result of the Kantian criticism was that it emancipated mental philosophy from the 'soul-thing', from the categories, and, consequently, from questions about the simplicity, complexity, materiality, etc., of the soul. But even for the common sense of ordinary men, the true point of view, from which the inadmissibility of these forms best appears, will be not that they are thoughts, but that thoughts of such a stamp neither can nor do retain truth.

If thought and phenomenon do not perfectly correspond to one another, we are free at least to choose which of the two shall be held the defaulter. The Kantian idealism, where it touches on the world of Reason, throws the blame on the thoughts; saying that the thoughts are defective, as not being exactly fitted to the sensations and to a mode of mind wholly restricted within the range of sensation, in which as such there are no traces of the presence of these thoughts. But as to the actual content of the thought, no question is raised.

Paralogisms are a species of unsound syllogism, the especial vice of which consists in employing one and the same word in the two premisses with a different meaning. According to Kant the method adopted by the rational psychology of the old metaphysicians, when they assumed that the qualities of the phenomenal soul, as given in experience, formed part of its own real essence, was based upon such a Paralogism. Nor can it be denied that predicates like simplicity, permanence, etc., are inapplicable to the soul. But their unfitness is not due to the ground assigned by Kant, that Reason, by applying them, would exceed its appointed bounds. The true ground is that this style of abstract terms is not good enough for the soul, which is very much more than a mere simple or unchangeable sort of thing. And thus, for example, while the soul may be admitted to be simple self-sameness, it is at the same time active and institutes distinctions in its own nature. But whatever is merely or abstractly simple is as such also a mere dead thing. By his polemic against the metaphysic of the past Kant discarded those predicates from the soul or mind. He did well; but when he came to state his reasons, his failure is apparent.

§ 48

(β) The second unconditioned object is the World (§ 35). In the attempt which reason makes to comprehend the unconditioned nature of the World, it falls into what are called Antinomies. In other words it maintains two opposite propositions about the same object, and in such a way that each of them has to be maintained with equal necessity. From this it follows that the body of cosmical fact, the specific statements descriptive of which run into contradiction, cannot be a self-subsistent reality, but only an appearance. The explanation offered by Kant alleges that the contradiction does not affect the object in its own proper essence, but attaches only to the Reason which seeks to comprehend it.

In this way the suggestion was broached that the contradiction is occasioned by the subject-matter itself, or by the intrinsic quality of the categories. And to offer the idea that the contradiction introduced into the world of Reason by the categories of Understanding is inevitable and essential was to make one of the most important steps in the progress of Modern Philosophy. But the more important the issue thus raised the more trivial was the solution. Its only motive was an excess of tenderness for the things of the world. The blemish of contradiction, it seems, could not be allowed to mar the essence of the world; but there could be no objection to attach it to the thinking Reason, to the essence of mind. Probably nobody will feel disposed to deny that the phenomenal world presents contradictions to the observing mind; meaning by 'phenomenal' the world as it presents itself to the senses and understanding, to the subjective mind. But if a comparison is instituted between the esssence of the world and the essence of the mind, it does seem strange to hear how calmly and confidently the modest dogma has been advanced by one, and repeated by others, that thought or Reason, and not the World, is the seat of contradiction. It is no escape to turn round and explain that Reason falls into contradiction only by applying the categories. For this application of the categories is maintained to be necessary, and Reason is not supposed to be equipped with any other forms but the categories for the purpose of cognition. But cognition is determining and determinate thinking: so that, if Reason be mere empty indeterminate thinking, it thinks nothing. And if in the end Reason be reduced to mere identity without diversity (see next §), it will in the end also win a happy release from contradiction at the slight sacrifice of all its facets and contents.

It may also be noted that his failure to make a more thorough study of Antinomy was one of the reasons why Kant enumerated only *four* Antinomies. These four attracted his notice, because, as may be seen in his discussion of the so-called Paralogisms of

Reason, he assumed the list of the categories as a basis of his argument. Employing what has subsequently become a favourite fashion, he simply put the object under a rubric otherwise ready to hand, instead of deducing its characteristics from its notion. Further deficiencies in the treatment of the Antinomies I have pointed out, as occasion offered, in my *Science of Logic*. Here it will be sufficient to say that the Antinomies are not confined to the four special objects taken from Cosmology: they appear in all objects of every kind, in all conceptions, notions, and Ideas. To be aware of this and to know objects in this property of theirs makes a vital part in a philosophical theory. For the property thus indicated is what we shall afterwards describe as the Dialectical influence in logic.

The principles of the metaphysical philosophy gave rise to the belief that, when cognition lapsed into contradictions, it was a mere accidental aberration, due to some subjective mistake in argument and inference. According to Kant, however, thought has a natural tendency to issue in contradictions or antinomies, whenever it seeks to apprehend the infinite. We have in the latter part of the above paragraph referred to the philosophical importance of the antinomies of reason, and shown how the recognition of their existence helped largely to get rid of the rigid dogmatism of the metaphysic of understanding, and to direct attention to the Dialectical movement of thought. But here too Kant, as we must add, never got beyond the negative result that the thing-in-itself is unknowable, and never penetrated to the discovery of what the antinomies really and positively mean. That true and positive meaning of the antinomies is this: that every actual thing involves a coexistence of opposed elements. Consequently to know, or, in other words, to comprehend an object is equivalent to being conscious of it as a concrete unity of opposed determinations. The old metaphysic, as we have already seen, when it studied the objects of which it sought a metaphysical knowledge, went to work by applying categories abstractly and to the exclusion of their opposites. Kant, on the other hand, tried to prove that the statements issuing through this method could be met by other statements of contrary import with equal warrant and equal necessity. In the enumeration of these antinomies he narrowed his ground to the cosmology of the old metaphysical system, and in his discussion made out four antinomies, a number which rests upon the list of the categories. The first antinomy is on the question: Whether we are or are not to think the world limited in space and time. In the second antinomy we have a discussion of the dilemma: Matter must be conceived either as endlessly divisible, or as consisting of atoms. The third antinomy bears upon the antithesis of freedom and necessity, to such extent as it is embraced in the question, Whether everything in the world must be supposed subject to the condition of causality, or if we can also assume free beings, in other words, absolute initial points of action, in the world. Finally, the fourth antinomy is the dilemma: Either the world as a whole has a cause or it is uncaused.

The method which Kant follows in discussing these antinomies is as follows. He puts the two propositions implied in the dilemma over against each other as thesis and antithesis, and seeks to prove both: that is to say he tries to exhibit them as inevitably issuing from reflection on the question. He particularly protests against the charge of being a special pleader and of grounding his reasoning on illusions. Speaking honestly, however, the arguments which Kant offers for his thesis and antithesis are mere shams of demonstration. The thing to be proved is invariably implied in the assumption he starts from, and the speciousness of his proofs is only due to his prolix and apagogic mode of procedure. Yet it was, and still is, a great achievement for the Critical philosophy when it exhibited these antinomies: for in this way it gave some expression (at first certainly subjective and unexplained) to the actual unity of those categories which are kept persistently separate by the understanding. The first of the cosmological antinomies, for example, implies a recognition of the doctrine that space and time present a discrete as well as a continuous aspect: whereas the old metaphysic, laying exclusive emphasis on the continuity, had been led to treat the world as unlimited in space and time. It is quite correct to say that we can go beyond every *definite* space and beyond every *definite* time: but it is no less correct that space and time are real and actual only when they are defined or specialized into 'here' and 'now'—a specialization which is involved in the very notion of them. The same observations apply to the rest of the antinomies. Take, for example, the antinomy of freedom and necessity. The main gist of it is that freedom and necessity as understood by abstract thinkers are not independently real, as these thinkers suppose, but merely ideal factors (moments) of the true freedom and the true necessity, and that to abstract and isolate either conception is to make it false.

§ 49

(γ) The third object of the Reason is God (§ 36): he also must be known and defined in terms of thought. But in comparison with an unalloyed identity, every defining term as such seems to the understanding to be only a limit and a negation: every reality accordingly must be taken as limitless, i.e. undefined. Accordingly God, when he is defined to be the sum of all realities, the most real of beings, turns into a *mere abstract*. And the only term under which that most real of real things can be defined is that of Being—itself the height of abstraction. These are the two elements, abstract identity, on one hand, which is spoken of in this place as the notion; and Being on the other—which Reason seeks to unify. And their union is the *Ideal* of Reason.

§ 50

To carry out this unification two ways or two forms are admissible. Either we may begin with Being and proceed to the *abstractum* of Thought: or the movement may begin with the abstraction and end in Being.

We shall, in the first place, start from Being. But Being, in its natural aspect, presents itself to view as a Being of infinite variety, a World in all its plentitude. And this world may be regarded in two ways: first, as a collection of innumerable unconnected facts; and second, as a collection of innumerable facts in mutual relation, giving evidence of design. The first aspect is emphasized in the Cosmological proof; the latter in the proofs of Natural Theology. Suppose now that this fullness of being passes under the agency of thought. Then it is stripped of its isolation and unconnectedness, and viewed as a universal and absolutely necessary being which determines itself and acts by general purposes or laws. And this necessary and self-determined being, different from the being at the commencement, is God.

The main force of Kant's criticism on this process attacks it for being a syllogizing, i.e. a transition. Perceptions, and that aggregate of perceptions we call the world, exhibit as they stand no traces of that universality which they afterwards receive from the purifying act of thought. The empirical conception of the world therefore gives no warrant for the idea of universality. And so any attempt on the part of thought to ascend from the empirical conception of the world to God is checked by the argument of Hume (as in the paralogisms, § 47), according to which we have no right to think sensations, that is, to elicit universality and necessity from them.

Man is essentially a thinker: and therefore sound Common Sense, as well as Philosophy, will not yield up their right of rising to God from and out of the empirical view of the world. The only basis on which this rise is possible is the thinking study of the world, not the bare sensuous, animal, attuition of it. Thought and thought alone has eyes for the essence, substance, universal power, and ultimate design of the world. And what men call the proofs of God's existence are, rightly understood, ways of describing and analysing the native course of the mind, the course of *thought* thinking the *data* of the senses. The rise of thought beyond the world of sense, its passage from the finite to the infinite, the leap into the supersensible which it takes when it snaps asunder the chain of sense, all this transition is thought and nothing but thought. Say there must be no such passage, and you say there is to be no thinking. And in sooth, animals make no such transition. They never get further than sensation and the perception of the senses, and in consequence they have no religion.

Both on general grounds, and in the particular case, there are two remarks to be made upon the criticism of this exaltation in thought. The first remark deals with the question of form. When the exaltation is exhibited in a syllogistic process, in the shape of what we call *proofs* of the being of God, these reasonings cannot but start from some sort of theory of the world, which makes it an aggregate either of contingent facts or of final causes and relations involving design. The merely syllogistic thinker may deem this starting-point a solid basis and suppose that it remains throughout in the same empirical light, left at last as it was at the first. In this case, the bearing of the beginning upon the conclusion to which it leads has a purely affirmative aspect, as if we were only reasoning from one thing which *is* and continues to *be*, to another thing which in like manner is. But the great error is to restrict our notions of the nature of thought to its form in understanding alone. To think the phenomenal world rather means to recast its form, and transmute it into a universal. And thus the action of thought has also a *negative* effect upon its basis: and the matter of sensation, when it receives the stamp of universality, at once loses its first and phenomenal shape. By the removal and negation of the shell, the kernel within the sense-percept is brought to the light (§§ 13 and 23). And it is because they do not, with sufficient prominence, express the negative features implied in the exaltation of the mind from the world to God that the metaphysical proofs of the being of a God are defective interpretations and descriptions of the process. If the world is only a sum of incidents, it follows that it is also deciduous and phenomenal, in *esse* and *posse* null. That upward spring of the mind signifies that the being which the world has is only a semblance, no real being, no absolute truth; it signifies that, beyond and above that appearance, truth abides in God, so that true being is another name for God. The process of exaltation might thus appear to be transition and to involve a means, but it is not a whit less true that every trace of transition and means is absorbed; since the world, which might have seemed to be the means of reaching God, is explained to be a nullity. Unless the being of the world is nullified, the *point d'appui* for the exaltation is lost. In this way the apparent means vanishes, and the process of derivation is cancelled in the very act by which it proceeds. It is the affirmative aspect of this relation, as supposed to subsist between two things, either of which *is* as much as the other, which Jacobi mainly has in his eye when he attacks the demonstrations of the understanding. Justly censuring them for seeking conditions (i.e. the world) for the unconditioned, he remarks that the Infinite or God must on such a method be presented as dependent and derivative. But that elevation, as it takes place in the mind, serves to correct this semblance: in fact, it has no other meaning than to correct that semblance. Jacobi, however, failed to recognize the genuine nature of essential thought—by which it cancels the mediation in the very act of mediating; and consequently, his objection, though it tells against the merely 'reflective' understanding, is false when applied to thought as a whole, and in particular to reasonable thought.

To explain what we mean by the neglect of the negative factor in thought, we may refer by way of illustration to the charges of Pantheism and Atheism brought against the doctrines of Spinoza. The absolute Substance of Spinoza certainly falls short of absolute spirit, and it is a right and proper requirement that God should be defined as absolute spirit. But when the definition in Spinoza is said to identify the world with God, and to confound God with nature and the finite world, it is implied that the finite world possesses a genuine actuality and affirmative reality. If this assumption be admitted, of course a union of God with the world renders God completely finite, and degrades Him to the bare finite and adventitious congeries of existence. But there are two objections to be noted. In the first place Spinoza does not define God as the unity of God with the world, but as the union of thought with extension, that is, with the material world. And secondly, even if we accept this awkward popular statement as to this unity, it would still be true that the system of Spinoza was not Atheism but Acosmism, defining the world to be an appearance lacking in true reality. A philosophy which affirms that God and God alone is should not be stigmatized as atheistic, when even those nations which worship the ape, the cow, or images of stone and brass, are credited with some religion. But as things stand the imagination of ordinary men feels a vehement reluctance to surrender its dearest conviction, that this aggregate of finitude, which it calls a world, has actual reality; and to hold that there is no world is a way of thinking they are fain to believe impossible, or at least much less possible than to entertain the idea that there is no God. Human nature, not much to its credit, is more ready to believe that a system denies God, than that it denies the world. A denial of God seems so much more intelligible than a denial of the world.

The second remark bears on the criticism of the material propositions to which that elevation in thought in the first instance leads. If these propositions have for their predicate such terms as substance of the world, its necessary essence, cause which regulates and directs it according to design, they are certainly inadequate to express what is or ought to be understood by God. Yet apart from the trick of adopting a preliminary popular conception of God, and criticizing a result by this assumed standard, it is certain that these characteristics have great value, and are necessary factors in the idea of God. But if we wish in this way to bring before thought the genuine idea of God, and give its true value and expression to the central truth, we must be careful not to start from a subordinate level of facts. To speak of the 'merely contingent' things of the world is a very inadequate description of the premisses. The organic structures, and the evidence they afford of mutual adaptation, belong to a higher province, the province of animated nature. But even without taking into consideration the possible blemish which the study of animated nature and of the other teleological aspects of existing things may contract from the pettiness of the final causes, and from puerile instances of them and their bearings, merely animated nature is, at the best, incapable of supplying the material for a truthful expression to the idea to God. God is more than life: he is Spirit. And therefore if the thought of the Absolute takes a starting-point for its rise, and desires to take the nearest, the most true and adequate starting-point will be found in the nature of spirit alone.

§ 51

The other way of unification by which to realize the Ideal of Reason is to set out from the *abstractum* of Thought and seek to characterize it: for which purpose Being is the only available term. This is the method of the Ontological proof. The opposition, here presented from a merely subjective point of view, lies between Thought and Being; whereas in the first way of junction, being is common to the two sides of the antithesis, and the contrast lies only between its individualization and universality. Understanding meets this second way with what is implicitly the same objection as it made to the first. It denied that the empirical involves the universal; so it denies that the universal involves the specialization, which specialization in this instance is being. In other words it says: Being cannot be deduced from the notion by any analysis.

The uniformly favourable reception and acceptance which attended Kant's criticism of the Ontological proof was undoubtedly due to the illustration which he made use of. To explain the difference between thought and being, he took the instance of a hundred sovereigns, which, for anything it matters to the notion, are the same hundred whether they are real or only possible, though the difference of the two cases is very perceptible in their effect on a man's purse. Nothing can be more obvious than that anything we only think or conceive is not on that account actual; that mental representation, and even notional comprehension, always falls short of being. Still it may not unfairly be styled a barbarism in language, when the name of notion is given to things like a hundred sovereigns. And, putting that mistake aside, those who perpetually urge against the philosophic Idea the difference between Being and Thought might have admitted that philosophers were not wholly ignorant of the fact. Can there be any proposition more trite than this? But after all, it is well to remember, when we speak of God, that we have an object of another kind than any hundred sovereigns, and unlike any one particular notion, representation, or however else it may be styled. It is in fact this and this alone which marks everything finite: its being in time and space is discrepant from its notion. God, on the contrary, expressly has to be what can only be 'thought as existing'; his notion involves being. It is this unity of the notion and being that constitutes the notion of God.

If this were all, we should have only a formal expression of the divine nature which would not really go beyond a statement of the nature of the notion itself. And that the notion, in its most abstract terms, involves being is plain. For the notion, whatever other determination it may receive, is at least reference back on itself, which results by abolishing the intermediation, and thus is immediate. And what is that reference to self, but being? Certainly it would be strange if the notion, the very inmost of mind, if even the 'Ego', or above all the concrete totality we call God, were not rich enough to include so poor a category as being, the very poorest and most abstract of all. For, if we look at the thought it holds, nothing can be more insignificant than being. And yet there may be something still more insignificant than being—that which at first sight is perhaps supposed to *be*, an external and sensible existence, like that of the paper lying before me. However, in this matter, nobody proposes to speak of the sensible existence of a limited and perishable thing. Besides, the petty stricture of the *Kritik* that 'thought and being are different' can at most molest the path of the human mind from the thought of God to the certainty that he *is*: it cannot take it away. It is this process of transition, depending on the absolute inseparability of the *thought* of God from his being, for which its proper authority has been revindicated in the theory of faith or immediate knowledge—whereof hereafter.

§ 52

In this way thought, at its highest pitch, has to go outside for any determinateness; and although it is continually termed Reason, is out-and-out abstract thinking. And the result of all is that Reason supplies nothing beyond the formal unity required to simplify and systematize experiences; it is a *canon*, not an *organon*, of truth, and can furnish only a *criticism* of knowledge, not a *doctrine* of the infinite. In its final analysis this criticism is summed up in the assertion that in strictness thought is only the indeterminate unity and the action of this indeterminate unity.

Kant undoubtedly held reason to be the faculty of the unconditioned; but if reason be reduced to abstract identity only, it by implication renounces its unconditionality and is in reality no better than empty understanding. For reason is unconditioned only in so far as its character and quality are not due to an extraneous and foreign content, only in so far as it is self-characterizing, and thus, in point of content, is its own master. Kant, however, expressly explains that the action of reason consists solely in applying the categories to systematize the matter given by perception, i.e. to place it in an outside order, under the guidance of the principle of non-contradiction.

§ 53

(b) The **Practical Reason** is understood by Kant to mean a *thinking* Will, i.e. a Will that determines itself on universal principles. Its office is to give objective, imperative laws of freedom—laws, that is, which state what ought to happen. The warrant for thus assuming thought to be an activity which makes itself felt objectively, that is, to be really a Reason, is the alleged possibility of proving practical freedom by experience, that is, of showing it in the phenomenon of self-consciousness. This experience in consciousness is at once met by all that the Necessitarian produces from contrary experience, particularly by the sceptical induction (employed among others by Hume) from the endless diversity of what men regard as right and duty—i.e. from the diversity apparent in those professedly objective laws of freedom.

§ 54

What, then, is to serve as the law which the Practical Reason embraces and obeys, and as the criterion in its act of self-determination? There is no rule at hand but the same abstract identity of understanding as before: there must be no contradiction in the act of self-determination. Hence the Practical Reason never shakes off the formalism which is represented as the climax of the Theoretical Reason.

But this Practical Reason does not confine the universal principle of the Good to its own inward regulation: it first becomes *practical*, in the true sense of the word, when it insists on the Good being manifested in the world with an outward objectivity, and requires that the thought shall be objective throughout, and not merely subjective. We shall speak of this postulate of the Practical Reason afterwards.

The free self-determination which Kant denied to the speculative, he has expressly vindicated for the practical reason. To many minds this particular aspect of the Kantian philosophy made it welcome; and that for good reasons. To estimate rightly what we owe to Kant in the matter, we ought to set before our minds the form of practical philosophy and in particular of 'moral philosophy' which prevailed in his time. It may be generally described as a system of Eudaemonism, which, when asked what man's chief end ought to be, replied Happiness. And by happiness Eudaemonism understood the satisfaction of the private appetites, wishes, and wants of the man: thus raising the contingent and particular into a principle for the will and its actualization. To this Eudaemonism, which was destitute of stability and consistency, and which left the 'door and gate' wide open for every whim and caprice, Kant opposed the practical reason, and thus emphasized the need for a principle of will which should be universal and lay the same obligation on all. The theoretical reason, as has been made evident in the preceding paragraphs, is identified by Kant with the negative faculty of the infinite; and as it has no positive content of its own, it is restricted to the function of detecting the finitude of experiential knowledge. To the practical reason, on the contrary, he has expressly allowed a positive infinity, by ascribing to the will the power of modifying itself in universal modes, i.e. by thought. Such a power the will undoubtedly has: and it is well to remember that man is free only in so far as he possesses it and avails himself of it in his conduct. But a recognition of the existence of this power is not enough and does not avail to tell us what are the contents of the will or practical reason. Hence to say that a man must make the Good the content of his will raises the question, what that content is, and what are the means of ascertaining what good is. Nor does one get over the difficulty by the principle that the will must be consistent with itself, or by the precept to do duty for the sake of duty.

§ 55

(c) The **Reflective Power of Judgement** is invested by Kant with the function of an Intuitive Understanding. That is to say, whereas the particulars had hitherto appeared, so far as the universal or abstract identity was concerned, adventitious and incapable of being deduced from it, the *Intuitive* Understanding apprehends the particulars as moulded and formed by the universal itself. Experience presents such universalized particulars in the products of Art and of *organic* nature.

The capital feature in Kant's Criticism of the Judgement is, that in it he gave a representation and a name, if not even an intellectual expression, to the Idea. Such a representation, as an Intuitive Understanding, or an inner adaptation, suggests a universal which is at the same time apprehended as essentially a concrete unity. It is in these *aperçus* alone that the Kantian philosophy rises to the speculative height. Schiller, and others, have found in the idea of artistic beauty, where thought and sensuous conception have grown together into one, a way of escape from the abstract and separatist understanding. Others have found the same relief in the perception and consciousness of life and of living things, whether that life be natural or intellectual. The work of Art, as well as the living individual, is, it must be owned, of limited content. But in the postulated harmony of nature (or necessity) and free purpose—in the final purpose of the world conceived as realized, Kant has put before us the Idea, comprehensive even in its content. Yet what may be called the laziness of thought, when dealing with the supreme Idea, finds a too easy mode of evasion in the 'ought to be': instead of the actual realization of the ultimate end, it clings hard to the disjunction of the notion from reality. Yet if thought will not *think* the ideal realized, the senses and the intuition can at any rate *see* it in the present reality of living organisms and of the beautiful in Art. And consequently Kant's remarks on these objects were well adapted to lead the mind on to grasp and think the concrete Idea.

§ 56

We are thus led to conceive a different relation between the universal of understanding and the particular of perception, than that on which the theory of the Theoretical and Practical Reason is founded. But while this is so, it is not supplemented by a recognition that the former is the genuine relation and the very truth. Instead of that, the unity (of universal with particular) is accepted only as it exists in finite phenomena, and is adduced only as a fact of experience. Such experience, at first only personal, may come from two sources. It may spring from Genius, the faculty which produces 'aesthetic ideas'; meaning by aesthetic ideas, the picture-thoughts of the free imagination which subserve an idea and suggest thoughts, although their content is not expressed in a notional form, and even admits of no such expression. It may also be due to Taste, the feeling of congruity between the free play of intuition or imagination and the uniformity of understanding.

§ 57

The principle by which the Reflective faculty of Judgement regulates and arranges the products of animated nature is described as the End or final cause—the notion in action, the universal at once determining and determinate in itself. At the same time Kant is careful to discard the conception of external or finite adaptation, in which the End is only an adventitious form for the means and material in which it is realized. In the living organism, on the contrary, the final cause is a moulding principle and an energy immanent in the matter, and every member is in its turn a means as well as an end.

§ 58

Such an Idea evidently radically transforms the relation which the understanding institutes between means and ends, between subjectivity and objectivity. And yet in the face of this unification, the End or design is subsequently explained to be a cause which exists and acts subjectively, i.e. as our idea only: and teleology is accordingly explained to be only a principle of criticism, purely personal to *our* understanding.

After the Critical philosophy had settled that Reason can know phenomena only, there would still have been an option for animated nature between two equally subjective modes of thought. Even according to Kant's own exposition, there would have been an obligation to admit, in the case of natural productions, a knowledge not confined to the categories of quality, cause and effect, composition, constituents, and so on. The principle of inward adaptation or design, had it been kept to and carried out in scientific application, would have led to a different and a higher method of observing nature.

§ 59

If we adopt this principle, the Idea, when all limitations were removed from it, would appear as follows. The universality moulded by Reason, and described as the absolute and final end or the Good, would be realized in the world, and realized moreover by means of a third thing, the power which proposes this End as well as realizes it—that is, God. Thus in him, who is the absolute truth, those oppositions of universal and individual, subjective and objective, are solved and explained to be neither self-subsistent nor true.

§ 60

But Good—which is thus put forward as the final cause of the world—has been already described as only *our* good, the moral law of *our* Practical Reason. This being so, the unity in question goes no further than make the state of the world and the course of its events harmonize with our moral standards.[1] Besides, even with this limitation, the final cause, or Good, is a vague abstraction, and

[1] In Kant's own words (*Criticism of the Power of Judgement*, p. 427): 'Final Cause is merely a notion of our practical reason. It cannot be deduced from any data of experience as a theoretical criterion of nature, nor can it be applied to know nature. No employment of this notion is possible except solely for the practical reason, by moral laws. The final purpose of the Creation is that constitution of the world which harmonizes with that to which alone we can give definite expression on universal principles, viz. the final purpose of our pure practical reason, and with that in so far as it means to be practical.'

the same vagueness attaches to what is to be Duty. But, further, this harmony is met by the revival and reassertion of the antithesis, which it by its own principle had nullified. The harmony is then described as merely subjective, something which merely ought to be, and which at the same time is not real—a mere article of faith, possessing a subjective certainty, but without truth, or that objectivity which is proper to the Idea. This contradiction may seem to be disguised by adjourning the realization of the Idea to a future, to a *time* when the Idea will also be. But a sensuous condition like time is the reverse of a reconciliation of the discrepancy; and an infinite progression—which is the corresponding image adopted by the understanding—on the very face of it only repeats and re-enacts the contradiction.

A general remark may still be offered on the result to which the Critical philosophy led as to the nature of knowledge; a result which has grown one of the current 'idols' or axiomatic beliefs of the day. In every dualistic system, and especially in that of Kant, the fundamental defect makes itself visible in the inconsistency of unifying at one moment what a moment before had been explained to be independent and therefore incapable of unification. And then, at the very moment after unification has been alleged to be the truth, we suddenly come upon the doctrine that the two elements, which, in their true status of unification, had been refused all independent subsistence, are only true and actual in their state of separation. Philosophizing of this kind wants the little penetration needed to discover, that this shuffling only evidences how unsatisfactory each one of the two terms is. And it fails simply because it is incapable of bringing two thoughts together. (And in point of form there are never more than two.) It argues an utter want of consistency to say, on the one hand, that the understanding only knows phenomena, and, on the other, assert the absolute character of this knowledge, by such statements as 'Cognition can go no further'; 'Here is the *natural* and absolute limit of human knowledge.' But 'natural' is the wrong word here. The things of nature are limited and are natural things only to such extent as they are not aware of their universal limit, or to such extent as their mode or quality is a limit from our point of view, and not from their own. No one knows, or even feels, that anything is a limit or defect, until he is at the same time above and beyond it. Living beings, for example, possess the privilege of pain which is denied to the inanimate: even with living beings, a single mode or quality passes into the feeling of a negative. For living beings as such possess within them a universal vitality, which overpasses and includes the single mode; and thus, as they maintain themselves in the negative of themselves, they feel the contradiction to *exist* within them. But the contradiction is within them only in so far as one and the same subject includes both the universality of their sense of life, and the individual mode which is in negation with it. This illustration will show how a limit or imperfection in knowledge comes to be termed a limit or imperfection, only when it is compared with the actually present Idea of the universal, of a total and perfect. A very little consideration might show that to call a thing finite or limited proves by implication the very presence of the infinite and unlimited, and that our knowledge of a limit can only be when the unlimited is *on this side* in consciousness.

The result however of Kant's view of cognition suggests a second remark. The philosophy of Kant could have no influence on the method of the sciences. It leaves the categories and method of ordinary knowledge quite unmolested. Occasionally, it may be, in the first sections of a scientific work of that period, we find propositions borrowed from the Kantian philosophy; but the course of the treatise renders it apparent that these propositions were superfluous decoration, and that the few first pages might have been omitted without producing the least change in the empirical contents.[1]

We may next institute a comparison of Kant with the metaphysics of the empirical school. Natural plain Empiricism, though it unquestionably insists most upon sensuous perception, still allows a supersensible world or spiritual reality, whatever may be its structure and constitution, and whether derived from intellect, or from imagination, etc. So far as form goes, the facts of this super-

[1] Even Hermann's *Handbook of Prosody* begins with paragraphs of Kantian philosophy. In § 8 it is argued that a law of rhythm must be (1) objective, (2) formal, and (3) determined *a priori*. With these requirements and with the principles of Causality and Reciprocity which follow later, it were well to compare the treatment of the various measures, upon which those formal principles do not exercise the slightest influence.

sensible world rest on the authority of mind, in the same way as the other facts embraced in empirical knowledge rest on the authority of external perception. But when Empiricism becomes reflective and logically consistent, it turns its arms against this dualism in the ultimate and highest species of fact; it denies the independence of the thinking principle and of a spiritual world which develops itself in thought. Materialism or Naturalism, therefore, is the consistent and thoroughgoing system of Empiricism. In direct opposition to such an Empiricism, Kant asserts the principle of thought and freedom, and attaches himself to the first-mentioned form of empirical doctrine, the general principles of which he never departed from. There is a dualism in his philosophy also. On one side stands the world of sensation, and of the understanding which reflects upon it. This world, it is true, he alleges to be a world of appearances. But that is only a title or formal description; for the source, the facts, and the modes of observation continue quite the same as in Empiricism. On the other side and independent stands a self-apprehending thought, the principle of freedom, which Kant has in common with ordinary and bygone metaphysic, but emptied of all that it held, and without his being able to infuse into it anything new. For, in the Critical doctrine, thought, or, as it is there called, Reason, is divested of every specific form, and thus bereft of all authority. The main effect of the Kantian philosophy has been to revive the consciousness of Reason, or the absolute inwardness of thought. Its abstractness indeed prevented that inwardness from developing into anything, or from originating any special forms, whether cognitive principles or moral laws; but nevertheless it absolutely refused to accept or indulge anything possessing the character of an externality. Henceforth the principle of the independence of Reason, or of its absolute self-subsistence, is made a general principle of philosophy, as well as a foregone conclusion of the time.

(1) The Critical philosophy has one great negative merit. It has brought home the conviction that the categories of understanding are finite in their range, and that any cognitive process confined within their pale falls short of the truth. But Kant had only a sight of half the truth. He explained the finite nature of the categories to mean that they were subjective only,

valid only for our thought, from which the thing-in-itself was divided by an impassable gulf. In fact, however, it is not because they are subjective that the categories are finite: they are finite by their very nature, and it is on their own selves that it is requisite to exhibit their finitude. Kant however holds that what we think is false, because it is we who think it. A further deficiency in the system is that it gives only a historical description of thought, and a mere enumeration of the factors of consciousness. The enumeration is in the main correct: but not a word touches upon the necessity of what is thus empirically colligated. The observations made on the various stages of consciousness culminate in the summary statement that the content of all we are acquainted with is only an appearance. And as it is true at least that all finite thinking is concerned with appearances, so far the conclusion is justified. This stage of 'appearance' however—the phenomenal world—is not the terminus of thought: there is another and a higher region. But that region was to the Kantian philosophy an inaccessible 'other world'.

(2) After all it was only formally that the Kantian system established the principle that thought is spontaneous and self-determining. Into details of the manner and the extent of this self-determination of thought, Kant never went. It was Fichte who first noticed the omission; and who, after he had called attention to the want of a deduction for the categories, endeavoured really to supply something of the kind. With Fichte, the 'Ego' is the starting-point in the philosophical development: and the outcome of its action is supposed to be visible in the categories. But in Fichte the 'Ego' is not really presented as a free, spontaneous energy; it is supposed to receive its first excitation by a shock or impulse from without. Against this shock the 'Ego' will, it is assumed, react, and only through this reaction does it first become conscious of itself. Meanwhile, the nature of the impulse remains a stranger beyond our pale: and the 'Ego', with something else always confronting it, is weighted with a condition. Fichte, in consequence, never advanced beyond Kant's conclusion, that the finite only is knowable, while the infinite transcends the range of thought. What Kant calls the thing-by-itself, Fichte calls the impulse from without —that abstraction of something else than 'I', not otherwise describable or definable than as the negative or non-Ego in general. The 'I' is thus looked at as standing in essential relation with the not-I, through which its act of self-determination is first awakened. And in this manner the 'I' is but the continuous act of self-liberation from this impulse, never gaining a real freedom, because with the surcease of the impulse the 'I', whose being is its action, would also cease to be. Nor is the content produced by the action of the 'I' at all different from the ordinary content of experience, except by the supplementary remark, that this content is mere appearance.

V

THIRD ATTITUDE OF THOUGHT TO OBJECTIVITY

IMMEDIATE OR INTUITIVE KNOWLEDGE

§ 61

If we are to believe the Critical philosophy, thought is subjective, and its ultimate and invincible mode is *abstract universality* or formal identity. Thought is thus set in opposition to Truth, which is no abstraction, but concrete universality. In this highest mode of thought, which is entitled Reason, the Categories are left out of account. The extreme theory on the opposite side holds thought to be an act of the *particular* only, and on that ground declares it incapable of apprehending the Truth. This is the Intuitional theory.

§ 62

According to this theory, thinking, a private and particular operation, has its whole scope and product in the Categories. But these Categories, as arrested by the understanding, are limited vehicles of thought, forms of the conditioned, of the dependent and derivative. A thought limited to these modes has no sense of the Infinite and the True, and cannot bridge over the gulf that separates it from them. (This stricture refers to the proofs of God's existence.) These inadequate modes or categories are also spoken of as *notions*: and to get a notion of an object therefore can only mean, in this language, to grasp it under the form of being conditioned and derivative. Consequently, if the object in question be the True, the Infinite, the Unconditioned, we change it by our notions into a finite and conditioned; whereby, instead of apprehending the truth by thought, we have perverted it into untruth.

Such is the one simple line of argument advanced for the thesis that the knowledge of God and of truth must be immediate, or intuitive. At an earlier period all sort of anthropomorphic conceptions, as they are termed, were banished from God, as being finite and therefore unworthy of the infinite; and in this way God had been reduced to a tolerably blank being. But in those days the thought-forms were in general not supposed to come under the head of anthropomorphism. Thought was believed rather to strip finitude from the conceptions of the Absolute—in agreement with the above-mentioned conviction of all ages, that reflection is the only road to truth. But now, at length, even the thought-forms are pronounced anthropomorphic, and thought itself is described as a mere faculty of finitization.

Jacobi has stated this charge most distinctly in the seventh supplement to his Letters on Spinoza—borrowing his line of argument from the works of Spinoza himself, and applying it as a weapon against knowledge in general. In his attack knowledge is taken to mean knowledge of the finite only, a process of thought from one condition in a series to another, each of which is at once conditioning and conditioned. According to such a view, to explain and to get the notion of anything, is the same as to show it to be derived from something else. Whatever such knowledge embraces, consequently, is partial, dependent, and finite, while the infinite or true, i.e. God, lies outside of the mechanical interconnection to which knowledge is said to be confined. It is important to observe that, while Kant makes the finite nature of the Categories consist mainly in the formal circumstance that they are subjective, Jacobi discusses the Categories in their own proper character, and pronounces them to be in their very import finite. What Jacobi chiefly had before his eyes, when he thus described science, was the brilliant successes of the physical or 'exact' sciences in ascertaining natural forces and laws. It is certainly not on the finite ground occupied by these sciences that we can expect to meet the in-dwelling presence of the infinite. Lalande was right when he said he had swept the whole heaven with his glass, and seen no God. (See note to § 60.) In the field of physical science, the universal, which is the final result of analysis, is only the indeterminate aggregate—of the external finite—in one word, Matter:

and Jacobi well perceived that there was no other issue obtainable in the way of a mere advance from one explanatory clause or law to another.

§ 63

All the while the doctrine that truth exists for the mind was so strongly maintained by Jacobi, that Reason alone is declared to be that by which man lives. This Reason is the knowledge of God. But, seeing that derivative knowledge is restricted to the compass of finite facts, Reason is knowledge underivative, or Faith.

Knowledge, Faith, Thought, Intuition are the categories that we meet with on this line of reflection. These terms, as presumably familiar to every one, are only too frequently subjected to an arbitrary use, under no better guidance than the conceptions and distinctions of psychology, without any investigation into their nature and notion, which is the main question after all. Thus, we often find knowledge contrasted with faith, and faith at the same time explained to be an underivative or intuitive knowledge—so that it must be at least some sort of knowledge. And, besides, it is unquestionably a fact of experience, firstly, that what we believe is in our consciousness—which implies that we *know about it*; and secondly, that this belief is a certainty in our consciousness—which implies that we *know it*. Again, and especially, we find thought opposed to immediate knowledge and faith, and, in particular, to intuition. But if this intuition be qualified as intellectual, we must really mean intuition which thinks, unless, in a question about the nature of God, we are willing to interpret intellect to mean images and representations of imagination. The word faith or belief, in the dialect of this system, comes to be employed even with reference to common objects that are present to the senses. We believe, says Jacobi, that we have a body—we believe in the existence of the things of sense. But if we are speaking of faith in the True and Eternal, and saying that God is given and revealed to us in immediate knowledge or intuition, we are concerned not with the things of sense, but with objects special to our thinking mind, with truths of inherently universal significance. And when the individual 'I', or in other words personality, is under discussion—not the 'I' of experience, or a single private person—

above all, when the personality of God is before us, we are speaking of personality unalloyed—of a personality in its own nature universal. Such personality is a thought, and falls within the province of thought only. More than this. Pure and simple intuition is completely the same as pure and simple thought. Intuition and belief, in the first instance, denote the definite conceptions we attach to these words in our ordinary employment of them: and to this extent they differ from thought in certain points which nearly every one can understand. But here they are taken in a higher sense, and must be interpreted to mean a belief in God, or an intellectual intuition of God; in short, we must put aside all that especially distinguishes thought on the one side from belief and intuition on the other. How belief and intuition, when transferred to these higher regions, differ from thought, it is impossible for any one to say. And yet, such are the barren distinctions of words, with which men fancy that they assert an important truth; even while the formulae they maintain are identical with those which they impugn.

The term *Faith* brings with it the special advantage of suggesting the faith of the Christian religion; it seems to include Christian faith, or perhaps even to coincide with it; and thus the Philosophy of Faith has a thoroughly orthodox and Christian look, on the strength of which it takes the liberty of uttering its arbitrary dicta with greater pretension and authority. But we must not let ourselves be deceived by the semblance surreptiously secured by a merely verbal similarity. The two things are radically distinct. Firstly, the Christian faith comprises in it an authority of the Church: but the faith of Jacobi's philosophy has no other authority than that of a personal revelation. And, secondly, the Christian faith is a copious body of objective truth, a system of knowledge and doctrine: while the scope of the philosophic faith is so utterly indefinite, that, while it has room for the faith of the Christian, it equally admits a belief in the divinity of the Dalai Lama, the ox, or the monkey—thus, so far as it goes, narrowing Deity down to its simplest terms, a 'Supreme Being'. Faith itself, taken in this professedly philosophical sense, is nothing but the sapless abstract of immediate knowledge—a purely formal category applicable to very different facts; and it ought never to be confused or identified with the spiritual fullness of Christian faith, whether we look at that faith in the heart of the believer and the indwelling of the Holy Spirit, or in the system of theological doctrine.

With what is here called faith or immediate knowledge must also be identified inspiration, the heart's revelations, the truths implanted in man by nature, and also in particular, healthy reason or Common Sense, as it is called. All these forms agree in adopting as their leading principle the immediacy, or self-evident way, in which a fact or body of truths is presented in consciousness.

§ 64

This immediate knowledge, consists in knowing that the Infinite, the Eternal, the God which is in our Idea, really *is*: or, it asserts that in our consciousness there is immediately and inseparably bound up with this idea the certainty of its actual being.

To seek to controvert these maxims of immediate knowledge is the last thing philosophers would think of. They may rather find occasion for self-gratulation when these ancient doctrines, expressing as they do the general tenor of philosophic teaching, have, even in this unphilosophical fashion, become to some extent universal convictions of the age. The true marvel rather is that any one could suppose that these principles were opposed to philosophy—the maxims, viz., that whatever is held to be true is immanent in the mind, and that there is truth for the mind (§ 63). From a formal point of view, there is a peculiar interest in the maxim that the being of God is immediately and inseparately bound up with the thought of God, that objectivity is bound up with the subjectivity which the thought originally presents. Not content with that, the philosophy of immediate knowledge goes so far in its one-sided view, as to affirm that the attribute of existence, even in perception, is quite as inseparably connected with the conception we have of our own bodies and of external things, as it is with the thought of God. Now it is the endeavour of philosophy to *prove* such a unity, to show that it lies in the very nature of thought and subjectivity, to be inseparable from being and objectivity. In these circumstances therefore, philosophy, whatever estimate may be formed of the character of these proofs, must in any case be glad to see it shown and maintained that its maxims are facts of consciousness, and thus in harmony with experience. The difference between philosophy and the asseverations of immediate knowledge rather centres in the exclusive attitude which immediate knowledge adopts, when it sets itself up against philosophy.

And yet it was as a self-evident or immediate truth that the *cogito, ergo sum* of Descartes, the maxim on which may be said to hinge the whole interest of Modern Philosophy, was first stated by its author. The man who calls this a syllogism, must know little more about a syllogism than that the word 'ergo' occurs in it. Where shall we look for the middle term? And a middle term is a much more essential point of a syllogism than the word 'ergo'. If we try to justify the name, by calling the combination of ideas in Descartes an 'immediate' syllogism, this superfluous variety of syllogism is a mere name for an utterly unmediated synthesis of distinct terms of thought. That being so, the synthesis of being with our ideas, as stated in the maxim of immediate knowledge, has no more and no less claim to the title of syllogism than the axiom of Descartes has. From Hotho's '*Dissertation on the Cartesian Philosophy*' (published 1826), I borrow the quotation in which Descartes himself distinctly declares that the maxim *cogito, ergo sum* is no syllogism. The passages are *Respons. ad II Object.*; *De Methodo* iv; *Ep.* i. 118. From the first passage I quote the words more immediately to the point. Descartes says: 'That we are thinking beings is *prima quaedam notio quae ex nullo syllogismo concluditur*' (a certain primary notion, which is deduced from no syllogism); and goes on: '*neque cum quis dicit: Ego cogito, ergo sum sive existo, existentiam ex cogitatione per syllogismum deducit*' (nor, when one says, I think, therefore I am or exist, does he deduce existence from thought by means of a syllogism). Descartes knew what it implied in a syllogism, and so he adds that, in order to make the maxim admit of a deduction by syllogism, we should have to add the major premiss: *Illud omne quod cogitat, est sive existit* (Everything which thinks, is or exists). Of course, he remarks, this major premiss itself has to be deduced from the original statement.

The language of Descartes on the maxim that the 'I' which *thinks* must also at the same time *be*, his saying that this connection is given and implied in the simple perception of consciousness—that this connection is the absolute first, the principle, the most certain and evident of all things, so that no scepticism can be conceived so monstrous as not to admit it—all this language is so vivid and distinct, that the modern statements of Jacobi and others on this immediate connection can only pass for needless repetitions.

§ 65

The theory of which we are speaking is not satisfied when it has shown that mediate knowledge taken separately is an adequate vehicle of truth. Its distinctive doctrine is that immediate knowledge alone, to the total exclusion of mediation, can possess a content which is true. This exclusiveness is enough to show that the theory is a relapse into the metaphysical understanding, with its pass-words 'either—or'. And thus it is really a relapse into the habit of external mediation, the gist of which consists in clinging to those narrow and one-sided categories of the finite, which it falsely imagined itself to have left for ever behind. This point, however, we shall not at present discuss in detail. An exclusively immediate knowledge is asserted as a fact only, and in the present Introduction we can only study it from this external point of view. The real significance of such knowledge will be explained when we come to the logical question of the opposition between mediate and immediate. But it is characteristic of the view before us to decline to examine the nature of the fact, that is, the notion of it; for such an examination would itself be a step towards mediation and even towards knowledge. The genuine discussion on logical ground, therefore, must be deferred till we come to the proper province of Logic itself.

The whole of the second part of Logic, the Doctrine of Essential Being, is a discussion of the intrinsic and self-affirming unity of immediacy and mediation.

§ 66

Beyond this point then we need not go: immediate knowledge is to be accepted as a *fact*. Under these circumstances examination is directed to the field of experience, to a psychological phenomenon. If that be so, we need only note, as the commonest of experiences, that truths which we well know to be results of complicated and highly mediated trains of thought present themselves immediately and without effort to the mind of any man who is familiar with the subject. The mathematician, like everyone who has mastered a particular science, meets any problem with ready-made solutions which presuppose most complicated analyses: and every educated man has a number of general views and maxims which he can muster without trouble, but which can only have sprung from frequent reflection and long experience. The facility we attain in any sort of knowledge, art, or technical expertness, consists in having the particular knowledge or kind of action present to our mind in any case that occurs, even, we may say, immediate in our very limbs, in an outgoing activity. In all these instances, immediacy of knowledge is so far from excluding mediation, that the two things are linked together—immediate knowledge being actually the product and result of mediated knowledge.

It is no less obvious that immediate *existence* is bound up with its mediation. The seed and the parents are immediate and initial existences in respect of the offspring which they generate. But the seed and the parents, though they exist and are therefore immediate, are yet in their turn generated; and the child, without prejudice to the mediation of its existence, is immediate, because it *is*. The fact that I am in Berlin, my immediate presence here, is mediated by my having made the journey hither.

§ 67

One thing may be observed with reference to the immediate knowledge of God, of legal and ethical principles (including under the head of immediate knowledge what is otherwise termed Instinct, Implanted or Innate Ideas, Common Sense, Natural Reason, or whatever form, in short, we give to the original spontaneity). It is a matter of general experience that education or development is required to bring out into consciousness what is therein contained. It was so even with the Platonic reminiscence; and the Christian rite of baptism, although a sacrament, involves the additional obligation of a Christian upbringing. In short, religion and morals, however much they may be faith or immediate knowledge, are still on every side conditioned by the mediating process which is termed development, education, training.

The adherents, no less than the assailants, of the doctrine of Innate Ideas have been guilty throughout of the like exclusiveness and narrowness as is here noted. They have drawn a hard and fast line between the essential and immediate union (as it may be described) of certain universal principles with the soul, and another union which has to be brought about in an external fashion, and through the channel of *given* objects and conceptions. There is one objection, borrowed from experience, which was raised against the doctrine of Innate Ideas. All men, it was said, must have these ideas; they must have, for example, the maxim of contradiction present in the mind—they must be aware of it; for this maxim and others like it were included in the class of Innate Ideas. The objection may be set down to misconception; for the principles in question, though innate, need not on that account have the form of ideas or conceptions of something we are aware of. Still, the objection completely meets and overthrows the crude theory of immediate knowledge, which expressely maintains its formulae in so far as they are in consciousness. Another point calls for notice. We may suppose it admitted by the intuitive school, that the special case of religious faith involves supplementing by a Christian or religious education and development. In that case it is acting capriciously when it seeks to ignore this admission when speaking about faith, or it betrays a want of reflection not to know, that, if the necessity of education be once admitted, mediation is pronounced indispensable.

The reminiscence of ideas spoken of by Plato is equivalent to saying that ideas implicitly exist in man, instead of being, as the Sophists assert, a foreign importation into his mind. But to conceive knowledge as reminiscence does not interfere with, or set aside as useless, the development of what is implicitly in man; which development is another word for mediation. The same holds good of the innate ideas that we find in Descartes and the Scotch philosophers. These ideas are only potential in the first instance, and should be looked at as being a sort of mere capacity in man.

§ 68

In the case of these experiences the appeal turns upon something that shows itself bound up with immediate consciousness. Even if this combination be in the first instance taken as an external and empirical connection, still, even for empirical observation, the fact of its being constant shows it to be essential and inseparable. But, again, if this immediate consciousness, as exhibited in experience, be taken separately, so far as it is a consciousness of God and the divine nature, the state of mind which it implies is generally described as an exaltation above the finite, above the senses, and above the instinctive desires and affections of the natural heart: which exaltation passes over into, and terminates in, faith in God and a divine order. It is apparent, therefore, that, though faith may be an immediate knowledge and certainty, it equally implies the interposition of this process as its antecedent and condition.

It has been already observed, that the so-called proofs of the being of God, which start from finite being, give an expression to this exaltation. In that light they are no inventions of an over-subtle reflection, but the necessary and native channel in which the movement of mind runs: though it may be that, in their ordinary form, these proofs have not their correct and adequate expression.

§ 69

It is the passage (§ 64) from the subjective Idea to being which forms the main concern of the doctrine of immediate knowledge. A primary and self-evident interconnection is declared to exist between our Idea and being. Yet precisely this central point of transition, utterly irrespective of any connections which show in experience, clearly involves a mediation. And the mediation is of no imperfect or unreal kind, where the mediation takes place with and through something external, but one comprehending both antecedent and conclusion.

§ 70

For, what this theory asserts is that truth lies neither in the Idea as a merely subjective thought, nor in mere being on its own account—that mere being *per se*, a being that is not of the Idea, is the sensible finite being of the world. Now all this only affirms, without demonstration, that the Idea has truth only by means of being, and being has truth only by means of the Idea. The maxim of immediate knowledge rejects an indefinite empty immediacy (and such is abstract being, or pure unity taken by itself), and affirms in its stead the unity of the Idea with being. And it acts rightly in so doing. But it is stupid not to see that the unity of distinct terms or modes is not merely a purely immediate unity, i.e. unity empty and indeterminate, but that—with equal emphasis—the one term is shown to have truth only as mediated through the other—or, if the phrase be preferred, that either term is only mediated with truth through the other. That the quality of mediation is involved in the very immediacy of intuition is thus exhibited as a fact, against which understanding, conformably to the fundamental maxim of immediate knowledge that the evidence of consciousness is infallible, can have nothing to object. It is only ordinary abstract understanding which takes the terms of mediation and immediacy, each by itself absolutely, to represent an inflexible line of distinction, and thus draws upon its own head the hopeless task of reconciling them. The difficulty, as we have shown, has no existence in the fact, and it vanishes in the speculative notion.

§ 71

The one-sidedness of the intuitional school has certain characteristics attending upon it, which we shall proceed to point out in their main features, now that we have discussed the fundamental principle. The *first* of these corollaries is as follows. Since the criterion of truth is found, not in the nature of the content, but in the mere fact of consciousness, every alleged truth has no other basis than subjective certitude and the assertion that we discover a certain fact in our consciousness. What I discover in my consciousness is thus exaggerated into a fact of the consciousness of all, and even passed off for the very nature of consciousness.

Among the so-called proofs of the existence of God, there used to stand the *consensus gentium*, to which appeal is made as early as Cicero. The *consensus gentium* is a weighty authority, and the transition is easy and natural, from the circumstance that a certain fact is found in the consciousness of every one to the conclusion that it is a necessary element in the very nature of consciousness. In this category of general agreement there was latent the deep-rooted perception, which does not excape even the least cultivated mind, that the consciousness of the individual is at the same time particular and accidental. Yet unless we examine the nature of this consciousness itself, stripping it of its particular and accidental elements and, by the toilsome operation of reflection, disclosing the universal in its entirety and purity, it is only a *unanimous* agreement upon a given point that can authorize a decent presumption that that point is part of the very nature of consciousness. Of course, if thought insists on seeing the necessity of what is presented as a fact of general occurrence, the *consensus gentium* is certainly not sufficient. Yet even granting the universality of the fact to be a satisfactory proof, it has been found impossible to establish the belief in God on such an argument, because experience shows that there are individuals and nations without any such faith.[1] But there can be nothing shorter and more convenient

[1] In order to judge of the greater or less extent to which Experience shows cases of Atheism or of the belief in God, it is all-important to know if the mere general conception of deity suffices, or if a more definite knowledge of God is required. The Christian world would certainly refuse the title of God to the idols of the Hindus and the Chinese, to the fetishes of the Africans, and even to the gods of Greece themselves. If so, a believer in these idols would not be a believer in God. If it were contended, on the other hand, that such a belief in idols implies some sort of belief in God, as the species implies the genus, then idolatry would argue not faith in an idol merely, but faith in God. The Athenians took an opposite view. The poets and philosophers who explained Zeus to be a cloud, and maintained that there was only one God, were treated as atheists at Athens.

The danger in these questions lies in looking at what the mind may make out of an object, and not what that object actually and explicitly is. If we fail to note this distinction, the commonest perceptions of men's senses will be religion: for every such perception, and indeed every act of mind, implicitly contains the principle which, when it is purified and developed, rises to religion. But to be capable of religion is one thing, to have it another. And religion yet implicit is only a capacity or a possibility.

Thus in modern times, travellers have found tribes (as Captains Ross and Parry found the Esquimaux) which, as they tell us, have not even that small modicum of religion possessed by African sorcerers, the *goetes* of Herodotus. On the other hand, an Englishman, who spent the first months of the last Jubilee at Rome, says, in his account of the modern Romans, that the common people are bigots, whilst those who can read and write are atheists to a man.

The charge of Atheism is seldom heard in modern times: principally because the facts and the requirements of religion are reduced to a minimum. (See § 73.)

than to have the bare assertion to make, that we discover a fact in our consciousness, and are certain that it is true: and to declare that this certainty, instead of proceeding from our particular mental constitution only, belongs to the very nature of the mind.

§ 72

A *second* corollary which results from holding immediacy of consciousness to be the criterion of truth is that all superstition or idolatry is allowed to be truth, and that an apology is prepared for any contents of the will, however wrong and immoral. It is because he believes in them, and not from the reasoning and syllogism of what is termed mediate knowledge, that the Hindu finds God in the cow, the monkey, the Brahmin, or the Lama. But the natural desires and affections spontaneously carry and deposit their interests in consciousness, where also immoral aims make themselves naturally at home: the good or bad character would thus express the *definite being* of the will, which would be known, and that most immediately, in the interests and aims.

§ 73

Thirdly and lastly, the immediate consciousness of God goes no further than to tell us *that* he is: to tell us *what* he is would be an act of cognition, involving mediation. So that God as an object of religion is expressly narrowed down to the indeterminate supersensible, God in general: and the significance of religion is reduced to a minimum.

If it were really needful to win back and secure the bare belief that there is a God, or even to create it, we might well wonder at the poverty of the age which can see a gain in the merest pittance of religious consciousness, and which in its church has sunk so low as to worship at the altar that stood in Athens long ago, dedicated to the 'Unknown God'.

§ 74

We have still briefly to indicate the general nature of the form of immediacy. For it is the essential one-sidedness of the category which makes whatever comes under it one-sided and, for that reason, finite. And, first, it makes the universal no better than an abstraction external to the particulars, and God a being without determinate quality. But God can only be called a spirit when he is known to be at once the beginning and end, as well as the mean, in the process of mediation. Without this unification of elements he is neither concrete, nor living, nor a spirit. Thus the knowledge of God as a spirit necessarily implies mediation. The form of immediacy, secondly, invests the particular with the character of independent or self-centred being. But such predicates contradict the very essence of the particular—which is to be referred to something else outside. They thus invest the finite with the character of an absolute. But, besides, the form of immediacy is altogether abstract: it has no preference for one set of contents more than another, but is equally susceptible of all: it may as well sanction what is idolatrous and immoral as the reverse. Only when we discern that the content—the particular—is not self-subsistent, but derivative from something else, are its finitude and untruth shown in their proper light. Such discernment, where the content we discern carries with it the ground of its dependent nature, is a knowledge which involves mediation. The only content which can be held to be the truth is one not mediated with something else, not limited by other things: or, otherwise expressed, it is one mediated by itself, where mediation and immediate reference-to-self coincide. The understanding that fancies it has got clear of finite knowledge, the identity of the analytical metaphysicians and the old 'rationalists', abruptly takes again as principle and criterion of truth that immediacy which, as an abstract reference-to-self, is the same as abstract identity. Abstract thought (the scientific form used by 'reflective' metaphysic) and abstract intuition (the form used by immediate knowledge) are one and the same.

The stereotyped opposition between the form of immediacy and that of mediation gives to the former a halfness and inadequacy that affects every content which is brought under it. Immediacy means, upon the whole, an abstract reference-to-self, that is, an abstract identity or abstract universality. Accordingly the essential and real universal, when taken merely in its immediacy, is a mere abstract universal; and from this point of view God is conceived as a being altogether without determinate quality. To call God spirit is in that case only a phrase: for the consciousness and self-consciousness which spirit implies are impossible without a distinguishing of it from itself and from something else, i.e. without mediation.

§ 75

It was impossible for us to criticize this, the third attitude which thought has been made to take towards objective truth, in any other mode than what is naturally indicated and admitted in the doctrine itself. The theory asserts that immediate knowledge is a fact. It has been shown to be untrue in fact to say that there is an immediate knowledge, a knowledge without mediation either by means of something else or in itself. It has also been explained to be false in fact to say that thought advances through finite and conditioned categories only, which are always mediated by a something else, and to forget that in the very act of mediation the mediation itself vanishes. And to show that, in point of fact, there is a knowledge which advances neither by unmixed immediacy nor by unmixed mediation, we can point to the example of Logic and the whole of philosophy.

§ 76

If we view the maxims of immediate knowledge in connection with the uncritical metaphysic of the past from which we started, we shall learn from the comparison the reactionary nature of the school of Jacobi. His doctrine is a return to the modern starting-point of this metaphysic in the Cartesian philosophy. Both Jacobi and Descartes maintain the following three points:

(1) The simple inseparability of the thought and being of the thinker. *Cogito, ergo sum* is the same doctrine as that the being, reality, and existence of the 'Ego' is immediately revealed to me in consciousness. (Descartes, in fact, is careful to state that by thought he means consciousness in general. *Princip. Phil.* i. 9.) This inseparability is the absolutely first and most certain knowledge, not mediated or demonstrated.

(2) The inseparability of existence from the conception of God: the former is necessarily implied in the latter, or the conception

never can be without the attribute of existence, which is thus necessary and eternal.[1]

(3) The immediate consciousness of the existence of external things. By this nothing more is meant than sense-consciousness. To have such a thing is the slightest of all cognitions: and the only thing worth knowing about it is that such immediate knowledge of the being of things external is error and delusion, that the sensible world as such is altogether void of truth; that the being of these external things is accidental and passes away as a show; and that their very nature is to have only an existence which is separable from their essence and notion.

§ 77

There is however a distinction between the two points of view:

(1) The Cartesian philosophy, from these unproved postulates, which it assumes to be unprovable, proceeds to wider and wider details of knowledge, and thus gave rise to the sciences of modern times. The modern theory (of Jacobi), on the contrary, (§ 62) has

[1] Descartes, *Princip. Phil.* i. 15: *Magis hoc* (*ens summe perfectum existere*) *credet, si attendat, nullius alterius rei ideam apud se inveniri, in qua eodem modo necessariam existentiam contineri animadvertat; intelliget illam ideam exhibere veram et immutabilem naturam, quaeque non potest non existere, cum necessaria existentia in ea contineatur.* (The reader will be more disposed to *believe* that there exists a being supremely perfect, if he notes that in the case of nothing else is there found in him an idea, in which he notices necessary existence to be contained in the same way. He will see that that idea exhibits a true and unchangeable nature —a nature which *cannot but exist*, since necessary existence is *contained in it*.) A remark which immediately follows, and which sounds like mediation or demonstration, does not really prejudice the original principle.

In Spinoza we come upon the same statement that the essence or abstract conception of God implies existence. The first of Spinoza's definitions, that of the *Causa Sui* (or Self-Cause), explains it to be *cujus essentia involvit existentiam, sive id cujus natura non potest concipi nisi existens* (that of which the essence involves existence, or that whose nature cannot be conceived except as existing). The inseparability of the notion from being is the main point and fundamental hypothesis in his system. But what notion is thus inseparable from being? Not the notion of finite things, for they are so constituted as to have a contingent and a created existence. Spinoza's eleventh proposition, which follows with a proof that God exists necessarily, and his twentieth, showing that God's existence and his essence are one and the same, are really superfluous, and the proof is more in form than in reality. To say that God is Substance, the only Substance, and that, as Subtance is *Causa Sui*, God therefore exists necessarily, is merely stating that God is that of which the notion and the being are inseparable.

come to what is intrinsically a most important conclusion that cognition, proceeding as it must by finite mediations, can know only the finite, and never embody the truth; and would fain have the consciousness of God go no further than the aforesaid very abstract belief that God *is*.[1]

(2) The modern doctrine on the one hand makes no change in the Cartesian method of the usual scientific knowledge, and conducts on the same plan the experimental and finite sciences that have sprung from it. But, on the other hand, when it comes to the science which has infinity for its scope, it throws aside that method and thus, as it knows no other, it rejects all methods. It abandons itself to wild vagaries of imagination and assertion, to a moral priggishness and sentimental arrogance, or to a reckless dogmatizing and lust of argument, which is loudest against philosophy and philosophic doctrines. Philosophy of course tolerates no mere assertions or conceits, and checks the free play of argumentative see-saw.

§ 78

We must then reject the opposition between an independent immediacy in the contents or facts of consciousness and an equally independent mediation, supposed incompatible with the former. The incompatibility is a mere assumption, an arbitrary assertion. All other assumptions and postulates must in like manner be left behind at the entrance to philosophy, whether they are derived from the intellect or the imagination. For philosophy is the science in which every such proposition must first be scrutinized and its meaning and oppositions be ascertained.

Scepticism, made a negative science and systematically applied to all forms of knowledge, might seem a suitable introduction, as pointing out the nullity of such assumptions. But a sceptical introduction would be not only an ungrateful but also a useless

[1] Anselm on the contrary says: *Negligentiae mihi videtur, si postquam confirmati sumus in fide, non studemus, quod credimus, intelligere.* (Methinks it is *carelessness*, if, after we have been confirmed in the faith, we do not *exert ourselves to see the meaning of what we believe.*) [*Tractat. Cur Deus Homo?*] These words of Anselm, in connection with the concrete truths of Christian doctrine, offer a far harder problem for investigation, than is contemplated by this modern faith.

course; and that because Dialectic, as we shall soon make appear, is itself an essential element of affirmative science. Scepticism, besides, could only get hold of the finite forms as they were suggested by experience, taking them as given, instead of deducing them scientifically. To require such a scepticism accomplished is the same as to insist on science being preceded by universal doubt, or a total absence of presupposition. Strictly speaking, in the resolve that *wills pure thought*, this requirement is accomplished by freedom which, abstracting from everything, grasps its pure abstraction, the simplicity of thought.

VI

LOGIC FURTHER DEFINED AND DIVIDED

§ 79

In point of form Logical doctrine has three sides: (α) the Abstract side, or that of understanding; (β) the Dialectical, or that of negative reason; (γ) the Speculative, or that of positive reason.

These three sides do not make three *parts* of logic, but are stages or 'moments' in every logical entity, that is, of every notion and truth whatever. They may all be put under the first stage, that of understanding, and so kept isolated from each other; but this would give an inadequate conception of them. The statement of the dividing lines and the characteristic aspects of logic is at this point no more than historical and anticipatory.

§ 80

(α) Thought, as *Understanding*, sticks to fixity of characters and their distinctness from one another: every such limited abstract it treats as having a subsistence and being of its own.

In our ordinary usage of the term thought and even notion, we often have before our eyes nothing more than the operation of Understanding. And no doubt thought is primarily an exercise of Understanding; only it goes further, and the notion is not a function of Understanding merely. The action of Understanding may be in general described as investing its subject-matter with the form of universality. But this universal is an abstract universal: that is to say, its opposition to the particular is so rigorously maintained, that it is at the same time also reduced to the character of a particular again. In this separating and abstracting attitude towards its objects, Understanding is the reverse of immediate perception and sensation, which, as such, keep completely to their native sphere of action in the concrete.

It is by referring to this opposition of Understanding to sensation or feeling that we must explain the frequent attacks made upon thought for being hard and narrow, and for leading, if consistently developed, to ruinous and pernicious results. The answer to these charges, in so far as they are warranted by the facts, is that they do not touch thinking in general, certainly not the thinking of Reason, but only the exercise of Understanding. It must be added, however, that the merit and rights of the mere Understanding should unhesitatingly be admitted. And that merit lies in the fact that apart from Understanding there is no fixity or accuracy in the region of theory or of practice.

Thus, in theory, knowledge begins by apprehending existing objects in their specific differences. In the study of nature, for example, we distinguish matters, forces, genera, and the like, and stereotype each in its isolation. Thought is here acting in its analytic capacity, where its canon is identity, a simple reference of each attribute to itself. It is under the guidance of the same identity that the process in knowledge is effected from one scientific truth to another. Thus, for example, in mathematics magnitude is the feature which, to the neglect of any other, determines our advance. Hence in geometry we compare one figure with another, so as to bring out their identity. Similarly in other fields of knowledge, such as jurisprudence, the advance is primarily regulated by identity. In it we argue from one specific law or precedent to another: and what is this but to proceed on the principle of identity?

But Understanding is as indispensable in practice as it is in theory. Character is an essential in conduct, and a man of character is an understanding man, who in that capacity has definite ends in view and undeviatingly pursues them. The man who will do something great must learn, as Goethe says, to limit himself. The man who, on the contrary, would do everything, really would do nothing, and fails. There is a host of interesting things in the world: Spanish poetry, chemistry, politics, and music are all very interesting, and if any one takes an interest in them we need not find fault. But for a person in a given situation to accomplish anything, he must stick to one definite point, and not dissipate his forces in many directions. In every calling, too, the great thing is to pursue it with understanding. Thus the judge must stick to the law, and give his verdict in accordance with it, undeterred by one motive or another, allowing no excuses, and looking neither left nor right. Understanding, too, is always an element in thorough training. The trained intellect is not satisfied with cloudy and indefinite impressions, but grasps the objects in their fixed character: whereas the uncultivated man wavers unsettled, and it often costs a deal of trouble to come to an understanding with him on the matter under discussion, and to bring him to fix his eye on the definite point in question.

It has been already explained that the Logical principle in general, far from being merely a subjective action in our minds, is rather the very universal, which as such is also objective. This doctrine is illustrated in the case of understanding, the first form of logical truths. Understanding in this larger sense corresponds to what we call the goodness of God, so far as that means that finite things are and subsist. In nature, for example, we recognize the goodness of God in the fact that the various classes or species of animals and plants are provided with whatever they need for their preservation and welfare. Nor is man excepted, who, both as an individual and as a nation, possesses partly in the given circumstances of climate, or quality and products of soil, and partly in his natural parts or talents, all that is required for his maintenance and development. Under this shape Understanding is visible in every department of the objective world; and no object in that world can ever be wholly perfect which does not give full satisfaction to the canons of understanding. A state, for example, is imperfect, so long as it has not reached a clear differentiation of orders and callings, and so long as those functions of politics and government, which are different in principle, have not evolved for themselves special organs, in the same way as we see, for example, the developed animal organism provided with separate organs for the functions of sensation, motion, digestion, &c.

The previous course of the discussion may serve to show that understanding is indispensable even in those spheres and regions of action which the popular fancy would deem furthest from it, and that in proportion as understanding is absent from them, imperfection is the result. This particularly holds good of Art, Religion, and Philosophy. In Art, for example, understanding is visible where the forms of beauty, which differ in principle, are kept distinct and exhibited in their purity. The same thing holds good also of single works of art. It is part of the beauty and perfection of a dramatic poem that the characters of the several persons should be closely and faithfully maintained, and that the different aims and interests involved should be plainly and decidedly exhibited. Or again, take the province of Religion. The superiority of Greek over Northern mythology (apart from other differences of subject-matter and conception) mainly consists in this: that in the former the individual gods are fashioned into forms of sculpture-like distinctness of outline, while in the latter the figures fade away vaguely and hazily into one another. Lastly comes Philosophy. That Philosophy never can get on without the understanding hardly calls for special remark after what has been said. Its foremost requirement is that every thought shall be grasped in its full precision, and nothing allowed to remain vague and indefinite.

It is usually added that understanding must not go too far. Which is so far correct, that understanding is not an ultimate, but on the contrary finite, and so constituted that when carried to extremes it veers round to its opposite. It is the fashion of youth to dash about in abstractions; but the man who has learnt to know life steers clear of the abstract 'either—or', and keeps to the concrete.

§ 81

(β) In the Dialectical stage these finite characterizations or formulae supersede themselves, and pass into their opposites.

(1) But when the Dialectical principle is employed by the understanding separately and independently—especially as seen in its application to philosophical theories—Dialectic becomes Scepticism; in which the result that ensues from its action is presented as a mere negation.

(2) It is customary to treat Dialectic as an adventitious art, which for very wantonness introduces confusion and a mere semblance of contradiction into definite notions. And in that light, the semblance is the nonentity, while the true reality is supposed to belong to the original dicta of understanding. Often, indeed, Dialectic is nothing more than a subjective see-saw of arguments *pro* and *con*, where the absence of sterling thought is disguised by the subtlety which gives birth to such arguments. But in its true and proper character, Dialectic is the very nature and essence of everything predicated by mere understanding—the law of things and of the finite as a whole. Dialectic is different from 'Reflection'. In the first instance, Reflection is that movement out beyond the isolated predicate of a thing which gives it some reference, and brings out its relativity, while still in other respects leaving it its isolated validity. But by Dialectic is meant the indwelling tendency outwards by which the one-sidedness and limitation of the predicates of understanding is seen in its true light, and shown to be the negation of them. For anything to be finite is just to suppress itself and put itself aside. Thus understood the Dialectical principle constitutes the life and soul of scientific progress, the dynamic which alone gives immanent connection and necessity to the body of science; and, in a word, is seen to constitute the real and true, as opposed to the external, exaltation above the finite.

(1) It is of the highest importance to ascertain and understand rightly the nature of Dialectic. Wherever there is movement, wherever there is life, wherever anything is carried into effect in the actual world, there Dialectic is at work. It is also the soul of all knowledge which is truly scientific. In the popular way of looking at things, the refusal to be bound by the abstract deliverances of understanding appears as fairness, which, according to the proverb Live and let live, demands that each should have its turn; we admit the one, but we admit the other also. But when we look more closely, we find that the limitations of the finite do not merely come from without; that its own nature is the cause of its abrogation, and that by its own act it passes into its counterpart. We say, for instance, that

man is mortal, and seem to think that the ground of his death is in external circumstances only; so that if this way of looking were correct, man would have two special properties, vitality and—also—mortality. But the true view of the matter is that life, as life, involves the germ of death, and that the finite, being radically self-contradictory, involves its own self-suppression.

Nor, again, is Dialectic to be confounded with mere Sophistry. The essence of Sophistry lies in giving authority to a partial and abstract principle, in its isolation, as may suit the interest and particular situation of the individual at the time. For example, a regard to my existence, and my having the means of existence, is a vital motive of conduct, but if I exclusively emphasize this consideration or motive of my welfare, and draw the conclusion that I may steal or betray my country, we have a case of Sophistry. Similarly, it is a vital principle in conduct that I should be subjectively free, that is to say, that I should have an insight into what I am doing, and a conviction that it is right. But if my pleading insists on this principle alone I fall into Sophistry, such as would overthrow all the principles of morality. From this sort of party-pleading Dialectic is wholly different; its purpose is to study things in their own being and movement and thus to demonstrate the finitude of the partial categories of understanding.

Dialectic, it may be added, is no novelty in philosophy. Among the ancients Plato is termed the inventor of Dialectic; and his right to the name rests on the fact that the Platonic philosophy first gave the free scientific, and thus at the same time the objective, form to Dialectic. Socrates, as we should expect from the general character of his philosophizing, has the dialectical element in a predominantly subjective shape, that of Irony. He used to turn his Dialectic, first against ordinary consciousness, and then especially against the Sophists. In his conversations he used to simulate the wish for some clearer knowledge about the subject under discussion, and after putting all sorts of questions with that intent, he drew on those with whom he conversed to the opposite of what their first impressions had pronounced correct. If, for instance, the Sophists claimed to be teachers, Socrates by a series of questions forced the Sophist Protagoras to confess that all learning is only recollection. In his more strictly scientific dialogues Plato employs the dialectical method to show the finitude of all hard and fast terms of understanding. Thus in the *Parmenides* he deduces the many from the one, and shows nevertheless that the many cannot but define itself as the one. In this grand style did Plato treat Dialectic. In modern times it was, more than any other, Kant who resuscitated the name of Dialectic, and restored it to its post of honour. He did it, as we have seen (§ 48), by working out the Antinomies of the reason. The problem of these Antinomies is no mere subjective piece of work oscillating between one set of grounds and another; it really serves to show that every abstract proposition of understanding, taken precisely as it is given, naturally veers round into its opposite.

However reluctant Understanding may be to admit the action of Dialectic, we must not suppose that the recognition of its existence is peculiarly confined to the philosopher. It would be truer to say that Dialectic gives expression to a law which is felt in all other grades of consciousness, and in general experience. Everything that surrounds us may be viewed as an instance of Dialectic. We are aware that everything finite, instead of being stable and ultimate, is rather changeable and transient; and this is exactly what we mean by that Dialectic of the finite, by which the finite, as implicitly other than what it is, is forced beyond its own immediate or natural being to turn suddenly into its opposite. We have before this (§ 80) identified Understanding with what is implied in the popular idea of the goodness of God; we may now remark of Dialectic, in the same objective signification, that its principle answers to the idea of his power. All things, we say—that is, the finite world as such—are doomed; and in saying so, we have a vision of Dialectic as the universal and irresistible power before which nothing can stay, however secure and stable it may deem itself. The category of power does not, it is true, exhaust the depth of the divine nature or the notion of God; but it certainly forms a vital element in all religious consciousness.

Apart from this general objectivity of Dialectic, we find traces of its presence in each of the particular provinces and phases of the natural and spiritual world. Take as an illustration the motion of the heavenly bodies. At this moment the planet stands in this spot, but implicitly it is the possibility of being in another spot; and that possibility of being otherwise the planet brings into existence by moving. Similarly the 'physical' elements prove to be Dialectical. The process of meteorological action is the exhibition of their Dialectic. It is the same dynamic that lies at the root of every natural process, and, as it were, forces nature out of itself. To illustrate the presence of Dialectic in the spiritual world, especially in the provinces of law and morality, we have only to recollect how general experience shows us the extreme of one state or action suddenly shifting into its opposite: a Dialectic which is recognized in many ways in common proverbs. Thus *summum jus summa injuria*, which means that to drive an abstract right to its extremity is to do a wrong. In political life, as every one knows, extreme anarchy and extreme despotism naturally lead to one another. The perception of Dialectic in the province of individual Ethics is seen in the well-known adages: Pride comes before a fall; Too much wit outwits itself. Even feeling, bodily as well as mental, has its Dialectic. Every one knows how the extremes of pain and pleasure pass into each other: the heart overflowing with joy seeks relief in tears, and the deepest melancholy will at times betray its presence by a smile.

(2) Scepticism should not be looked upon merely as a doctrine of doubt. It would be more correct to say that the Sceptic has no doubt of his point, which is the nothingness of all finite existence. He who only doubts still clings to the hope that his doubt may be resolved, and that

one or other of the definite views, between which he wavers, will turn out solid and true. Scepticism properly so called is a very different thing: it is complete hopelessness about all which understanding counts stable, and the feeling to which it gives birth is one of unbroken calmness and inward repose. Such at least is the noble Scepticism of antiquity, especially as exhibited in the writings of Sextus Empiricus, when in the later times of Rome it had been systematized as a complement to the dogmatic systems of Stoic and Epicurean. Of far other stamp, and to be strictly distinguished from it, is the modern Scepticism already mentioned (§ 39), which partly preceded the Critical Philosophy, and partly sprang out of it. That later Scepticism consisted solely in denying the truth and certitude of the supersensible, and in pointing to the facts of sense and of immediate sensations as what we have to keep to.

Even to this day Scepticism is often spoken of as the irresistible enemy of all positive knowledge, and hence of philosophy, in so far as philosophy is concerned with positive knowledge. But in these statements there is a misconception. It is only the finite thought of abstract understanding which has to fear Scepticism, because unable to withstand it: philosophy includes the sceptical principle as a subordinate function of its own, in the shape of Dialectic. In contradistinction to mere Scepticism, however, philosophy does not remain content with the purely negative result of Dialectic. The sceptic mistakes the true value of his result, when he supposes it to be no more than a negation pure and simple. For the negative which emerges as the result of dialectic is, because a result, at the same time the positive: it contains what it results from, absorbed into itself, and made part of its own nature. Thus conceived, however, the dialectical stage has the features characterizing the third grade of logical truth, the speculative form, or form of positive reason.

§ 82

(γ) The Speculative stage, or stage of Positive Reason, apprehends the unity of terms (propositions) in their opposition—the affirmative, which is involved in their disintegration and in their transition.

(1) The result of Dialectic is positive, because it has a definite content, or because its result is not empty and abstract nothing, but the negation of certain specific propositions which are contained in the result—for the very reason that it is a resultant and not an immediate nothing. (2) It follows from this that the 'reasonable' result, though it be only a thought and abstract, is still a concrete, being not a plain formal unity, but a unity of distinct propositions. Bare abstractions or formal thoughts are therefore

no business of philosophy, which has to deal only with concrete thoughts. (3) The logic of mere Understanding is involved in Speculative logic, and can at will be elicited from it, by the simple process of omitting the dialectical and 'reasonable' element. When that is done, it becomes what the common logic is, a descriptive collection of sundry thought-forms and rules which, finite though they are, are taken to be something infinite.

If we consider only what it contains, and not how it contains it, the true reason-world, so far from being the exclusive property of philosophy, is the right of every human being on whatever grade of culture or mental growth he may stand; which would justify man's ancient title of rational being. The general mode by which experience first makes us aware of the reasonable order of things is by accepted and unreasoned belief; and the character of the rational, as already noted (§ 45), is to be unconditioned, self-contained, and thus to be self-determining. In this sense man above all things becomes aware of the reasonable order when he knows of God, and knows him to be the completely self-determined. Similarly, the consciousness a citizen has of his country and its laws is a perception of the reason-world, so long as he looks up to them as unconditioned and likewise universal powers, to which he must subject his individual will. And in the same sense, the knowledge and will of the child is rational, when he knows his parents' will, and wills it.

Now, to turn these rational (of course positively rational) realities into speculative principles, the only thing needed is that they be *thought*. The expression 'Speculation' in common life is often used with a very vague and at the same time secondary sense, as when we speak of a matrimonial or a commercial speculation. By this we only mean two things: first, that what is immediately at hand has to be passed and left behind; and secondly, that the subject-matter of such speculations, though in the first place only subjective, must not remain so, but be realized or translated into objectivity.

What was some time ago remarked respecting the Idea may be applied to this common usage of the term 'speculation'; and we may add that people who rank themselves among the educated expressly speak of speculation even as if it were something purely subjective. A certain theory of some conditions and circumstances of nature or mind may be, say these people, very fine and correct as a matter of speculation, but it contradicts experience and nothing of the sort is admissible in reality. To this the answer is, that the speculative is in its true signification, neither preliminarily nor even definitively, something merely subjective: that, on the contrary, it expressly rises above such oppositions as that between subjective and objective, which the understanding cannot get over, and absorbing them in itself, evinces its own concrete and all-embracing nature. A one-sided proposition therefore can never even give expression to a speculative truth. If we say, for example, that the absolute is the unity of subjective and objective, we are undoubtedly in the right, but so far one-sided, as we enunciate the unity only and lay the accent upon it, forgetting that in reality the subjective and objective are not merely identical but also distinct.

Speculative truth, it may also be noted, means very much the same as what, in special connection with religious experience and doctrines, used to be called Mysticism. The term Mysticism is at present used, as a rule, to designate what is mysterious and incomprehensible: and in proportion as their general culture and way of thinking vary, the epithet is applied by one class to denote the real and the true, by another to name everything connected with superstition and deception. On which we first of all remark that there is mystery in the mystical, only however for the understanding which is ruled by the principle of abstract identity; whereas the mystical, as synonymous with the speculative, is the concrete unity of those propositions which understanding only accepts in their separation and opposition. And if those who recognize Mysticism as the highest truth are content to leave it in its original utter mystery, their conduct only proves that for them too, as well as for their antagonists, thinking means abstract identification, and that in their opinion, therefore, truth can only be won by renouncing thought, or as it is frequently expressed, by leading the reason captive. But, as we have seen, the abstract thinking of understanding is so far from being either ultimate or stable, that it shows a perpetual tendency to work its own dissolution and swing round into its opposite. Reasonableness, on the contrary, just consists in embracing within itself these opposites as unsubstantial elements. Thus the reason-world may be equally styled mystical—not however because thought cannot both reach and comprehend it, but merely because it lies beyond the compass of understanding.

§ 83

Logic is subdivided into three parts:

I. The Doctrine of Being.
II. The Doctrine of Essence.
III. The Doctrine of Notion and Idea.

That is, into the Theory of Thought:

I. In its immediacy: the notion implicit and in germ.

II. In its reflection and mediation: the being-for-self and show of the notion.

III. In its return into itself, and its developed abiding by itself: the notion in and for itself.

The division of Logic now given, as well as the whole of the previous discussion on the nature of thought, is anticipatory; and the justification, or proof of it, can only result from the detailed treatment of thought itself. For in philosophy, to prove means to show how the subject by and from itself makes itself what it is. The relation in which these three leading grades of thought, or of the logical Idea, stand to each other must be conceived as follows. Truth comes only with the notion; or, more precisely, the notion is the truth of being and essence, both of which, when separately maintained in their isolation, cannot but be untrue, the former because it is exclusively immediate, and the latter because it is exclusively mediate. Why then, it may be asked, begin with the false and not at once with the true? To which we answer that truth, to deserve the name, must authenticate its own truth: which authentication, here within the sphere of logic, is given, when the notion demonstrates itself to be what is mediated by and with itself, and thus at the same time to be truly immediate. This relation between the three stages of the logical Idea appears in a real and concrete shape thus: God, who is the truth, is known by us in His truth, that is, as absolute spirit, only in so far as we at the same time recognize that the world which He created, nature and the finite spirit, are, in their difference from God, untrue.

VII

FIRST SUBDIVISION OF LOGIC

THE DOCTRINE OF BEING

§ 84

Being is the notion implicit only: its special forms have the predicate 'is'; when they are distinguished they are each of them an 'other': and the shape which dialectic takes in them, i.e. their further specialization, is a passing over into another. This further determination, or specialization, is at once a forth-putting and in that way a disengaging of the notion implicit in being; and at the same time the withdrawing of being inwards, its sinking deeper into itself. Thus the explication of the notion in the sphere of being does two things: it brings out the totality of being, and it abolishes the immediacy of being, or the form of being as such.

§ 85

Being itself and the special sub-categories of it which follow, as well as those of logic in general, may be looked upon as definitions of the Absolute, or metaphysical definitions of God: at least the first and third category in every triad may—the first, where the thought-form of the triad is formulated in its simplicity, and the third, being the return from differentiation to a simple self-reference. For a metaphysical definition of God is the expression of his nature in thoughts as such: and logic embraces all thoughts so long as they continue in the thought-form. The second sub-category in each triad, where the grade of thought is in its differentiation, gives, on the other hand, a definition of the finite. The objection to the form of definition is that it implies a something in the mind's eye on which these predicates may fasten. Thus even the Absolute (though it purports to express God in the style and character of thought) in comparison with its predicate (which really and distinctly expresses in thought what the subject does not) is as yet only an inchoate pretended thought—the indeterminate subject of predicates yet to come. The thought, which is here the matter of sole importance, is contained only in the predicate: and hence the propositional form, like the said subject, viz. the Absolute, is a mere superfluity (cf. § 31, and below, on the Judgement).

Each of the three spheres of the logical idea proves to be a systematic whole of thought-terms, and a phase of the Absolute. This is the case with Being, containing the three grades of quality, quantity, and measure. Quality is, in the first place, the character identical with being: so identical that a thing ceases to be what it is, if it loses its quality. Quantity, on the contrary, is the character external to being, and does not affect the being at all. Thus e.g. a house remains what it is, whether it be greater or smaller; and red remains red, whether it be brighter or darker. Measure, the third grade of being, which is the unity of the first two, is a qualitative quantity. All things have their measure: i.e. the quantitative terms of their existence, their being so or so great, does not matter within certain limits; but when these limits are exceeded by an additional more or less, the things cease to be what they were. From measure follows the advance to the second subdivision of the idea, Essence.

The three forms of being here mentioned, just because they are the first, are also the poorest, i.e. the most abstract. Immediate (sensible) consciousness, in so far as it simultaneously includes an intellectual element, is especially restricted to the abstract categories of quality and quantity. The sensuous consciousness is in ordinary estimation the most concrete and thus also the richest; but that is only true as regards materials, whereas, in reference to the thought it contains, it is really the poorest and most abstract.

A. QUALITY

(*a*) *Being*

§ 86

Pure **Being** makes the beginning: because it is on one hand pure thought, and on the other immediacy itself, simple and indeterminate; and the first beginning cannot be mediated by anything, or be further determined.

All doubts and admonitions, which might be brought against beginning the science with abstract empty being, will disappear if we only perceive what a beginning naturally implies. It is possible to define being as 'I=I', as 'Absolute Indifference' or Identity, and so on. Where it is felt necessary to begin either with what is absolutely certain, i.e. the certainty of oneself, or with a definition or intuition of the absolute truth, these and other forms of the kind may be looked on as if they must be the first. But each of these forms contains a mediation, and hence cannot be the real first: for all mediation implies advance made from a first on to a second, and proceeding from something different. If I=I, or even the intellectual intuition, are really taken to mean no more than the first, they are in this mere immediacy identical with being: while conversely, pure being, if abstract no longer, but including in it mediation, is pure thought or intuition.

If we enunciate Being as a predicate of the Absolute, we get the first definition of the latter. The Absolute is Being. This is (in thought) the absolutely initial definition, the most abstract and stinted. It is the definition given by the Eleatics, but at the same time is also the well-known definition of God as the sum of all realities. It means, in short, that we are to set aside that limitation which is in every reality, so that God shall be only the real in all reality, the superlatively real. Or, if we reject reality, as implying a reflection, we get a more immediate or unreflected statement of the same thing, when Jacobi says that the God of Spinoza is the *principium* of being in all existence.

(1) When thinking is to begin, we have nothing but thought in its merest indeterminateness: for we cannot determine unless there is both one and another; and in the beginning there is yet no other. The indeterminate, as we here have it, is the blank we begin with, not a featurelessness reached by abstraction, not the elimination of all character, but the original featurelessness which precedes all definite character and is the very first of all. And this we call Being. It is not to be felt, or perceived by sense, or pictured in imagination: it is only and merely thought, and as such it forms the beginning. Essence also is indeterminate, but in another sense: it has traversed the process of mediation and contains implicit the determination it has absorbed.

(2) In the history of philosophy the different stages of the logical Idea assume the shape of successive systems, each based on a particular definition of the Absolute. As the logical Idea is seen to unfold itself in a process from the abstract to the concrete, so in the history of philosophy the earliest systems are the most abstract, and thus at the same time the poorest. The relation too of the earlier to the later systems of philosophy

is much like the relation of the corresponding stages of the logical Idea: in other words, the earlier are preserved in the later; but subordinated and submerged. This is the true meaning of a much misunderstood phenomenon in the history of philosophy—the refutation of one system by another, of an earlier by a later. Most commonly the refutation is taken in a purely negative sense to mean that the system refuted has ceased to count for anything, has been set aside and done for. Were it so, the history of philosophy would be of all studies most saddening, displaying, as it does, the refutation of every system which time has brought forth. Now although it may be admitted that every philosophy has been refuted, it must be in an equal degree maintained that no philosophy has been refuted, nay, or can be refuted. And that in two ways. For first, every philosophy that deserves the name always embodies the Idea: and secondly, every system represents one particular factor or particular stage in the evolution of the Idea. The refutation of a philosophy, therefore, only means that its barriers are crossed, and its special principle reduced to a factor in the completer principle that follows. Thus the history of philosophy, in its true meaning, deals not with a past, but with an eternal and veritable present: and, in its results, resembles not a museum of the aberrations of the human intellect, but a Pantheon of godlike figures. These figures of gods are the various stages of the Idea, as they come forward one after another in dialectical development. To the historian of philosophy it belongs to point out more precisely how far the gradual evolution of his theme coincides with, or swerves from, the dialectical unfolding of the pure logical Idea. It is sufficient to mention here, that logic begins where the proper history of philosophy begins. Philosophy began in the Eleatic school, especially with Parmenides. Parmenides, who conceives the absolute as Being, says that 'Being alone is and Nothing is not.' Such was the true starting-point of philosophy, which is always knowledge by thought: and here for the first time we find pure thought seized and made an object to itself.

Men indeed thought from the beginning (for thus only were they distinguished from the animals). But thousands of years had to elapse before they came to apprehend thought in its purity, and to see it in the truly objective. The Eleatics are celebrated as daring thinkers. But this nominal admiration is often accompanied by the remark that they went too far, when they made Being alone true, and denied the truth of every other object of consciousness. We must go further than mere Being, it is true: and yet it is absurd to speak of the other contents of our consciousness as somewhat as it were outside and beside Being, or to say that there are other things, as well as Being. The true state of the case is rather as follows. Being, as Being, is nothing fixed or ultimate: it yields to dialectic and sinks into its opposite, which, also taken immediately, is Nothing. After all, the point is that Being is the first pure Thought; whatever else you may begin with (the I=I, the absolute indifference, or God himself), you begin with a figure of materialized conception, not a product of thought; and that, so far as its thought-content is concerned, such beginning is merely Being.

§ 87

But this mere Being, as it is mere abstraction, is therefore the absolutely negative: which, in a similarly immediate aspect, is just **Nothing.**

(1) Hence was derived the second definition of the Absolute: the Absolute is the Nought. In fact this definition is implied in saying that the thing-in-itself is the indeterminate, utterly without form and so without content—or in saying that God is only the supreme Being and nothing more; for this is really declaring him to be the same negativity as above. The Nothing which the Buddhists make the universal principle, as well as the final aim and goal of everything, is the same abstraction.

(2) If the opposition in thought is stated in this immediacy as Being and Nothing, the shock of its nullity is too great not to stimulate the attempt to fix Being and secure it against the transition into Nothing. With this intent, reflection has recourse to the plan of discovering some fixed predicate for Being, to mark it off from Nothing. Thus we find Being identified with what persists amid all change, with *matter*, susceptible of innumerable determinations—or even, unreflectingly, with a single existence, any chance object of the senses or of the mind. But every additional and more concrete characterization causes Being to lose that integrity and simplicity it has in the beginning. Only in, and by virtue of, this mere generality is it Nothing, something inexpressible, whereof the distinction from Nothing is a mere intention or *meaning*.

All that is wanted is to realize that these beginnings are nothing but these empty abstractions, one as empty as the other. The instinct that induces us to attach a settled import to Being, or to both, is the very necessity which leads to the onward movement of Being and Nothing, and gives them a true or concrete significance. This advance is the logical deduction and the movement of thought exhibited in the sequel. The reflection which finds a profounder connotation for Being and Nothing is nothing but logical thought, through which such connotation is evolved, not, however, in an accidental, but a necessary way. Every signification, therefore, in which they afterwards appear, is only a more precise specification and truer definition of the Absolute. And when that is done, the mere abstract Being and Nothing are replaced by a concrete in which both these elements form an organic part. The supreme form of Nought as a separate principle would be Freedom: but Freedom is negativity in that stage, when it sinks self-absorbed to supreme intensity, and is itself an affirmation, and even absolute affirmation.

The distinction between Being and Nought is, in the first place, only implicit, and not yet actually made: they only *ought* to be distinguished. A distinction of course implies two things, and that one of them possesses an attribute which is not found in the other. Being however is an absolute absence of attributes, and so is Nought. Hence the distinction between the two is only meant to be; it is a quite nominal distinction, which is at the same time no distinction. In all other cases of difference there is some common point which comprehends both things. Suppose e.g. we speak of two different species: the genus forms a common ground for both. But in the case of mere Being and Nothing, distinction is without a bottom to stand upon: hence there can be no distinction, both determinations being the same bottomlessness. If it be replied that Being and Nothing are both of them thoughts, so that thought may be reckoned common ground, the objector forgets that Being is not a particular or definite thought, and hence, being quite indeterminate, is a thought not to be distinguished from Nothing. It is natural too for us to represent Being as absolute riches, and Nothing as absolute poverty. But if when we view the whole world we can only say that everything *is*, and nothing more, we are neglecting all speciality and, instead of absolute plenitude, we have absolute emptiness. The same stricture is applicable to those who define God to be mere Being; a definition not a whit better than that of the Buddhists, who make God to be Nought, and who from that principle draw the further conclusion that self-annihilation is the means by which man becomes God.

§ 88

Nothing, if it be thus immediate and equal to itself, is also conversely the same as Being is. The truth of Being and of Nothing is accordingly the unity of the two: and this unity is **Becoming.**

(1) The proposition that Being and Nothing is the same seems so paradoxical to the imagination or understanding, that it is perhaps taken for a joke. And indeed it is one of the hardest things

thought expects itself to do: for Being and Nothing exhibit the fundamental contrast in all its immediacy—that is, without the one term being invested with any attribute which would involve its connection with the other. This attribute, however, as the above paragraph points out, is implicit in them—the attribute which is just the same in both. So far the deduction of their unity is complety analytical: indeed the whole progress of philosophizing in every case, if it be a methodical, that is to say a necessary, progress, merely renders explicit what is implicit in a notion. It is as correct however to say that Being and Nothing are altogether different, as to assert their unity. The one is *not* what the other is. But since the distinction has not at this point assumed definite shape (Being and Nothing are still the immediate), it is, in the way that they have it, something unutterable, which we merely *mean*.

(2) No great expenditure of wit is needed to make fun of the maxim that Being and Nothing are the same, or rather to adduce absurdities which, it is erroneously asserted, are the consequences and illustrations of that maxim.

If Being and Nought are identical, say these objectors, it follows that it makes no difference whether my home, my property, the air I breathe, this city, the sun, the law, mind, God, are or are not. Now in some of these cases, the objectors foist in private aims, the utility a thing has for me, and then ask, whether it be all the same to me if the thing exist and if it do not. For that matter indeed, the teaching of philosophy is precisely what frees man from the endless crowd of finite aims and intentions, by making him so insensible to them that their existence or non-existence is to him a matter of indifference. But it is never to be forgotten that, once mention something substantial, and you thereby create a connection with other existences and other purposes which are *ex hypothesi* worth having: and on such hypothesis it comes to depend whether the Being and not-Being of a determinate subject are the same or not. A substantial distinction is in these cases secretly substituted for the empty distinction of Being and Nought. In others of the cases referred to, it is virtually absolute existences and vital ideas and aims, which are placed under the mere category of Being or not-Being. But there is more to be said of these concrete objects, than that they merely are or are not. Barren abstractions, like Being and Nothing—the intial categories which, for that reason, are the scantiest anywhere to be found—are utterly inadequate to the nature of these objects. Substantial truth is something far above these abstractions and their oppositions. And always when a concrete existence is disguised under the name of Being and not-Being, empty-headedness makes its usual mistake of speaking about, and having in the mind an image of, something else than what is in question: and in this place the question is about abstract Being and Nothing.

(3) It may perhaps be said that nobody can form a notion of the unity of Being and Nought. As for that, the notion of the unity is stated in the sections preceding, and that is all: apprehend that, and you have comprehended this unity. What the objector really means by comprehension—by a notion—is more than his language properly implies: he wants a richer and more complex state of mind, a pictorial conception which will propound the notion as a concrete case and one more familiar to the ordinary operations of thought. And so long as incomprehensibility means only the want of habituation for the effort needed to grasp an abstract thought, free from all sensuous admixture, and to seize a speculative truth, the reply to the criticism is that philosophical knowledge is undoubtedly distinct in kind from the mode of knowledge best known in common life, as well as from that which reigns in the other sciences. But if to have no notion merely means that we cannot represent in imagination the oneness of Being and Nought, the statement is far from being true; for every one has countless ways of envisaging this unity. To say that we have no such conception can only mean, that in none of these images do we recognize the notion in question, and that we are not aware that they exemplify it. The readiest example of it is Becoming. Every one has a mental idea of Becoming, and will even allow that it is *one* idea: he will further allow that, when it is analysed, it involves the attribute of Being, and also what is the very reverse of Being, viz. Nothing: and that these two attributes lie undivided in the one idea: so that Becoming is the unity of Being and Nothing. Another tolerably plain example is a Beginning. In its beginning, the thing is not yet, but it is more than merely nothing, for its Being is already in the beginning. Beginning is itself a case of Becoming;

only the former term is employed with an eye to the further advance. If we were to adopt logic to the more usual method of the sciences, we might start with the representation of a Beginning as abstractly thought, or with Beginning as such, and then analyse this representation; and perhaps people would more readily admit, as a result of this analysis, that Being and Nothing present themselves as undivided in unity.

(4) It remains to note that such phrases as 'Being and Nothing are the same', or 'The unity of Being and Nothing'—like all other such unities, that of subject and object, and others—give rise to reasonable objection. They misrepresent the facts, by giving an exclusive prominence to the unity, and leaving the difference which undoubtedly exists in it (because it is Being and Nothing, for example, the unity of which is declared) without any express mention or notice. It accordingly seems as if the diversity had been unduly put out of court and neglected. The fact is, no speculative principle can be correctly expressed by any such propositional form, for the unity has to be conceived *in* the diversity, which is all the while present and explicit. 'To become' is the true expression for the resultant of 'to be' and 'not to be'; it is the unity of the two; but not only is it the unity, it is also inherent unrest—the unity, which is no mere reference-to-self and therefore without movement, but which, through the diversity of Being and Nothing that is in it, is at war within itself. Determinate being, on the other hand, is this unity, or Becoming in this form of unity: hence all that 'is there and so' is one-sided and finite. The opposition between the two factors seems to have vanished; it is only implied in the unity, it is not explicitly put in it.

(5) The maxim of Becoming, that Being is the passage into Nought, and Nought the passage into Being, is controverted by the maxim of Pantheism, the doctrine of the eternity of matter, that from nothing comes nothing, and that something can only come out of something. The ancients saw plainly that the maxim, 'From nothing comes nothing, from something something', really abolishes Becoming: for what it comes from and what it becomes are one and the same. Thus explained, the proposition is the maxim of abstract identity as upheld by the understanding. It cannot but seem strange, therefore, to hear such maxims as 'Out

of nothing comes nothing: Out of something comes something' calmly taught in these days, without the teacher being in the least aware that they are the basis of Pantheism, and even without his knowing that the ancients have exhausted all that is to be said about them.

Becoming is the first concrete thought, and therefore the first notion: whereas Being and Nought are empty abstractions. The notion of Being, therefore, of which we sometimes speak, must mean Becoming; not the mere point of Being, which is empty Nothing, any more than Nothing, which is empty Being. In Being then we have Nothing, and in Nothing Being; but this Being which does not lose itself in Nothing is Becoming. Nor must we omit the distinction, while we emphasize the unity of Becoming: without that distinction we should once more return to abstract Being. Becoming is only the explicit statement of what Being is in its truth.

We often hear it maintained that thought is opposed to being. Now in the face of such a statement, our first question ought to be, what is meant by being. If we understand being as it is defined by reflection, all that we can say of it is that it is what is wholly identical and affirmative. And if we then look at thought, it cannot escape us that thought also is at least what is absolutely identical with itself. Both therefore, being as well as thought, have the same attribute. This identity of being and thought is not however to be taken in a concrete sense, as if we could say that a stone, so far as it has being, is the same as a thinking man. A concrete thing is always very different from the abstract category as such. And in the case of being, we are speaking of nothing concrete: for being is the utterly abstract. So far then the question regarding the *being* of God—a being which is in itself concrete above all measure—is of slight importance.

As the first concrete thought-term, Becoming is the first adequate vehicle of truth. In the history of philosophy, this stage of the logical Idea finds its analogue in the system of Heraclitus. When Heraclitus says 'All is flowing' (πάντα ῥεῖ), he enunciates Becoming as the fundamental feature of all existence, whereas the Eleatics, as already remarked, saw the only truth in Being, rigid processless Being. Glancing at the principle of the Eleatics, Heraclitus then goes on to say: Being no more is than not-Being (οὐδὲν μᾶλλον τὸ ὂν τοῦ μὴ ὄντος ἐστί); a statement expressing the negativity of abstract Being, and its identity with not-Being, as made explicit in Becoming; both abstractions being alike untenable. This may be looked at as an instance of the real refutation of one system by another. To refute a philosophy is to exhibit the dialectical movement in its principle, and thus reduce it to a constituent member of a higher concrete form of the Idea. Even Becoming, however, taken at its best on its own ground, is an extremely poor term: it needs to grow in depth and weight of meaning.

Such deepened force we find e.g. in Life. Life is a Becoming; but that is not enough to exhaust the notion of life. A still higher form is found in Mind. Here too is Becoming, but richer and more intensive than mere logical Becoming. The elements whose unity constitutes mind are not the bare abstracts of Being and of Nought, but the system of the logical Idea and of Nature.

(*b*) *Being Determinate*

§ 89

In Becoming the Being which is one with Nothing, and the Nothing which is one with Being, are only vanishing factors; they are and they are not. Thus by its inherent contradiction Becoming collapses into the unity in which the two elements are absorbed. This result is accordingly **Being Determinate** (Being there and so).

In this first example we must call to mind, once for all, what was stated in § 82 and in the note there: the only way to secure any growth and progress in knowledge is to hold results fast in their truth. There is absolutely nothing whatever in which we cannot and must not point to contradictions or opposite attributes; and the abstraction made by understanding therefore means a forcible insistence on a single aspect, and a real effort to obscure and remove all consciousness of the other attribute which is involved. Whenever such contradiction, then, is discovered in any object or notion, the usual inference is, *Hence* this object is *nothing*. Thus Zeno, who first showed the contradiction native to motion, concluded that there is no motion: and the ancients, who recognized origin and decease, the two species of Becoming, as untrue categories, made use of the expression that the One or Absolute neither arises nor perishes. Such a style of dialectic looks only at the negative aspect of its result, and fails to notice, what is at the same time really present, the definite result, in the present case a pure nothing, but a Nothing which includes Being, and, in like manner, a Being which includes Nothing. Hence Being Determinate is (1) the unity of Being and Nothing, in which we get rid of the immediacy in these determinations, and their contradiction vanishes in their mutual connection—the unity in which they are only constituent elements. And (2) since the result is the abolition of the contradiction, it comes in the shape of a simple unity with itself: that is to say, it also is Being, but Being with negation or determinateness: it is Becoming expressly put in the form of one of its elements, viz. Being.

Even our ordinary conception of Becoming implies that somewhat comes out of it, and that Becoming therefore has a result. But this conception gives rise to the question, how Becoming does not remain mere Becoming, but has a result? The answer to this question follows from what Becoming has already shown itself to be. Becoming always contains Being and Nothing in such a way, that these two are always changing into each other, and reciprocally cancelling each other. Thus Becoming stands before us in utter restlessness—unable however to maintain itself in this abstract restlessness: for since Being and Nothing vanish in Becoming (and that is the very notion of Becoming), the latter must vanish also. Becoming is as it were a fire, which dies out in itself, when it consumes its material. The result of this process however is not an empty Nothing, but Being identical with the negation—what we call Being Determinate (being then and there): the primary import of which evidently is that it *has become*.

§ 90

(α) Determinate Being is Being with a character or mode—which simply *is*; and such unmediated character is **Quality.** And as reflected into itself in this its character or mode, Determinate Being is a somewhat, as existent. The categories, which issue by a closer analysis of Determinate Being, need only be mentioned briefly.

Quality may be described as the determinate mode immediate and identical with Being—as distinguished from Quantity (to come afterwards), which, although a mode of Being, is no longer immediately identical with Being, but a mode indifferent and external to it. A Something is what it is in virtue of its quality, and losing its quality it ceases to be what it is. Quality, moreover, is completely a category only of the finite, and for that reason too it has its proper place in Nature, not in the world of Mind. Thus, for example, in Nature what are styled the elementary bodies, oxygen, nitrogen, etc., should be regarded as existing qualities. But in the sphere of mind, Quality appears in a subordinate way only, and not as if its qualitativeness could exhaust any specific aspect of mind. If, for example, we consider the subjective mind, which forms the object of psychology, we may describe what is called (moral and mental) character, as in logical language identical with Quality. This however does not mean that character is a mode of being which pervades the soul and is immediately identical with it, as is the case in the natural world with the elementary bodies before mentioned. Yet a more distinct manifestation of Quality as such, in mind even, is found in the case of besotted or morbid conditions, especially in states of passion and when the passion rises to derangement. The state of mind of a deranged person, being one mass of jealousy, fear, etc., may suitably be described as Quality.

§ 91

Quality, as determinateness which *is*, as contrasted with the **Negation** which is involved in it but distinguished from it, is **Reality.** Negation is no longer an abstract nothing, but, as a determinate being and somewhat, is only a form of such being—it is as Otherness. Since this otherness, though a determination of Quality itself, is in the first instance distinct from it, Quality is **Being-for-another**—an expansion of the mere point of Determinate Being, or of Somewhat. The Being as such of Quality, contrasted with this reference to somewhat else, is **Being-by-self.**

The foundation of all determinateness is negation (as Spinoza says, *Omnis determinatio est negatio*). The unreflecting observer supposes that determinate things are merely positive, and pins them down under the form of being. Mere being however is not the end of the matter: it is, as we have already seen, utter emptiness and instability besides. Still, when abstract being is confused in this way with being modified and determinate, it implies some perception of the fact that, though in determinate being there is involved an element of negation, this element is at first wrapped up, as it were, and only comes to the front and receives its due in Being-for-self. If we go on to consider determinate Being as a determinateness which *is*, we get in this way what is called Reality. We speak, for example, of the reality of a plan or a purpose, meaning thereby that they are no longer inner and subjective, but have passed into being-there-and-then. In the same sense the body may be called the reality of the soul, and the law the reality of freedom, and the world altogether the reality of the divine idea. The word 'reality' is however used in another acceptation to mean that something behaves conformably to its essential characteristic or notion. For example, we use the expression: This is a real occupation; This is a real man. Here the term does not merely mean outward and immediate existence: but rather that some existence agrees with its notion. In which sense, be it added, reality is not distinct from the ideality which we shall in the first instance become acquainted with in the shape of Being-for-self.

§ 92

(β) Being, if kept distinct and apart from its determinate mode, as it is in Being-by-self (Being implicit), would be only the vacant abstraction of Being. In Being (determinate there and then), the determinateness is one with Being; yet at the same time, when explicitly made a negation, it is a **Limit,** a Barrier. Hence the otherness is not something indifferent and outside it, but a function proper to it. Somewhat is by its quality, firstly **finite**, secondly **alterable**; so that finitude and variability appertain to its being.

In Being-there-and-then, the negation is still directly one with the Being, and this negation is what we call a Limit (Boundary). A thing is what it is, only in and by reason of its limit. We cannot therefore regard the limit as only external to being which is then and there. It rather goes through and through the whole of such existence. The view of limit, as merely an external characteristic of being-there-and-then, arises from a confusion of quantitative with qualitative limit. Here we are speaking primarily of the qualitative limit. If, for example, we observe a piece of ground, three acres large, that circumstance is its quantitative limit. But, in addition, the ground is, it may be, a meadow, not a wood or a pond. This is its qualitative limit. Man, if he wishes to be actual, must be-there-and-then, and to this end he must set a limit to himself. People who are too fastidious towards the finite never reach actuality, but linger lost in abstraction, and their light dies away.

If we take a closer look at what a limit implies, we see it involving a contradiction in itself, and thus evincing its dialectical nature. On the one side the limit makes the reality of a thing; on the other it is negation. But, again, the limit, as the negation of something, is not an abstract nothing but a nothing which *is*—what we call an 'other'. Given something, and up starts an other to us: we know that there is not something only, but an other as well. Nor, again, is the other of such a nature that we can think something apart from it; a something is implicitly the other of itself, and the somewhat sees its limit become objective to it in the other. If we now ask for the difference between something and another, it turns out that they are the same: which sameness is expressed in Latin by calling the pair *aliud . . . aliud*. The other, as opposed to the something, is itself a something, and hence we say some other, or something else; and so on the other hand the first something when opposed to the other, also defined as something, is itself an other. When we say 'something else' our first impression is that something taken separately is only something, and that the quality of being another attaches to it only from outside considerations. Thus we suppose that the moon, being something else than the sun, might very well exist without the sun. But really the moon, as a something, has its other implicit in it: Plato says: God made the world out of the nature of the 'one' and the 'other' (τοῦ ἑτέρου): having brought these together, he formed from them a third, which is of the nature of the 'one' and the 'other'. In these words we have in general terms a statement of the nature of the finite, which, as something, does not meet the nature of the other as if it had no affinity to it, but, being implicitly the other of itself, thus undergoes alteration. Alteration thus exhibits the inherent contradiction which originally attaches to determinate being, and which forces it out of its own bounds. To materialized conception existence stands in the character of something solely positive, and quietly abiding within its own limits: though we also know, it is true, that everything finite (such as existence) is subject to change. Such changeableness in existence is to the superficial eye a mere possibility, the realization of which is not a consequence of its own nature. But the fact is, mutability lies in the notion of existence, and change is only the manifestation of what it implicitly is. The living die, simply because as living they bear in themselves the germ of death.

§ 93

Something becomes an other; this other is itself somewhat; therefore it likewise becomes an other, and so on *ad infinitum*.

§ 94

This **Infinity** is the wrong or negative infinity: it is only a negation of a finite: but the finite rises again the same as ever, and is never got rid of and absorbed. In other words, this infinite only expresses the *ought-to-be* elimination of the finite. The progression to infinity never gets further than a statement of the contradiction involved in the finite, viz. that it is somewhat as well as somewhat else. It sets up with endless iteration the alternation between these two terms, each of which calls up the other.

If we let somewhat and another, the elements of determinate Being, fall asunder, the result is that some becomes other, and this other is itself a somewhat, which then as such changes likewise, and so on *ad infinitum*. This result seems to superficial reflection something very grand, the grandest possible. But such a progression to infinity is not the real infinite. That consists in being at home with itself in its other, or, if enunciated as a process, in coming to itself in its other. Much depends on rightly apprehending the notion of infinity, and not stopping short at the wrong infinity of endless progression. When time and space, for example, are spoken of as infinite, it is in the first place the infinite progression on which our thoughts fasten. We say, Now, This time, and then we keep continually going forwards and backwards beyond this limit. The case is the same with space, the infinity of which has formed the theme of barren declamation to astronomers with a talent for edification. In the attempt to contemplate such an infinite, our thought, we are commonly informed, must sink exhausted. It is true indeed that we must abandon the unending contemplation, not however because the occupation is too sublime, but because it is too tedious. It is tedious to expatiate in the contemplation of this infinite progression, because the same thing is constantly recurring. We lay down a limit: then we pass it: next we have a limit once more, and so on for ever. All this is but superficial alternation, which never leaves the region of the finite behind. To suppose that by stepping out and away into that infinity we release ourselves from the finite, is in truth but to seek the release which comes by flight. But the man who flees is not yet free: in fleeing he is still conditioned by that from which he flees. If it be also said that the infinite is unattainable, the statement is true, but only because to the idea of infinity has been attached the circumstance of being simply and solely negative. With such empty and other-world stuff philosophy has nothing to do. What philosophy has to do with is always something concrete and in the highest sense present.

No doubt philosophy has also sometimes been set the task of finding an answer to the question, how the infinite comes to the resolution of issuing out of itself. This question, founded, as it is, upon the assumption of a rigid opposition between finite and infinite, may be answered by saying that the opposition is false, and that in point of fact the infinite eternally proceeds out of itself, and yet does not proceed out of itself. If we further say that the infinite is the not-finite, we have in point of fact virtually expressed the truth: for as the finite itself is the first negative, the not-finite is the negative of that negation, the negation which is identical with itself and thus at the same time a true affirmation.

The infinity of reflection here discussed is only an *attempt* to reach the true infinity, a wretched neither-one-thing-nor-another. Generally speaking, it is the point of view which has in recent times been emphasized in Germany. The finite, this theory tells us, *ought* to be absorbed; the infinite *ought* not to be a negative merely, but also a positive. That 'ought to be' betrays the incapacity of actually making good a claim which is at the same time recognized to be right. This stage was never passed by the systems of Kant and Fichte, so far as ethics are concerned. The utmost to which this way brings us is only the postulate of a never-ending approximation to the law of Reason: which postulate has been made an argument for the immortality of the soul.

§ 95

(γ) What we now in point of fact have before us, is that somewhat comes to be an other, and that the other generally comes to be an other. Thus essentially relative to another, somewhat is virtually an other against it: and since what is passed into is quite the same as what passes over, since both have one and the same attribute, viz. to be an other, it follows that something in its passage into other only joins with itself. To be thus self-related in the passage, and in the other, is the genuine Infinity. Or, under a negative aspect: what is altered is the other, it becomes the other of the other. Thus Being, but as negation of the negation, is restored again: it is now **Being-for-self.**

Dualism, in putting an insuperable opposition between finite and infinite, fails to note the simple circumstance that the infinite is thereby only one of two, and is reduced to a particular, to which the finite forms the other particular. Such an infinite, which is only a particular, is co-terminous with the finite which makes for it a limit and a barrier: it is not what it ought to be, that is, the infinite, but is only finite. In such circumstances, where the finite is on this side, and the infinite on that—this world as the finite and the other world as the infinite—an equal dignity of permanence and independence is ascribed to finite and to infinite. The being of the finite is made an absolute being, and by this dualism gets independence and stability. Touched, so to speak, by the infinite, it would be annihilated. But it must not be touched by the infinite. There must be an abyss, an impassable gulf between the two, with the infinite abiding on yonder side and the finite steadfast on this. Those who attribute to the finite this inflexible persistence in comparison with the infinite are not, as they imagine, far above metaphysic: they are still on the level of the most ordinary metaphysic of understanding. For the same thing occurs here as in the infinite progression. At one time it is admitted that the finite has no independent actuality, no absolute being, no root and development of its own, but is only a transient. But next moment this is straightway forgotten; the finite, made a mere counterpart to the infinite, wholly separated from it, and rescued from annihilation, is conceived to be persistent in its independence. While thought thus imagines itself elevated to the infinite, it meets with the opposite fate: it comes to an infinite which is only a finite, and the finite, which it had left behind, has always to be retained and made into an absolute.

After this examination (with which it were well to compare Plato's *Philebus*), tending to show the nullity of the distinction made by understanding between the finite and the infinite, we are liable to glide into the statement that the infinite and the finite are therefore one, and that the genuine infinity, the truth, must be defined and enunciated as the unity of the finite and infinite. Such a statement would be to some extent correct; but is just as open to perversion and falsehood as the unity of Being and Nothing already noticed. Besides it may very fairly be charged with reducing the infinite to finitude and making a finite infinite. For, so far as the expression goes, the finite seems left in its place—it is not expressly stated to be absorbed. Or, if we reflect that the finite, when identified with the infinite, certainly cannot remain what it was out of such unity, and will at least suffer some change in its characteristics (as an alkali, when combined with an acid, loses some of its properties), we must see that the same fate awaits the infinite, which, as the negative, will on its part likewise have its edge, as it were, taken off on the other. And this does really happen with the abstract one-sided infinite of understanding. The genuine infinite however is not merely in the position of the one-sided acid, and so docs not lose itself. The negation of negation is not a neutralization: the infinite is the affirmative, and it is only the finite which is absorbed.

In Being-for-self enters the category of **Ideality**. Being-there-and-then, as in the first instance apprehended in its being or affirmation, has reality (§ 91); and thus even finitude in the first instance is in the category of reality. But the truth of the finite is rather its ideality. Similarly, the infinite of understanding, which is co-ordinated with the finite, is itself only one of two finites, no whole truth, but a non-substantial element. This ideality of the finite is the chief maxim of philosophy; and for that reason every genuine philosophy is idealism. But everything depends upon not taking for the infinite what, in the very terms of its characterization, is at the same time made a particular and finite. For this reason we have bestowed a greater amount of attention on this distinction. The fundamental notion of philosophy, the genuine infinite, depends upon it. The distinction is cleared up by the simple, and for that reason seemingly insignificant, but incontrovertible reflections contained in the first paragraph of this section.

(c) *Being-for-self*

§ 96

(*α*) Being-for-self, as reference to itself, is immediacy, and as reference of the negative to itself, is a self-subsistent, the **One**. This unit, being without distinction in itself, thus excludes the other from itself.

To be for self—to be one—is completed Quality, and as such, contains abstract Being and Being modified as non-substantial elements. As simple Being, the One is simple self-reference; as Being modified it is determinate: but the determinateness is not in this case a finite determinateness—a somewhat in distinction from an other—but infinite, because it contains distinction absorbed and annulled in itself.

The readiest instance of Being-for-self is found in the 'I'. We know ourselves as existents, distinguished in the first place from other existents, and with certain relations thereto. But we also come to know this expansion of existence (in these relations) reduced, as it were, to a point in the simple form of being-for-self. When we say 'I', we express the reference-to-self which is infinite, and at the same time negative. Man, it may be said, is distinguished from the animal world, and in that way from nature altogether, by knowing himself as 'I': which amounts to saying that natural things never attain a free Being-for-self, but as limited to Being-there-and-then, are always and only Being for an other. Again, Being-for-self may be described as ideality, just as Being-there-and-then was described as reality. It is said, that besides reality there is *also* an ideality. Thus the two categories are made equal and parallel. Properly speaking, ideality is not somewhat outside of and beside reality: the notion of ideality just lies in its being the truth of reality. That is to say, when reality is explicitly put as what it implicitly is, it is at once seen to be ideality. Hence ideality has not received its proper estimation, when you allow that reality is not all in all, but that an ideality must be recognized outside of it. Such an ideality, external to or it may be even beyond reality, would be no better than an empty name. Ideality only has a meaning when it is the ideality of something: but this something is not a mere indefinite this or that, but existence characterized as reality, which, if retained in isolation, possesses no truth. The distinction between Nature and Mind is not improperly conceived, when the former is traced back to reality, and the latter to ideality as a fundamental category. Nature however is far from being so fixed and complete, as to subsist even without Mind: in Mind it first, as it were, attains its goal and its truth. And similarly, Mind on its part is not merely a world beyond Nature and nothing more: it is really, and with full proof, seen to be mind, only when it involves Nature as absorbed in itself. Apropos of this, we should note the double meaning of the German word *aufheben* (to put by, or set aside). We mean by it (1) to clear away, or annul: thus, we say, a law or a regulation is set aside; (2) to keep, or preserve: in which sense we use it when we say: something is well put by. This double usage of language, which gives to the same word a positive and negative meaning, is not an accident, and gives no ground for reproaching language as a cause of confusion. We should rather recognize in it the speculative spirit of our language rising above the mere 'either—or' of understanding.

§ 97

(β) The relation of the negative to itself is a negative relation, and so a distinguishing of the One from itself, the repulsion of the One; that is, it makes **Many** Ones. So far as regards the immediacy of the self-existents, these Many *are*: and the repulsion of every One of them becomes to that extent their repulsion against each other as existing units—in other words, their reciprocal exclusion.

Whenever we speak of the One, the Many usually come into our mind at the same time. Whence, then, we are forced to ask, do the Many come? This question is unanswerable by the consciousness which pictures the Many as a primary datum, and treats the One as only one among the Many. But the philosophic notion teaches, contrariwise, that the One forms the presupposition of the Many: and in the thought of the One is implied that it explicitly make itself Many. The self-existing unit is not, like Being, void of all connective reference: it is a reference, as well as Being-there-and-then was, not however a reference connecting somewhat with an other, but, as unity of the some and the other, it is a connection with itself, and this connection, be it noted, is a negative connection. Hereby the One manifests an utter incompatibility with itself, a self-repulsion: and what it makes itself explicitly be, is the Many. We may denote this side in the process of Being-for-self by the figurative term Repulsion. Repulsion is a term originally employed in the study of matter, to mean that matter, as a Many, in each of these many Ones, behaves as exclusive to all the others. It would be wrong however to view the process of repulsion, as if the One were the repellent and the Many the repelled. The One, as already remarked, just is self-exclusion and explicit putting itself as the Many. Each of the Many however is itself a One, and in virtue of its so behaving, this all-round repulsion is by one stroke converted into its opposite—Attraction.

§ 98

(γ) But the Many are one the same as another: each is One, or even one of the Many; they are consequently one and the same. Or when we study all that **Repulsion** involves, we see that as a negative attitude of many Ones to one another, it is just as essentially a connective reference of them to each other; and as those to which the One is related in its act of repulsion are ones, it is in them thrown into relation with itself. The repulsion therefore has an equal right to be called **Attraction**; and the exclusive One, or Being-for-self, suppresses itself. The qualitative character, which in the One or unit has reached the extreme point of its characterization, has thus passed over into determinateness (quality) suppressed, i.e. into Being as Quantity.

The philosophy of the Atomists is the doctrine in which the Absolute is formulated as Being-for-self, as One, and many ones. And it is the repulsion, which shows itself in the notion of the One, which is assumed as the fundamental force in these atoms. But instead of attraction, it is Accident, that is, mere unintelligence, which is expected to bring them together. So long as the One is fixed as one, it is certainly impossible to regard its congression with others as anything but external and mechanical. The Void, which is assumed as the complementary principle to the atoms, is repulsion and nothing else, presented under the image of the nothing existing between the atoms. Modern Atomism—and physics is still in principle atomistic—has surrendered the atoms so far as to pin its faith on molecules or particles. In doing so, science has come closer to sensuous conception, at the cost of losing the precision of thought. To put an attractive by the side of a repulsive force, as the moderns have done, certainly gives completeness to the contrast: and the discovery of this natural force, as it is called, has been a source of much pride. But the mutual implication of the two, which makes what is true and concrete in them, would have to be wrested from the obscurity and confusion in which they were left even in Kant's Metaphysical Rudiments of Natural Science. In modern times the importance of the atomic theory is even more evident in political than in physical science. According to it, the will of individuals as such is the creative principle of the State: the attracting force is the special wants and inclinations of individuals; and the Universal, or the State itself, is the external nexus of a compact.

(1) The Atomic philosophy forms a vital stage in the historical evolution of the Idea. The principle of that system may be described as Being-for-self in the shape of the Many. At present, students of nature who are anxious to avoid metaphysics turn a favourable ear to Atomism. But it is not possible to escape metaphysics and cease to trace nature back to terms of thought, by throwing ourselves into the arms of Atomism. The atom, in fact, is itself a thought; and hence the theory which holds matter to consist of atoms is a metaphysical theory. Newton gave physics an express warning to beware of metaphysics, it is true; but, to his honour be it said, he did not by any means obey his own warning. The only mere physicists are the animals: they alone do not think: while man is a thinking being and a born metaphysician. The real question is not whether we shall apply metaphysics, but whether our metaphysics are of the right kind: in other words, whether we are not, instead of the concrete logical Idea, adopting one-sided forms of thought, rigidly fixed by understanding, and making these the basis of our theoretical as well as our practical work. It is on this ground that one objects to the Atomic philosophy. The old Atomists viewed the world as a many, as their successors often do to this day. On chance they laid the task of collecting the atoms which float about in the void. But, after all, the nexus binding the many with one another is by no means a mere accident: as we have already remarked, the nexus is founded on their very nature. To Kant we owe the completed theory of matter as the unity of repulsion and attraction. The theory is correct, so far as it recognizes attraction to be the other of the two elements involved in the notion of Being-for-self: and to be an element no less essential than repulsion to constitute matter. Still this dynamical construction of matter, as it is termed, has the fault of taking for granted, instead of deducing, attraction and repulsion. Had they been deduced, we should then have seen the How and the Why of a unity which is merely asserted. Kant indeed was careful to inculcate that Matter must not be taken to be in existence *per se*, and then as it were incidentally to be provided with the two forces mentioned, but must be regarded as consisting solely in their unity. German physicists for some time accepted this pure dynamic. But in spite of this, the majority of these physicists in modern times have found it more convenient to return to the Atomic point of view, and in spite of the warnings of Kästner, one of their number, have begun to regard Matter as consisting of infinitesimally small particles, termed 'atoms'—which atoms have then to be brought into relation with one another by the play of forces attaching to them—attractive, repulsive, or whatever they may be. This too is metaphysics; and metaphysics which, for its utter unintelligence, there would be sufficient reason to guard against.

(2) The transition from Quality to Quantity, indicated in the paragraph before us, is not found in our ordinary way of thinking, which deems each of these categories to exist independently beside the other. We are in the habit of saying that things are not merely qualitatively, but also quantitatively defined; but whence these categories originate, and how they are related to each other, are questions not further examined. The fact is, quantity just means quality superseded and absorbed: and it is by the dialectic of quality here examined that this supersession is effected. First of all, we had Being: as the truth of Being, came Becoming: which formed the passage to Being Determinate: and the truth of that we found to be Alteration. And in its result Alteration showed itself to be Being-for-self, exempt from implication of another and from passage into another—which Being-for-self, finally, in the two sides of its process, Repulsion and Attraction, was clearly seen to annul itself, and thereby to annul quality in the totality of its stages. Still this superseded and absorbed quality is neither an abstract nothing, nor an equally abstract and featureless being: it is only being as indifferent to determinateness or character. This aspect of being is also what appears as quantity in our ordinary conceptions. We observe things, first of all, with an eye to their quality—which we take to be the character identical with the being of the thing. If we proceed to consider their quantity, we get the conception of an indifferent and external character or mode, of such a kind that a thing remains what it is, though its quantity is altered, and the thing becomes greater or less.

B. QUANTITY

(a) *Pure Quantity*

§ 99

Quantity is pure being, where the mode or character is no longer taken as one with the being itself, but explicitly put as superseded or indifferent.

(1) The expression **Magnitude** especially marks *determinate* Quantity, and is for that reason not a suitable name for Quantity in general. (2) Mathematics usually define magnitude as what can be increased or diminished. This definition has the defect of containing the thing to be defined over again: but it may serve to show that the category of magnitude is explicitly understood to be changeable and indifferent, so that, in spite of its being altered by an increased extension or intension, the thing, a house, for example, does not cease to be a house, and red to be red. (3) The Absolute is pure Quantity. This point of view is upon the whole the same as

when the Absolute is defined to be Matter, in which, though form undoubtedly is present, the form is a characteristic of no importance one way or another. Quantity too constitutes the main characteristic of the Absolute, when the Absolute is regarded as absolute indifference, and only admitting of quantitative distinction. Otherwise pure space, time, etc., may be taken as examples of Quantity, if we allow ourselves to regard the real as whatever fills up space and time, it matters not with what.

The mathematical definition of magnitude as what may be increased or diminished, appears at first sight to be more plausible and perspicuous than the exposition of the notion in the present section. When closely examined, however, it involves, under cover of presuppositions and images, the same elements as appear in the notion of quantity reached by the method of logical development. In other words, when we say that the notion of magnitude lies in the possibility of being increased or diminished, we state that magnitude (or more correctly, quantity), as distinguished from quality, is a characteristic of such kind that the characterized thing is not in the least affected by any change in it. What then, it may be asked, is the fault which we have to find with this definition? It is that to increase and to diminish is the same thing as to characterize magnitude otherwise. If this aspect then were an adequate account of it, quantity would be described merely as whatever can be altered. But quality is no less than quantity open to alteration; and the distinction here given between quantity and quality is expressed by saying increase *or* diminution: the meaning being that, towards whatever side the determination of magnitude be altered, the thing still remains what it is.

One remark more. Throughout philosophy we do not seek merely for correct, still less for plausible definitions, whose correctness appeals directly to the popular imagination; we seek approved or verified definitions, the content of which is not assumed merely as given, but is seen and known to warrant itself, because warranted by the free self-evolution of thought. To apply this to the present case: however correct and self-evident the definition of quantity usual in Mathematics may be, it will still fail to satisfy the wish to see how far this particular thought is founded in universal thought, and in that way necessary. This difficulty, however, is not the only one. If quantity is not reached through the action of thought, but taken uncritically from our generalized image of it, we are liable to exaggerate the range of its validity, or even to raise it to the height of an absolute category. And that such a danger is real, we see when the title of exact science is restricted to those sciences the objects of which can be submitted to mathematical calculation. Here we have another trace of the bad metaphysics (mentioned in § 98, note) which replace the concrete idea by partial and inadequate categories of understanding. Our knowledge would be in a very awkward predicament if such objects as freedom, law, morality, or even God himself, because they cannot be measured and calculated, or expressed in a mathematical formula, were to be reckoned beyond the reach of exact knowledge, and we had to put up with a vague generalized image of them, leaving their details or particulars to the pleasure of each individual, to make out of them what he will. The pernicious consequences, to which such a theory gives rise in practice, are at once evident. And this mere mathematical view, which identifies with the Idea one of its special stages, viz. quantity, is no other than the principle of Materialism. Witness the history of the scientific modes of thought, especially in France since the middle of last century. Matter, in the abstract, is just what, though of course there is form in it, has that form only as an indifferent and external attribute.

The present explanation would be utterly misconceived if it were supposed to disparage mathematics. By calling the quantitative characteristic merely external and indifferent, we provide no excuse for indolence and superficiality, nor do we assert that quantitative characteristics may be left to mind themselves, or at least require no very careful handling. Quantity, of course, is a stage of the Idea: and as such it must have its due, first as a logical category, and then in the world of objects, natural as well as spiritual. Still, even so, there soon emerges the different importance attaching to the category of quantity according as its objects belong to the natural or to the spiritual world. For in Nature, where the form of the Idea is to be other than, and at the same time outside, itself, greater importance is for that very reason attached to quantity than in the spiritual world, the world of free inwardness. No doubt we regard even spiritual facts under a quantitative point of view; but it is at once apparent that in speaking of God as a Trinity, the number three has by no means the same prominence, as when we consider the three dimensions of space or the three sides of a triangle—the fundamental feature of which last is just to be a surface bounded by three lines. Even inside the realm of Nature we find the same distinction of greater or less importance of quantitative features. In the inorganic world, Quantity plays, so to say, a more prominent part than in the organic. Even in organic nature, when we distinguish mechanical functions from what are called chemical, and in the narrower sense physical, there is the same difference. Mechanics is of all branches of science, confessedly, that in which the aid of mathematics can be least dispensed with—where indeed we cannot take one step without them. On that account mechanics is regarded, next to mathematics, as the science *par excellence*; which leads us to repeat the remark about the coincidence of the materialist with the exclusively mathematical point of view. After all that has been said, we cannot but hold it, in the interest of exact and thorough knowledge, one of the most hurtful prejudices, to seek all distinction and determinateness of objects merely in quantitative considerations. Mind to be sure is more than Nature and the animal is more than the plant: but we know very little of these objects and the distinction between them, if a more and less is enough for us, and if we do not proceed to comprehend them in their peculiar, that is their qualitative character.

§ 100

Quantity, as we saw, has two sources: the exclusive unit, and the identification or equalization of these units. When we look therefore at its immediate relation to self, or at the characteristic of self-sameness made explicit by attraction, quantity is **Continuous** magnitude; but when we look at the other characteristic, the One implied in it, it is **Discrete** magnitude. Still continuous quantity has also a certain discreteness, being but a continuity of the Many; and discrete quantity is no less continuous, its continuity being the One or Unit, that is, the self-same point of the many Ones.

(1) Continuous and Discrete magnitude, therefore, must not be supposed two species of magnitude, as if the characteristic of the one did not attach to the other. The only distinction between them is that the same whole (of quantity) is at one time explicitly put under the one, at another under the other of its characteristics. (2) The Antinomy of space, of time, or of matter, which discusses the question of their being divisible for ever, or of consisting of indivisible units, just means that we maintain quantity as at one time Discrete, at another Continuous. If we explicitly invest time, space, or matter with the attribute of Continuous quantity alone, they are divisible *ad infinitum*. When, on the contrary, they are invested with the attribute of Discrete quantity, they are potentially divided already, and consist of indivisible units. The one view is as inadequate as the other.

Quantity, as the proximate result of Being-for-self, involves the two sides in the process of the latter, attraction and repulsion, as constitutive elements of its own idea. It is consequently Continuous as well as Discrete. Each of these two elements involves the other also, and hence there is no such thing as a merely Continuous or a merely Discrete quantity. We may speak of the two as two particular and opposite species of magnitude; but that is merely the result of our abstracting reflection, which in viewing definite magnitudes waives now the one, now the other, of the elements contained in inseparable unity in the notion of quantity. Thus, it may be said, the space occupied by this room is a continuous magnitude, and the hundred men assembled in it form a discrete magnitude.

And yet the space is continuous and discrete at the same time; hence we speak of points of space, or we divide space, a certain length, into so many feet, inches, etc., which can be done only on the hypothesis that space is also potentially discrete. Similarly, on the other hand, the discrete magnitude, made up of a hundred men, is also continuous; and the circumstance on which this continuity depends is the common element, the species man, which pervades all the individuals and unites them with each other.

(*b*) *Quantum* (*How Much*)

§ 101

Quantity, essentially invested with the exclusionist character which it involves, is **Quantum** (or How Much): i.e. limited quantity.

Quantum is, as it were, the determinate Being of quantity: whereas mere quantity corresponds to abstract Being, and the Degree, which is next to be considered, corresponds to Being-for-self. As for the details of the advance from mere quantity to quantum, it is founded on this: that while in mere quantity the distinction, as a distinction of continuity and discreteness, is at first only implicit, in a quantum the distinction is actually made, so that quantity in general now appears as distinguished or limited. But in this way the quantum breaks up at the same time into an indefinite multitude of quanta or definite magnitudes. Each of these definite magnitudes, as distinguished from the others, forms a unity, while on the other hand, viewed *per se*, it is a many. And, when that is done, the quantum is described as Number.

§ 102

In **Number** the quantum reaches its development and perfect mode. Like the One, the medium in which it exists, Number involves two qualitative factors or functions; Annumeration or Sum, which depends on the factor discreteness, and Unity, which depends on continuity.

In arithmetic the several kinds of operation are usually presented as accidental modes of dealing with numbers. If necessary and meaning is to be found in these operations, it must be by a principle: and that must come from the characteristic element in the notion of number itself. (This principle must here be briefly exhibited.) These characteristic elements are Annumeration on the one hand, and Unity on the other, of which number is the unity. But this latter Unity, when applied to empirical numbers, is only the equality of these numbers: hence the principle of arithmetical operations must be to put numbers in the ratio of Unity and Sum (or amount), and to elicit the equality of these two modes.

The Ones or the numbers themselves are indifferent towards each other, and hence the unity into which they are translated by the arithmetical operation takes the aspect of an external colligation. All reckoning is therefore making up the tale: and the difference between the species of it lies only in the qualitative constitution of the numbers of which we make up the tale. The principle for this constitution is given by the way we fix Unity and Annumeration.

Numeration comes first: what we may call, making number; a colligation of as many units as we please. But to get a *species* of calculation, it is necessary that what we count up should be numbers already, and no longer a mere unit.

First, and as they naturally come to hand, Numbers are quite vaguely numbers in general, and so, on the whole, unequal. The colligation, or telling the tale of these, is Addition.

The second point of view under which we regard numbers is as equal, so that they make one unity, and of such there is an annumeration or sum before us. To tell the tale of these is Multiplication. It makes no matter in the process, how the functions of Sum and Unity are distributed between the two numbers, or factors of the product; either may be Sum and either may be Unity.

The third and final point of view is the equality of Sum (amount) and Unity. To number together numbers when so characterized is Involution; and in the first instance raising them to the square power. To raise the number to a higher power means in point of form to go on multiplying a number with itself an indefinite amount of times. Since this third type of calculation exhibits the complete equality of the sole existing distinction in number, viz. the distinction between Sum or amount and Unity, there can be no more than these three modes of calculation. Corresponding to the integration we have the dissolution of numbers according to the same features. Hence besides the three species mentioned, which may to that extent be called positive, there are three negative species of arithmetical operation.

Number, in general, is the quantum in its complete specialization. Hence we may employ it not only to determine what we call discrete, but what are called continuous magnitudes as well. For that reason even geometry must call in the aid of number, when it is required to specify definite figurations of space and their ratios.

(*c*) *Degree*

§ 103

The limit (in a quantum) is identical with the whole of the quantum itself. As *in itself* multiple, the limit is Extensive magnitude; as in itself *simple* determinateness (qualitative simplicity), it is Intensive magnitude or **Degree.**

The distinction between Continuous and Discrete magnitude differs from that between Extensive and Intensive in the circumstance that the former apply to quantity in general, while the latter apply to the limit or determinateness of it as such. Intensive and Extensive magnitude are not, any more than the other, two species, of which the one involves a character not possessed by the other: what is Extensive magnitude is just as much Intensive, and vice versa.

Intensive magnitude or Degree is in its notion distinct from Extensive magnitude or the Quantum. It is therefore inadmissible to refuse, as many do, to recognize this distinction, and without scruple to identify the two forms of magnitude. They are so identified in physics, when difference of specific gravity is explained by saying that a body with a specific gravity twice that of another contains within the same space twice as many material parts (or atoms) as the other. So with heat and light, if the various degrees of temperature and brilliance were to be explained by the greater or less number of particles (or molecules) of heat and light. No doubt the physicists, who employ such a mode of explanation, usually excuse themselves, when they are remonstrated with on its untenableness, by saying that the expression is without prejudice to the confessedly unknowable essence of such phenomena, and employed merely for greater convenience. This greater convenience is meant to point to the easier application of the calculus: but it is hard to see why Intensive magnitudes, having, as they do, a definite numerical expression of their own, should not be as convenient for calculation as Extensive magnitudes. If convenience be all that is desired, surely it would be more convenient to banish calculation and thought altogether. A further point against the apology offered by the physicists is that to engage in explanations of this kind is to overstep the sphere of perception and experience, and resort to the realm of metaphysics and of what at other times would be called idle or even pernicious speculation. It is certainly a fact of experience that, if one of two purses filled with shillings is twice as heavy as the other, the reason must be, that the one contains, say, two hundred, and the other only one hundred shillings. These pieces of money we can see and feel with our senses: atoms, molecules, and the like, are on the contrary beyond the range of sensuous perception; and thought alone can decide whether they are admissible, and have a meaning. But (as already noticed in § 98, note) it is abstract understanding which stereotypes the factor of multeity (involved in the notion of Being-for-self) in the shape of atoms, and adopts it as an ultimate principle. It is the same abstract understanding which, in the present instance, at equal variance with unprejudiced perception and with real concrete thought, regards Extensive magnitude as the sole form of quantity, and, where Intensive magnitudes occur, does not recognize them in their own character, but makes a violent attempt by a wholly untenable hypothesis to reduce them to Extensive magnitudes.

Among the charges made against modern philosophy, one is heard more than another. Modern philosophy, it is said, reduces everything to identity. Hence its nickname, the Philosophy of Identity. But the present discussion may teach that it is philosophy, and philosophy alone, which insists on distinguishing what is logically as well as in experience different; while the professed devotees of experience are the people who erect abstract identity into the chief principle of knowledge. It is their philosophy which might more appropriately be termed one of identity. Besides it is quite correct that there are no merely Extensive and merely Intensive magnitudes, just as little as there are merely continuous and merely discrete magnitudes. The two characteristics of quantity are not opposed as independent kinds. Every Intensive magnitude is also Extensive, and vice versa. Thus a certain degree of temperature is an Intensive magnitude, which has a perfectly simple sensation corresponding to it as such. If we look at a thermometer, we find this degree of temperature has a certain expansion of the column of mercury corresponding to it; which Extensive magnitude changes simultaneously with the temperature or Intensive magnitude. The case is similar in the world of mind: a more intensive character has a wider range with its effects than a less intensive.

§ 104

In Degree the notion of quantum is explicitly put. It is magnitude as indifferent on its own account and simple: but in such a way that the character (or modal being) which makes it a quantum lies quite outside it in other magnitudes. In this contradiction, where the *independent* indifferent limit is absolute *externality*, the **Infinite Quantitative Progression** is made explicit—an immediacy which immediately veers round into its counterpart, into mediation (the passing beyond and over the quantum just laid down), and vice versa.

Number is a thought, but thought in its complete self-externalization. Becuase it is a thought, it does not belong to perception: but it is a thought which is characterized by the externality of perception. Not only therefore *may* the quantum be increased or diminished without end: the very notion of quantum is thus to push out and out beyond itself. The infinite quantitative progression is only the meaningless repetition of one and the same contradiction, which attaches to the quantum, both generally and, when explicitly invested with its special character, as degree. Touching the futility of enunciating this contradiction in the form of infinite progression, Zeno, as quoted by Aristotle, rightly says, 'It is the same to say a thing once, and to say it for ever.'

(1) If we follow the usual definition of the mathematicians, given in § 99, and say that magnitude is what can be increased or diminished, there may be nothing to urge against the correctness of the perception on which it is founded; but the question remains, how we come to assume such a capacity of increase or diminution. If we simply appeal for an answer to experience, we try an unsatisfactory course; because apart from the fact that we should merely have a material image of magnitude, and not the thought of it, magnitude would come out as a bare possibility (of increasing or diminishing) and we should have no key to the necessity for its exhibiting this behaviour. In the way of our logical evolution, on the contrary, quantity is obviously a grade in the process of self-determining thought; and it has been shown that it lies in the very notion of quantity to shoot out beyond itself. In that way, the increase or diminution (of which we have heard) is not merely possible, but necessary.

(2) The quantitative infinite progression is what the reflective understanding usually relies upon when it is engaged with the general question of Infinity. The same thing however holds good of this progression, as was already remarked on the occasion of the qualitatively infinite progression. As was then said, it is not the expression of a true, but of a wrong infinity; it never gets further than a bare 'ought', and thus really remains within the limits of finitude. The quantitative form of this infinite progression, which Spinoza rightly calls a mere imaginary infinity

(*infinitum imaginationis*), is an image often employed by poets, such as Haller and Klopstock, to depict the infinity, not of Nature merely, but even of God Himself. Thus we find Haller, in a famous description of God's infinity, saying:

Ich häufe ungeheure Zahlen,
Gebirge Millionen auf,
Ich setze Zeit auf Zeit
Und Welt auf Welt zu Hauf,
Und wenn ich von der grausen Höh'
Mit Schwindel wieder nach Dir seh:
Ist alle Macht der Zahl,
Vermehrt zu Tausendmal,
Noch nicht ein Theil von Dir.

[I heap up monstrous numbers, mountains of millions; I pile time upon time, and world on the top of world; and when from the awful height I cast a dizzy look towards Thee, all the power of number, multiplied a thousand times, is not yet one part of Thee.]

Here then we meet, in the first place, that continual extrusion of quantity, and especially of number, beyond itself, which Kant describes as 'eery'. The only really 'eery' thing about it is the wearisomeness of ever fixing, and anon unfixing a limit, without advancing a single step. The same poet however well adds to that description of false infinity the closing line:

Ich zieh sie ab, und Du liegst ganz vor mir.

[These I remove, and Thou liest all before me.]

Which means, that the true infinite is more than a mere world beyond the finite, and that we, in order to become conscious of it, must renounce that *progressus in infinitum*.

(3) Pythagoras, as is well known, philosophized in numbers, and conceived number as the fundamental principle of things. To the ordinary mind this view must at first glance seem an utter paradox, perhaps a mere craze. What then, are we to think of it? To answer this question, we must, in the first place, remember that the problem of philosophy consists in tracing back things to thoughts, and, of course, to definite thoughts. Now number is undoubtedly a thought: it is the thought nearest the sensible, or, more precisely expressed, it is the thought of the sensible itself, if we take the sensible to mean what is many, and in reciprocal exclusion. The attempt to apprehend the universe as number is therefore the first step to metaphysics. In the history of philosophy, Pythagoras, as we know, stands between the Ionian philosophers and the Eleatics. While the former, as Aristotle says, never get beyond viewing the essence of things as material (ὕλη), and the latter, especially Parmenides, advanced as far as pure thought, in the shape of Being, the principle

of the Pythagorean philosophy forms, as it were, the bridge from the sensible to the supersensible.

We may gather from this, what is to be said of those who suppose that Pythagoras undoubtedly went too far, when he conceived the essence of things as mere number. It is true, they admit, that we can number things; but, they contend, things are far more than mere numbers. But in what respect are they more? The ordinary sensuous consciousness, from its own point of view, would not hesitate to answer the question by handing us over to sensuous perception, and remarking that things are not merely numerable, but also visible, odorous, palpable, etc. In the phrase of modern times, the fault of Pythagoras would be described as an excess of idealism. As may be gathered from what has been said on the historical position of the Pythagorean school, the real state of the case is quite the reverse. Let it be conceded that things are more than numbers; but the meaning of that admission must be that the bare thought of number is still insufficient to enunciate the definite notion or essence of things. Instead, then, of saying that Pythagoras went too far with his philosophy of number, it would be nearer the truth to say that he did not go far enough; and in fact the Eleatics were the first to take the further step to pure thought.

Besides, even if there are not things, there are states of things, and phenomena of nature altogether, the character of which mainly rests on definite numbers and proportions. This is especially the case with the difference of tones and their harmonic concord, which, according to a well-known tradition, first suggested to Pythagoras to conceive the essence of things as number. Though it is unquestionably important to science to trace back these phenomena to the definite numbers on which they are based, it is wholly inadmissible to view the characterization by thought as a whole as merely numerical. We may certainly feel ourselves prompted to associate the most general characteristics of thought with the first numbers: saying, 1 is the simple and immediate; 2 is difference and mediation; and 3 the unity of both of these. Such associations however are purely external: there is nothing in the mere numbers to make them express these definite thoughts. With every step in this method, the more arbitrary grows the association of definite numbers with definite thoughts. Thus, we may view 4 as the unity of 1 and 3, and of the thoughts associated with them, but 4 is just as much the double of 2; similarly 9 is not merely the square of 3, but also the sum of 8 and 1, of 7 and 2, and so on. To attach, as do some secret societies of modern times, importance to all sorts of numbers and figures, is to some extent an innocent amusement, but it is also a sign of deficiency of intellectual resource. These numbers, it is said, conceal a profound meaning, and suggest a deal to think about. But the point in philosophy is, not what you may think, but what you do think: and the genuine air of thought is to be sought in thought itself, and not in arbitrarily selected symbols.

§ 105

That the Quantum in its independent character is external to itself, is what constitutes its quality. In that externality it is itself and referred connectively to itself. There is a union in it of externality, i.e. the quantitative, and of independency (Being-for-self)—the qualitative. The Quantum when explicitly put thus in its own self is the **Quantitative Ratio**, a mode of being which, while, in its Exponent, it is an immediate quantum, is also mediation, viz. the reference of some one quantum to another, forming the two sides of the ratio. But the two quanta are not reckoned at their immediate value: their value is only in this relation.

The quantitative infinite progression appears at first as a continual extrusion of number beyond itself. On looking closer, it is, however, apparent that in this progression quantity returns to itself: for the meaning of this progression, so far as thought goes, is the fact that number is determined by number. And this gives the quantitative ratio. Take, for example, the ratio 2:4. Here we have two magnitudes (not counted in their several immediate values) in which we are only concerned with their mutual relations. This relation of the two terms (the exponent of the ratio) is itself a magnitude, distinguished from the related magnitudes by this, that a change in it is followed by a change of the ratio, whereas the ratio is unaffected by the change of both its sides, and remains the same so long as the exponent is not changed. Consequently, in place of 2:4, we can put 3:6 without changing the ratio; as the exponent 2 remains the same in both cases.

§ 106

The two sides of the ratio are still immediate quanta: and the qualitative and quantitative characteristics still external to one another. But in their truth, seeing that the quantitative itself in its externality is relation to self, or seeing that the independence and the indifference of the character are combined, it is **Measure.**

Thus quantity by means of the dialectical movement so far studied through its several stages, turns out to be a return to quality. The first notion of quantity presented to us was that of quality abrogated and absorbed. That is to say, quantity seemed an external character not identical with Being, to which it is quite immaterial. This notion, as we have seen, underlies the mathematical definition of magnitude as what can be increased or diminished. At first sight this definition may create the impression that quantity is merely whatever can be altered—increase and diminution alike implying determination of magnitude otherwise—and may tend to confuse it with determinate Being, the second stage of quality, which in its notion is similarly conceived as alterable. We can, however, complete the definition by adding that in quantity we have an alterable, which in spite of alterations still remains the same. The notion of quantity, it thus turns out, implies an inherent contradiction. This contradiction is what forms the dialectic of quantity. The result of the dialectic however is not a mere return to quality, as if that were the true and quantity the false notion, but an advance to the unity and truth of both, to qualitative quantity, or Measure.

It may be well, therefore, at this point to observe that whenever in our study of the objective world we are engaged in quantitative determinations, it is in all cases Measure which we have in view, as the goal of our operations. This is hinted at even in language, when the ascertainment of quantitative features and relations is called measuring. We measure, e.g. the length of different chords that have been put into a state of vibration, with an eye to the qualitative difference of the tones caused by their vibration, corresponding to this difference of length. Similarly, in chemistry, we try to ascertain the quantity of the matters brought into combination, in order to find out the measures or proportions conditioning such combinations, that is to say, those quantities which give rise to definite qualities. In statistics, too, the numbers with which the study is engaged are important only from the qualitative results conditioned by them. Mere collection of numerical facts, prosecuted without regard to the ends here noted, is justly called an exercise of idle curiosity, of neither theoretical nor practical interest.

C. MEASURE

§ 107

Measure is the qualitative quantum, in the first place as immediate—a quantum, to which a determinate being or a quality is attached.

Measure, where quality and quantity are in one, is thus the completion of Being. Being, as we first apprehend it, is something utterly abstract and characterless; but it is the very essence of Being to characterize itself, and its complete characterization is reached in Measure. Measure, like the other stages of Being, may serve as a definition of the Absolute: God, it has been said, is the Measure of all things. It is this idea which forms the ground-note of many of the ancient Hebrew hymns, in which the glorification of God tends in the main to show that he has appointed to everything its bound: to the sea and the solid land, to the rivers and mountains; and also to the various kinds of plants and animals. To the religious sense of the Greeks the divinity of measure, especially in respect of social ethics, was represented by Nemesis. That conception implies a general theory that all human things, riches, honour, and power, as well as joy and pain, have their definite measure, the transgression of which brings ruin and destruction. In the world of objects, too, we have measure. We see, in the first place, existences in Nature, of which measure forms the essential structure. This is the case, for example, with the solar system, which may be described as the realm of free measures. As we next proceed to the study of inorganic nature, measure retires, as it were, into the background; at least we often find the quantitative and qualitative characteristics showing indifference to each other. Thus the quality of a rock or a river is not tied to a definite magnitude. But even these objects when closely inspected are found not to be quite measureless: the water of a river, and the single constituents of a rock, when chemically analysed, are seen to be qualities conditioned by quantitative ratios between the matters they contain. In organic nature, however, measure again rises into immediate perception. The various kinds of plants and animals, in the whole as well as in their parts, have a certain measure: though it is worth noticing that the more imperfect forms, those which are least removed from inorganic nature, are partly distinguished from the higher forms by the greater indefiniteness of their measure. Thus among fossils, we find some ammonites discernible only by the microscope, and others as large as a cart-wheel. The same vagueness of measure appears in several plants, which stand on a low level of organic development—for instance, ferns.

§ 108

In so far as in Measure quality and quantity are only in *immediate* unity, to that extent their difference presents itself in a manner equally immediate. Two cases are then possible. Either the specific quantum or measure is a bare quantum, and the definite being (there-and-then) is capable of an increase or a diminution, without Measure (which to that extent is a **Rule**) being thereby set completely aside. Or the alteration of the quantum is also an alteration of the quality.

The identity between quantity and quality, which is found in Measure, is at first only implicit, and not yet explicitly realized. In other words, these two categories, which unite in Measure, each claim an independent authority. On the one hand, the quantitative features of existence may be altered, without affecting its quality. On the other hand, this increase and diminution, immaterial though it be, has its limit, by exceeding which the quality suffers change. Thus the temperature of water is, in the first place, a point of no consequence in respect of its liquidity: still, with the increase or diminution of the temperature of the liquid water, there comes a point where this state of cohesion suffers a qualitative change, and the water is converted into steam or ice. A quantitative change takes place, apparently without any further significance: but there is something lurking behind, and a seemingly innocent change of quantity acts as a kind of snare, to catch hold of the quality. The antinomy of Measure which this implies was exemplified under more than one garb among the Greeks. It was asked, for example, whether a single grain makes a heap of wheat, or whether it makes a bald-tail to tear out a single hair from the horse's tail. At first, no doubt, looking at the nature of quantity as an indifferent and external character of Being, we are disposed to answer these questions in the negative. And yet, as we must admit, this indifferent increase and diminution has its limit: a point is finally reached, where a single additional grain makes a heap of wheat; and the bald-tail is produced, if we continue plucking out single hairs. These examples find a parallel in the story of the peasant who, as his ass trudged cheerfully along, went on adding ounce after ounce to its load, till at length it sank under the unendurable burden. It would be a mistake to treat these examples as pedantic futility; they really turn on thoughts, an acquaintance with which is of great importance in practical life, especially in ethics. Thus in the matter of expenditure, there is a certain latitude within which a more or less does not matter; but when the Measure, imposed by the individual circumstances of the special case, is exceeded on the one side or the other, the qualitative nature of Measure (as in the above examples of the different temperature of water) makes itself felt, and a course, which a moment before was held good economy, turns into avarice or prodigality. The same principle may be applied in politics, when the constitution of a state has to be looked at as independent of, no less than as dependent on, the extent of its territory, the number of its inhabitants, and other quantitative points of the same kind. If we look e.g. at a state with a territory of ten thousand square miles and a population of four millions we should, without hesitation, admit that a few square miles of land or a few thousand inhabitants more or less could exercise no essential influence on the character of its constitution. But, on the other hand, we must not forget, that by the continual increase or diminishing of a state, we finally get to a point where, apart from all other circumstances, this quantitative alteration alone necessarily draws with it an alteration in the quality of the constitution. The constitution of a little Swiss canton does not suit a great kingdom; and, similarly, the constitution of the Roman republic was unsuitable when transferred to the small imperial towns of Germany.

§ 109

In this second case, when a measure through its quantitative nature has gone in excess of its qualitative character, we meet what is at first an absence of measure, the **Measureless.** But seeing that the second quantitative ratio, which in comparison with the first is measureless, is none the less qualitative, the measureless is also a measure. These two transitions, from quality to quantum, and from the latter back again to quality, may be represented under the image of an infinite progression—as the self-abrogation and restoration of measure in the measureless.

Quantity, as we have seen, is not only capable of alteration, i.e. of increase or diminution: it is naturally and necessarily a tendency to exceed itself. This tendency is maintained even in measure. But if the quantity present in measure exceeds a certain limit, the quality corresponding to it is also put in abeyance. This however is not a negation of quality altogether, but only of this definite quality, the place of which is at once occupied by another. This process of measure, which appears alternately as a mere change in quantity, and then as a sudden revulsion of quantity into quality, may be envisaged under the figure of a nodal (knotted) line. Such lines we find in Nature under a variety of forms. We have already referred to the qualitatively different states of aggregation water exhibits under increase or diminution of temperature. The same phenomenon is presented by the different degrees in the oxidation of metals. Even the difference of musical notes may be regarded as an example of what takes place in the process of measure—the revulsion from what is at first merely quantitative into qualitative alteration.

§ 110

What really takes place here is that the immediacy, which still attaches to measure as such, is set aside. In measure, at first, quality and quantity itself are immediate, and measure is only their 'relative' identity. But measure shows itself absorbed and superseded in the measureless: yet the measureless, although it be the negation of measure, is itself a unity of quantity and quality. Thus in the measureless the measure is still seen to meet only with itself.

§ 111

Instead of the more abstract factors, Being and Nothing, some and other, etc., the Infinite, which is affirmation as a negation of negation, now finds its factors in quality and quantity. These (α) have in the first place passed over quality into quantity (§ 98), and quantity into quality (§ 105), and thus are both shown up as negations. (β) But in their unity, that is, in measure, they are originally distinct, and the one is only through the instrumentality of the other. And (γ) after the immediacy of this unity has turned out to be self-annulling, the unity is explicitly put as what it implicitly is, simple relation-to-self, which contains in it being and all its forms absorbed. Being or immediacy, which by the negation of itself is a mediation with self and a reference to self—which consequently is also a mediation which cancels itself into reference-to-self, or immediacy—is Essence.

The process of measure, instead of being only the wrong infinite of an endless progression, in the shape of an ever-recurrent recoil from quality to quantity, and from quantity to quality, is also the true infinity of coincidence with self in another. In measure, quality and quantity originally confront each other, like some and other. But quality is implicitly quantity, and conversely quantity is implicitly quality. In the processs of measure, therefore, these two pass into each other: each of them becomes what it already was implicitly: and thus we get Being thrown into abeyance and absorbed, with its several characteristics negatived. Such Being is Essence. Measure is implicitly Essence; and its process consists in realizing what it is implicitly. The ordinary consciousness conceives things as being, and studies them in quality, quantity, and measure. These immediate characteristics, however, soon show themselves to be not fixed but transient; and Essence is the result of their dialectic. In the sphere of Essence one category does not pass into another, but refers to another merely. In Being, the form of reference is purely due to our reflection on what takes place: but it is the special and proper characteristic of Essence. In the sphere of Being, when somewhat becomes another, the somewhat has vanished. Not so in Essence: here there is no real other, but only diversity, reference of the one to *its* other. The transition of Essence is therefore at the same time no transition: for in the passage of different into different, the different does not vanish: the different terms remain in their relation. When we speak of Being and Nought, Being is independent, so is Nought. The case is otherwise with the Positive and the Negative. No doubt these possess the characteristic of Being and Nought. But the positive by itself has no sense; it is wholly in reference to the negative. And it is the same with the negative. In the sphere of Being the reference of one term to another is only implicit; in Essence on the contrary it is explicit. And this in general is the distinction between the forms of Being and Essence: in Being everything is immediate, in Essence everything is relative.

VIII

SECOND SUBDIVISION OF LOGIC

THE DOCTRINE OF ESSENCE

§ 112

The terms in **Essence** are always mere pairs of correlatives, and not yet absolutely reflected in themselves: hence in essence the actual unity of the notion is not realized, but only postulated by reflection. Essence—which is Being coming into mediation with itself through the negativity of itself—is self-relatedness, only in so far as it is relation to an Other—this Other however coming to view at first not as something which *is*, but as postulated and hypothetized. Being has not vanished: but, firstly, Essence, as simple self-relation, is Being, and secondly as regards its one-sided characteristic of immediacy, Being is deposed to a mere negative, to a seeming or reflected light—Essence accordingly is Being thus reflecting light into itself.

The Absolute is the Essence. This is the same definition as the previous one that the Absolute is Being, in so far as Being likewise is simple self-relation. But it is at the same time higher, because Essence is Being that has gone into itself: that is to say, the simple self-relation (in Being) is expressly put as negation of the negative, as immanent self-mediation. Unfortunately when the Absolute is defined to be the Essence, the negativity which this implies is often taken only to mean the withdrawal of all determinate predicates. This negative action of withdrawal or abstraction thus falls outside of the Essence—which is thus left as a mere result apart from its premisses—the *caput mortuum* of abstraction. But as this negativity, instead of being external to Being, is its own dialectic, the truth of the latter, viz. Essence, will be Being as retired within itself—immanent Being. That reflection, or light thrown into itself, constitutes the distinction between Essence and immediate Being, and is the peculiar characteristic of Essence itself.

Any mention of Essence implies that we distinguish it from Being: the latter is immediate, and, compared with the Essence, we look upon it as mere seeming. But this seeming is not an utter nonentity and nothing at all, but Being superseded and put by. The point of view given by the Essence is in general the standpoint of 'Reflection'. This word 'reflection' is originally applied, when a ray of light in a straight line impinging upon the surface of a mirror is thrown back from it. In this phenomenon we have two things—first an immediate fact which is, and secondly the deputed, derivated, or transmitted phase of the same. Something of this sort takes place when we reflect, or think upon an object; for here we want to know the object, not in its immediacy, but as derivative or mediated. The problem or aim of philosophy is often represented as the ascertainment of the essence of things: a phrase which only means that things, instead of being left in their immediacy, must be shown to be mediated by, or based upon, something else. The immediate Being of things is thus conceived under the image of a rind or curtain behind which the Essence lies hidden.

Everything, it is said, has an Essence; that is, things really are not what they immediately show themselves. There is therefore something more to be done than merely rove from one quality to another, and merely to advance from qualitative to quantitative, and vice versa: there is a permanent in things, and that permanent is in the first instance their Essence. With respect to other meanings and uses of the category of Essence, we may note that in the German auxiliary verb, *sein*, the past tense is expressed by the term for Essence (*Wesen*): we designate past being as *gewesen*. This anomaly of language implies to some extent a correct perception of the relation between Being and Essence. Essence we may certainly regard as past Being, remembering however meanwhile that the past is not utterly denied, but only laid aside and thus at the same time preserved. Thus, to say, Caesar *was* in Gaul, only denies the immediacy of the event, but not his sojourn in Gaul altogether. That sojourn is just what forms the import of the proposition, in which however it is represented as over and gone. *Wesen* in ordinary life frequently means only a collection or aggregate: *Zeitungswesen* (the Press), *Postwesen* (the Post Office), *Steuerwesen* (the Revenue). All that these terms mean is that the things in question are not to be taken single, in their immediacy, but as a complex, and then, perhaps, in addition, in their various bearings. This usage of the term is not very different in its implications from our own.

People also speak of *finite* Essences, such as man. But the very term Essence implies that we have made a step beyond finitude: and the title as applied to man is so far inexact. It is often added that there is a supreme Essence (Being): by which is meant God. On this two remarks may be made. In the first place the phrase 'there is' suggests a finite only: as when we say there are so many planets, or there are plants of such a constitution and plants of such another. In these cases we are speaking of something which has other things beyond and beside it. But God, the absolutely infinite, is not something outside and beside whom there are other essences. All else outside God, if separated from him, possesses no essentiality: in its isolation it becomes a mere show or seeming, without stay or essence of its own. But, secondly, it is a poor way of talking to call God the *highest* or supreme Essence. The category of quantity which the phrase employs has its proper place within the compass of the finite. When we call one mountain the highest on the earth, we have a vision of other high mountains beside it. So too when we call any one the richest or most learned in his country. But God, far from being *a* Being, even the highest, is *the* Being. This definition, however, though such a representation of God is an important and necessary stage in the growth of the religious consciousness, does not by any means exhaust the depth of the ordinary Christian idea of God. If we consider God as the Essence only, and nothing more, we know Him only as the universal and irresistible Power; in other words, as the Lord. Now the fear of the Lord is, doubtless, the beginning, but *only* the beginning, of wisdom. To look at God in this light, as the Lord, and the Lord alone, is especially characteristic of Judaism and also of Mohammedanism. The defect of these religions lies in their scant recognition of the finite, which, be it as natural things or as finite phases of mind, it is characteristic of the heathen and (as they also for that reason are) polytheistic religions to maintain intact. Another not uncommon assertion is that God, as the supreme Being, cannot be known. Such is the view taken by modern 'enlightenment' and abstract understanding, which is content to say *Il y a un être suprême*: and there lets the matter rest. To speak thus, and treat God merely as the supreme other-world Being, implies that we look upon the world before us in its immediacy as something permanent and positive, and forget that true Being is just the superseding of all that is immediate. If God be the abstract supersensible Being, outside whom therefore lies all difference and all specific character, he is only a bare name, a mere *caput mortuum* of abstracting understanding. The true knowledge of God begins when we know that things, as they immediately are, have no truth.

In reference also to other subjects besides God the category of Essence is often liable to an abstract use, by which, in the study of anything, its Essence is held to be something unaffected by, and subsisting in independence of, its definite phenomenal embodiment. Thus we say, for example, of people, that the great thing is not what they do or how they behave, but what they are. This is correct, if it means that a man's conduct should be looked at, not in its immediacy, but only as it is explained by his inner self, and as a revelation of that inner self. Still it should be remembered that the only means by which the Essence and the inner self can be verified is their appearance in outward reality; whereas the appeal which men make to the essential life, as distinct from the material facts of conduct, is generally prompted by a desire to assert their own subjectivity and to elude an absolute and objective judgment.

§ 113

Self-relation in Essence is the form of **Identity** or of reflection-into-self, which has here taken the place of the immediacy of Being. They are both the same abstraction—self-relation.

The unintelligence of sense, to take everything limited and finite for Being, passes into the obstinacy of understanding, which views the finite as self-identical, not inherently self-contradictory.

§ 114

This identity, as it has descended from Being, appears in the first place only charged with the characteristics of Being, and referred to Being as to something external. This external Being, if taken in separation from the true Being (of Essence), is called the **Unessential.** But that turns out a mistake. Because Essence is Being-in-self, it is essential only to the extent that it has in itself its negative, i.e. reference to another, or mediation. Consequently, it has the unessential as its own proper seeming (reflection) in itself. But in seeming or mediation there is distinction involved: and since what is distinguished (as distinguished from the identity out of which it arises, and in which it is not, or lies as seeming) receives itself the form of identity, the semblance is still in the mode of Being, or of self-related immediacy. The sphere of Essence thus turns out to be a still imperfect combination of immediacy and mediation. In it every term is expressly invested with the character of self-relatedness, while yet at the same time one is forced beyond it. It has Being—reflected being, a being in which another shows, and which shows in another. And so it is also the sphere in which the contradiction, still implicit in the sphere of Being, is made explicit.

As the one notion is the common principle underlying all logic, there appear in the development of Essence the same attributes or terms as in the development of Being, but in a reflex form. Instead of Being and Nought we have now the forms of Positive and Negative; the former at first as Identity corresponding to pure and uncontrasted Being, the latter developed (showing in itself) as

Difference. So also, we have Becoming represented by the Ground of determinate Being: which itself, when reflected upon the Ground, is Existence.

The theory of Essence is the most difficult branch of Logic. It includes the categories of metaphysic and of the sciences in general. These are products of reflective understanding, which, while it assumes the differences to possess a footing of their own, and at the same time also expressly affirms their relativity, still combines the two statements, side by side, or one after the other, by an 'also', without bringing these thoughts into one, or unifying them into the notion.

A. ESSENCE AS GROUND OF EXISTENCE

(*a*) *The pure principles or categories of Reflection*

(α) *Identity*

§ 115

The Essence lights up *in itself* or is mere reflection: and therefore is only self-relation, not as immediate but as reflected. And that reflex relation is **self-Identity.**

This Identity becomes an Identity, in form only, or of the understanding, if it be held hard and fast, quite aloof from difference. Or, rather, abstraction is the imposition of this Identity of form, the transformation of something inherently concrete into this form of elementary simplicity. And this may be done in two ways. Either we may neglect a part of the multiple features which are found in the concrete thing (by what is called analysis) and select only one of them; or, neglecting their variety, we may concentrate the multiple characters into one.

If we associate Identity with the Absolute, making the Absolute the subject of a proposition, we get: The Absolute is what is identical with itself. However true this proposition may be, it is doubtful whether it be meant in its truth: and therefore it is at least imperfect in the expression. For it is left undecided, whether it means the abstract Identity of understanding—abstract, that is, because constrasted with the other characteristics of Essence—or the Identity which is inherently concrete. In the latter case, as will be seen, true Identity is first discoverable in the Ground, and, with a higher truth, in the Notion. Even the word Absolute is often used to mean no more than 'abstract'. Absolute space and absolute time, for example, is another way of saying abstract space and abstract time.

When the principles of Essence are taken as essential principles of thought they become predicates of a presupposed subject, which, because they are essential, is 'everything'. The propositions thus arising have been stated as universal Laws of Thought. Thus the first of them, the maxim of Identity, reads: Everything is identical with itself, A=A: and, negatively, A cannot at the same time be A and not A. This maxim, instead of being a true law of thought, is nothing but the law of abstract understanding. The propositional form itself contradicts it: for a proposition always promises a distinction between subject and predicate; while the present one does not fulfil what its form requires. But the Law is particularly set aside by the following so-called Laws of Thought, which make laws out of its opposite. It is asserted that the maxim of Identity, though it cannot be proved, regulates the procedure of every consciousness, and that experience shows it to be accepted as soon as its terms are apprehended. To this alleged experience of the logic-books may be opposed the universal experience that no mind thinks or forms conceptions or speaks in accordance with this law, and that no existence of any kind whatever conforms to it. Utterances after the fashion of this pretended law (A planet is a planet; Magnetism is magnetism; Mind is mind) are, as they deserve to be, reputed silly. That is certainly matter of general experience. The logic which seriously propounds such laws and the scholastic world in which alone they are valid have long been discredited with practical common sense as well as with the philosophy of reason.

Identity is, in the first place, the repetition of what we had earlier as Being, but as *become*, through supersession of its character of immediateness. It is therefore Being as Ideality. It is important to come to a proper understanding on the true meaning of Identity: and, for that purpose, we must especially guard against taking it as abstract Identity, to the exclusion of all Difference. That is the touchstone for distinguishing all bad philosophy from what alone deserves the name of philosophy. Identity in its truth, as an Ideality of what immediately is, is a high category for our religious modes of mind as well as all other forms of thought and mental activity. The true knowledge of God, it may be said, begins when we know him as identity—as absolute identity. To know so much is to see that all the power and glory of the world sinks into nothing in God's presence, and subsists only as the reflection of his power and his glory. In the same way, Identity, as self-consciousness, is what distinguishes man from nature, particularly from the brutes which never reach the point of comprehending themselves as 'I', that is, pure self-contained unity. So again, in connection with thought, the main thing is not to confuse the true Identity, which contains Being and its characteristics ideally transfigured in it, with an abstract Identity, identity of bare form. All the charges of narrowness, hardness, meaninglessness, which are so often directed against thought from the quarter of feeling and immediate perception rest on the perverse assumption that thought acts only as a faculty of abstract Identification. The Formal Logic itself confirms this assumption by laying down the supreme law of thought (so-called) which has been discussed above. If thinking were no more than an abstract Identity, we could not but own it to be a most futile and tedious business. No doubt the notion, and the idea too, are identical with themselves: but identical only in so far as they at the same time involve distinction.

(β) *Difference*

§ 116

Essence is mere Identity and reflection in itself only as it is self-relating negativity, and in that way self-repulsion. It contains therefore essentially the characteristic of **Difference.**

Other-being is here no longer qualitative, taking the shape of the character or limit. It is now in Essence, in self-relating essence, and therefore the negation is at the same time a relation—is, in short, Distinction, Relativity, Mediation.

To ask, 'How Identity comes to Difference', assumes that Identity as mere abstract Identity is something of itself, and Difference also something else equally independent. This supposition renders an answer to the question impossible. If identity is viewed as diverse from Difference, all that we have in this way is but Difference; and hence we cannot demonstrate the advance to difference, because the person who asks for the How of the progress thereby implies that for him the starting-point is non-existent. The question then when put to the test has obviously no meaning, and its proposer may be met with the question what he means by Identity; whereupon we should soon see that he attaches no idea to it at all, and that Identity is for him an empty name. As we have seen, besides, Identity is undoubtedly a negative—not however an abstract empty Nought, but the negation of Being and its characteristics. Being so, Identity is at the same time self-relation, and, what is more, negative self-relation; in other words, it draws a distinction between it and itself.

§ 117

Difference is, first of all (1) immediate difference, i.e. **Diversity** or Variety. In Diversity the different things are each individually what they are, and unaffected by the relation in which they stand to each other. This relation is therefore external to them. In consequence of the various things being thus indifferent to the difference between them, it falls outside them into a third thing, the agent of Comparison. This external difference, as an identity of the objects related, is Likeness; as a non-identity of them, is Unlikeness.

The gap which understanding allows to divide these characteristics is so great that although comparison has one and the same substratum for likeness and unlikeness, which are explained to be different aspects and points of view in it, still likeness by itself is the first of the elements alone, viz. identity, and unlikeness by itself is difference.

Diversity has, like Identity, been transformed into a maxim: 'Everything is various or different': or, 'There are no two things completely like each other'. Here Everything is put under a predicate, which is the reverse of the identity attributed to it in the first maxim; and therefore under a law contradicting the first. However there is an explanation. As the diversity is supposed due only to external comparison, anything taken *per se* is expected and understood always to be identical with itself, so that the second law need not interfere with the first. But, in that case, variety does not belong to the something or everything in question: it constitutes no intrinsic characteristic of the subject: and the second maxim on this showing does not admit of being stated at all. If, on the other hand, the something *itself* is, as the maxim says, diverse, it must be in virtue of its own proper character: but in this case the specific difference, and not variety as such, is what is intended. And this is the meaning of the maxim of Leibniz.

When understanding sets itself to study Identity, it has already passed beyond it, and is looking at Difference in the shape of bare Variety. If we follow the so-called law of Identity, and say, The sea is the sea, The air is the air, The moon is the moon, these objects pass for having no bearing on one another. What we have before us therefore is not Identity, but Difference. We do not stop at this point, however, or regard things merely as different. We compare them one with another, and thus discover the features of likeness and unlikeness. The work of the finite sciences lies to a great extent in the application of these categories, and the phrase 'scientific treatment' generally means no more than the method which has for its aim comparison of the objects under examination. This method has undoubtedly led to some important results; we may particularly mention the great advance of modern times in the provinces of comparative anatomy and comparative linguistics. But it is going too far to suppose that the comparative method can be employed with equal success in all branches of knowledge. Nor—and this must be emphasized—can mere comparison ever ultimately satisfy the requirements of science. Its results are indeed indispensable, but they are still labours only preliminary to truly intelligent cognition.

If it be the office of comparison to reduce existing differences to Identity, the science which most perfectly fulfils that end is mathematics. The reason of that is that quantitative difference is only the difference which is quite external. Thus, in geometry, a triangle and a quadrangle, figures qualitatively different, have this qualitative difference discounted by abstraction, and are equalized to one another in magnitude. It follows from what has been formerly said about the mere Identity of understanding that, as has also been pointed out (§ 99, note), neither philosophy nor the empirical sciences need envy this superiority of Mathematics.

The story is told that when Leibniz propounded the maxim of Variety, the cavaliers and ladies of the court, as they walked round the garden, made efforts to discover two leaves indistinguishable from each other, in order to confute the law stated by the philosopher. Their device was unquestionably a convenient method of dealing with metaphysics—one which has not ceased to be fashionable. All the same, as regards the principle of Leibniz, difference must be understood to mean not an external and indifferent diversity merely, but difference essential. Hence the very nature of things implies that they must be different.

§ 118

Likeness is an Identity only of those things which are not the same, not identical with each other: and **Unlikeness** is a relation of things unlike. The two therefore do not fall on different aspects or points of view in the thing, without any mutual affinity, but one throws light into the other. Variety thus comes to be reflexive difference, or difference (distinction) implicit and essential, **determinate** or **specific difference.**

While things merely various show themselves unaffected by each other, likeness and unlikeness on the contrary are a pair of characteristics which are in completely reciprocal relation. The one of them cannot be thought without the other. This advance from simple variety to opposition appears in our common acts of thought, when we allow that comparison has a meaning only upon the hypothesis of an existing difference, and that on the other hand we can distinguish only on the hypothesis of existing similarity. Hence, if the problem be the discovery of a difference, we attribute no great cleverness to the man who only distinguishes those objects, of which the difference is palpable, e.g. a pen and a camel: and similarly it implies no very advanced faculty of comparison, when the objects compared, e.g. a beech and an oak, a temple and a church, are near akin. In the case of difference, in short, we like to see identity, and in the case of identity we like to see difference. Within the range of the empirical sciences, however, the one of these two categories is often allowed to put the other out of sight and mind. Thus the scientific problem at one time is to reduce existing differences to identity; on another occasion, with equal one-sidedness, to discover new differences. We see this especially in physical science. There the problem consists, in the first place, in the continual search for new 'elements', new forces, new genera and species. Or, in another direction, it seeks to show that all bodies hitherto believed to be simple are compound: and modern physicists and chemists smile at the ancients, who were satisfied with four elements, and these not simple. Secondly, and on and the other hand, mere identity is made the chief question. Thus electricity and chemical affinity are regarded as the same, and even the organic processes of digestion and assimilation are looked upon as a mere chemical operation. Modern philosophy has often been nicknamed the Philosophy of Identity. But, as was already remarked (§ 103, note), it is precisely philosophy, and in particular speculative logic, which lays bare the nothingness of the abstract, undifferentiated identity, known to understanding; though it also undoubtedly urges its disciples not to rest at mere diversity, but to ascertain the inner unity of all existence.

§ 119

Difference implicit is essential difference, the **Positive** and the **Negative**: and that is this way. The Positive is the identical self-relation in such a way as not to be the Negative, and the Negative is the different by itself so as not to be the Positive. Thus either has an existence of its own in proportion as it is not the other. The one is made visible in the other, and is only in so far as that other is. Essential difference is therefore Opposition; according to which the different is not confronted by *any* other but by *its* other. That is, either of these two (Positive and Negative) is stamped with a characteristic of its own only in its relation to the other: the one is only reflected into itself as it is reflected into the other. And so with the other. Either in this way is the other's *own* other.

Difference implicit or essential gives the maxim, Everything is essentially distinct; or, as it has also been expressed, Of two opposite predicates the one only can be assigned to anything, and there is no third possible. This maxim of Contrast or Opposition most expressly controverts the maxim of Identity: the one says a thing should be only self-relation, the other says that it must be an opposite, a relation to its other. The native unintelligence of abstraction betrays itself by setting in juxtaposition two contrary maxims, like these, as laws, without even so much as comparing them. The Maxim of Excluded Middle is the maxim of the definite understanding, which would fain avoid contradiction, but in so doing falls into it. A must be either +A or −A, it says. It virtually declares in these words a third A which is neither + nor −, and which at the same time is yet invested with + and − characters. If + W mean 6 miles to the West, and −W mean 6 miles to the East, and if the + and − cancel each other, the 6 miles of way or space remain what they were with and without the contrast. Even the mere *plus* and *minus* of number or abstract direction have, if we like, zero, for their third: but it need not be denied that the empty contrast, which understanding institutes between *plus* and *minus*, is not without its value in such abstractions as number, direction, &c.

In the doctrine of contradictory concepts, the one notion is, say, blue (for in this doctrine even the sensuous generalized image of a colour is called a notion) and the other not-blue. This other then would not be an affirmative, say, yellow, but would merely be kept at the abstract negative. That the Negative in its own nature is quite as much Positive (see next §), is implied in saying that what is opposite to another is *its* other. The inanity of the opposition between what are called contradictory notions is fully exhibited in what we may call the grandiose formula of a general law, that Everything has the one and not the other of *all* predicates which are in such opposition. In this way, mind is either white or not-white, yellow or not-yellow, etc., *ad infinitum*.

It was forgotten that Identity and Opposition are themselves opposed, and the maxim of Opposition was taken even for that of Identity, in the shape of the principle of Contradiction. A notion, which possesses neither or both of two mutually contradictory marks, e.g. a quadrangular circle, is held to be logically false. Now though a multangular circle and a rectilineal arc no less contradict this maxim, geometers never hesitate to treat the circle as a polygon with rectilineal sides. But anything like a circle (that is to say its mere character or nominal definition) is still no notion. In the notion of a circle, centre and circumference are equally essential; both marks belong to it: and yet centre and circumference are opposite and contradictory to each other.

The conception of Polarity, which is so dominant in physics, contains by implication the more correct definition of Opposition. But physics for its theory of the laws of thought adheres to the ordinary logic; it might therefore well be horrified in case it should ever work out the conception of Polarity, and get at the thoughts which are implied in it.

(1) With the positive we return to identity, but in its higher truth as identical self-relation, and at the same time with the note that it is not the negative. The negative *per se* is the same as difference itself. The identical as such is primarily the yet uncharacterized: the positive on the other hand is what is self-identical, but with the mark of antithesis to an other. And the negative is difference as such, characterized as not identity. This is the difference of difference within its own self.

Positive and negative are supposed to express an absolute difference. The two however are at bottom the same: the name of either might be transferred to the other. Thus, for example, debts and assets are not two particular, self-subsisting species of property. What is negative to the debtor is positive to the creditor. A way to the east is also a way to the west. Positive and negative are therefore intrinsically conditioned by one another, and are only in relation to each other. The north pole of the magnet cannot be without the south pole, and vice versa. If we cut a magnet in two, we have not a north pole in one piece, and a south pole in the other. Similarly, in electricity, the positive and the negative are not two diverse and independent fluids. In opposition, the different is not confronted by any other, but by its other. Usually we regard different things as unaffected by each other. Thus we say: I am a human being, and around me are air, water, animals, and all sorts of things. Everything is thus put outside of every other. But the aim of philosophy is to banish indifference, and to ascertain the necessity of things. By that means the other is seen to stand over against *its* other. Thus, for example, inorganic nature is not to be considered merely something else than organic nature, but the necessary antithesis of it. Both are in essential relation to one another; and the one of the two is, only in so far as it excludes the other from it, and thus relates itself thereto. Nature in like manner is not without mind, nor mind without nature. An important step has been taken, when we cease in thinking to use phrases like: Of course something else is also possible. While we so speak, we are still tainted with contingency: and all true thinking, we have already said, is a thinking of necessity.

In modern physical science the opposition, first observed to exist in magnetism as polarity, has come to be regarded as a universal law pervading the whole of nature. This would be a real scientific advance, if care were at the same time taken not to let mere variety revert without explanation, as a valid category, side by side with opposition. Thus at one time the colours are regarded as in polar opposition to one another, and called complementary colours: at another time they are looked at in their indifferent and merely quantitative difference of red, yellow, green, etc.

(2) Instead of speaking by the maxim of Excluded Middle (which is the maxim of abstract understanding) we should rather say: Everything is opposite. Neither in heaven nor in earth, neither in the world of mind nor of nature, is there anywhere such an abstract 'either—or' as the understanding maintains. Whatever exists is concrete, with difference and opposition in itself. The finitude of things will then lie in the want of correspondence between their immediate being, and what they essentially are. Thus, in inorganic nature, the acid is implicitly at the same time the base: in other words, its only being consists in its relation to its other. Hence also the acid is not something that persists quietly in the contrast: it is always in effort to realize what it potentially is. Contradiction is the very moving principle of the world: and it is ridiculous to say that contradiction is unthinkable. The only thing correct in that statement is that contradiction is not the end of the matter, but cancels itself. But contradiction, when cancelled, does not leave abstract identity; for that is itself only one side of the contrariety. The proximate result of opposition (when realized as contradiction) is the Ground, which contains identity as well as difference superseded and deposited to elements in the completer notion.

§ 120

Contrariety then has two forms. The Positive is the aforesaid various (different) which is understood to be independent, and yet at the same not to be unaffected by its relation to its other. The Negative is to be, no less independently, negative self-relating, self-subsistent, and yet at the same time as Negative must on every point have this its self-relation, i.e. its Positive, only in the other. Both Positive and Negative are therefore explicit contradiction; both are potentially the same. Both are so actually also; since either is the abrogation of the other and of itself. Thus they fall to the Ground. Or as is plain, the essential difference, as a difference, is only the difference of it from itself, and thus contains the identical: so that to essential and actual difference there belongs itself as well as identity. As self-relating difference it is likewise virtually enunciated as the self-identical. And the opposite is in general that which includes the one and its other, itself and its opposite. The immanence of essence thus defined is the Ground.

(γ) *The Ground*

§ 121

The **Ground** is the unity of identity and difference, the truth of what difference and identity have turned out to be—the reflection-into-self, which is equally a reflection-into-an-other, and vice versa. It is essence put explicitly as a totality.

The maxim of the Ground runs thus: Everything has its Sufficient Ground: that is, the true essentiality of any thing is not the predication of it as identical with itself, or as different (various), or merely positive, or merely negative, but as having its Being in an other, which, being its selfsame, is its essence. And to this extent the essence is not abstract reflection into self, but into an other. The Ground is the essence in its own inwardness; the essence is intrinsically a ground; and it is a ground only when it is a ground of somewhat, of an other.

We must be careful, when we say that the ground is the unity of identity and difference, not to understand by this unity an abstract identity. Otherwise we only change the name, while we still think the identity (of understanding) already seen to be false. To avoid this misconception we may say that the ground, besides being the unity, is also the difference of identity and difference. In that case in the ground, which promised at first to supersede contradiction, a new contradiction seems to arise. It is, however, a contradiction, which, so far from persisting quietly in itself, is rather the expulsion of it from itself. The ground is a ground only to the extent that it affords ground: but the result which thus issued from the ground is only itself. In this lies its formalism. The ground and what is grounded are one and the same content: the difference between the two is the mere difference of form which separates simple self-relation, on the one hand, from mediation or derivativeness on the other. Inquiry into the grounds of things goes with the point of view which, as already noted (note to § 112), is adopted by Reflection. We wish, as it were, to see the matter double, first in its immediacy, and secondly in its ground, where it is no longer immediate. This is the plain meaning of the law of sufficient ground, as it is called; it asserts that things should essentially be viewed as mediated. The manner in which Formal Logic establishes this law of thought, sets a bad example to other sciences. Formal Logic asks these sciences not to accept their subject-matter as it is immediately given; and yet herself lays down a law of thought without deducing it—in other words, without exhibiting its mediation. With the same justice as the logician maintains our faculty of thought to be so constituted that we must ask for the ground of everything, might the physicist, when asked why a man who falls into water is drowned, reply that man happens to be so organized that he cannot live under water; or the jurist, when asked why a criminal is punished, reply that civil society happens to be so constituted that crimes cannot be left unpunished.

Yet even if logic be excused the duty of giving a ground for the law of the sufficient ground, it might at least explain what is to be understood by a ground. The common explanation, which describes the ground as what has a consequence, seems at the first glance more lucid and intelligible than the preceding definition in logical terms. If you ask however what the consequence is, you are told that it is what has a ground; and it becomes obvious that the explanation is intelligible only because it assumes what in our case has been reached as the termination of an antecedent movement of thought. And this is the true business of logic: to show that those thoughts, which as usually employed merely float before consciousness neither understood nor demonstrated, are really grades in the self-determination of thought. It is by this means that they are understood and demonstrated.

In common life, and it is the same in the finite sciences, this reflective form is often employed as a key to the secret of the real condition of the objects under investigation. So long as we deal with what may be termed the household needs of knowledge, nothing can be urged against this method of study. But it can never afford definitive satisfaction, either in theory or practice. And the reason why it fails is that the ground is yet without a definite content of its own; so that to regard anything as resting upon a ground merely gives the formal difference of mediation in place of immediacy. We see an electrical phenomenon, for example, and we ask for its ground (or reason): we are told that electricity is the ground of this phenomenon. What is this but the same content as we had immediately before us, only translated into the form of inwardness?

The ground however is not merely simple self-identity, but also different: hence various grounds may be alleged for the same sum of fact. This variety of grounds, again, following the logic of difference, culminates in opposition of grounds *pro* and *contra*. In any action, such as a theft, there is a sum of fact in which several aspects may be distinguished. The theft has violated the rights of property: it has given the means of satisfying his wants to the needy thief: possibly too the man, from whom the theft was made, misused his property. The violation of property is unquestionably the decisive point of view before which the others must give way: but the bare law of the ground cannot settle that question. Usually indeed the law is interpreted to speak of a sufficient ground, not of any ground whatever: and it might be supposed therefore, in the action referred to, that, although other points of view besides the violation of property might be held as grounds, yet they would not be sufficient grounds. But here comes a dilemma. If we use the phrase 'sufficient ground', the epithet is either otiose, or of such a kind as to carry us past the mere category of ground. The predicate is otiose and tautological, if it only states the capability of giving a ground or reason: for the ground is a ground, only in so far as it has this capability. If a soldier runs away from battle to save his life, his conduct is certainly a violation of duty; but it cannot be held that the ground which led him so to act was insufficient, otherwise he would have remained at his post. Besides, there is this also to be said. On one hand any ground suffices: on the other no ground suffices as mere ground; because, as already said, it is yet void of a content objectively and intrinsically determined, and is therefore not self-acting and productive. A content thus objectively and intrinsically determined, and hence self-acting, will hereafter come before us as the notion: and it is the notion which Leibniz had in his eye when he spoke of sufficient ground, and urged the study of things under its point of view. His remarks were originally directed against that merely mechanical method of conceiving things so much in vogue even now; a method which he justly pronounces insufficient. We may see an instance of this mechanical theory of investigation when the organic process of the circulation of the blood is traced back merely to the contraction of the heart; or when certain theories of criminal law explain the purpose of punishment to lie in deterring people from crime, in rendering the criminal harmless, or in other extraneous grounds of the same kind. It is unfair to Leibniz to suppose that he was content with anything so poor as this formal law of the ground. The method of investigation which he inaugurated is the very reverse of a formalism which acquiesces in mere grounds, where a full and concrete knowledge is sought. Considerations to this effect led Leibniz to contrast *causae efficientes* and *causae finales*, and to insist on the place of final causes as the conception to which the efficient were to lead up. If we adopt this distinction, light, heat, and moisture would be the *causae efficientes*, not the *causa finalis* of the growth of plants: the *cause finalis* is the notion of the plant itself.

To get no further than mere grounds, especially on questions of law and morality, is the position and principle of the Sophists. Sophistry, as we ordinarily conceive it, is a method of investigation which aims at distorting what is just and true, and exhibiting things in a false light. Such however is not the proper or primary tendency of Sophistry: the standpoint of which is no other than that of *raisonnement*. The Sophists came on the scene at a time when the Greeks had begun to grow dissatisfied with mere authority and tradition and felt the need of intellectual justification for what they were to accept as obligatory. That desideratum the Sophists supplied by teaching their countrymen to seek for the various points of view under which things may be considered: which points of view are the same as grounds. But the ground, as we have seen, has no essential and objective principles of its own, and it is as easy to discover grounds for what is wrong and immoral as for what is moral and right. Upon the observer therefore it depends to decide what points are to have most weight. The decision in such circumstances is prompted by his individual views and sentiments. Thus the objective foundation of what ought to have been of absolute and essential obligation, accepted by all, was undermined: and Sophistry by this destructive action deservedly brought upon itself the bad name previously mentioned. Socrates, as we all know, met the Sophists at every point, not by a bare reassertion of authority and tradition against their argumentations, but by showing dialectically how untenable the mere grounds were, and by vindicating the obligations of justice and goodness—by reinstating the universal or notion of the will. In the present day such a method of argumentation is not quite out of fashion. Nor is that the case only in the discussion of secular matters. It occurs even in sermons, such as those where every possible ground of gratitude to God is propounded. To such pleading Socrates and Plato would not have scrupled to apply the name of Sophistry. For Sophistry has nothing to do with what is taught: that may very possibly be true. Sophistry lies in the formal circumstance of teaching it by grounds which are as available for attack as for defence. In a time so rich in reflection and so devoted to *raisonnement* as our own, he must be a poor creature who cannot advance a good ground for everything, even for what is worst and most depraved. Everything in the world that has become corrupt has had good ground for its corruption. An appeal to grounds at first makes the hearer think of beating a retreat: but when experience has taught him the real state of these matters, he closes his ears against them, and refuses to be imposed upon any more.

§ 122

As it first comes, the chief feature of Essence is show in itself and intermediation in itself. But when it has completed the circle of intermediation, its unity with itself is explicitly put as the self-annulling of difference, and therefore of intermediation. Once more then we come back to immediacy or Being—but Being in so far as it is intermediated by annulling the intermediation. And that Being is **Existence**.

The ground is not yet determined by objective principles of its own, nor is it an end or final cause: hence it is not active, not productive. An Existence only *proceeds from* the ground. The determinate ground is therefore a formal matter: that is to say, any point will do, so long as it is expressly put as self-relation, as affirmation, in correlation with the immediate existence depending on it. If it be a ground at all, it is a good ground: for the term 'good' is employed abstractly as equivalent to affirmative; and any point (or feature) is good which can in any way be enunciated as confessedly affirmative. So it happens that a ground can be found and adduced for everything: and a good ground (for example, a good motive for action) may effect something or may not, it may have a consequence or it may not. It becomes a motive (strictly so called) and effects something, e.g. through its reception into a will; there and there only it becomes active and is made a cause.

(*b*) *Existence*

§ 123

Existence is the immediate unity of reflection-into-self and reflection-into-another. It follows from this that existence is the indefinite multitude of existents as reflected-into-themselves, which at the same time equally throw light upon one another—which, in short, are co-relative, and form a world of reciprocal dependence and of infinite interconnection between grounds and consequents. The grounds are themselves existences: and the existents in like manner are in many directions grounds as well as consequents.

The phrase 'Existence' (derived from *existere*) suggests the fact of having proceeded from something. Existence is Being which has proceeded from the ground, and has reinstated by annulling its intermediation. The Essence, as Being set aside and absorbed, originally came before us as shining or showing in self, and the categories of this reflection are identity, difference, and ground. The last is the unity of identity and difference; and because it unifies them it has at the same time to distinguish itself from itself. But that which is in this way distinguished from the ground is as little mere difference as the ground itself is abstract sameness. The ground works its own suspension: and when suspended, the result of its negation is existence. Having issued from the ground, existence contains the ground in it; the ground does not remain, as it were, behind existence, but by its very nature supersedes itself and translates itself into existence. This is exemplified even in our ordinary mode of thinking, when we look upon the ground of a thing, not as something abstractly inward, but as itself also an existent. For example, the lightning-flash which has set a house on fire would be considered the ground of the conflagration; or the manners of a nation and the condition of its life would be regarded as the ground of its constitution. Such indeed is the ordinary aspect in which the existent world originally appears to reflection—an indefinite crowd of things existent, which being simultaneously reflected on themselves and on one another are related reciprocally as ground and consequence. In this motley play of the world, if we may so call the sum of existents, there is nowhere a firm footing to be found: everything bears an aspect of relativity, conditioned by and conditioning something else. The reflective understanding makes it its business to elicit and trace these connections running out in every direction; but the question touching an ultimate design is so far left unanswered, and therefore the craving of the reason after knowledge passes with the further development of the logical Idea beyond this position of mere relativity.

§ 124

The reflection-on-another of the existent is however inseparable from the reflection-on-self: the ground is their unity, from which existence has issued. The existent therefore includes relativity, and has on its own part its multiple interconnections with other existents: it is reflected on itself as its ground. The existent is, when so described, a **Thing**.

The 'thing-by-itself' (or thing in the abstract), so famous in the philosophy of Kant, shows itself here in its genesis. It is seen to be the abstract reflection-on-self, which is clung to, to the exclusion of reflection-on-other-things and of all predication of difference.

The thing-by-itself therefore is the empty substratum for these predicates of relation.

If to know means to comprehend an object in its concrete character, then the thing-by-itself, which is nothing but the quite abstract and indeterminate thing in general, must certainly be as unknowable as it is alleged to be. With as much reason however as we speak of the thing-by-itself, we might speak of quality-by-itself or quantity-by-itself, and of any other category. The expression would then serve to signify that these categories are taken in their abstract immediacy, apart from their development and inward character. It is no better than a whim of the understanding, therefore, if we attach the qualificatory 'in or by-itself' to the *thing* only. But this 'in or by-itself' is also applied to the facts of the mental as well as the natural world: as we speak of electricity or of a plant in itself, so we speak of man or the state in itself. By this 'in-itself' in these objects we are meant to understand what they strictly and properly are. This usage is liable to the same criticism as the phrase 'thing-in-itself'. For if we stick to the mere 'in-itself' of an object, we apprehend it not in its truth, but in the inadequate form of mere abstraction. Thus the man, by or in himself, is the child. And what the child has to do is to rise out of this abstract and undeveloped 'in-himself', and become 'for himself' what he is at first only 'in-himself'—a free and reasonable being. Similarly, the state-in-itself is the yet immature and patriarchal state, where the various political functions, latent in the notion of the state, have not received the full logical constitution which the logic of political principles demands. In the same sense, the germ may be called the plant-in-itself. These examples may show the mistake of supposing that the 'thing-in-itself' or the 'in-itself' of things is something inaccessible to our cognition. All things are originally in-themselves, but that is not the end of the matter. As the germ, being the plant-in-itself, means self-development, so the thing in general passes beyond its in-itself (the abstract reflection on self) to manifest itself further as a reflection on other things. It is in this sense that it has properties.

(*c*) *The Thing*

§ 125

(*a*) The Thing is the totality—the development in explicit unity—of the categories of the ground and of existence. On the side of one of its factors, viz. reflection-on-other-things, it has in it the differences, in virtue of which it is a characterized and concrete thing. These characteristics are different from one another; they have their reflection-into-self not on their own part, but on the part of the thing. They are **Properties** of the thing: and their relation to the thing is expressed by the word 'have'.

As a term of relation, 'to have' takes the place of 'to be'. True, somewhat has qualities on its part too: but this transference of 'having' into the sphere of Being is inexact, because the character as quality is directly one with the somewhat, and the somewhat ceases to be when it loses its quality. But the thing is reflection-into-self: for it is an identity which is also distinct from the difference, i.e. from its attributes. In many languages 'have' is employed to denote past time. And with reason: for the past is absorbed or suspended being, and the mind is its reflection-into-self; in the mind only it continues to subsist—the mind, however, distinguishing from itself this being in it which has been absorbed or suspended.

In the Thing all the characteristics of reflection recur as existent. Thus the thing, in its initial aspect, as the thing-by-itself, is the selfsame or identical. But identity, it was proved, is not found without difference: so the properties, which the thing has, are the existent difference in the form of diversity. In the case of diversity of variety each diverse member exhibited an indifference to every other, and they had no other relation to each other, save what was given by a comparison external to them. But now in the thing we have a bond which keeps the various properties in union. Property, besides, should not be confused with quality. No doubt, we also say, a thing has qualities. But the phraseology is a misplaced one: 'having' hints at an independence, foreign to the 'somewhat', which is still directly identical with its quality. Somewhat is what it is only by its quality: whereas, though the thing indeed exists only as it has its properties, it is not confined to this or that definite property, and can therefore lose it, without ceasing to be what it is.

§ 126

(*β*) Even in the ground, however, the reflection-on-something-else is directly convertible with reflection-on-self. And hence the properties are not merely different from each other; they are also self-identical, independent, and relieved from their attachment to the thing. Still, as they are the characters of the thing distinguished from one another (as reflected-into-self), they are not themselves things, if things be concrete; but only existences reflected into themselves as abstract characters. They are what are called **Matters.**

Nor is the name 'things' given to Matters, such as magnetic and electric matters. They are qualities proper, a reflected Being—one with their Being—they are the character that has reached immediacy, existence: they are 'entities'.

To elevate the properties, which the Thing has, to the independent position of matters, or materials of which it consists, is a proceeding based upon the notion of a Thing: and for that reason is also found in experience. Thought and experience however alike protest against concluding from the fact that certain properties of a thing, such as colour, or smell, may be represented as particular colouring or odorific matters, that we are then at the end of the inquiry, and that nothing more is needed to penetrate to the true secret of things than a disintegration of them into their component materials. This disintegration into independent matters is properly restricted to inorganic nature only. The chemist is in the right, therefore, when, for example, he analyses common salt or gypsum into its elements, and finds that the former consists of muriatic acid and soda, the latter of sulphuric acid and calcium. So too the geologist does well to regard granite as a compound of quartz, felspar, and mica. These matters, again, of which the thing consists, are themselves partly things, which in that way may be once more reduced to more abstract matters. Sulphuric acid, for example, is a compound of sulphur and oxygen. Such matters or bodies can as a matter of fact be exhibited as subsisting by themselves: but frequently we find other properties of things, entirely wanting this self-subsistence, also regarded as particular matters. Thus we hear caloric, and electrical or magnetic matters spoken of. Such matters are at the best figments of understanding. And we see here the usual procedure of the abstract reflection of understanding. Capriciously adopting single categories, whose value entirely depends on their place in the gradual evolution of the logical idea, it employs them in the pretended interests of explanation, but in the face of plain, unprejudiced perception and experience, so as to trace back to them every object investigated. Nor is this all. The theory, which makes things consist of independent matters, is frequently applied in a region where it has neither meaning nor force. For within the limits of nature even, wherever there is organic life, this category is obviously inadequate. An animal may be said to consist of bones, muscles, nerves, etc.: but evidently we are here using the term 'consist' in a very different sense from its use when we spoke of the piece of granite as consisting of the above-mentioned elements. The elements of granite are utterly indifferent to their combination: they could subsist as well without it. The different parts and members of an organic body on the contrary subsist only in their union: they cease to exist as such, when they are separated from each other.

§ 127

Thus Matter is the mere abstract or indeterminate reflection-into-something-else, or reflection-into-self at the same time as determinate; it is consequently Thinghood which then and there is—the subsistence of the thing. By this means the thing has on the part of the matters its reflection-into-self (the reverse of § 125); it subsists not on its own part, but consists of the matters, and is only a superficial association between them, an external combination of them.

§ 128

(γ) Matter, being the immediate unity of existence with itself, is also indifferent towards specific character. Hence the numerous diverse matters coalesce into the one **Matter,** or into existence under the reflective characteristic of identity. In contrast to this one Matter these distinct properties and their external relation which they have to one another in the thing, constitute the **Form**—the reflective category of difference, but a difference which exists and is a totality.

This one featureless Matter is also the same as the Thing-by-itself was: only the latter is intrinsically quite abstract, while the former essentially implies relation to something else, and in the first place to the Form.

The various matters of which the thing consists are potentially the same as one another. Thus we get one Matter in general to which the difference is expressly attached externally and as a bare form. This theory which holds things all round to have one and the same matter at bottom, and merely to differ externally in respect of form, is much in vogue with the reflective understanding. Matter in that case counts for naturally indeterminate, but susceptible of any determination; while at the same time it is perfectly permanent, and continues the same amid all change and alteration. And in finite things at least this disregard of matter for any determinate form is certainly exhibited. For example, it matters not to a block of marble, whether it receive the form of this or that statue or even the form of a pillar. Be it noted however that a block of marble can disregard form only relatively, that is, in reference to the sculptor: it is by no means purely formless. And so the mineralogist considers the relatively formless marble as a special formation of rock, differing from other equally special formations, such as sandstone or porphyry. Therefore we say it is an abstraction of the understanding which isolates matter into a certain natural formlessness. For properly speaking the thought of matter includes the principle of form throughout, and no formless matter therefore appears anywhere even in experience as existing. Still the conception of matter as original and pre-existent, and as naturally formless, is a very ancient one; it meets us even among the Greeks, at first in the mythical shape of Chaos, which is supposed to represent the unformed substratum of the existing world. Such a conception must of necessity tend to make God not the Creator of the world, but a mere world-moulder or demiurge. A deeper insight into nature reveals God as creating the world out of nothing. And that teaches two things. On the one hand it enunciates that matter, as such, has no independent subsistence, and on the other that the form does not supervene upon matter from without, but as a totality involves the principle of matter in itself. This free and infinite form will hereafter come before us as the notion.

§ 129

Thus the Thing suffers a disruption into Matter and Form. Each of these is the totality of thinghood and subsists for itself. But Matter, which is meant to be the positive and indeterminate existence, contains, as an existence, reflection-on-another, every whit as much as it contains self-enclosed being. Accordingly as uniting these characteristics, it is itself the totality of Form. But Form, being a complete whole of characteristics, *ipso facto* involves reflection-into-self; in other words, as self-relating Form it has the very function attributed to Matter. Both are at bottom the same. Invest them with this unity, and you have the relation of Matter and Form, which are also no less distinct.

§ 130

The Thing, being this totality, is a contradiction. On the side of its negative unity it is Form in which Matter is determined and deposed to the rank of properties (§ 125). At the same time it consists of Matters, which in the reflection-of-the-thing-into-itself are as much independent as they are at the same time negatived. Thus the thing is the essential existence, in such a way as to be an existence that suspends or absorbs itself in itself. In other words, the thing is an Appearance or Phenomenon.

The negation of the several matters, which is insisted on in the thing no less than their independent existence, occurs in Physics as *porosity*. Each of the several matters (coloured matter, odorific matter, and if we believe some people, even sound-matter—not excluding caloric, electric matter, etc.) is also negated: and in this negation of theirs, or as interpenetrating their pores, we find the numerous other independent matters, which, being similarly porous, make room in turn for the existence of the rest. Pores are not empirical facts; they are figments of the understanding, which uses them to represent the element of negation in independent matters. The further working-out of the contradictions is concealed by the nebulous imbroglio in which all matters are independent and all no less negated in each other. If the faculties or activities are similarly hypostatized in the mind, their living unity similarly turns to the imbroglio of an action of the one on the others.

These pores (meaning thereby not the pores in an organic body, such as the pores of wood or of the skin, but those in the so-called 'matters', such as colouring matter, caloric, or metals, crystals, etc.) cannot be verified by observation. In the same way matter itself—furthermore form which is separated from matter—whether that be the thing as consisting of matters, or the view that the thing itself subsists and only has proper ties, is all a product of the reflective understanding which, while it observes and professes to record only what it observes, is rather creating a metaphysic, bristling with contradictions of which it is unconscious.

B. APPEARANCE

§ 131

The Essence must appear or shine forth. Its shining or reflection in it is the suspension and translation of it to immediacy, which, while as reflection-on-self it is matter or subsistence, is also form, reflection-on-something-else, a subsistence which sets itself aside. To show or shine is the characteristic by which essence is distinguished from being—by which it is essence; and it is this show which, when it is developed, shows itself, and is Appearance. Essence accordingly is not something beyond or behind appearance, but—just because it is the essence which exists—the existence is **Appearance** (Forth-shining).

Existence stated explicitly in its contradiction is Appearance. But appearance (forth-shining) is not to be confused with a mere show (shining). Show is the proximate truth of Being or immediacy. The immediate, instead of being, as we suppose, something independent, resting on its own self, is a mere show, and as such it is packed or summed up under the simplicity of the immanent essence. The essence is, in the first place, the sum total of the showing itself, shining in itself (inwardly); but, far from abiding in this inwardness, it comes as a ground forward into existence; and this existence being grounded not in itself, but on something else, is just appearance. In our imagination we ordinarily combine with the term appearance or phenomenon the conception of an indefinite congeries of things existing, the being of which is purely relative, and which consequently do not rest on a foundation of their own, but are esteemed only as passing stages. But in this conception it is no less implied that essence does not linger behind or beyond appearance. Rather it is, we may say, the infinite kindness which lets its own show freely issue into immediacy, and graciously allows it the joy of existence. The appearance which is thus created does not stand on its own feet, and has its being not in itself but in something else. God who is the essence, when he lends existence to the passing stages of his own show in himself, may be described as the goodness that creates a world: but he is also the power above it, and the righteousness, which manifests the merely phenomenal character of the content of this existing world, whenever it tries to exist in independence.

Appearance is in every way a very important grade of the logical idea. It may be said to be the distinction of philosophy from ordinary consciousness that it sees the merely phenomenal character of what the latter supposes to have a self-subsistent being. The significance of appearance however must be properly grasped, or mistakes will arise. To say that anything is a *mere* appearance may be misinterpreted to mean that, as compared with what is merely phenomenal, there is greater truth in the immediate, in that which *is*. Now in strict fact, the case is precisely the reverse. Appearance is higher than mere Being—a richer category because it holds in combination the two elements of reflection-into-self and reflection-into-another: whereas Being (or immediacy) is still mere relationlessness, and apparently rests upon itself alone. Still, to say that anything is *only* an appearance suggests a real flaw, which consists in this, that Appearance is still divided against itself and without intrinsic stability. Beyond and above mere appearance comes in the first place Actuality, the third grade of Essence, of which we shall afterwards speak.

In the history of Modern Philosophy, Kant has the merit of first rehabilitating this distinction between the common and the philosophic modes of thought. He stopped half-way, however, when he attached to Appearance a subjective meaning only, and put the abstract essence immovable outside it as the thing-in-itself beyond the reach of our cognition.

For it is the very nature of the world of immediate objects to be appearance only. Knowing it to be so, we know at the same time the essence, which, far from staying behind or beyond the appearance, rather manifests its own essentiality by deposing the world to a mere appearance. One can hardly quarrel with the plain man who, in his desire for totality, cannot acquiesce in the doctrine of subjective idealism, that we are solely concerned with phenomena. The plain man, however, in his desire to save the objectivity of knowledge, may very naturally return to abstract immediacy, and maintain that immediacy to be true and actual. In a little work published under the title, *A Report, Clear as Day, to the Larger Public touching the Proper Nature of the Latest Philosophy: an Attempt to force the Reader to understand*, Fichte examined the opposition between subjective idealism and immediate consciousness in a popular form, under the shape of a dialogue between the author and the reader, and tried hard to prove that the subjective idealist's point of view was right. In this dialogue the reader complains to the author that he has completely failed to place himself in the idealist's position, and is inconsolable at the thought that things around him are no real things but mere appearances. The affliction of the reader can scarcely be blamed when he is expected to consider himself hemmed in by an impervious circle of purely subjective conceptions. Apart from this subjective view of Appearance, however, we have all reason to rejoice that the things which environ us are appearances and not steadfast and independent existences; since in that case we should soon perish of hunger, both bodily and mental.

(*a*) *The World of Appearance*

§ 132

The Apparent or Phenomenal exists in such a way, that its subsistence is *ipso facto* thrown into abeyance or suspended and is only one stage in the form itself. The form embraces in it the matter or subsistence as one of its characteristics. In this way the phenomenal has its ground in this (form) as its essence, its reflection-into-self in contrast with its immediacy, but, in so doing, has it only in another aspect of the form. This ground of its is no less phenomenal than itself, and the phenomenon accordingly goes on to an endless mediation of subsistence by means of form, and thus equally by non-subsistence. This endless intermediation is at the same time a unity of self-relation; and existence is developed into a totality, into a world of phenomena—of reflected finitude.

(*b*) *Content and Form*

§ 133

Outside one another as the phenomena in this phenomenal world are, they form a totality, and are wholly contained in their self-relatedness. In this way the self-relation of the phenomenon is completely specified, it has the **Form** in itself: and because it is in this identity, has it as essential subsistence. So it comes about that the form is **Content**: and in its mature phase is the **Law of the Phenomenon.** When the form, on the contrary, is not reflected into self, it is equivalent to the negative of the phenomenon, to the non-independent and changeable: and that sort of form is the indifferent or External Form.

The essential point to keep in mind about the opposition of Form and Content is that the content is not formless, but has the form in its own self, quite as much as the form is external to it. There is thus a doubling of form. At one time it is reflected into itself; and then is identical with the content. At another time it is not reflected into itself, and then is the external existence, which does not at all affect the content. We are here in presence, implicitly, of the absolute correlation of content and form: viz. their reciprocal revulsion, so that content is nothing but the revulsion of form into content, and form nothing but the revulsion of content into form. This mutual revulsion is one of the most important laws of thought. But it is not explicitly brought out before the Relations of Substance and Causality.

Form and content are a pair of terms frequently employed by the reflective understanding, especially with a habit of looking on the content as the essential and independent, the form on the contrary as the unessential and dependent. Against this it is to be noted that both are in fact equally essential; and that, while a formless *content* can be as little found as a formless *matter*, the two (content and matter) are distinguished by this circumstance, that matter, though implicitly not without form, still in its existence manifests a disregard of form, whereas the content, as such, is what it is only because the matured form is included in it. Still the form comes before us sometimes as an existence indifferent and external to content, and does so for the reason that the whole range of Appearance still suffers from externality. In a book, for instance, it certainly has no bearing upon the content, whether it be written or printed, bound in paper or in leather. That however does not in the least imply that apart from such an indifferent and external form, the content of the book is itself formless. There are undoubtedly books enough which even in reference to their content may well be styled formless: but want of form in this case is the same as bad form, and means the defect of the right form, not the absence of all form whatever. So far is this right form from being unaffected by the content that it is rather the content itself. A work of art that wants the right form is for that very reason no right or true work of art: and it is a bad way of excusing an artist, to say that the content of his works is good and even excellent, though they want the right form. Real works of art are those where content and form exhibit a thorough identity. The content of the *Iliad*, it may be said, is the Trojan war, and especially the wrath of Achilles. In that we have everything, and yet very little after all; for the *Iliad* is made an *Iliad* by the poetic form, in which that content is moulded. The content of *Romeo and Juliet* may similarly be said to be the ruin of two lovers through the discord between their families: but something more is needed to make Shakespeare's immortal tragedy.

In reference to the relation of form and content in the field of science, we should recollect the difference between philosophy and the rest of the sciences. The latter are finite, because their mode of thought, as a merely formal act, derives its content from without. Their content therefore is not known as moulded from within through the thoughts which lie at the ground of it, and form and content do not thoroughly interpenetrate each other. This partition disappears in philosophy, and thus justifies its title of infinite knowledge. Yet even philosophic thought is often held to be a merely formal act; and that logic, which confessedly deals only with thoughts *qua* thoughts, is merely formal, is especially a foregone conclusion. And if content means no more than what is palpable and obvious to the senses, all philosophy and logic in particular must be at once acknowledged to be void of content, that is to say, of content perceptible to the senses. Even ordinary forms of thought, however, and the common usage of language, do not in the least restrict the appellation of content to what is perceived by the senses, or to what has a being in place and time. A book without content is, as every one knows, not a book with empty leaves, but one of which the content is as good as none. We shall find as the last result on closer analysis, that by what is called content an educated mind means nothing but the presence and power of thought. But this is to admit that thoughts are not empty forms without affinity to their content, and that in other spheres as well as in art the truth and the sterling value of the content essentially depend on the content showing itself identical with the form.

§ 134

But immediate existence is a character of the subsistence itself as well as of the form: it is consequently external to the character of the content; but in an equal degree this externality, which the content has through the factor of its subsistence, is essential to it. When thus explicitly stated, the phenomenon is relativity or correlation: where one and the same thing, viz. the content or the developed form, is seen as the externality and antithesis of independent existences, and as their reduction to a relation of identity, in which identification alone the two things distinguished are what they are.

(*c*) *Relation or Correlation*

§ 135

(*a*) The immediate relation is that of the **Whole** and the **Parts.** The content is the whole, and consists of the parts (the form), its counterpart. The parts are diverse one from another. It is they that possess independent being. But they are parts, only when they are identified by being related to one another; or, in so far as they make up the whole, when taken together. But this 'together' is the counterpart and negation of the part.

Essential correlation is the specific and completely universal phase in which things appear. Everything that exists stands in correlation, and this correlation is the veritable nature of every existence. The existent thing in this way has no being of its own, but only in something else: in this other however it is self-relation; and correlation is the unity of the self-relation and relation-to-others.

The relation of the whole and the parts is untrue to this extent, that the notion and the reality of the relation are not in harmony. The notion of the whole is to contain parts: but if the whole is taken and made what its notion implies, *i.e.* if it is divided, it at once ceases to be a whole. Things there are, no doubt, which correspond to this relation: but for that very reason they are low and untrue existences. We must remember, however, what 'untrue' signifies. When it occurs in a philosophical discussion, the term 'untrue' does not signify that the thing to which it is applied is non-existent. A bad state or a sickly body may exist all the same; but these things are untrue, because their notion and their reality are out of harmony.

The relation of whole and parts, being the immediate relation, comes easy to reflective understanding; and for that reason it often satisfies when the question really turns on profounder ties. The limbs and organs, for instance, of an organic body are not merely parts of it: it is only in their unity that they are what they are, and they are unquestionably affected by that unity, as they also in turn affect it. These limbs and organs become mere parts, only when they pass under the hands of the anatomist, whose occupation, be it remembered, is not with the living body but with the corpse. Not that such analysis is illegitimate: we only mean that the external and mechanical relation of whole and parts is not sufficient for us, if we want to study organic life in its truth. And if this be so in organic life, it is the case to a much greater extent when we apply this relation to the mind and the formations of the spiritual world. Psychologists may not expressly speak of parts of the soul or mind, but the mode in which this subject is treated by the analytic understanding is largely founded on the analogy of this finite relation. At least that is so, when the different forms of mental activity are enumerated and described merely in their isolation one after another, as so-called special powers and faculties.

§ 136

(β) The one-and-same of this correlation (the self-relation found in it) is thus immediately a negative self-relation. The correlation is in short the mediating process whereby one and the same is first unaffected towards difference, and secondly is the negative self-relation, which repels itself as reflection-into-self to difference, and invests itself (as reflection-into-something-else) with existence, whilst it conversely leads back this reflection-into-other to self-relation and indifference. This gives the correlation of **Force** and its **Expression.**

The relationship of whole and part is the immediate and therefore unintelligent (mechanical) relation—a revulsion of self-identity into mere variety. Thus we pass from the whole to the parts, and from the parts to the whole: in the one we forget its opposition to the other, while each on its own account, at one time the whole, at another the parts, is taken to be an independent existence. In other words, when the parts are declared to subsist in the whole, and the whole to consist of the parts, we have either member of the relation at different times taken to be permanently subsistent, while the other is non-essential. In its superficial form the mechanical nexus consists in the parts being independent of each other and of the whole.

This relation may be adopted for the progression *ad infinitum*, in the case of the divisibility of matter: and then it becomes an unintelligent alternation with the two sides. A thing at one time is taken as a whole: then we go on to specify the parts: this specifying is forgotten, and what was a part is regarded as a whole: then the specifying of the part comes up again, and so on for ever. But if this infinity be taken as the negative which it is, it is the *negative* self-relating element in the correlation—Force, the self-identical whole, or immanency—which yet supersedes this immanency and gives itself expression; and conversely the expression which vanishes and returns into Force.

Force, notwithstanding this infinity, is also finite: for the content, or the one and the same of the Force and its out-putting, is this identity at first only for the observer: the two sides of the relation are not yet, each on its own account, the concrete identity of that one and same, not yet the totality. For one another they are therefore different, and the relationship is a finite one. Force consequently requires solicitation from without: it works blindly: and on account of this defectiveness of form, the content is also limited and accidental. It is not yet genuinely identical with the form: not yet is it *as* a notion and an end; that is to say, it is not intrinsically and actually determinate. This difference is most vital, but not easy to apprehend: it will assume a clearer formulation when we reach Design. If it be overlooked, it leads to the confusion of conceiving God as Force, a confusion from which Herder's God especially suffers.

It is often said that the nature of Force itself is unknown and only its manifestation apprehended. But, in the first place, it may be replied, every article in the import of Force is the same as what is specified in the Exertion: and the explanation of a phenomenon by a Force is to that extent a mere tautology. What is supposed to remain unknown, therefore, is really nothing but the empty form of reflection-into-self, by which alone the Force is distinguished from the Exertion—and that form too is something familiar. It is a form that does not make the slightest addition to the content and to the law, which have to be discovered from the phenomenon alone. Another assurance always given is that to speak of forces implies no theory as to their nature: and that being so, it is impossible to see why the form of Force has been introduced into the sciences at all. In the second place the nature of Force is undoubtedly unknown: we are still without any necessity binding and connecting its content together in itself, as we are without necessity in the content, in so far as it is expressly limited and hence has its character by means of another thing outside it.

(1) Compared with the immediate relation of whole and parts, the relation between force and its putting-forth may be considered infinite. In it that identity of the two sides is realized, which in the former relation only existed for the observer. The whole, though we can see that it consists of parts, ceases to be a whole when it is divided: whereas force is only shown to be force when it exerts itself, and in its exercise only comes back to itself. The exercise is only force once more. Yet, on further examination even this relation will appear finite, and finite in virtue of this mediation: just as, conversely, the relation of whole and parts is obviously finite in virtue of its immediacy. The first and simplest evidence for the finitude of the mediated relation of force and its exercise is, that each and every force is conditioned and requires something else than itself for its subsistence. For instance, a special vehicle of magnetic force, as is well known, is iron, the other properties of which, such as its colour, specific weight, or relation to acids, are independent of this connection with magnetism. The same thing is seen in all other forces, which from one end to the other are found to be conditioned and mediated by something else than themselves. Another proof of the finite nature of force is that it requires solicitation before it can put itself forth. That through which the force is solicited, is itself another exertion of force, which cannot put itself forth without similar solicitation. This brings us either to a repetition of the infinite progression, or to a reciprocity of soliciting and being solicited. In either case we have no absolute beginning of motion. Force is not as yet, like the final cause, inherently self-determining: the content is given to it as determined, and force, when it exerts itself, is, according to the phrase, blind in its working. That phrase implies the distinction between abstract force-manifestation and teleological action.

(2) The oft-repeated statement, that the exercise of the force and not the force itself admits of being known, must be rejected as groundless. It is the very essence of force to manifest itself, and thus in the totality of manifestation, conceived as a law, we at the same time discover the force itself. And yet this assertion that force in its own self is unknowable betrays a well-grounded presentiment that this relation is finite. The several manifestations of a force at first meet us in indefinite multiplicity, and in their isolation seem accidental: but, reducing this multiplicity to its inner unity, which we term force, we see that the apparently contingent is necessary, by recognizing the law that rules it. But the different forces themselves are a multiplicity again, and in their mere juxtaposition seem to be contingent. Hence in empirical physics, we speak of the forces of gravity, magnetism, electricity, etc., and in empirical psychology of the forces of memory, imagination, will, and all the other faculties.

All this multiplicity again excites a craving to know these different forces as a single whole, nor would this craving be appeased even if the several forces were traced back to one common primary force. Such a primary force would be really no more than an empty abstraction, with as little content as the abstract thing-in-itself. And besides this, the correlation of force and manifestation is essentially a mediated correlation (of reciprocal dependence), and it must therefore contradict the notion of force to view it as primary or resting on itself.

Such being the case with the nature of force, though we may consent to let the world be called a manifestation of divine forces, we should object to have God himself viewed as a mere force. For force is after all a subordinate and finite category. At the so-called renaissance of the sciences, when steps were taken to trace the single phenomena of nature back to underlying forces, the Church branded the enterprise as impious. The argument of the Church was as follows. If it be the forces of gravitation, of vegetation, etc., which occasion the movements of the heavenly bodies, the growth of plants, etc., there is nothing left for divine providence, and God sinks to the level of a leisurely onlooker, surveying this play of forces. The students of nature, it is true, and Newton more than others, when they employed the reflective category of force to explain natural phenomena, have expressly pleaded that the honour of God, as the Creator and Governor of the world, would not thereby be impaired. Still the logical issue of this explanation by means of forces is that the inferential understanding proceeds to fix each of these forces, and to maintain them in their finitude as ultimate. And contrasted with this de-infinitized world of independent forces and matters, the only terms in which it is possible still to describe God will present him in the abstract infinity of an unknowable supreme Being in some other world far away. This is precisely the position of materialism, and of modern 'free-thinking', whose theology ignores what God is and restricts itself to the mere fact *that* he is. In this dispute therefore the Church and the religious mind have to a certain extent the right on their side. The finite forms of understanding certainly fail to fulfil the conditions for a knowledge either of Nature or of the formations in the world of Mind as they truly are. Yet on the other side it is impossible to overlook the formal right which, in the first place, entitles the empirical sciences to vindicate the right of thought to know the existent world in all the speciality of its content, and to seek something further than the bare statement of mere abstract faith that God created and governs the world. When our religious consciousness, resting on the authority of the Church, teaches us that God created the world by his almighty will, that he guides the stars in their courses, and vouchsafes to all his creatures their existence and their well-being, the question Why? is still left to answer. Now it is the answer to this question which forms the common task of empirical science and of philosophy. When religion refuses to recognize this problem, or the right to put it, and appeals to the unsearchableness of the decrees of God, it is taking up the same agnostic ground as is taken by the mere Enlightenment of understanding. Such an appeal is no better than an arbitrary dogmatism, which contravenes the express command of Christianity, to know God in spirit and in truth, and is prompted by a humility which is not Christian, but born of ostentatious bigotry.

§ 137

Force is a whole, which is in its own self negative self-relation; and as such a whole it continually pushes itself off from itself and puts itself forth. But since this reflection-into-another (corresponding to the distinction between the Parts of the Whole) is equally a reflection-into-self, this out-putting is the way and means by which Force that returns back into itself is as a Force. The very act of out-putting accordingly sets in abeyance the diversity of the two sides which is found in this correlation, and expressly states the identity which virtually constitutes their content. The truth of Force and utterance therefore is that relation, in which the two sides are distinguished only as Outward and Inward.

§ 138

(γ) The **Inward** (Interior) is the ground, when it stands as the mere form of the one side of the Appearance and the Correlation—the empty form of reflection-into-self. As a counterpart to it stands the **Outward** (Exterior)—Existence—also as the form of the other side of the correlation, with the empty characteristic of reflection-into-something-else. But Inward and Outward are identified: and their identity is identity brought to fullness in the content, that unity of reflection-into-self and reflection-into-other which was forced to appear in the movement of force. Both are the same one totality, and this unity makes them the content.

§ 139

In the first place then, Exterior is the same content as Interior. What is inwardly is also found outwardly, and vice versa. The appearance shows nothing that is not in the essence, and in the essence there is nothing but what is manifested.

§ 140

In the second place, Inward and Outward, as formal terms, are also reciprocally opposed, and that thoroughly. The one is the abstraction of identity with self; the other, of mere multiplicity or reality. But as stages of the one form, they are essentially identical so that whatever is at first explicitly put only in the one abstraction, is also as plainly and at one step only in the other. Therefore what is only internal is also only external: and what is only external, is so far only at first internal.

It is the customary mistake of reflection to take the essence to be merely the interior. If it be so taken, even this way of looking at it is purely external, and that sort of essence is the empty external abstraction.

Ins Innere der Natur
Dringt kein erschaffner Geist,
Zu glücklich wenn er nur
Die äußere Schaale weißt.[1]

It ought rather to have been said that, if the essence of nature is ever described as the inner part, the person who so decribes it only knows its outer shell. In Being as a whole, or even in mere sense-perception, the notion is at first only an inward, and for that very reason is something external to Being, a subjective thinking and being, devoid of truth. In Nature as well as in Mind, so long as the notion, design, or law are at first the inner capacity, mere possibilities, they are first only an external, inorganic nature, the knowledge of a third person, alien force, and the like. As a man is outwardly, that is to say in his actions (not of course in his merely bodily outwardness), so is he inwardly: and if his virtue, morality, etc. are only inwardly his—that is if they exist only in his intentions and sentiments, and his outward acts are not identical with them—the one half of him is as hollow and empty as the other.

[1] Compare Goethe's indignant outcry 'To Natural Science' (vol. i, pt. 3):

Das hör' ich sechzig Jahre wiederholen,
Und fluche drauf, aber verstohlen,—
Natur hat weder Kern noch Schaale,
Alles ist sie mit einem Male.

The relation of Outward and Inward unites the two relations that precede, and at the same time sets in abeyance mere relativity and phenomenality in general. Yet so long as understanding keeps the Inward and Outward fixed in their separation, they are empty forms, the one as null as the other. Not only in the study of nature, but also of the spiritual world, much depends on a just appreciation of the relation of inward and outward, and especially on avoiding the misconception that the former only is the essential point on which everything turns, while the latter is unessential and trivial. We find this mistake made when, as is often done, the difference between nature and mind is traced back to the abstract difference between inner and outer. As for nature, it certainly is in the gross external, not merely to the mind, but even on its own part. But to call it external 'in the gross' is not to imply an abstract externality—for there is no such thing. It means rather that the Idea which forms the common content of nature and mind, is found in nature as outward only, and for that very reason only inward. The abstract understanding, with its 'either—or', may struggle against this conception of nature. It is none the less obviously found in our other modes of consciousness, particularly in religion. It is the lesson of religion that nature, no less than the spiritual world, is a revelation of God: but with this distinction, that while nature never gets so far as to be conscious of its divine essence, that consciousness is the express problem of the mind, which in the matter of that problem is as yet finite. Those who look upon the essence of nature as mere inwardness, and therefore inaccessible to us, take up the same line as that ancient creed which regarded God as envious and jealous; a creed which both Plato and Aristotle pronounced against long ago. All that God is, he imparts and reveals; and he does so, at first, in and through nature.

Any object indeed is faulty and imperfect when it is only inward, and thus at the same time only outward, or (which is the same thing) when it is only an outward and thus only an inward. For instance, a child, taken in the gross as human being, is no doubt a rational creature; but the reason of the child as child is at first a mere inward, in the shape of his natural ability or vocation, etc. This mere inward, at the same time, has for the child the form of a mere outward, in the shape of the will of his parents, the attainments of his teachers, and the whole world of reason that environs him. The education and instruction of a child aim at making him actually and for himself what he is at first potentially and therefore for others, viz. for his grown-up friends. The reason, which at first exists in the child only as an inner possibility, is actualized through education: and conversely, the child by these means becomes conscious that the goodness, religion, and science which he had at first looked upon as an outward authority, are his own and inward nature. As with the child so it is in this matter with the adult, when, in opposition to his true destiny, his intellect and will remain in the bondage of the natural man. Thus, the criminal sees the punishment to which he has to submit as an act of violence from without: whereas in fact the penalty is only the manifestation of his own criminal will.

From what has now been said, we may learn what to think of a man who, when blamed for his shortcomings, or, it may be, his discreditable acts, appeals to the (professedly) excellent intentions and sentiments of the inner self he distinguishes therefrom. There certainly may be individual cases where the malice of outward circumstances frustrates well-meant designs, and disturbs the execution of the best-laid plans. But in general even here the essential unity between inward and outward is maintained. We are thus justified in saying that a man is what he does; and the lying vanity which consoles itself with the feeling of inward excellence may be confronted with the words of the Gospel: 'By their fruits ye shall know them.' That grand saying applies primarily in a moral and religious aspect, but it also holds good in reference to performances in art and science. The keen eye of a teacher who perceives in his pupil decided evidences of talent, may lead him to state his opinion that a Raphael or a Mozart lies hidden in the boy: and the result will show how far such an opinion was well-founded. But if a daub of a painter, or a poetaster, soothe themselves by the conceit that their head is full of high ideals, their consolation is a poor one; and if they insist on being judged not by their actual works but by their projects, we may safely reject their pretensions as unfounded and unmeaning. The converse case however also occurs. In passing judgment on men who have accomplished something great and good, we often make use of the false distinction between inward and outward. All that they have accomplished, we say, is outward merely; inwardly they were acting from some very different motive, such as a desire to gratify their vanity or other unworthy passion. This is the spirit of envy. Incapable of any great action of its own, envy tries hard to depreciate greatness and to bring it down to its own level. Let us, rather, recall the fine expression of Goethe, that there is no remedy but Love against great superiorities of others. We may seek to rob men's great actions of their grandeur, by the insinuation of hypocrisy; but, though it is possible that men in an instance now and then may dissemble and disguise a good deal, they cannot conceal the whole of their inner self, which infallibly betrays itself in the *decursus vitae*. Even here it is true that a man is nothing but the series of his actions.

What is called the 'pragmatic' writing of history has in modern times frequently sinned in its treatment of great historical characters, and defaced and tarnished the true conception of them by this fallacious separation of the outward from the inward. Not content with telling the unvarnished tale of the great acts which have been wrought by the heroes of the world's history, and with acknowledging that their inward being corresponds with the import of their acts, the pragmatic historian fancies himself justified and even obliged to trace the supposed secret motives that lie behind the open facts of the record. The historian, in that case, is supposed to write with more depth in proportion as he succeeds in tearing away the aureole from all that has been heretofore held grand and glorious, and in depressing it, so far as its origin and proper significance are concerned, to the level of vulgar mediocrity. To make these pragmatic researches in history easier, it is usual to recommend the study of psychology, which is supposed to make us acquainted with the real motives of human actions. The psychology in question however is only that petty knowledge of men, which looks away from the essential and permanent in human nature to fasten its glance on the casual and private features shown in isolated instincts and passions. A pragmatic psychology ought at least to leave the historian, who investigates the motives at the ground of great actions, a choice between the 'substantial' interests of patriotism, justice, religious truth, and the like, on the one hand, and the subjective and 'formal' interests of vanity, ambition, avarice, and the like, on the other. The latter, however, are the motives which must be viewed by the pragmatist as really efficient, otherwise the assumption of a contrast between the inward (the disposition of the agent) and the outward (the import of the action) would fall to the ground. But inward and outward have in truth the same content; and the right doctrine is the very reverse of this pedantic judiciality. If the heroes of history had been actuated by subjective and formal interests alone, they would never have accomplished what they have. And if we have due regard to the unity between the inner and the outer, we must own that great men willed what they did, and did what they willed.

§ 141

The empty abstractions, by means of which the one identical content perforce continues in the two correlatives, suspend themselves in the immediate transition, the one in the other. The content is itself nothing but their identity (§ 138): and these abstractions are the seeming of essence, put as seeming. By the manifestation of force the inward is put into existence: but this putting is the mediation by empty abstractions. In its own self the intermediating process vanishes to the immediacy, in which the inward and the outward are absolutely identical and their difference is distinctly no more than assumed and imposed. This identity is Actuality.

C. ACTUALITY

§ 142

Actuality is the unity, become immediate, of essence with existence, or of inward with outward. The utterance of the actual is the actual itself: so that in this utterance it remains just as essential, and only is essential, in so far as it is in immediate external existence.

We have ere this met Being and Existence as forms of the immediate. Being is, in general, unreflected immediacy and transition into another. Existence is immediate unity of being and reflection; hence appearance: it comes from the ground, and falls to the ground. In actuality this unity is explicitly put, and the two sides of the relation identified. Hence the actual is exempted from transition, and its externality is its energizing. In that energizing it is reflected into itself: its existence is only the manifestation of itself, not of an other.

Actuality and thought (or Idea) are often absurdly opposed. How commonly we hear people saying that, though no objection can be urged against the truth and correctness of a certain thought, there is nothing of the kind to be seen in actuality, or it cannot be actually carried out! People who use such language only prove that they have not properly apprehended the nature either of thought or of actuality. Thought in such a case is, on one hand, the synonym for a subjective conception, plan, intention, or the like, just as actuality, on the other, is made synonymous with external and sensible existence. This is all very well in common life, where great laxity is allowed in the categories and the names given to them; and it may of course happen that, e.g., the plan, or so-called idea, say, of a certain method of taxation, is good and advisable in the abstract, but that nothing of the sort is found in so-called actuality, or could possibly be carried out under the given conditions. But when the abstract understanding gets hold of these categories and exaggerates the distinction they imply into a hard and fast line of contrast, when it tells us that in this actual world we must knock ideas out of our heads, it is necessary energetically to protest against these doctrines, alike in the name of science and of sound reason. For on the one hand Ideas are not confined to our heads merely, nor is the Idea, on the whole, so feeble as to leave the question of its actualization or non-actualization dependent on our will. The Idea is rather the absolutely active as well as actual. And on the other hand actuality is not so bad and irrational, as purblind or wrong-headed and muddle-brained would-be reformers imagine. So far is actuality, as distinguished from mere appearance, and primarily presenting a unity of inward and outward, from being in contrariety with reason, that it is rather thoroughly reasonable, and everything which is not reasonable must on that very ground cease to be held actual. The same view may be traced in the usages of educated speech, which declines to give the name of real poet or real statesman to a poet or a statesman who can do nothing really meritorious or reasonable.

In that vulgar conception of actuality which mistakes for it what is palpable and directly obvious to the senses, we must seek the ground of a widespread prejudice about the relation of the philosophy of Aristotle to that of Plato. Popular opinion makes the difference to be as follows. While Plato recognizes the idea and only the idea as the truth, Aristotle, rejecting the idea, keeps to what is actual, and is on that account to be considered the founder and chief of empiricism. On this it may be remarked: that although actuality certainly is the principle of the Aristotelian philosophy, it is not the vulgar actuality of what is immediately at hand, but the idea as actuality. Where then lies the controversy of Aristotle against Plato? It lies in this. Aristotle calls the Platonic idea a mere *δύναμις*, and establishes in opposition to Plato that the idea, which both equally recognize to be the only truth, is essentially to be viewed as an *ἐνέργεια*, in other words, as the inward which is quite to the fore, or as the unity of inner and outer, or as actuality, in the emphatic sense here given to the word.

§ 143

Such a concrete category as Actuality includes the characteristics aforesaid and their difference, and is therefore also the development of them, in such a way that, as it has them, they are at the same time plainly understood to be a show, to be assumed or imposed (§ 141).

(*α*) Viewed as an identity in general, Actuality is first of all **Possibility**—the reflection-into-self which, as in contrast with the concrete unity of the actual, is taken and made an abstract and unessential essentiality. Possibility is what is essential to reality, but in such a way that it is at the same time only a possibility.

It was probably the import of Possibility which induced Kant to regard it along with necessity and actuality as Modalities, 'since these categories do not in the least increase the notion as object, but only express its relation to the faculty of knowledge'. For Possibility is really the bare abstraction of reflection-into-self—what was formerly called the Inward, only that it is now taken to mean the external inward, lifted out of reality and with the being of a mere supposition, and is thus, sure enough, supposed only as a bare modality, an abstraction which comes short, and, in more concrete terms, belongs only to subjective thought. It is otherwise with Actuality and Necessity. They are anything but a mere sort and mode for something else: in fact the very reverse of that. If they are supposed, it is as the concrete, not merely suppositious, but intrinsically complete.

As Possibility is, in the first instance, the mere form of identity-with-self (as compared with the concrete which is actual), the rule for it merely is that a thing must not be self-contradictory. Thus everything is possible; for an act of abstraction can give any content this form of identity. Everything however is as impossible as it is possible. In every content—which is and must be concrete—the speciality of its nature may be viewed as a specialized contrariety and in that way as a contradiction. Nothing therefore can be more meaningless than to speak of such possibility and impossibility. In philosophy, in particular, there should never be a word said of showing that 'It is possible', or 'There is still another possibility', or, to adopt another phraseology, 'It is conceivable'. The same consideration should warn the writer of history against employing a category which has now been explained to be on its own merits untrue: but the subtlety of the empty understanding finds its chief pleasure in the fantastic ingenuity of suggesting possibilities and lots of possibilities.

Our picture-thought is at first disposed to see in possibility the richer and more comprehensive, in actuality the poorer and narrower category. Everything, it is said, is possible, but everything which is possible is not on that account actual. In real truth, however, if we deal with them as thoughts, actuality is the more comprehensive, because it is the concrete thought which includes possibility as an abstract element. And that superiority is to some extent expressed in our ordinary mode of thought when we speak of the possible, in distinction from the actual, as *only* possible. Possibility is often said to consist in a thing's being thinkable. 'Think', however, in this use of the word, only means to conceive any content under the form of an abstract identity. Now every content can be brought under this form, since nothing is required except to separate it from the relations in which it stands. Hence any content, however absurd and nonsensical, can be viewed as possible. It is possible that the moon might fall upon the earth tonight; for the moon is a body separate from the earth—and may as well fall down upon it as a stone thrown into the air does. It is possible that the Sultan may become Pope; for, being a man, he may be converted to the Christian faith, may become a Catholic priest, and so on. In language like this about possibilities, it is chiefly the law of the sufficient ground or reason which is manipulated in the style already explained. Everything, it is said, is possible, for which you can state some ground. The less education a man has, or, in other words, the less he knows of the specific connections of the objects to which he directs his observations, the greater is his tendency to launch out into all sorts of empty possibilities. An instance of this habit in the political sphere is seen in the pot-house politician. In practical life too it is no uncommon thing to see ill will and indolence slink behind the category of possibility, in order to escape definite obligations. To such conduct the same remarks apply as were made in connection with the law of sufficient ground. Reasonable and practical men refuse to be imposed upon by the possible, for the simple ground that it is possible only. They stick to the actual (not meaning by that word merely whatever immediately is now and here). Many of the proverbs of common life express the same contempt for what is abstractly possible. 'A bird in the hand is worth two in the bush.'

After all there is as good reason for taking everything to be impossible, as to be possible: for every content (a content is always concrete) includes not only diverse but even opposite characteristics. Nothing is so impossible, for instance, as this, that I am: for 'I' is at the same time simple self-relation and, as undoubtedly, relation to something else. The same may be seen in every other fact in the natural or spiritual world. Matter, it may be said, is impossible: for it is the unity of attraction and repulsion. The same is true of life, law, freedom, and above all of God himself, as the true, i.e. the triune God—a notion of God, which the abstract 'Enlightenment' of Understanding, in conformity with its canons, rejected on the allegation that it was contradictory in thought. Generally speaking, it is the empty understanding which haunts these empty forms: and the business of philosophy in the matter is to show how null and meaningless they are. Whether a thing is possible or impossible, depends altogether on the subject-matter: that is, on the sum total of the elements in actuality, which, as it opens itself out, discloses itself to be necessity.

§ 144

(β) But the Actual in its distinction from possibility (which is reflection-into-self) is itself only the outward concrete, the unessential immediate. In other words, to such extent as the actual is primarily (§ 142) the simple merely immediate unity of Inward and Outward, it is obviously made an unessential outward, and thus at the same time (§ 140) it is merely inward, the abstraction of reflection-into-self. Hence it is itself characterized as a merely possible. When thus valued at the rate of a mere possibility, the actual is a **Contingent** or Accidental, and, conversely, possibility is mere Accident itself or **Chance.**

§ 145

Possibility and Contingency are the two factors of Actuality—Inward and Outward, put as mere forms which constitute the externality of the actual. They have their reflection-into-self on the body of actual fact, or content, with its intrinsic definiteness which gives the essential ground of their characterization. The finitude of the contingent and the possible lies, therefore, as we now see, in the distinction of the form-determination from the content: and, therefore, it depends on the content alone whether anything is contingent and possible.

As possibility is the mere *inside* of actuality, it is for that reason a mere *outside* actuality, in other words, Contingency. The contingent, roughly speaking, is what has the ground of its being not in itself but in somewhat else. Such is the aspect under which actuality first comes before consciousness, and which is often mistaken for actuality itself. But the contingent is only one side of the actual—the side, namely, of reflection on somewhat else. It is the actual, in the signification of something merely possible. Accordingly we consider the contingent to be what may or may not be, what may be in one way or in another, whose being or not-being, and whose being on this wise or otherwise, depends not upon itself but on something else. To overcome this contingency is, roughly speaking, the problem of science on the one hand; as in the range of practice, on the other, the end of action is to rise above the contingency of the will, or above caprice. It has however often happened, most of all in modern times, that contingency has been unwarrantably elevated, and had a value attached to it, both in nature and the world of mind, to which it has no just claim. Frequently Nature—to take it first—has been chiefly admired for the richness and variety of its structures. Apart, however, from what disclosure it contains of the Idea, this richness gratifies none of the higher interests of reason, and in its vast variety of structures, organic and inorganic, affords us only the spectacle of a contingency losing itself in vagueness. At any rate, the chequered scene presented by the several varieties of animals and plants, conditioned as it is by outward circumstances—the complex changes in the figuration and grouping of clouds, and the like—ought not to be ranked higher than the equally casual fancies of the mind which surrenders itself to its own caprices. The wonderment with which such phenomena are welcomed is a most abstract frame of mind, from which one should advance to a closer insight into the inner harmony and uniformity of nature.

Of contingency in respect of the Will it is especially important to form a proper estimate. The Freedom of the Will is an expression that often means mere free choice, or the will in the form of contingency. Freedom of choice, or the capacity for determining ourselves towards one thing or another, is undoubtedly a vital element in the will (which in its very notion is free); but instead of being freedom itself, it is only in the first instance a freedom in form. The genuinely free will, which includes free choice as suspended, is conscious to itself that its content is intrinsically firm and fast, and knows it at the same time to be thoroughly its own. A will, on the contrary, which remains standing on the grade of option, even supposing it does decide in favour of what is in import right and true, is always haunted by the conceit that it might, if it had so pleased, have decided in favour of the reverse course. When more narrowly examined, free choice is seen to be a contradiction, to this extent that its form and content stand in antithesis. The matter of choice is given, and known as a content dependent not on the will itself, but on outward circumstances. In reference to such a given content, freedom lies only in the form of choosing, which, as it is only a freedom in form, may consequently be regarded as freedom only in supposition. On an ultimate analysis it will be seen that the same outwardness of circumstances, on which is founded the content that the will finds to its hand, can alone account for the will giving its decision for the one and not the other of the two alternatives.

Although contingency, as it has thus been shown, is only one aspect in the whole of actuality, and therefore not to be mistaken for actuality itself, it has no less than the rest of the forms of the idea its due office in the world of objects. This is, in the first place, seen in Nature. On the surface of Nature, so to speak, Chance ranges unchecked, and that contingency must simply be recognized, without the pretension sometimes erroneously ascribed to philosophy, of seeking to find in it a could-only-be-so-and-not-otherwise. Nor is contingency less visible in the world of Mind. The will, as we have already remarked, includes contingency under the shape of option or free choice, but only as a vanishing and abrogated element. In respect of Mind and its works, just as in the case of Nature, we must guard against being so far misled by a well-meant endeavour after rational knowledge, as to try to exhibit the necessity of phenomena which are marked by a decided contingency, or, as the phrase is, to construe them *a priori*. Thus in language (although it be, as it were, the body of thought) Chance still unquestionably plays a decided part; and the same is true of the creations of law, of art, etc. The problem of science, and especially of philosophy, undoubtedly consists in eliciting the necessity concealed under the semblance of contingency. That, however, is far from meaning that the contingent belongs to our subjective conception alone, and must therefore be simply set aside, if we wish to get at the truth. All scientific researches which pursue this tendency exclusively lay themselves fairly open to the charge of mere jugglery and an over-strained precisianism.

§ 146

When more closely examined, what the aforesaid outward side of actuality implies is this. Contingency, which is actuality in its immediacy, is the self-identical, essentially only as a supposition which is no sooner made than it is revoked and leaves an existent externality. In this way, the external contingency is something presupposed, the immediate existence of which is at the same time a possibility, and has the vocation to be suspended, to be the possibility of something else. Now this possibility is the **Condition.**

The Contingent, as the immediate actuality, is at the same time the possibility of somewhat else—no longer however that abstract possibility which we had at first, but the possibility which *is*. And a possibility existent is a Condition. By the Condition of a thing we mean first, an existence, in short an immediate, and secondly the vocation of this immediate to be suspended and subserve the actualizing of something else. Immediate actuality is in general as such never what it ought to be; it is a finite actuality with an inherent flaw, and its vocation is to be consumed. But the other aspect of actuality is its essentiality. This is primarily the inside which as a mere possibility is no less destined to be suspended. Possibility thus suspended is the issuing of a new actuality, of which the first immediate actuality was the presupposition. Here we see the alternation which is involved in the notion of a Condition. The Conditions of a thing seem at first sight to involve no bias any way. Really however an immediate actuality of this kind includes in it the germ of something else altogether. At first this something else is only a possibility: but the form of possibility is soon suspended and translated into actuality. This new actuality thus issuing is the very inside of the immediate actuality which it uses up. Thus there comes into being quite another shape of things, and yet it is not an other: for the first actuality is only put as what it in essence was. The conditions which are sacrificed, which fall to the ground and are spent, only unite with themselves in the other actuality. Such in general is the nature of the process of actuality. The actual is no mere case of immediate Being, but, as essential Being, a suspension of its own immediacy, and thereby mediating itself with itself.

§ 147

(γ) When this externality (of actuality) is thus developed into a circle of the two categories of possibility and immediate actuality, showing the intermediation of the one by the other, it is what is called **Real Possibility.** Being such a circle, further, it is the totality, and thus the content, the actual fact or affair in its all-round definiteness. While in like manner, if we look at the distinction between the two characteristics in this unity, it realizes the concrete totality of the form, the immediate self-translation of inner into outer, and of outer into inner. This self-movement of the form is **Activity,** carrying into effect the fact or affair as a *real* ground which is self-suspended to actuality, and carrying into effect the contingent actuality, the conditions; i.e. it is their reflection-in-self, and their self-suspension to another actuality, the actuality of the actual fact. If all the conditions are at hand, the fact (event) *must* be actual; and the fact itself is one of the conditions: for being in the first place only inner, it is at first itself only presupposed. Developed actuality, as the coincident alternation of inner and outer, the alternation of their opposite motions combined into a single motion, is **Necessity.**

Necessity has been defined, and rightly so, as the union of possibility and actuality. This mode of expression, however, gives a superficial and therefore unintelligible description of the very difficult notion of necessity. It is difficult because it is the notion itself, only that its stages or factors are still as actualities, which are yet at the same time to be viewed as forms only, collapsing and transient. In the two following paragraphs, therefore, an exposition of the factors which constitute necessity must be given at greater length.

When anything is said to be necessary, the first question we ask is, Why? Anything necessary accordingly comes before us as something due to a supposition, the result of certain antecedents. If we go further than mere derivation from antecedents, however, we have not gained a complete notion of what necessity means. What is merely derivative, is what it is, not through itself, but through something else; and in this way it too is merely contingent. What is necessary, on the other hand, we would have be what it is through itself; and thus, although derivative, it must still contain the antecedent whence it is derived as a vanishing element in itself. Hence we say of what is necessary, 'It is'. We thus hold it to be simple self-relation, in which all dependence on something else is removed.

Necessity is often said to be blind. If that means that in the process of necessity the End or final cause is not explicitly and overtly present, the statement is correct. The process of necessity begins with the existence of scattered circumstances which appear to have no interconnection and no concern one with another. These circumstances are an immediate actuality which collapses, and out of this negation a new actuality proceeds. Here we have a content which in point of form is doubled, once as content of the final realized fact, and once as content of the scattered circumstances which appear as if they were positive, and make themselves at first felt in that character. The latter content is in itself nought and is accordingly inverted into its negative, thus becoming content of the realized fact. The immediate circumstances fall to the ground as contitions, but are at the same time retained as content of the ultimate reality. From such circumstances and conditions there has, as we say, proceeded quite another thing, and it is for that reason that we call this process of necessity blind. If on the contrary we consider teleological action, we have in the end of action a content which is already foreknown. This activity therefore is not blind but seeing. To say that the world is ruled by Providence implies that design, as what has been absolutely predetermined, is the active principle, so that the issue corresponds to what has been foreknown and forewilled.

The theory however which regards the world as determined through necessity and the belief in a divine providence are by no means mutually excluding points of view. The intellectual principle underlying the idea of divine providence will hereafter be shown to be the notion. But the notion is the truth of necessity, which it contains in suspension in itself; just as, conversely, necessity is the notion implicit. Necessity is blind only so long as it is not understood. There is nothing therefore more mistaken than the charge of blind fatalism made against the Philosophy of History, when it takes for its problem to understand the necessity of every event. The philosophy of history rightly understood takes the rank of a Théodicée; and those, who fancy they honour Divine Providence by excluding necessity from it, are really degrading it by this exclusiveness to a blind and irrational caprice. In the simple language of the religious mind which speaks of God's eternal and immutable decrees, there is implied an express recognition that necessity forms part of the essence of God. In his difference from God, man, with his own private opinion and will, follows the call of caprice and arbitrary humour, and thus often finds his acts turn out something quite different from what he had meant and willed. But God knows what he wills, is determined in his eternal will neither by accident from within nor from without, and what he wills he also accomplishes, irresistibly.

Necessity gives a point of view which has important bearings upon our sentiments and behaviour. When we look upon events as necessary, our situation seems at first sight to lack freedom completely. In the creed of the ancients, as we know, necessity figured as Destiny. The modern point of view, on the contrary, is that of Consolation. And Consolation means that, if we renounce our aims and interests, we do so only in prospect of receiving compensation. Destiny, on the contrary, leaves no room for Consolation. But a close examination of the ancient feeling about destiny will not by any means reveal a sense of bondage to its power. Rather the reverse. This will clearly appear, if we remember that the sense of bondage springs from inability to surmount the antithesis, and from looking at what *is*, and what happens, as contradictory to what *ought* to be and happen. In the ancient mind the feeling was more of the following kind: Because such a thing is, it is, and as it is, so ought it to be. Here there is no contrast to be seen, and therefore no sense of bondage, no pain, and no sorrow. True, indeed, as already remarked, this attitude towards destiny is void of consolation. But then, on the other hand, it is a frame of mind which does not need consolation, so long as personal subjectivity has not acquired its infinite significance. It is this point on which special stress should be laid in comparing the ancient sentiment with that of the modern and Christian world.

By Subjectivity, however, we may understand, in the first place, only the natural and finite subjectivity, with its contingent and arbitrary content of private interests and inclinations—all, in short, that we call person as distinguished from thing: taking 'thing' in the emphatic sense of the word (in which we use the (correct) expression that it is a question of *things* and not of *persons*). In this sense of subjectivity we cannot help admiring the tranquil resignation of the ancients to destiny, and feeling that it is a much higher and worthier mood than that of the moderns, who obstinately pursue their subjective aims, and when they find themselves constrained to resign the hope of reaching them, console themselves with the prospect of a reward in some other shape. But the term subjectivity is not to be confined merely to the bad and finite kind of it which is contrasted with the thing (fact). In its truth subjectivity is immanent in the fact, and as a subjectivity thus infinite is the very truth of the fact. Thus regarded, the doctrine of consolation receives a newer and a higher significance. It is in this sense that the Christian religion is to be regarded as the religion of consolation, and even of absolute consolation. Christianity, we know, teaches that God wishes all men to be saved. That teaching declares that subjectivity has an infinite value. And that consoling power of Christianity just lies in the fact that God himself is in it known as the absolute subjectivity, so that, inasmuch as subjectivity involves the element of particularity, *our* particular personality too is recognized not merely as something to be solely and simply nullified, but as at the same time something to be preserved. The gods of the ancient world were also, it is true, looked upon as personal; but the personality of a Zeus and an Apollo is not a real personality: it is only a figure in the mind. In other words, these gods are mere personifications, which, being such, do not know themselves, and are only known. An evidence of this defect and this powerlessness of the old gods is found even in the religious beliefs of antiquity. In the ancient creeds not only men, but even gods, were represented as subject to destiny (*πεπρωμένον* or *εἱμαρμένη*), a destiny which we must conceive as necessity not unveiled, and thus as something wholly impersonal, selfless, and blind. On the other hand, the Christian God is God not known merely, but also self-knowing; he is a personality not merely figured in our minds, but rather absolutely actual.

We must refer to the Philosophy of Religion for a further discussion of the points here touched. But we may note in passing how important it is for any man to meet everything that befalls him with the spirit of the old proverb which describes each man as the architect of his own fortune. That means that it is only himself after all of which a man has the usufruct. The other way would be to lay the blame of whatever we experience upon other men, upon unfavourable circumstances, and the like. And this is a fresh example of the language of unfreedom, and at the same time the spring of discontent. If man saw, on the contrary, that whatever happens to him is only the outcome of himself, and that he only bears his own guilt, he would stand free, and in everything that came upon him would have the consciousness that he suffered no wrong. A man who lives in dispeace with himself and his lot commits much that is perverse and amiss, for no other reason than because of the false opinion that he is wronged by others. No doubt too there is a great deal of chance in what befalls us. But the chance has its root in the 'natural' man. So long however as a man is otherwise conscious that he is free, his harmony of soul and peace of mind will not be destroyed by the disagreeables that befall him. It is their view of necessity, therefore, which is at the root of the discontent of men, and which in that way determines their destiny itself.

§ 148

Among the three elements in the process of necessity, the Condition, the Fact, and the Activity:

a. The Condition is (α) what is presupposed or ante-stated, i.e. it is not only supposed or stated, and so only a correlative to the fact, but also prior, and so independent, a contingent and external circumstance which exists without respect to the fact. While thus contingent, however, this presupposed or ante-stated term, in respect withal of the fact, which is the totality, is a complete circle of conditions. (β) The conditions are passive, are used as materials for the fact, into the content of which they thus enter. They are likewise intrinsically conformable to this content, and already contain its whole characteristic.

b. The Fact is also (α) something presupposed or ante-stated, i.e. it is at first, and as supposed, only inner and possible, and also, being prior, an independent content by itself. (β) By using up the conditions, it receives its external existence, the realization of the articles of its content, which reciprocally correspond to the conditions, so that while it presents itself out of these as the facts, it also proceeds from them.

c. The Activity similarly has (α) an independent existence of its own (as a man, a character), and at the same time it is possible only where the conditions are and the fact. (β) It is the movement which translates the conditions into fact, and the latter into the former as the side of existence, or rather the movement which educes the fact from the conditions in which it is potentially present, and which gives existence to the fact by abolishing the existence possessed by the conditions.

In so far as these three elements stand to each other in the shape of independent existences, this process has the aspect of an outward necessity. Outward necessity has a limited content for its fact. For the fact is this whole, in phase of singleness. But since in its form this whole is external to itself, it is self-externalized even in its own self and in its content, and this externality, attaching to the fact, is a limit of its content.

§ 149

Necessity, then, is potentially the one essence, self-same but not full of content, in the reflected light of which its distinctions take the form of independent realities. This self-sameness is at the same time, as absolute form, the activity which reduces into dependency and mediates into immediacy. Whatever is necessary is through an other, which is broken up into the mediating ground (the Fact and the Activity) and an immediate actuality or accidental circumstance, which is at the same time a Condition. The necessary, being through an other, is not in and for itself: hypothetical, it is a mere result of assumption. But this intermediation is just as immediate however the abrogation of itself. The ground and contingent condition is translated into immediacy, by which that dependency is now lifted up into actuality, and the fact has closed with itself. In this return to itself the necessary simply and positively *is*, as unconditioned actuality. The necessary is so, mediated through a circle of circumstances: it is so, because the circumstances are so, and at the same time it is so, unmediated: it is so, because it is.

(a) *Relationship of Substantiality*

§ 150

The necessary is in itself an absolute correlation of elements, i.e. the process developed (in the preceding paragraphs), in which the correlation also suspends itself to absolute identity.

In its immediate form it is the relationship of Substance and Accident. The absolute self-identity of this relationship is Substance as such, which as necessity gives the negative to this form of inwardness, and thus invests itself with actuality, but which also gives the negative to this outward thing. In this negativity, the actual, as immediate, is only an accidental which through this bare possibility passes over into another actuality. This transition is the identity of substance, regarded as form-activity (§§ 148, 149).

§ 151

Substance is accordingly the totality of the **Accidents**, revealing itself in them as their absolute negativity (that is to say, as absolute power) and at the same time as the wealth of all content. This content however is nothing but that very revelation, since the character (being reflected in itself to make content) is only a passing stage of the form which passes away in the power of substance. Substantiality is the absolute form-activity and the power of necessity: all content is but a vanishing element which merely belongs to this process, where there is an absolute revulsion of form and content into one another.

In the history of philosophy we meet with Substance as the principle of Spinoza's system. On the import and value of that much-praised and no less decried philosophy there has been great misunderstanding and a deal of talking since the days of Spinoza. The atheism and, as a further charge, the pantheism of the system has formed the commonest ground of accusation. These cries arise because of Spinoza's conception of God as substance, and substance only. What we are to think of this charge follows, in the first instance, from the place which substance takes in the system of the logical idea. Though an essential stage in the evolution of the idea, substance is not the same with absolute Idea, but the idea under the still limited form of necessity. It is true that God is necessity, or, as we may also put it, that he is the absolute Thing: he is however no less the absolute Person. That he is the absolute Person however is a point which the philosophy of Spinoza never reached: and on that side it falls short of the true notion of God which forms the content of religious consciousness in Christianity. Spinoza was by descent a Jew; and it is upon the whole the Oriental way of seeing things, according to which the nature of the finite world seems frail and transient, that has found its intellectual expression in his system. This Oriental view of the unity of substance certainly gives the basis for all real further development. Still it is not the final idea. It is marked by the absence of the principle of the Western world, the principle of individuality, which first appeared under a philosophic shape, contemporaneously with Spinoza, in the Monadology of Leibniz.

From this point we glance back to the alleged atheism of Spinoza. The charge will be seen to be unfounded if we remember that his system, instead of denying God, rather recognizes that he alone really is. Nor can it be maintained that the God of Spinoza, although he is described as alone true, is not the true God, and therefore as good as no God. If that were a just charge, it would only prove that all other systems, where speculation has not gone beyond a subordinate stage of the idea—that the Jews and Mohammedans who know God only as the Lord—and that even the many Christians for whom God is merely the most high, unknowable, and transcendent being, are as much atheists as Spinoza. The so-called atheism of Spinoza is merely an exaggeration of the fact that he defrauds the principle of difference or finitude of its due. Hence his system, as it holds that there is properly speaking no world, at any rate that the world has no positive being, should rather be styled Acosmism. These considerations will also show what is to be said of the charge of Pantheism. If Pantheism means, as it often does, the doctrine which takes finite things in their finitude and in the complex of them to be God, we must acquit the system of Spinoza of the crime of Pantheism. For in that system, finite things and the world as a whole are denied all truth. On the other hand, the philosophy which is Acosmism is for that reason certainly pantheistic.

The shortcoming thus acknowledged to attach to the content turns out at the same time to be a shortcoming in respect of form. Spinoza puts substance at the head of his system, and defines it to be the unity of thought and extension, without demonstrating how he gets to this distinction, or how he traces it back to the unity of substance. The further treatment of the subject proceeds in what is called the mathematical method. Definitions and axioms are first laid down: after them comes a series of theorems, which are proved by an analytical reduction of them to these unproved postulates. Although the system of Spinoza, and that even by those who altogether reject its contents and results, is praised for the strict sequence of its method, such unqualified praise of the form is as little justified as an unqualified rejection of the content. The defect of the content is that the form is not known as immanent in it, and therefore only approaches it as an outer and subjective form. As intuitively accepted by Spinoza without a previous mediation by dialectic, Substance, as the universal negative power, is as it were a dark shapeless abyss which engulfs all definite content as radically null, and produces from itself nothing that has a positive subsistence of its own.

§ 152

At the stage where substance, as absolute power, is the self-relating power (itself a merely inner possibility), which thus determines itself to accidentality—from which power the externality it thereby creates is distinguished—necessity is a correlation strictly so called, just as in the first form of necessity it is substance. This is the correlation of Causality.

(*b*) *Relationship of Causality*

§ 153

Substance is **Cause**, in so far as substance reflects into self as against its passage into accidentality and so stands as the *primary* fact, but again no less suspends this reflection-into-self (its bare possibility), lays itself down as the negative of itself, and thus produces an **Effect**, an actuality, which, though so far only assumed as a sequence, is through the process that effectuates it at the same time necessary.

As primary fact, the cause is qualified as having absolute independence and a subsistence maintained in face of the effect: but in the necessity, whose identity constitutes that primariness itself, it is wholly passed into the effect. So far again as we can speak of a definite content, there is no content in the effect that is not in the cause. That identity in fact is the absolute content itself: but it is no less also the form-characteristic. The primariness of the cause is suspended in the effect in which the cause makes itself a dependent being. The cause however does not for that reason vanish and leave the effect to be alone actual. For this dependency is in like manner directly suspended, and is rather the reflection of the cause in itself, its primariness: in short, it is in the effect that the cause first becomes actual and a cause. The cause consequently is in its full truth *causa sui*. Jacobi, sticking to the partial conception of mediation (in his *Letters on Spinoza*, second edit., p. 416), has treated the *causa sui* (and the *effectus sui* is the same), which is the absolute truth of the cause, as a mere formalism. He has also made the remark that God ought to be defined not as the ground of things, but essentially as cause. A more thorough consideration of the nature of cause would have shown that Jacobi did not by this means gain what he intended. Even in the finite cause and its conception we can see this identity between cause and effect in point of content. The rain (the cause) and the wet (the effect) are the self-same existing water. In point of form the cause (rain) is dissipated or lost in the effect (wet): but in that case the result can no longer be described as effect; for without the cause it is nothing, and we should have only the unrelated wet left.

In the common acceptation of the causal relation the cause is finite, to such extent as its content is so (as is also the case with finite substance), and so far as cause and effect are conceived as two several independent existences: which they are, however, only when we leave the causal relation out of sight. In the finite sphere we never get over the difference of the form-characteristics in their relation: and hence we turn the matter round and define the cause also as something dependent or as an effect. This again has another cause, and thus there grows up a progress from effects to causes *ad infinitum*. There is a descending progress too: the effect, looked at in its identity with the cause, is itself defined as a cause, and at the same time as another cause, which again has other effects, and so on for ever.

The way understanding bristles up against the idea of substance is equalled by its readiness to use the relation of cause and effect. Whenever it is proposed to view any sum of fact as necessary, it is especially the relation of causality to which the reflective understanding makes a point of tracing it back. Now, although this relation does undoubtedly belong to necessity, it forms only one aspect in the process of that category. That process equally requires the suspension of the mediation involved in causality and the exhibition of it as simple self-relation. If we stick to causality as such, we have it not in its truth. Such a causality is merely finite, and its finitude lies in retaining the distinction between cause and effect unassimilated. But these two terms, if they are distinct, are also identical. Even in ordinary consciousness that identity may be found. We say that a cause is a cause, only when it has an effect, and vice versa. Both cause and effect are thus one and the same content: and the distinction between them is primarily only that the one lays down, and the other is laid down. This formal difference however again suspends itself, because the cause is not only a cause of something else, but also a cause of itself; while the effect is not only an effect of something else, but also an effect of itself. The finitude of things consists accordingly in this. While cause and effect are in their notion identical, the two forms present themselves severed so that, though the cause is also an effect, and the effect also a cause, the cause is not an effect in the same connection as it is a cause, nor the effect a cause in the same connection as it is an effect. This again gives the infinite progress, in the shape of an endless series of causes, which shows itself at the same time as an endless series of effects.

§ 154

The effect is different from the cause. The former as such has a being dependent on the latter. But such a dependence is likewise reflection-into-self and immediacy: and the action of the cause, as it constitutes the effect, is at the same time the pre-constitution of the effect, so long as effect is kept separate from cause. There is already in existence another substance on which the effect takes place. As immediate, this substance is not a self-related negativity and *active*, but *passive*. Yet it is a substance, and it is therefore active also: it therefore suspends the immediacy it was originally put forward with, and the effect which was put into it: it reacts, i.e. suspends the activity of the first substance. But this first substance also in the same way sets aside its own immediacy, or the effect which is put into it; it thus suspends the activity of the other substance and reacts. In this manner causality passes into the relation of **Action and Reaction**, or **Reciprocity**.

In Reciprocity, although causality is not yet invested with its true characteristic, the rectilinear movement out from causes to effects, and from effects to causes, is bent round and back into itself, and thus the progress *ad infinitum* of causes and effects is, as a progress, really and truly suspended. This bend, which transforms the infinite progression into a self-contained relationship, here as always the plain reflection that in the above meaningless repetition there is only one and the same thing, viz. one cause and another, and their connection with one another. Reciprocity—which is the development of this relation—itself however only distinguishes turn and turn about—not causes, but factors of causation, in each of which, just because they are inseparable (on the principle of the identity that the cause is cause in the effect, and vice versa), the other factor is also equally supposed.

(*c*) *Reciprocity or Action and Reaction*

§ 155

The characteristics which in Reciprocal Action are retained as distinct are (α) potentially the same. The one side is a cause, is primary, active, passive, etc., just as the other is. Similarly the presupposition of another side and the action upon it, the immediate primariness and the dependence produced by the alternation, are one and the same on both sides. The cause assumed to be first is on account of its immediacy passive, a dependent being, and an effect. The distinction of the causes spoken of as two is accordingly void: and properly speaking there is only one cause, which, while it suspends itself (as substance) in its effect, also rises in this operation only to independent existence as a cause.

§ 156

But this unity of the double cause is also (β) actual. All this alternation is properly the cause in act of constituting itself and in such constitution lies its being. The nullity of the distinctions is not only potential, or a reflection of ours (§ 155). Reciprocal action just means that each characteristic we impose is also to be suspended and inverted into its opposite, and that in this way the essential nullity of the 'moments' is explicitly stated. An effect is introduced into the primariness; in other words, the primariness is abolished: the action of a cause becomes reaction, and so on.

Reciprocal action realizes the causal relation in its complete development. It is this relation, therefore, in which reflection usually takes shelter when the conviction grows that things can no longer be studied satisfactorily from a causal point of view, on account of the infinite progress already spoken of. Thus in historical research the question may be raised in a first form, whether the character and manners of a nation are the cause of its constitution and its laws, or if they are not rather the effect. Then, as the second step, the character and manners on one side and the constitution and laws on the other are conceived on the principle of reciprocity: and in that case the cause in the same connection as it is a cause will at the same time be an effect, and vice versa. The same thing is done in the study of Nature, and especially of living organisms. There the several organs and functions are similarly seen to stand to each other in the relation of reciprocity. Reciprocity is undoubtedly the proximate truth of the relation of cause and effect, and stands, so to say, on the threshold of the notion; but on that very ground, supposing that our aim is a thoroughly comprehensive idea, we should not rest content with applying this relation. If we get no further than studying a given content under the point of view of reciprocity, we are taking up an attitude which leaves matters utterly incomprehensible. We are left with a mere dry fact; and the call for mediation, which is the chief motive in applying the relation of causality, is still unanswered. And if we look more narrowly into the dissatisfaction felt in applying the relation of reciprocity, we shall see that it consists in the circumstance that this relation, instead of being treated as an equivalent for the notion, ought, first of all, to be known and understood in its own nature. And to understand the relation of action we must not let the two sides rest in their state of mere given facts, but recognize them, as has been shown in the two paragraphs preceding, for factors of a third and higher, which is the notion and nothing else. To make, for example, the manners of the Spartans the cause of their constitution and their constitution conversely the cause of their manners, may no doubt be in a way correct. But, as we have comprehended neither the manners nor the constitution of the nation, the result of such reflections can never be final or satisfactory. The satisfactory point will be reached only when these two, as well as all other, special aspects of Spartan life and Spartan history are seen to be founded in this notion.

§ 157

This pure self-reciprocation is therefore **Necessity** unveiled or realized. The link of necessity *qua* necessity is identity, as still inward and concealed, because it is the identity of what are esteemed actual things, although their very self-subsistence is bound to be necessity. The circulation of substance through causality and reciprocity therefore only expressly makes out or states that self-subsistence is the infinite negative self-relation—a relation *negative* in general, for in it the act of distinguishing and intermediating becomes a primariness of actual things independent one against the other—and *infinite self-relation*, because their independence only lies in their identity.

§ 158

This truth of necessity, therefore, is **Freedom**: and the truth of substance is the Notion—an independence which, though self-repulsive into distinct independent elements, yet in that repulsion is self-identical, and in the movement of reciprocity still at home and conversant only with itself.

Necessity is often called hard, and rightly so, if we keep only to necessity as such, i.e. to its immediate shape. Here we have, first of all, some state or, generally speaking, fact, possessing an independent subsistence: and necessity primarily implies that there falls upon such a fact something else by which it is brought low. This is what is hard and sad in necessity immediate or abstract. The identity of the two things, which necessity presents as bound to each other and thus bereft of their independence, is at first only inward, and therefore has no existence for those under the yoke of necessity. Freedom too from this point of view is only abstract, and is preserved only by renouncing all that we immediately are and have. But, as we have seen already, the process of necessity is so directed that it overcomes the rigid externality which it first had and reveals its inward nature. It then appears that the members, linked to one another, are not really foreign to each other, but only elements of one whole, each of them, in its connection with the other, being, as it were, at home, and combining with itself. In this way necessity is transfigured into freedom—not the freedom that consists in abstract negation, but freedom concrete and positive. From which we may learn what a mistake it is to regard freedom and necessity as mutually exclusive. Necessity indeed, *qua* necessity, is far from being freedom: yet freedom presupposes necessity, and contains it as an unsubstantial element in itself. A good man is aware that the tenor of his conduct is essentially obligatory and necessary. But this consciousness is so far from making any abatement from his freedom, that without it real and reasonable freedom could not be distinguished from arbitrary choice—a freedom which has no reality and is merely potential. A criminal, when punished, may look upon his punishment as a restriction of his freedom. Really the punishment is not foreign constraint to which he is subjected, but the manifestation of his own act: and if he recognizes this, he comports himself as a free man. In short, man is most independent when he knows himself to be determined by the absolute idea throughout. It was this phase of mind and conduct which Spinoza called *Amor intellectualis Dei*.

§ 159

Thus the Notion is the truth of Being and Essence, inasmuch as the shining or show of self-reflection is itself at the same time independent immediacy, and this being of a different actuality is immediately only a shining or show on itself.

The Notion has exhibited itself as the truth of Being and Essence as the ground to which the regress of both leads. Conversely it has been developed out of being as its ground. The former aspect of the advance may be regarded as a concentration of being into its depth, thereby disclosing its inner nature: the latter aspect as an issuing of the more perfect from the less perfect. When such development is viewed on the latter side only, it does prejudice to the method of philosophy. The special meaning which these superficial thoughts of more imperfect and more perfect have in this place is to indicate the distinction of being, as an immediate unity with itself, from the notion, as free mediation with itself. Since being has shown that it is an element in the notion, the latter has thus exhibited itself as the truth of being. As this its reflection in itself and as an absorption of the mediation, the notion is the presupposition of the immediate—a presupposition which is identical with the return to self; and in this identity lie freedom and the notion. If the partial element therefore be called the imperfect, then the notion, or the perfect, is certainly a development from the imperfect; since its very nature is thus to suspend its presupposition. At the same time it is the notion alone which, in the act of supposing itself, makes its presupposition; as has been made apparent in causality in general and especially in reciprocal action.

Thus in reference to Being and Essence the Notion is defined as Essence reverted to the simple immediacy of Being—the shining or show of Essence thereby having actuality, and its actuality being at the same time a free shining or show in itself. In this manner the notion has being as its simple self-relation, or as the immediacy of its immanent unity. Being is so poor a category that it is the least thing which can be shown to be found in the notion.

The passage from necessity to freedom, or from actuality into the notion, is the very hardest, because it proposes that independent actuality shall be thought as having all its substantiality in the passing over and identity with the other independent actuality. The notion, too, is extremely hard, because it is itself just this very identity. But the actual substance as such, the cause, which in its exclusiveness resists all invasion, is *ipso facto* subjected to necessity or the destiny of passing into dependency: and it is this subjection rather where the chief hardness lies. To think necessity, on the contrary, rather tends to melt that hardness. For thinking means that, in the other, one meets with one's self. It means a liberation, which is not the flight of abstraction, but consists in that which is actual having itself not as something else, but as its own being and creation, in the other actuality with which it is bound up by the force of necessity. As existing in an individual form, this liberation is called I: as developed to its totality, it is free Spirit; as feeling, it is Love; and as enjoyment, it is Blessedness. The great vision of substance in Spinoza is only a potential liberation from finite exclusiveness and egotism: but the notion itself realizes for its own both the power of necessity and actual freedom.

When, as now, the notion is called the truth of Being and Essence, we must expect to be asked, why we do not begin with the notion? The answer is that, where knowledge by thought is our aim, we cannot begin with the truth, because the truth, when it forms the beginning, must rest on mere assertion. The truth when it is thought must as such verify itself to thought. If the notion were put at the head of Logic, and defined, quite correctly in point of content, as the unity of Being and Essence, the following question would come up: What are we to think under the terms 'Being' and 'Essence', and how do they come to be embraced in the unity of the Notion? But if we answered these questions, then our beginning with the notion would be merely nominal. The real start would be made with Being, as we have here done: with this difference, that the characteristics of Being as well as those of Essence would have to be accepted uncritically from figurate conception, whereas we have observed Being and Essence in their own dialectical development and learnt how they lose themselves in the unity of the notion.

IX

THIRD SUBDIVISION OF LOGIC

THE DOCTRINE OF THE NOTION

§ 160

The **Notion** is the principle of freedom, the power of substance self-realized. It is a systematic whole, in which each of its constituent functions is the very total which the notion is, and is put as indissolubly one with it. Thus in its self-identity it has original and complete determinateness.

The position taken up by the notion is that of absolute idealism. Philosophy is a knowledge through notions because it sees that what on other grades of consciousness is taken to have Being, and to be naturally or immediately independent, is but a constituent stage in the Idea. In the logic of understanding, the notion is generally reckoned a mere form of thought, and treated as a general conception. It is to this inferior view of the notion that the assertion refers, so often urged on behalf of the heart and sentiment, that notions as such are something dead, empty, and abstract. The case is really quite the reverse. The notion is, on the contrary, the principle of all life, and thus possesses at the same time a character of thorough concreteness. That it is so follows from the whole logical movement up to this point, and need not be here proved. The contrast between form and content, which is thus used to criticize the notion when it is alleged to be merely formal, has, like all the other contrasts upheld by reflection, been already left behind and overcome dialectically or through itself. The notion, in short, is what contains all the earlier categories of thought merged in it. It certainly is a form, but an infinite and creative form, which includes, but at the same time releases from itself, the fullness of all content. And so too the notion may, if it be wished, be styled abstract, if the name concrete is restricted to the concrete facts of sense or of immediate perception. For the notion is not palpable to the touch, and when we are engaged with it, hearing and seeing must quite fail us. And yet, as it was before remarked, the notion is a true concrete; for the reason that it involves Being and Essence, and the total wealth of these two spheres with them, merged in the unity of thought.

If, as was said at an earlier point, the different stages of the logical idea are to be treated as a series of definitions of the Absolute, the definition which now results for us is that the Absolute is the Notion. That necessitates a higher estimate of the notion, however, than is found in formal conceptualist Logic, where the notion is a mere form of our subjective thought, with no original content of its own. But if Speculative Logic thus attaches a meaning to the term notion so very different from that usually given, it may be asked why the same word should be employed in two contrary acceptations, and an occasion thus given for confusion and misconception. The answer is that, great as the interval is between the speculative notion and the notion of Formal Logic, a closer examination shows that the deeper meaning is not so foreign to the general usages of language as it seems at first sight. We speak of the deduction of a content from the notion, e.g. of the specific provisions of the law of property from the notion of property; and so again we speak of tracing back these material details to the notion. We thus recognize that the notion is no mere form without a content of its own: for if it were, there would be in the one case nothing to deduce from such a form, and in the other case to trace a given body of fact back to the empty form of the notion would only rob the fact of its specific character, without making it understood.

§ 161

The onward movement of the notion is no longer either a transition into, or a reflection on something else, but **Development**. For in the notion, the elements distinguished are without more ado at the same time declared to be identical with one another and with the whole, and the specific character of each is a free being of the whole notion.

Transition into something else is the dialectical process within the range of Being: reflection (bringing something else into light), in the range of Essence. The movement of the Notion is *development*: by which that only is explicit which is already implicitly present. In the world of nature it is organic life that corresponds to the grade of the notion. Thus e.g. the plant is developed from its germ. The germ virtually involves the whole plant, but does so only ideally or in thought: and it would therefore be a mistake to regard the development of the root, stem, leaves, and other different parts of the plant, as meaning that they were *realiter* present, but in a very minute form, in the germ. That is the so-called 'box-within-box' hypothesis; a theory which commits the mistake of supposing an actual existence of what is at first found only as a postulate of the completed thought. The truth of the hypothesis on the other hand lies in its perceiving that in the process of development the notion keeps to itself and only gives rise to alteration of form, without making any addition in point of content. It is this nature of the notion—this manifestation of itself in its process as a development of its own self—which is chiefly in view with those who speak of innate ideas, or who, like Plato, describe all learning merely as reminiscence. Of course that again does not mean that everything which is embodied in a mind, after that mind has been formed by instruction, had been present in that mind beforehand, in its definitely expanded shape.

The movement of the notion is as it were to be looked upon merely as play: the other which it sets up is in reality not an other. Or, as it is expressed in the teaching of Christianity: not merely has God created a world which confronts him as an other; he has also from all eternity begotten a Son in whom he, a Spirit, is at home with himself.

§ 162

The doctrine of the notion is divided into three parts. (1) The first is the doctrine of the **Subjective** or Formal **Notion**. (2) The second is the doctrine of the notion invested with the character of immediacy, or of **Objectivity**. (3) The third is the doctrine of the **Idea**, the subject-object, the unity of notion and objectivity, the absolute truth.

The Common Logic covers only the matters which come before us here as a portion of the third part of the whole system, together with the so-called Laws of Thought, which we have already met; and in the Applied Logic it adds a little about cognition. This is combined with psychological, metaphysical, and all sorts of empirical materials, which were introduced because, when all was done, those forms of thought could not be made to do all that was required of them. But with these additions the science lost its unity of aim. Then there was a further circumstance against the Common Logic. Those forms, which at least do belong to the proper domain of Logic, are supposed to be categories of conscious thought only, of thought too in the character of understanding, not of reason.

The preceding logical categories, those viz. of Being and Essence, are, it is true, no mere logical modes or entities: they are proved to be notions in their transition or their dialectical element, and in their return into themselves and totality. But they are only in a modified form notions (cf. §§ 84 and 112), notions rudimentary, or, what is the same thing, notions for us. The antithetical term into which each category passes, or in which it shines, so producing correlation, is not characterized as a particular. The third, in which they return to unity, is not characterized as a subject or an individual: nor is there any explicit statement that the category is identical in its antithesis—in other words, its freedom is not expressly stated: and all this because the category is not universality. What generally passes current under the name of a notion is a mode of understanding, or even a mere general representation, and therefore, in short, a finite mode of thought (cf. § 62).

The Logic of the Notion is usually treated as a science of form only, and understood to deal with the form of notion, judgement, and syllogism as form, without in the least touching the question whether anything is true. The answer to that question is supposed to depend on the content only. If the logical forms of the notion were really dead and inert receptacles of conceptions and thoughts, careless of what they contained, knowledge about them would be an idle curiosity which the truth might dispense with. On the contrary they really are, as forms of the notion, the vital spirit of the actual world. That only is true of the actual which is true in virtue of these forms, through them and in them. As yet, however, the truth of these forms has never been considered or examined on their own account any more than their necessary interconnection.

A. THE SUBJECTIVE NOTION

(*a*) *The Notion as Notion*

§ 163

The Notion as Notion contains the three following 'moments' or functional parts. (1) The first is **Universality**—meaning that it is in free equality with itself in its specific character. (2) The second is **Particularity**—that is, the specific character, in which the universal continues serenely equal to itself. (3) The third is **Individuality**—meaning the reflection-into-self of the specific characters of universality and particularity; which negative self-unity has complete and original determinateness, without any loss to its self-identity or universality.

Individual and actual are the same thing: only the former has issued from the notion, and is thus, as a universal, stated expressly as a negative identity with itself. The actual, because it is at first no more than a potential or immediate unity of essence or existence, *may* possibly have effect: but the individuality of the notion is the very source of effectiveness, effective moreover no longer as the cause is, with a show of effecting something else, but effective of itself. Individuality, however, is not to be understood to mean the immediate or natural individual, as when we speak of individual things or individual men: for that special phase of individuality does not appear till we come to the judgement. Every function and 'moment' of the notion is itself the whole notion (§ 160); but the individual or subject is the notion expressly put as a totality.

(1) The notion is generally associated in our minds with abstract generality, and on that account it is often described as a general conception. We speak, accordingly, of the notions of colour, plant, animal, etc. They are supposed to be arrived at by neglecting the particular features which distinguish the different colours, plants, and animals from each other, and by retaining those common to them all. This is the aspect of the notion which is familiar to understanding; and feeling is in the right when it stigmatizes such hollow and empty notions as mere phantoms and shadows. But the universal of the notion is not a mere sum of features common to several things, confronted by a particular which enjoys an existence of its own. It is, on the contrary, self-particularizing or self-specifying, and with undimmed clearness finds itself at home in its antithesis. For the sake both of cognition and of our practical conduct, it is of the utmost importance that the real universal should not be confused with what is merely held in common. All those charges which the devotees of feeling make against thought, and especially against philosophic thought, and the reiterated statement that is is dangerous to carry thought to what they call too great lengths, originate in the confusion of these two things.

The universal in its true and comprehensive meaning is a thought which, as we know, cost thousands of years to make it enter into the consciousness of men. The thought did not gain its full recognition till the days of Christianity. The Greeks, in other respects so advanced, knew neither God nor even man in their true universality. The gods of the Greeks were only particular powers of the mind; and the universal God, the God of all nations, was to the Athenians still a God concealed. They believed in the same way that an absolute gulf separated themselves from the barbarians. Man as man was not then recognized to be of infinite worth and to have infinite rights. The question has been asked, why slavery has vanished from modern Europe. One special circumstance after another has been adduced in explanation of this phenomenon. But the real ground why there are no more slaves in Christian Europe is only to be found in the very principle of Christianity itself, the religion of absolute freedom. Only in Christendom is man respected as man, in his infinitude and universality. What the slave is without, is the recognition that he is a person: and the principle of personality is universality. The master looks upon his slave not as a person, but as a selfless thing. The slave is not himself reckoned an 'I'—his 'I' is his master.

The distinction referred to above between what is merely in common, and what is truly universal, is strikingly expressed by Rousseau in his famous *Contrat social*, when he says that the laws of a state must spring from the universal will (*volonté générale*), but need not on that account be the will of all (*volonté de tous*). Rousseau would have made a sounder contribution towards a theory of the state, if he had always kept this distinction in sight. The general will is the notion of the will: and the laws are the special clauses of this will and based upon the notion of it.

(2) We add a remark upon the account of the origin and formation of notions which is usually given in the Logic of Understanding. It is not *we* who frame the notions. The notion is not something which is originated at all. No doubt the notion is not mere Being, or the immediate: it involves mediation, but the mediation lies in itself. In other words, the notion is what is mediated through itself and with itself. It is a mistake to imagine that the objects which form the content of our mental ideas come first and that our subjective agency then supervenes, and by the aforesaid operation of abstraction, and by colligating the points possessed in common by the objects, frames notions of them. Rather the notion is the genuine first; and things are what they are through the action of the notion, immanent in them, and revealing itself in them. In religious language we express this by saying that God created the world out of nothing. In other words, the world and finite things have issued from the fullness of the divine thoughts and the divine decrees. Thus religion recognizes thought and (more exactly) the notion to be the infinite form, or the free creative activity, which can realize itself without the help of a matter that exists outside it.

§ 164

The notion is concrete out and out: because the negative unity with itself, as characterization pure and entire, which is individuality, is just what constitutes its self-relation, its universality. The functions or 'moments' of the notion are to this extent indissoluble. The categories of 'reflection' are expected to be severally apprehended and separately accepted as current, apart from their opposites. But in the notion, where their identity is expressly assumed, each of its functions can be immediately apprehended only from and with the rest.

Universality, particularity, and individuality are, taken in the abstract, the same as identity, difference, and ground. But the universal is the self-identical, with the express qualification, that it simultaneously contains the particular and the individual. Again, the particular is the different or the specific character, but with the qualification that it is in itself universal and is as an individual. Similarly the individual must be understood to be a subject or substratum, which involves the genus and species in itself and possesses a substantial existence. Such is the explicit or realized inseparability of the functions of the notion in their difference (§ 160)—what may be called the clearness of the notion, in which each distinction causes no dimness or interruption, but is quite as much transparent.

No complaint is oftener made against the notion than that it is *abstract*. Of course it is abstract, if abstract means that the medium in which the notion exists is thought in general and not the sensible thing in its empirical concreteness. It is abstract also, because the notion falls short of the idea. To this extent the subjective notion is still formal. This however does not mean that it ought to have or receive another content than its own. It is itself the absolute form, and so is all specific character, but as that character is in its truth. Although it be abstract therefore, it is the concrete, concrete altogether, the subject as such. The absolutely concrete is the mind (see end of § 159)—the notion when it *exists* as notion distinguishing itself from its objectivity, which notwithstanding the distinction still continues to be its own. Everything else which is concrete, however rich it be, is not so intensely identical with itself and therefore not so concrete on its own part—least of all what is commonly supposed to be concrete, but is only a congeries held together by external influence. What are called notions, and in fact specific notions, such as man, house, animal, etc., are simply denotations and abstract representations. These abstractions retain out of all the functions of the notion only that of universality; they leave particularity and individuality out of account and have no development in these directions. By so doing they just miss the notion.

§ 165

It is the element of Individuality which first explicitly differentiates the elements of the notion. Individuality is the negative reflection of the notion into itself, and it is in that way at first the free differentiating of it as the first negation, by which the specific character of the notion is realized, but under the form of particularity. That is to say, the different elements are in the first place only qualified as the several elements of the notion, and, secondly, their identity is no less explicitly stated, the one being said to be the other. This realized particularity of the notion is the Judgement.

The ordinary classification of notions, as *clear*, *distinct*, and *adequate*, is no part of the notion; it belongs to psychology. Notions, in fact, are here synonymous with mental representations; a *clear* notion is an abstract simple representation: a *distinct* notion is one where, in addition to the simplicity, there is one 'mark' or character emphasized as a sign for subjective cognition. There is no more striking mark of the formalism and decay of Logic than the favourite category of the 'mark'. The *adequate* notion comes nearer the notion proper, or even the Idea: but after all it expresses only the formal circumstance that a notion or representation agrees with its object, that is, with an external thing. The division into what are called *subordinate* and *co-ordinate* notions implies a mechanical distinction of universal from particular which allows only a mere correlation of them in external comparison. Again, an enumeration of such kinds as *contrary* and *contradictory*, *affirmative* and *negative* notions, etc., is only a chance-directed gleaning of logical forms which properly belong to the sphere of Being or Essence (where they have been already examined) and which have nothing to do with the specific notional character as such. The true distinctions in the notion, universal, particular, and individual, may be said also to constitute species of it, but only when they are kept severed from each other by external reflection. The immanent differentiating and specifying of the notion come to sight in the judgement: for to judge is to specify the notion.

(*b*) *The Judgement*

§ 166

The **Judgement** is the notion in its particularity, as a connection which is also a distinguishing of its functions, which are put as independent and yet as identical with themselves, not with one another.

One's first impression about the Judgement is the independence of the two extremes, the subject and the predicate. The former we take to be a thing or term *per se*, and the predicate a general term outside the said subject and somewhere in our heads. The next point is for us to bring the latter into combination with the former, and in this way frame a Judgement. The copula 'is', however, enunciates the predicate *of* the subject, and so that external subjective subsumption is again put in abeyance, and the Judgement taken as a determination of the object itself. The etymological meaning of the Judgement (*Urtheil*) in German goes deeper, as it were declaring the unity of the notion to be primary, and its distinction to be the original partition. And that is what the Judgement really is.

In its abstract terms a Judgement is expressible in the proposition: 'The individual is the universal.' These are the terms under which the subject and the predicate first confront each other, when the functions of the notion are taken in their immediate character or first abstraction. (Propositions such as, 'The particular is the universal', and 'The individual is the particular', belong to the further specialization of the judgement.) It shows a strange want of observation in the logic-books, that in none of them is the fact stated, that in *every* judgement there is still a statement made, as, The individual is the universal, or still more definitely, The subject is the predicate (e.g. God is absolute spirit). No doubt there is also a distinction between terms like individual and universal, subject and predicate: but it is none the less the universal fact, that every judgement states them to be identical.

The copula 'is' springs from the nature of the notion, to be self-identical even in parting with its own. The individual and universal are *its* constituents, and therefore characters which cannot be isolated. The earlier categories (of reflection) in their correlations also refer to one another: but their interconnection is only 'having' and not 'being', i.e. it is not the identity which is realized as identity or universality. In the judgement, therefore, for the first time there is seen the genuine particularity of the notion: for it is the speciality or distinguishing of the latter, without thereby losing universality.

Judgements are generally looked upon as combinations of notions, and, be it added, of heterogeneous notions. This theory of judgement is correct, so far as it implies that it is the notion which forms the presupposition of the judgement, and which in the judgement comes up under the form of difference. But on the other hand, it is false to speak of notions differing in kind. The notion, although concrete, is still as a notion essentially one, and the functions which it contains are not different kinds of it. It is equally false to speak of a combination of the two sides in the judgement, if we understand the term 'combination' to imply the independent existence of the combining members apart from the combination. The same external view of their nature is more forcibly apparent when judgements are described as produced by the ascription of a predicate to the subject. Language like this looks upon the subject as self-subsistent outside, and the predicate as found somewhere in our head. Such a conception of the relation between subject and predicate however is at once contradicted by the copula 'is'. By saying 'This rose is red', or 'This picture is beautiful', we declare, that it is not we who from outside attach beauty to the picture or redness to the rose, but that these are the characteristics proper to these objects. An additional fault in the way in which Formal Logic conceives the judgement is, that it makes the judgement look as if it were something merely contingent, and does not offer any proof for the advance from notion on to judgement. For the notion does not, as understanding supposes, stand still in its own immobility. It is rather an infinite form, of boundless activity, as it were the *punctum saliens* of all vitality, and thereby self-differentiating. This disruption of the notion into the difference of its constituent functions—a disruption imposed by the native act of the notion—is the judgement. A judgement therefore means the particularizing of the notion. No doubt the notion is implicitly the particular. But in the notion as notion the particular is not yet explicit, and still remains in transparent unity with the universal. Thus, for example, as we remarked before (§ 160, note), the germ of a plant contains its particular, such as root, branches, leaves, etc.: but these details are at first present only potentially, and are not realized till the germ uncloses. This unclosing is, as it were, the judgement of the plant. The illustration may also serve to show how neither the notion nor the judgement are merely found in our head, or merely framed by us. The notion is the very heart of things, and makes them what they are. To form a notion of an object means therefore to become aware of its notion: and when we proceed to a criticism or judgement of the object, we are not performing a subjective act, and merely ascribing this or that predicate to the object. We are, on the contrary, observing the object in the specific character imposed by its notion.

§ 167

The Judgement is usually taken in a subjective sense as an operation and a form, occurring merely in self-conscious thought. This distinction, however, has no existence on purely logical principles, by which the judgement is taken in the quite universal signification that all things are a judgement. That is to say, they are individuals, which are a universality or inner nature in themselves—a universal which is individualized. Their universality and individuality are distinguished, but the one is at the same time identical with the other.

The interpretation of the judgement, according to which it is assumed to be merely subjective, as if *we* ascribed a predicate to a subject, is contradicted by the decidedly objective expression of the judgement. The rose *is* red; Gold *is* a metal. It is not by us that something is first ascribed to them. A judgement is however distinguished from a proposition. The latter contains a statement about the subject, which does not stand to it in any universal relationship, but expresses some single action, or some state, or the like. Thus, 'Caesar was born at Rome in such and such a year, waged war in Gaul for ten years, crossed the Rubicon, etc.', are propositions, but not judgements. Again it is absurd to say that such statements as 'I slept well last night' or 'Present arms!' may be turned into the form of a judgement. 'A carriage is passing by' would be a judgement, and a subjective one at best, only if it were doubtful, whether the passing object was a carriage, or whether it and not rather the point of observation was in motion: in short, only if it were desired to specify a conception which was still short of appropriate specification.

§ 168

The judgement is an expression of finitude. Things from its point of view are said to be finite, because they are a judgement, because their definite being and their universal nature (their body and their soul), though united indeed (otherwise the things would be nothing), are still elements in the constitution which are already different and also in any case separable.

§ 169

The abstract terms of the judgement, 'The individual is the universal', present the subject (as negatively self-relating) as what is immediately *concrete*, while the predicate is what is *abstract*, indeterminate, in short, the universal. But the two elements are connected together by an 'is': and thus the predicate (in its universality) must also contain the speciality of the subject, must, in short, have particularity: and so is realized the identity between subject and predicate; which, being thus unaffected by this difference in form, is the content.

It is the predicate which first gives the subject, which till then was on its own account a bare mental representation or an empty name, its specific character and content. In judgements like 'God is the most real of all things', or 'The Absolute is the self-identical', God and the Absolute are mere names; what they *are* we only learn in the predicate. What the subject may be in other respects, as a concrete thing, is no concern of *this* judgement. (Cf. § 31.)

To define the subject as that of which something is said, and the predicate as what is said about it, is mere trifling. It gives no information about the distinction between the two. In point of thought, the subject is primarily the individual, and the predicate the universal. As the judgement receives further development, the subject ceases to be merely the immediate individual, and the predicate merely the abstract universal: the former acquires the additional significations of particular and universal, the latter the additional significations of particular and individual. Thus while the same names are given to the two terms of the judgement, their meaning passes through a series of changes.

§ 170

We now go closer into the speciality of subject and predicate. The subject as negative self-relation (§§ 163, 166) is the stable substratum in which the predicate has its subsistence and where it is ideally present. The predicate, as the phrase is, *inheres* in the subject. Further, as the subject is in general and immediately concrete, the specific connotation of the predicate is only one of the numerous characters of the subject. Thus the subject is ampler and wider than the predicate.

Conversely, the predicate as universal is self-subsistent, and indifferent whether this subject is or not. The predicate outflanks the subject, subsuming it under itself: and hence on its side is wider than the subject. The specific content of the predicate (§ 169) alone constitutes the identity of the two.

§ 171

At first, subject, predicate, and the specific content or the identity are, even in their relation, still put in the judgement as different and divergent. By implication, however, that is, in their notion, they are identical. For the subject is a concrete totality, which means not any indefinite multiplicity, but individuality alone, the particular and the universal in an identity: and the predicate too in the very same unity (§ 170). The copula again, even while stating the identity of subject and predicate, does so at first only by an abstract 'is'. Conformably to such an identity the subject has to be *put* also in the characteristic of the predicate. By this means the latter also receives the characteristic of the former: so that the copula receives its full complement and full force. Such is the continuous specification by which the judgement, through a copula charged with content, comes to be a syllogism. As it is primarily exhibited in the judgement, this gradual specification consists in giving to an originally abstract, sensuous universality the specific character of allness, of species, of genus, and finally of the developed universality of the notion.

After we are made aware of this continuous specification of the judgement, we can see a meaning and an interconnection in what are usually stated as the kinds of judgement. Not only does the ordinary enumeration seem purely casual, but it is also superficial, and even bewildering in its statement of their distinctions. The distinction between positive, categorical, and assertory judgements is either a pure invention of fancy, or is left undetermined. On the right theory, the different judgements follow necessarily from one another, and present the continuous specification of the notion; for the judgement itself is nothing but the notion specified.

When we look at the two preceding spheres of Being and Essence, we see that the specified notions as judgements are reproductions of these spheres, but put in the simplicity of relation peculiar to the notion.

The various kinds of judgement are no empirical aggregate. They are a systematic whole based on a principle; and it was one of Kant's great merits to have first emphasized the necessity of showing this. His proposed division, according to the headings in his table of categories, into judgements of quality, quantity, relation, and modality, cannot be called satisfactory, partly from the merely formal application of this categorical rubric, partly on account of their content. Still it rests upon a true perception of the fact that the different species of judgement derive their features from the universal forms of the logical idea itself. If we follow this clue, it will supply us with three chief kinds of judgement parallel to the stages of Being, Essence, and Notion. The second of these kinds, as required by the character of Essence, which is the stage of differentiation, must be doubled. We find the inner ground for that systematization of judgements in the circumstance that when the Notion, which is the unity of Being and Essence in a comprehensive thought, unfolds, as it does in the judgement, it must reproduce these two stages in a transformation proper to the notion. The notion itself meanwhile is seen to mould and form the genuine grade of judgement.

Far from occupying the same level, and being of equal value, the different species of judgement form a series of steps, the difference of which rests upon the logical significance of the predicate. That judgements differ in value is evident in our ordinary ways of thinking. We should not hesitate to ascribe a very slight faculty of judgement to a person who habitually framed only such judgements as 'This wall is green', 'This stove is hot'. On the other hand we should credit with a genuine capacity of judgement the person whose criticisms dealt with such questions as whether a certain work of art was beautiful, whether a certain action was good, and so on. In judgements of the first-mentioned kind the content forms only an abstract quality, the presence of which can be sufficiently detected by immediate perception. To pronounce a work of art to be beautiful, or an action to be good, requires on the contrary a comparison of the objects with what they ought to be, i.e. with their notion.

(α) *Qualitative Judgement*

§ 172

The immediate judgement is the judgement of definite Being. The subject is invested with a universality as its predicate, which is an immediate, and therefore a sensible quality. It may be (1) a **Positive** judgement: The individual is a particular. But the individual is not a particular: or in more precise language, such a single quality is not congruous with the concrete nature of the subject. This is (2) a **Negative** judgement.

It is one of the fundamental assumptions of dogmatic Logic that Qualitative judgements such as 'The rose is red' or 'is not red' can contain *truth*. *Correct* they may be, i.e. in the limited circle of perception, of finite conception and thought: that depends on the content, which likewise is finite, and, on its own merits, untrue. Truth, however, as opposed to correctness, depends solely on the form, viz. on the notion as it is put and the reality corresponding to it. But truth of that stamp is not found in the Qualitative judgement.

In common life the terms *truth* and *correctness* are often treated as synonymous: we speak of the truth of a content, when we are only thinking of its correctness. Correctness, generally speaking, concerns only the formal coincidence between our conception and its content, whatever the constitution of this content may be. Truth, on the contrary, lies in the coincidence of the object with itself, that is, with its notion. That a person is sick, or that some one has committed a theft, may certainly be correct. But the content is untrue. A sick body is not in harmony with the notion of body, and there is a want of congruity between theft and the notion of human conduct. These instances may show that an immediate judgement in which an abstract quality is predicated of an immediately individual thing, however correct it may be, cannot contain truth. The subject and predicate of it do not stand to each other in the relation of reality and notion.

We may add that the untruth of the immediate judgement lies in the incongruity between its form and content. To say 'This rose is red' involves (in virtue of the copula 'is') the coincidence of subject and predicate. The rose however is a concrete thing, and so is not red only: it has also an odour, a specific form, and many other features not implied in the predicate red. The predicate on its part is an abstract universal, and does not apply to the rose alone. There are other flowers and other objects which are red too. The subject and predicate in the immediate judgement touch, as it were, only in a single point, but do not cover each other. The case is different with the notional judgement. In pronouncing an action to be good, we frame a notional judgement. Here, as we at once perceive, there is a closer and a more intimate relation than in the immediate judgement. The predicate in the latter is some abstract quality which may or may not be applied to the subject. In the judgement of the notion the predicate is, as it were, the soul of the subject, by which the subject, as the body of this soul, is characterized through and through.

§ 173

This negation of a particular quality, which is the first negation, still leaves the connection of the subject with the predicate subsisting. The predicate is in that manner a sort of relative universal, of which a special phase only has been negatived. (To say, that the rose is not red, implies that it is still coloured—in the first place with another colour; which however would be only one more positive judgement.) The individual, however, is not a universal. Hence (3) the judgement suffers disruption into one of two forms. It is either (*a*) the **Identical** judgement, an empty identical relation stating that the individual is the individual; or it is (*b*) what is called the **Infinite** judgement, in which we are presented with the total incompatibility of subject and predicate.

Examples of the latter are: 'The mind is no elephant'; 'A lion is no table'; propositions which are correct but absurd, exactly like the identical propositions: 'A lion is a lion'; 'Mind is mind.' Propositions like these are undoubtedly the truth of the immediate, or, as it is called, Qualitative judgement. But they are not judgements at all, and can only occur in a subjective thought where even an untrue abstraction may hold its ground. In their objective aspect, these latter judgements express the nature of what is, or of sensible things, which, as they declare, suffer disruption into an empty identity on the one hand, and on the other a fully-charged relation—only that this relation is the qualitative antagonism of the things related, their total incongruity.

The negatively infinite judgement, in which the subject has no relation whatever to the predicate, gets its place in the Formal Logic solely as a nonsensical curiosity. But the infinite judgement is not really a mere casual form adopted by subjective thought. It exhibits the proximate result of the dialectical process in the immediate judgements preceding (the positive and simply-negative), and distinctly displays their finitude and untruth. Crime may be quoted as an objective instance of the negatively infinite judgement. The person committing a crime, such as a theft, does not, as in a suit about civil rights, merely deny the particular right of another person to some one definite thing. He denies the right of that person in general, and therefore he is not merely forced to restore what he has stolen, but is punished in addition, because he has violated law as law, i.e. law in general. The civil-law suit on the contrary is an instance of the negative judgement pure and simple where merely the particular law is violated, while law in general is so far acknowledged. Such a dispute is precisely paralleled by a negative judgement, like, 'This flower is not red': by which we merely deny the particular colour of the flower, but not its colour in general, which may be blue, yellow, or any other. Similarly death, as a negatively infinite judgement, is distinguished from disease as simply-negative. In disease, merely this or that function of life is checked or negatived: in death, as we ordinarily say, body and soul part, i.e. subject and predicate utterly diverge.

(β) *Judgement of Reflection*

§ 174

The individual put as individual (i.e. as reflected-into-self) into the judgement, has a predicate, in comparison with which the subject, as self-relating, continues to be still *an other* thing. In existence the subject ceases to be immediately qualitative, it is in correlation, and interconnection with an other thing—with an external world. In this way the universality of the predicate comes to signify this relativity (e.g. useful, or dangerous; weight or acidity; or again, instinct; are examples of such relative predicates).

The Judgement of Reflection is distinguished from the Qualitative judgement by the circumstance that its predicate is not an immediate or abstract quality, but of such a kind as to exhibit the subject as in relation to something else. When we say, e.g. 'This rose is red', we regard the subject in its immediate individuality, and without reference to anything else. If, on the other hand, we frame the judgement, 'This plant is medicinal', we regard the subject, plant, as standing in connection with something else (the sickness which it cures), by means of its predicate (its medicinality). The case is the same with judgements like: This body is elastic; This instrument is useful; This punishment has a deterrent influence. In every one of these instances the predicate is some category of reflection. They all exhibit an advance beyond the immediate individuality of the subject, but none of them goes so far as to indicate the adequate notion of it. It is in this mode of judgement that ordinary *raisonnement* luxuriates. The greater the concreteness of the object in question, the more points of view does it offer to reflection; by which however its proper nature or notion is not exhausted.

§ 175

(1) Firstly then the subject, the individual as individual (in the **Singular** judgement), is a universal. But (2) secondly, in this relation it is elevated above its singularity. This enlargement is external, due to subjective reflection, and at first is an indefinite number of particulars. (This is seen in the **Particular** judgement, which is obviously negative as well as positive: the individual is divided in itself: partly it is self-related, partly related to something else.) (3) Thirdly, Some are the universal: particularity is thus enlarged to universality: or universality is modified through

the individuality of the subject, and appears as **allness** Community, the ordinary universality of reflection.

The subject, receiving, as in the Singular judgement, a universal predicate, is carried out beyond its mere individual self. To say, 'This plant is wholesome', implies not only that this single plant is wholesome, but that some or several are so. We have thus the particular judgement (some plants are wholesome, some men are inventive, etc.). By means of particularity the immediate individual comes to lose its independence, and enters into an interconnection with something else. Man, as *this* man, is not this single man alone: he stands beside other men and becomes one in the crowd. Just by this means however he belongs to his universal, and is consequently raised. The particular judgement is as much negative as positive. If only some bodies are elastic, it is evident that the rest are not elastic.

On this fact again depends the advance to the third form of the Reflective judgement, viz. the judgement of allness (all men are mortal, all metals conduct electricity). It is as 'all' that the universal is in the first instance generally encountered by reflection. The individuals form for reflection the foundation, and it is only our subjective action which collects and describes them as 'all'. So far the universal has the aspect of an external fastening, that holds together a number of independent individuals, which have not the least affinity towards it. This semblance of indifference is however unreal: for the universal is the ground and foundation, the root and substance of the individual. If e.g. we take Caius, Titus, Sempronius, and the other inhabitants of a town or country, the fact that all of them are men is not merely something which they have in common, but their universal or kind, without which these individuals would not be at all. The case is very different with that superficial generality falsely so called, which really means only what attaches, or is common, to all the individuals. It has been remarked, for example, that men, in contradistinction from the lower animals, possess in common the appendage of ear-lobes. It is evident, however, that the absence of these ear-lobes in one man or another would not affect the rest of his being, character, or capacities: whereas it would be nonsense to suppose that Caius, without being a man, would still be brave, learned, etc. The individual man is what he is in particular, only in so far as he is before all things a man as man and in general. And that generality is not something external to, or something in addition to, other abstract qualities, or to mere features discovered by reflection. It is what permeates and includes in it everything particular.

§ 176

This subject being thus likewise characterized as a universal, there is an express identification of subject and predicate, by which at the same time the speciality of the judgement-form is deprived of all importance. This unity of the content (the content being the universality which is identical with the negative reflection-in-self of the subject) makes the connection in judgement a necessary one.

The advance from the reflective judgement of allness to the judgement of necessity is found in our usual modes of thought, when we say that whatever appertains to all, appertains to the species, and is therefore necessary. To say all plants, or all men, is the same thing as to say *the* plant, or *the* man.

(γ) *Judgement of Necessity*

§ 177

The Judgement of Necessity, i.e. of the identity of the content in its difference (1), contains, in the predicate, partly the substance or nature of the subject, the concrete universal, the *genus*; partly, seeing that this universal also contains the specific character as negative, the predicate represents the exclusive essential character, the *species*. This is the **Categorical** judgement.

(2) Conformably to their substantiality, the two terms receive the aspect of independent actuality. Their identity is then inward only; and thus the actuality of the one is at the same time not its own, but the being of the other. This is the **Hypothetical** judgement.

(3) If, in this self-surrender and self-alienation of the notion, its inner identity is at the same time explicitly put, the universal is the genus which is self-identical in its mutually exclusive individualities. This judgement, which has this universal for both its terms, the one time as a universal, the other time as the circle of its self-excluding particularization in which the 'either—or' as much as the 'as well as' stands for the genus, is the **Disjunctive** judgement. Universality, at first as a genus, and now also as the circuit of its species, is thus described and expressly put as a totality.

The Categorical judgement (such as 'Gold is a metal', 'The rose is a plant') is the unmediated judgement of necessity, and finds within the sphere of Essence its parallel in the relation of substance. All things are a Categorical judgement. In other words, they have their substantial nature, forming their fixed and unchangeable substratum. It is only when things are studied from the point of view of their kind, and as with necessity determined by the kind, that the judgement first begins to be real. It betrays a defective logical training to place upon the same level judgements like 'gold is dear' and judgements like 'gold is a metal'. That 'gold is dear' is a matter of external connection between it and our wants or inclinations, the costs of obtaining it, and other circumstances. Gold remains the same as it was, though that external reference is altered or removed. Metalleity, on the contrary, constitutes the substantial nature of gold, apart from which it, and all else that is in it, or can be predicated of it, would be unable to subsist. The same is the case if we say, 'Caius is a man.' We express by that, that whatever else he may be has worth and meaning only when it corresponds to his substantial nature or manhood.

But even the Categorical judgement is to a certain extent defective. It fails to give due place to the function or element of particularity. Thus 'gold is a metal', it is true; but so are silver, copper, iron: and metalleity as such has no leanings to any of its particular species. In these circumstances we must advance from the Categorical to the Hypothetical judgement, which may be expressed in the formula: If *A* is, *B* is. The present case exhibits the same advance as formerly took place from the relation of substance to the relation of cause. In the Hypothetical judgement the specific character of the content shows itself mediated and dependent on something else: and this is exactly the relation of cause and effect. And if we were to give a general interpretation to the Hypothetical judgement, we should say that it expressly realizes the universal in its particularizing. This brings us to the third form of the Judgement of Necessity, the Disjunctive judgement. *A* is either *B* or *C* or *D*. A work of poetic art is either epic or lyric or dramatic. Colour is either yellow or blue or red. The two terms in the Disjunctive judgement are identical. The genus is the sum total of the species, and the sum total of the species is the genus. This unity of the universal and the particular is the notion: and it is the notion which, as we now see, forms the content of the judgement.

(δ) *Judgement of the Notion*

§ 178

The Judgement of the Notion has for its content the notion, the totality in simple form, the universal with its complete speciality, The subject is, (1) in the first place, an individual, which has for its predicate the reflection of the particular existence on its universal; or the judgement states the agreement or disagreement of these two aspects. That is, the predicate is such a term as good, true, correct. This is the **Assertory** judgement.

Judgements, such as whether an object, action, etc., is good, bad, true, beautiful, etc., are those to which even ordinary language first applies the name of judgement. We should never ascribe judgement to a person who framed positive or negative judgements like: This rose is red, This picture is red, green, dusty, etc.

The Assertory judgement, although rejected by society as out of place when it claims authority on its own showing, has however been made the single and all-essential form of doctrine, even in philosophy, through the influence of the principle of immediate knowledge and faith. In the so-called philosophic works which maintain this principle, we may read hundreds and hundreds of assertions about reason, knowledge, thought, etc., which, now that external authority counts for little, seek to accredit themselves by an endless restatement of the same thesis.

§ 179

On the part of its at first unmediated subject, the Assertory judgement does not contain the relation of particular with universal which is expressed in the predicate. This judgement is consequently a mere subjective particularity, and is confronted by a contrary assertion with equal right, or rather want of right. It is therefore at once turned into (2) a **Problematical** judgement. But when we explicitly attach the objective particularity to the subject and make its speciality the constitutive feature of its existence, the subject (3) then expresses the connection of that objective particularity with its constitution, i.e. with its genus; and thus expresses what forms the content of the predicate (see § 178). (This (*the immediate individuality*) house (*the genus*), being so and so constituted (*particularity*), is good or bad.) This is the **Apodeictic** judgement. All things are a genus (i.e. have a meaning and purpose) in an *individual* actuality of a *particular* constitution. And they are finite, because the particular in them may and also may not conform to the universal.

§ 180

In this manner subject and predicate are each the whole judgement. The immediate constitution of the subject is at first exhibited as the intermediating ground, where the individuality of the actual thing meets with its universality, and in this way as the ground of the judgement. What has been really made explicit is the oneness of subject and predicate, as the notion itself, filling up the empty 'is' of the copula. While its constituent elements are at the same time distinguished as subject and predicate, the notion is put as their unity, as the connection which serves to intermediate them: in short, as the Syllogism.

(*c*) *The Syllogism*

§ 181

The **Syllogism** brings the notion and the judgement into one. It is notion, being the simple identity into which the distinctions of form in the judgement have retired. It is judgement, because it is at the same time set in reality, that is, put in the distinction of its terms. The Syllogism is the reasonable, and everything reasonable.

Even the ordinary theories represent the Syllogism to be the form of reasonableness, but only a subjective form; and no interconnection whatever is shown to exist between it and any other reasonable content, such as a reasonable principle, a reasonable action, idea, etc. The name of reason is much and often heard, and appealed to: but no one thinks of explaining its specific character, or saying what it is, least of all that it has any connection with Syllogism. But formal Syllogism really presents what is reasonable in such a reasonless way that it has nothing to do with any reasonable matter. But as the matter in question can only be rational in virtue of the same quality by which thought is reason, it can be made so by the form only: and that form is Syllogism. And what is a Syllogism but an explicit putting, i.e. realizing of the notion, at first in form only, as stated above? Accordingly the Syllogism is the essential ground of whatever is true: and at the present stage the definition of the Absolute is that it is the Syllogism, or stating the principle in a proposition: Everything is a Syllogism. Everything is a notion, the existence of which is the differentiation of its members or functions, so that the universal nature of the Notion gives itself external reality by means of particularity, and thereby, and as a negative reflection-into-self, makes itself an individual. Or, conversely: the actual thing is an individual, which by means of particularity rises to universality and makes itself identical with itself. The actual is one: but it is also the divergence from each other of the constituent elements of the notion; and the Syllogism represents the orbit of intermediation of its elements, by which it realizes its unity.

The Syllogism, like the notion and the judgement, is usually described as a form merely of our subjective thinking. The Syllogism, it is said, is the process of proving the judgement. And certainly the judgement does in every case refer us to the syllogism. The step from the one to the other however is not brought about by our subjective action, but by the judgement itself which puts itself as Syllogism, and in the conclusion returns to the unity of the notion. The precise point by which we pass to the Syllogism is found in the Apodeictic judgement. In it we have an individual which by means of its qualities connects itself with its universal or notion. Here we see the particular becoming the mediating mean between the individual and the universal. This gives the fundamental form of the Syllogism, the gradual specification of which, formally considered, consists in the fact that universal and individual also occupy this place of mean. This again paves the way for the passage from subjectivity to objectivity.

§ 182

In the 'immediate' Syllogism the several aspects of the notion confront one another abstractly, and stand in an external relation only. We have first the two extremes, which are Individuality and Universality; and then the notion, as the mean for locking the two together, is in like manner only abstract Particularity. In this way the extremes are put as independent and without affinity either towards one another or towards their mean. Such a Syllogism contains reason, but in utter notionlessness—the formal Syllogism of Understanding. In it the subject is coupled with *an other* character; or the universal by this mediation subsumes a subject external to it. In the rational Syllogism, on the contrary, the subject is by means of the mediation coupled with itself. In this manner it first comes to be a subject: or, in the subject we have the first germ of the rational Syllogism.

In the following examination, the Syllogism of Understanding, according to the interpretation usually put upon it, is expressed in its subjective shape; the shape which it has when *we* are said to make such Syllogisms. And it really is only a subjective syllogizing. Such Syllogism however has also an objective meaning; it expresses only the finitude of things, but does so in the specific mode which the form has here reached. In the case of finite things their subjectivity, being only thinghood, is separable from their properties or their particularity, but also separable from their universality: not only when the universality is the bare quality of the thing and its external interconnection with other things, but also when it is its genus and notion.

On the above-mentioned theory of syllogism, as the rational form *par excellence*, reason has been defined as the faculty of syllogizing, while understanding is defined as the faculty of forming notions. We might object to the conception on which this depends, and according to which the mind is merely a sum of forces or faculties existing side by side. But apart from that objection, we may observe in regard to the parallelism of understanding with the notion, as well as of reason with syllogism, that the notion is as little a mere category of the understanding as the syllogism is without qualification definable as rational. For, in the first place, what the Formal Logic usually examines in its theory of syllogism, is really nothing but the mere syllogism of understanding, which has no claim to the honour of being made a form of rationality, still less to be held as the embodiment of all reason. The notion, in the second place, so far from being a form of understanding, owes its degradation to such a place entirely to the influence of that abstract mode of thought. And it is not unusual to draw such a distinction between a notion of understanding and a notion of reason. The distinction however does not mean that notions are of two kinds. It means that our own action often stops short at the mere negative and abstract form of the notion, when we might also have proceeded to apprehend the notion in its true nature, as at once positive and concrete. It is e.g. the mere understanding which thinks liberty to be the abstract contrary of necessity, whereas the adequate rational notion of liberty requires the element of necessity to be merged in it. Similarly the definition of God, given by what is called Deism, is merely the mode in which the understanding thinks God: whereas Christianity, to which he is known as the Trinity, contains the rational notion of God.

(α) *Qualitative Syllogism*

§ 183

The first syllogism is a syllogism of definite being—a Qualitative Syllogism, as stated in the last paragraph. Its form (1) is I—P—U:

i.e. a subject as Individual is coupled (concluded) with a Universal character by means of a (Particular) quality.

Of course the subject (*terminus minor*) has other characteristics besides individuality, just as the other extreme (the predicate of the conclusion, or *terminus major*) has other characteristics than mere universality. But here the interest turns only on the characteristics through which these terms make a syllogism.

The syllogism of existence is a syllogism of understanding merely, at least in so far as it leaves the individual, the particular, and the universal to confront each other quite abstractly. In this syllogism the notion is at the very height of self-estrangement. We have in it an immediately individual thing as subject: next some one particular aspect or property attaching to this subject is selected, and by means of this property the individual turns out to be a universal. Thus we may say, This rose is red: Red is a colour: Therefore, this rose is a coloured object. It is this aspect of the syllogism which the common logics mainly treat of. There was a time when the syllogism was regarded as an absolute rule for all cognition, and when a scientific statement was not held to be valid until it had been shown to follow from a process of syllogism. At present, on the contrary, the different forms of the syllogism are met nowhere save in the manuals of Logic; and an acquaintance with them is considered a piece of mere pedantry, of no further use either in practical life or in science. It would indeed be both useless and pedantic to parade the whole machinery of the formal syllogism on every occasion. And yet the several forms of syllogism make themselves constantly felt in our cognition. If any one, when awaking on a winter morning, hears the creaking of the carriages on the street, and is thus led to conclude that it has frozen hard in the night, he has gone through a syllogistic operation—an operation which is every day repeated under the greatest variety of conditions. The interest, therefore, ought at least not to be less in becoming expressly conscious of this daily action of our thinking selves, than confessedly belongs to the study of the functions of organic life, such as the processes of digestion, assimilation, respiration, or even the processes and structures of the nature around us. We do not, however, for a moment deny that a study of Logic is no more necessary to teach us how to draw correct conclusions, than a previous study of anatomy and physiology is required in order to digest or breathe.

Aristotle was the first to observe and describe the different forms, or, as they are called, figures of syllogism, in their subjective meaning: and he performed this work so exactly and surely, that no essential addition has ever been required. But while sensible of the value of what he has thus done, we must not forget that the forms of the syllogism of understanding, and of finite thought altogether, are not what Aristotle has made use of in his properly philosophical investigations. (See § 187.)

§ 184

This syllogism is completely contingent (i) in the matter of its terms. The Middle Term, being an abstract particularity, is nothing but any quality whatever of the subject: but the subject being immediate and thus empirically concrete, has several others, and could therefore be coupled with exactly as many other universalities as it possesses single qualities. Similarly a single particularity may have various characters in itself, so that the same *medius terminus* would serve to connect the subject with several different universals.

It is more a caprice of fashion, than a sense of its incorrectness, which has led to the disuse of ceremonious syllogizing. This and the following section indicate the uselessness of such syllogizing for the ends of truth.

The point of view indicated in the paragraph shows how this style of syllogism can 'demonstrate' (as the phrase goes) the most diverse conclusions. All that is requisite is to find a *medius terminus* from which the transition can be made to the proposition sought. Another *medius terminus* would enable us to demonstrate something else, and even the contrary of the last. And the more concrete an object is, the more aspects it has, which may become such middle terms. To determine which of these aspects is more essential than another, again, requires a further syllogism of this kind, which fixing on the single quality can with equal ease discover in it some aspect or consideration by which it can make good its claims to be considered necessary and important.

Little as we usually think on the Syllogism of Understanding in the daily business of life, it never ceases to play its part there. In a civil suit, for instance, it is the duty of the advocate to give due force to the legal titles which make in favour of his client. In logical language, such a legal title is nothing but a middle term. Diplomatic transactions afford another illustration of the same, when, for instance, different powers lay claim to one and the same territory. In such a case the laws of inheritance, the geographical position of the country, the descent and the language of its inhabitants, or any other ground, may be emphasized as a *medius terminus*.

§ 185

(ii) This syllogism, if it is contingent in point of its terms, is no less contingent in virtue of the form of relation which is found in it. In the syllogism, according to its notion, truth lies in connecting two distinct things by a Middle Term in which they are one. But connections of the extremes with the Middle Term (the so-called *premisses*, the major and the minor premiss) are in the case of this syllogism much more decidedly *immediate* connections. In other words, they have not a proper Middle Term.

This contradiction in the syllogism exhibits a new case of the infinite progression. Each of the premisses evidently calls for a fresh syllogism to demonstrate it: and as the new syllogism has two immediate premisses, like its predecessor, the demand for proof is doubled at every step, and repeated without end.

§ 186

On account of its importance for experience, there has been here noted a defect in the syllogism, to which in this form absolute correctness had been ascribed. This defect however must lose itself in the further specification of the syllogism. For we are now within the sphere of the notion; and here therefore, as well as in the judgement, the opposite character is not merely present potentially, but is explicit. To work out the gradual specification of the syllogism, therefore, there need only be admitted and accepted what is at each step realized by the syllogism itself.

Through the immediate syllogism I—P—U, the Individual is mediated (through a Particular) with the Universal, and in this conclusion put as a universal. It follows that the individual subject, becoming itself a universal, serves to unite the two extremes, and to form their ground of intermediation. This gives the second figure of the syllogism, (2) U—I—P. It expresses the truth of the first; it shows in other words that the intermediation has taken place in the individual, and is thus something contingent.

§ 187

The universal, which in the first conclusion was specified through individuality, passes over into the second figure and there now occupies the place that belonged to the immediate subject. In the second figure it is concluded with the particular. By this conclusion therefore the universal is explicitly put as particular—and is now made to mediate between the two extremes, the places of which are occupied by the two others (the particular and the individual). This is the third figure of the syllogism: (3) P—U—I.

What are called the **Figures** of the syllogism (being three in number, for the fourth is a superfluous and even absurd addition of the Moderns to the three known to Aristotle) are in the usual mode of treatment put side by side, without the slightest thought of showing their necessity, and still less of pointing out their import and value. No wonder then that the figures have been in later times treated as an empty piece of formalism. They have however a very real significance, derived from the necessity for every function or characteristic element of the notion to become the whole itself, and to stand as mediating ground. But to find out what 'moods' of the propositions (such as whether they may be universals, or negatives) are needed to enable us to draw a correct conclusion in the different figures, is a mechanical inquiry, which its purely mechanical nature and its intrinsic meaninglessness have very properly consigned to oblivion. And Aristotle would have been the last person to give any countenance to those who wish to attach importance to such inquiries or to the syllogism of understanding in general. It is true that he described these, as well as numerous other forms of mind and nature, and that he examined and expounded their specialities. But in his metaphysical theories, as well as his theories of nature and mind, he was very far from taking as basis, or criterion, the syllogistic forms of the 'understanding'. Indeed it might be maintained that not one of these theories would ever have come into existence, or been allowed to exist, if it had been compelled to submit to the laws of understanding. With all the descriptiveness and analytic faculty which Aristotle after his fashion is substantially strong in, his ruling principle is always the speculative notion; and that syllogistic of 'understanding' to which he first gave such a definite expression is never allowed to intrude in the higher domain of philosophy.

In their objective sense, the three figures of the syllogism declare that everything rational is manifested as a triple syllogism; that is to say, each one of the members takes in turn the place of the extremes, as well as of the mean which reconciles them. Such, for example, is the case with the three branches of philosophy: the Logical Idea, Nature, and Mind. As we first see them, Nature is the middle term which links the others together. Nature, the totality immediately before us, unfolds itself into the two extremes of the Logical Idea and Mind. But Mind is Mind only when it is mediated through nature. Then, in the second place, Mind, which we know as the principle of individuality, or as the actualizing principle, is the mean; and Nature and the Logical Idea are the extremes. It is Mind which cognizes the Logical Idea in Nature and which thus raises Nature to its essence. In the third place again the Logical Idea itself becomes the mean: it is the absolute substance both of mind and of nature, the universal and all-pervading principle. These are the members of the Absolute Syllogism.

§ 188

In the round by which each constituent function assumes successively the place of mean and of the two extremes, their specific difference from each other has been superseded. In this form, where there is no distinction between its constituent elements, the syllogism at first has for its connective link equality, or the external identity of understanding. This is the Quantitative or Mathematical Syllogism: if two things are equal to a third, they are equal to one another.

Everybody knows that this Quantitative syllogism appears as a mathematical axiom, which like other axioms is said to be a principle that does not admit of proof, and which indeed being self-evident does not require such proof. These mathematical axioms however are really nothing but logical propositions, which, so far as they enunciate definite and particular thoughts, are deducible from the universal and self-characterizing thought. To deduce them is to give their proof. That is true of the Quantitative syllogism, to which mathematics gives the rank of an axiom. It is really the proximate result of the qualitative or immediate syllogism. Finally, the Quantitative syllogism is the syllogism in utter formlessness. The difference between the terms which is required by the notion is suspended. Extraneous circumstances alone can decide what propositions are to be premisses here: and therefore in applying this syllogism we make a presupposition of what has been elsewhere proved and established.

§ 189

Two results follow as to the form. In the first place, each constituent element has taken the place and performed the function of the mean and therefore of the whole, thus implicitly losing its partial and abstract character (§ 182 and § 184); secondly, the mediation has been completed (§ 185), though the completion too is only implicit, that is, only as a circle of mediations which in turn presuppose each other. In the first figure I—P—U the two premisses I is P and P is U are yet without a mediation. The former premiss is mediated in the third, the latter in the second figure. But each of these two figures, again, for the mediation of its premisses presupposes the two others.

In consequence of this, the mediating unity of the notion must be put no longer as an abstract particularity, but as a developed unity of the individual and universal—and in the first place a reflected unity of these elements. That is to say, the individuality gets at the same time the character of universality. A mean of this kind gives the Syllogism of Reflection.

(β) *Syllogism of Reflection*

§ 190

If the mean, in the first place, be not only an abstract particular character of the subject, but at the same time all the individual concrete subjects which possess that character, but possess it only along with others, (1) we have the Syllogism of **Allness**. The major premiss, however, which has for its subject the particular character, the *terminus medius*, as allness, presupposes the very conclusion which ought rather to have presupposed it. It rests therefore (2) on an **Induction**, in which the mean is given by the complete list of individuals as such, *A*, *B*, *C*, *D*, etc. On account of the disparity, however, between universality and an immediate and empirical individuality, the list can never be complete. Induction therefore rests upon (3) **Analogy**. The middle term of Analogy is an individual, which however is understood as equivalent to its essential universality, its genus, or essential character. The first syllogism for its intermediation turns us over to the second, and the second turns us over to the third. But the third no less demands an intrinsically determinate Universality, or an individuality as type of the genus, after the round of the forms of external connection between individuality and universality has been run through in the figures of the Reflective Syllogism.

By the Syllogism of Allness the defect in the first form of the Syllogism of Understanding, noted in § 184, is remedied, but only to give rise to a new defect. This defect is that the major premiss itself presupposes what really ought to be the conclusion, and presupposes it as what is thus an 'immediate' proposition. All men are mortal, therefore Caius is mortal: All metals conduct electricity, therefore e.g. copper does so. In order to enunciate these major premisses, which when they say 'all' mean the 'immediate' individuals and are properly intended to be empirical propositions, it is requisite that the propositions about the individual man Caius, or the individual metal copper, should previously have been ascertained to be correct. Everybody feels not merely the pedantry, but the unmeaning formalism of such syllogisms as: All men are mortal, Caius is a man, therefore Caius is mortal.

The syllogism of Allness hands us over to the syllogism of Induction, in which the individuals form the coupling mean. 'All metals conduct electricity' is an empirical proposition derived from experiments made with each of the individual metals. We thus get the syllogism of Induction

```
                              I
in the following shape P—I—U.
                              I
                              :
                              :
```

Gold is a metal: silver is a metal: so is copper, lead, etc. This is the major premiss. Then comes the minor premiss: All these bodies conduct electricity; and hence results the conclusion, that all metals conduct electricity. The point which brings about a combination here is individuality in the shape of allness. But this syllogism once more hands us over to another syllogism. Its mean is constituted by the complete list of the individuals. That presupposes that over a certain region observation and experience are completed. But the things in question here are individuals; and as again we are landed in the progression *ad infinitum* (I, I, I, etc.). In other words, in no Induction can we ever exhaust the individuals. The 'all metals', 'all plants', of our statements, mean only all the metals, all the plants, which we have hitherto become acquainted with. Every Induction is consequently imperfect. One and the other observation, many it may be, have been made: but all the cases, all the individuals, have not been observed. By this defect of Induction we are led on to Analogy. In the syllogism of Analogy we conclude from the fact that some things of a certain kind possess a certain quality, that the same quality is possessed by other things of the same kind. It would be a syllogism of Analogy, for example, if we said: In all planets hitherto discovered this has been found to be the law of motion, consequently a newly discovered planet will probably move according to the same law. In the experiential sciences Analogy deservedly occupies a high place, and has led to results of the highest importance. Analogy is the instinct or reason, creating an anticipation that this or that characteristic, which experience has discovered, has its root in the inner nature or kind of an object, and arguing on the faith of that anticipation. Analogy it should be added may be superficial or it may be thorough. It would certainly be a very bad analogy to argue that since the man Caius is a scholar, and Titus also is a man, Titus will probably be a scholar too: and it would be bad because a man's learning is not an unconditional consequence of his manhood. Superficial analogies of this kind however are very frequently met with. It is often argued, for example: The earth is a celestial body, so is the moon, and it is therefore in all probability inhabited as well as the earth. The analogy is not one whit better than that previously mentioned. That the earth is inhabited does not depend on its being a celestial body, but on other conditions, such as the presence of an atmosphere, and of water in connection with the atmosphere, etc.: and these are precisely the conditions which the moon, so far as we know, does not possess. What has in modern times been called the Philosophy of Nature consists principally in a frivolous play with empty and external analogies, which, however, claim to be considered profound results. The natural consequence has been to discredit the philosophical study of nature.

(γ) *Syllogism of Necessity*

§ 191

The Syllogism of Necessity, if we look to its purely abstract characteristics or terms, has for its mean the Universal in the same way as the Syllogism of Reflection has the Individual, the latter being in the second, and the former in the third figure (§ 187). The Universal is expressly put as in its very nature intrinsically determinate. In the first place (1) the Particular, meaning by the particular the specific genus or species, is the term for mediating the extremes—as is done in the **Categorical** syllogism. (2) The same office is performed by the Individual, taking the individual as immediate being, so that it is as much mediating as mediated—as happens in the **Hypothetical** syllogism. (3) We have also the mediating Universal explicitly put as a totality of its particular members, and as a single particular, or exclusive individuality—

which happens in the **Disjunctive** syllogism. It is one and the same universal which is in these terms of the Disjunctive syllogism; they are only different forms for expressing it.

§ 192

The syllogism has been taken conformably to the distinctions which it contains; and the general result of the course of their evolution has been to show that these differences work out their own abolition and destroy the notion's outwardness to its own self. And, as we see, in the first place, (1) each of the dynamic elements has proved itself the systematic whole of these elements, in short, a whole syllogism—they are consequently implicitly identical. In the second place, (2) the negation of their distinctions and of the mediation of one through another constitutes independency; so that it is one and the same universal which is in these forms, and which is in this way also explicitly put as their identity. In this ideality of its dynamic elements, the syllogistic process may be described as essentially involving the negation of the characters through which its course runs, as being a mediative process through the suspension of mediation—as coupling the subject not with another, but with a suspended other, in one word, with itself.

In the common logic, the doctrine of syllogism is supposed to conclude the first part, or what is called the 'elementary' theory. It is followed by the second part, the doctrine of Method, which proposes to show how a body of scientific knowledge is created by applying to existing objects the forms of thought discussed in the elementary part. Whence these objects originate, and what the thought of objectivity generally speaking implies, are questions to which the Logic of Understanding vouchsafes no further answer. It believes thought to be a mere subjective and formal activity, and the objective fact, which confronts thought, to have a separate and permanent being. But this dualism is a half-truth: and there is a want of intelligence in the procedure which at once accepts, without inquiring into their origin, the categories of subjectivity and objectivity. Both of them, subjectivity as well as objectivity, are certainly thoughts—even specific thoughts: which must show themselves founded on the universal and self-determining thought. This has here been done—at least for subjectivity. We have recognized it, or the notion subjective (which includes the notion proper, the judgement, and the syllogism) as the dialectical result of the first two main stages of the Logical Idea, Being and Essence. To say that the notion is subjective and subjective only, is so far quite correct: for the notion certainly is subjectivity itself. Not less subjective than the notion are also the judgement and syllogism: and these forms, together with the so-called Laws of Thought (the Laws of Identity, Difference, and Sufficient Ground), make up the contents of what is called the 'Elements' in the common logic. But we may go a step further. This subjectivity, with its functions of notion, judgement, and syllogism, is not like a set of empty compartments which has to get filled from without by separately existing objects. It would be truer to say that it is subjectivity itself, which, as dialectical, breaks through its own barriers and opens out into objectivity by means of the syllogism.

§ 193

This 'realization' of the notion—a realization in which the universal is this one totality withdrawn back into itself (of which the different members are no less the whole, and which has given itself a character of 'immediate' unity by merging the mediation)—this realization of the notion is the **Object**.

This transition from the Subject, the notion in general, and especially the syllogism, to the Object, may, at the first glance, appear strange, particularly if we look only at the Syllogism of Understanding, and suppose syllogizing to be only an act of consciousness. But that strangeness imposes on us no obligation to seek to make the transition plausible to the image-loving conception. The only question which can be considered is, whether our usual conception of what is called an 'object' approximately corresponds to the object as here described. By 'object' is commonly understood not an abstract being, or an existing thing merely, or any sort of actuality, but something independent, concrete, and self-complete, this completeness being the totality of the notion. That the object (*Objekt*) is also an object to us (*Gegenstand*) and is external to something else, will be more precisely seen when it puts itself in contrast with the subjective. At present, as that into which the notion has passed from its mediation, it is only immediate object and nothing more, just as the notion is not describable as subjective, previous to the subsequent contrast with objectivity.

Further, the Object in general is the one total, in itself still unspecified, the Objective World as a whole, God, the Absolute

Object. The object, however, has also difference attaching to it: it falls into pieces, indefinite in their multiplicity (making an objective world); and each of these individualized parts is also an object, an intrinsically concrete, complete, and independent existence.

Objectivity has been compared with being, existence, and actuality; and so too the transition to existence and actuality (not to being, for *it* is the primary and quite abstract immediate) may be compared with the transition to objectivity. The ground from which existence proceeds, and the reflective correlation which is merged in actuality, are nothing but the as yet imperfectly realized notion. They are only abstract aspects of it—the ground being its merely essence-bred unity, and the correlation only the connection of real sides which are supposed to have only self-reflected being. The notion is the unity of the two; and the object is not a merely essence-like, but inherently universal unity, not only containing real distinctions, but containing them as totalities in itself.

It is evident that in all these transitions there is a further purpose than merely to show the indissoluble connection between the notion or thought and being. It has been more than once remarked that being is nothing more than simple self-relation, and this meagre category is certainly implied in the notion, or even in thought. But the meaning of these transitions is not to accept characteristics or categories, as only implied—a fault which mars even the Ontological argument for God's existence, when it is stated that being is one among realities. What such a transition does, is to take the notion, as it ought to be primarily characterized *per se* as a notion, with which this remote abstraction of being, or even of objectivity, has as yet nothing to do, and looking at its specific character as a notional character alone, to see when and whether it passes over into a form which is different from the character as it belongs to the notion and appears in it.

If the Object, the product of this transition, be brought into relation with the notion, which, so far as its special form is concerned, has vanished in it, we may give a correct expression to the result, by saying that notion (or, if it be preferred, subjectivity) and object are *implicitly* the same. But it is equally correct to say that they are different. In short, the two modes of expression are equally correct and incorrect. The true state of the case can be presented in no expressions of this kind. The 'implicit' is an abstraction, still more partial and inadequate than the notion itself, of which the inadequacy is on the whole suspended, by suspending itself to the object with its opposite inadequacy. Hence that implicitness also must, by its negation, give itself the character of explicitness. As in every case, speculative identity is not the above-mentioned triviality of an *implicit* identity of subject and object. This has been said often enough. Yet it could not be too often repeated, if the intention were really to put an end to the stale and purely malicious misconception in regard to this identity—of which however there can be no reasonable expectation.

Looking at that unity in a quite general way, and raising no objection to the one-sided form of its implicitness, we find it as the well-known presupposition of the ontological proof for the existence of God. There it appears as supreme perfection. Anselm, in whom the notable suggestion of this proof first occurs, no doubt originally restricted himself to the question whether a certain content was in our thinking only. His words are briefly these: *Certe id quo majus cogitari nequit, non potest esse in intellectu solo. Si enim vel in solo intellectu est, potest cogitari esse* **et in re:** *quod majus est. Si ergo id quo majus cogitari non potest, est in solo intellectu; id ipsum quo majus cogitari non potest, est quo major cogitari potest. Sed certe hoc esse non potest.* (Certainly that, than which nothing greater can be thought, cannot be in the intellect alone. For even if it is in the intellect alone, it can also be thought to exist in fact: and that is greater. If then that, than which nothing greater can be thought, is in the intellect alone; then the very thing, which is greater than anything which can be thought, can be exceeded in thought. But certainly this is impossible.) The same unity received a more objective expression in Descartes, Spinoza, and others: while the theory of immediate certitude or faith presents it, on the contrary, in somewhat the same subjective aspect as Anselm. These Intuitionalists hold that *in our consciousness* the attribute of being is indissolubly associated with the conception of God. The theory of faith brings even the conception of external finite things under the same inseparable nexus between the consciousness and the being of them, on the ground that *perception* presents them conjoined with the attribute of existence: and in so saying, it is no doubt correct. It would be utterly absurd, however, to suppose that the association in consciousness between existence and our conception of finite things is of the same description as the association between existence and the conception of God. To do so would be to forget that finite things are changeable and transient, i.e. that existence is associated with them for a season, but that the association is neither eternal nor inseparable. Speaking in the phraseology of the categories before us, we may say that, to call a thing finite, means that its objective existence is not in harmony with the thought of it, with its universal calling, its kind, and its end. Anselm, consequently, neglecting any such conjunction as occurs in finite things, has with good reason pronounced that only to be the Perfect which exists not merely in a subjective, but also in an objective mode. It does no good to put on airs against the Ontological proof, as it is called, and against Anselm thus defining the Perfect. The argument is one latent in every unsophisticated mind, and it recurs in every philosophy, even against its wish and without its knowledge—as may be seen in the theory of immediate belief.

The real fault in the argumentation of Anselm is one which is chargeable on Descartes and Spinoza, as well as on the theory of immediate knowledge. It is this. This unity which is enunciated as the supreme perfection or, it may be, subjectively, as the true knowledge, is presupposed, i.e. it is assumed only as potential. This identity, abstract as it thus appears, between the two categories may be at once met and opposed by their diversity; and this was the very answer given to Anselm long ago. In short, the conception and existence of the finite is set in antagonism to the infinite; for, as previously remarked, the finite possesses objectivity of such a kind as is at once incongruous with and different from the end or aim, its essence and notion. Or, the finite is such a conception and in such a way subjective, that it does not involve existence. This objection and this antithesis are got over, only by showing the finite to be untrue and these categories in their separation to be inadequate and null. Their identity is thus seen to be one into which they spontaneously pass over, and in which they are reconciled.

B. THE OBJECT

§ 194

The Object is immediate being, because insensible to difference, which in it has suspended itself. It is, further, a totality in itself, while at the same time (as this identity is only the *implicit* identity of its dynamic elements) it is equally indifferent to its immediate unity. It thus breaks up into distinct parts, each of which is itself the totality. Hence the object is the absolute contradiction between a complete independence of the multiplicity, and the equally complete non-independence of the different pieces.

The definition, which states that the Absolute is the Object, is most definitely implied in the Leibnizian Monad. The Monads are each an object, but an object implicitly 'representative', indeed the total representation of the world. In the simple unity of the Monad, all difference is merely ideal, not independent or real. Nothing from without comes into the monad: it is the whole notion in itself, only distinguished by its own greater or less development. None the less, this simple totality parts into the absolute multeity of differences, each becoming an independent monad. In the monad of monads, and the Pre-established Harmony of their inward developments, these substances are in like manner again reduced to 'identity' and unsubstantiality. The philosophy of Leibniz, therefore, represents contradiction in its complete development.

(1) As Fichte in modern times has especially and with justice insisted, the theory which regards the Absolute or God as the Object and there stops, expresses the point of view taken by superstition and slavish fear. No doubt God is the Object, and, indeed, the Object out and out, confronted with which our particular or subjective opinions and desires have no truth and no validity. As absolute object, however, God does not therefore take up the position of a dark and hostile power over against subjectivity. He rather involves it as a vital element in himself. Such also is the meaning of the Christian doctrine, according to which God has willed that all men should be saved and all attain blessedness. The salvation and the blessedness of men are attained when they come to feel themselves at one with God, so that God, on the other hand, ceases to be for them mere object, and, in that way, an object of fear and terror, as was especially the case with the religious consciousness of the Romans. But God in the Christian religion is also known as Love, because in his Son, who is one

with him, he has revealed himself to men as a man among men, and thereby redeemed them. All which is only another way of saying that the antithesis of subjective and objective is implicity overcome, and that it is our affair to participate in this redemption by laying aside our immediate subjectivity (putting off the old Adam), and learning to know God as our true and essential self.

Just as religion and religious worship consist in overcoming the antithesis of subjectivity and objectivity, so science too and philosophy have no other task than to overcome this antithesis by the medium of thought. The aim of knowledge is to divest the objective world that stands opposed to us of its strangeness, and, as the phrase is, to find ourselves at home in it: which means no more than to trace the objective world back to the notion—to our innermost self. We may learn from the present discussion the mistake of regarding the antithesis of subjectivity and objectivity as an abstract and permanent one. The two are wholly dialectical. The notion is at first only subjective: but without the assistance of any foreign material or stuff it proceeds, in obedience to its own action, to objectify itself. So, too, the object is not rigid and processless. Its process is to show itself as what is at the same time subjective, and thus form the step onwards to the idea. Any one who, from want of familiarity with the categories of subjectivity and objectivity, seeks to retain them in their abstraction will find that the isolated categories slip through his fingers before he is aware, and that he says the exact contrary of what he wanted to say.

(2) Objectivity contains the three forms of Mechanism, Chemism, and Teleology. The object of mechanical type is the immediate and undifferentiated object. No doubt it contains difference, but the different pieces stand, as it were, without affinity to each other, and their connection is only extraneous. In chemism, on the contrary, the object exhibits an essential tendency to differentiation, in such a way that the objects are what they are only by their relation to each other: this tendency to difference constitutes their quality. The third type of objectivity, the teleological relation, is the unity of mechanism and chemism. Design, like the mechanical object, is a self-contained totality, enriched however by the principle of differentiation which came to the fore in chemism, and thus referring itself to the object that stands over against it. Finally, it is the realization of design which forms the transition to the Idea.

(*a*) *Mechanism*

§ 195

The object (1) in its immediacy is the notion only potentially; the notion as subjective is primarily outside it; and all its specific character is imposed from without. As a unity of differents, therefore, it is a composite, an aggregate; and its capacity of acting on anything else continues to be an external relation. This is **Formal Mechanism**. Notwithstanding, and in this connection and non-independence, the objects remain independent and offer resistance, external to each other.

Pressure and impact are examples of mechanical relations. Our knowledge is said to be mechanical or by rote, when the words have no meaning for us, but continue external to sense, conception, thought; and when, being similarly external to each other, they form a meaningless sequence. Conduct, piety, etc., are in the same way mechanical, when a man's behaviour is settled for him by ceremonial laws, by a spiritual adviser, etc.; in short, when his own mind and will are not in his actions, which in this way are extraneous to himself.

Mechanism, the first form of objectivity, is also the category which primarily offers itself to reflection, as it examines the objective world. It is also the category beyond which reflection seldom goes. It is, however, a shallow and superficial mode of observation, one that cannot carry us through in connection with Nature and still less in connection with the world of Mind. In Nature it is only the veriest abstract relations of matter in its inert masses which obey the law of mechanism. On the contrary the phenomena and operations of the province to which the term 'physical' in its narrower sense is applied, such as the phenomena of light, heat, magnetism, and electricity, cannot be explained by any mere mechanical processes, such as pressure, impact, displacement of parts, and the like. Still less satisfactory is it to transfer these categories and apply them in the field of organic nature; at least if it be our aim to understand the specific features of that field, such as the growth and nourishment of plants, or, it may be, even animal sensation. It is at any rate a very deep-seated, and perhaps the main, defect of modern researches into nature, that, even where other and higher categories than those of mere mechanism are in operation, they still stick obstinately to the mechanical laws; although they thus conflict with the testimony of unbiased perception, and foreclose the gate to an adequate knowledge of nature. But even in considering the formations in the world of Mind, the mechanical theory has been repeatedly invested with an authority which it has no right to. Take as an instance the remark that man consists of soul and body. In this language, the two things stand each self-subsistent, and associated only from without. Similarly we find the soul regarded as a mere group of forces and faculties, subsisting independently side by side.

Thus decidedly must we reject the mechanical mode of inquiry when it comes forward and arrogates to itself the place of rational cognition in general, and seeks to get mechanism accepted as an absolute category. But we must not on that account forget expressly to vindicate for mechanism the right and import of a general logical category. It would be, therefore, a mistake to restrict it to the special physical department from which it derives its name. There is no harm done, for example, in directing attention to mechanical actions, such as that of gravity, the lever, etc., even in departments, notably in physics and in physiology, beyond the range of mechanics proper. It must however be remembered that within these spheres the laws of mechanism cease to be final or decisive, and sink, as it were, to a subservient position. To which may be added that in Nature, when the higher or organic functions are in any way checked or disturbed in their normal efficiency, the otherwise subordinate category of mechanism is immediately seen to take the upper hand. Thus a sufferer from indigestion feels pressure on the stomach, after partaking of certain food in slight quantity; whereas those whose digestive organs are sound remain free from the sensation, although they have eaten as much. The same phenomenon occurs in the general feeling of heaviness in the limbs, experienced in bodily indisposition. Even in the world of Mind, mechanism has its place; though there, too, it is a subordinate one. We are right in speaking of mechanical memory, and all sorts of mechanical operations, such as reading, writing, playing on musical instruments, etc. In memory, indeed, the mechanical quality of the action is essential: a circumstance of which the neglect has not unfrequently caused great harm in the training of the young, from the misapplied zeal of modern educationalists for the freedom of intelligence. It would betray bad psychology, however, to have recourse to mechanism for an explanation of the nature of memory, and to apply mechanical laws straight off to the soul. The mechanical feature in memory lies merely in the fact that certain signs, tones, etc., are apprehended in their purely external association, and then reproduced in this association, without attention being expressly directed to their meaning and inward association. To become acquainted with these conditions of mechanical memory requires no further study of mechanics, nor would that study tend at all to advance the special inquiry of psychology.

§ 196

The want of stability in itself which allows the object to suffer violence, is possessed by it (see preceding §) only in so far as it has a certain stability. Now as the object is implicitly invested with the character of notion, the one of these characteristics is not merged into its other; but the object, through the negation of itself (its lack of independence), closes with itself, and not till it so closes, is it independent. Thus at the same time in distinction from the outwardness, and negativing that outwardness in its independence, does this independence form a negative unity with self—**Centrality** (subjectivity). So conceived, the other itself has direction and reference towards the external. But this external object is similarly central in itself, and being so, is no less only referred towards the other centre; so that it no less has its centrality in the other. This is (2) **Mechanism with Affinity** (with bias, or 'difference'), and may be illustrated by gravitation, appetite, social instinct, etc.

§ 197

This relation, when fully carried out, forms a syllogism. In that syllogism the immanent negativity, as the central individuality of an object (abstract centre) relates itself to non-independent objects, as the other extreme, by a mean which unites the centrality with the non-independence of the objects (relative centre). This is (3) **Absolute Mechanism**.

§ 198

The syllogism thus indicated (I—P—U) is a triad of syllogisms. The wrong individuality of non-independent objects, in which formal Mechanism is at home, is, by reason of that non-independence, no less universality, though it be only external. Hence these objects also form the mean between the absolute and the relative centre (the form of syllogism being U—I—P): for it is by this want of independence that those two are kept asunder and made extremes, as well as related to one another. Similarly absolute centrality, as the permanently underlying universal substance (illustrated by the gravity which continues identical), which as pure negativity equally includes individuality in it, is what mediates between the relative centre and the non-independent objects (the form of syllogism being P—U—I). It does so no less essentially as a disintegrating force, in its character of immanent individuality, than in virtue of universality, acting as an identical bond of union and tranquil self-containedness.

Like the solar system, so for example in the practical sphere the state is a system of three syllogisms. (1) The Individual or person, through his particularity or physical or mental needs (which when carried out to their full development give *civil* society), is coupled with the universal, i.e. with society, law, right, government. (2) The will or action of the individuals is the intermediating force which procures for these needs satisfaction in society, in law, etc., and which gives to society, law, etc., their fulfilment and actualization. (3) But the universal, that is to say the state, government, and law, is the permanent underlying mean in which the individuals and their satisfaction have and receive their fulfilled reality, intermediation, and persistence. Each of the functions of the notion, as it is brought by intermediation to coalesce with the other extreme, is brought into union with itself and produces itself: which production is self-preservation. It is only by the nature of this triple coupling, by this triad of syllogisms with the same *termini*, that a whole is thoroughly understood in its organization.

§ 199

The immediacy of existence, which the objects have in Absolute Mechanism, is implicitly negatived by the fact that their independence is derived from, and due to, their connections with each other, and therefore to their own want of stability. Thus the object must be explicitly stated as in its existence having an **Affinity** (or a bias) towards its other—as not-indifferent.

(*b*) *Chemism*

§ 200

The not-indifferent (biased) object has an immanent mode which constitutes its nature, and in which it has existence. But as it is invested with the character of total notion, it is the contradiction between this totality and the special mode of its existence. Consequently it is the constant endeavour to cancel this contradiction and to make its definite being equal to the notion.

Chemism is a category of objectivity which, as a rule, is not particularly emphasized, and is generally put under the head of mechanism. The common name of mechanical relationship is applied to both, in contradistinction to the teleological. There is a reason for this in the common feature which belongs to mechanism and chemism. In them the notion exists, but only implicit and latent, and they are thus both marked off from teleology where the notion has real independent existence. This is true: and yet chemism and mechanism are very decidedly distinct. The object, in the form of mechanism, is primarily only an indifferent reference to self, while the chemical object is seen to be completely in reference to something else. No doubt even in mechanism, as it develops itself, there spring up references to something else: but the nexus of mechanical objects with one another is at first only an external nexus, so that the objects in connection with one another still retain the semblance of independence. In nature, for example, the several celestial bodies, which form our solar system, compose a kinetic system, and thereby show that they are related to one another. Motion, however, as the unity of time and space, is a connection which is purely abstract and external. And it seems therefore as if these celestial bodies, which are thus externally connected with each other, would continue to be what they are, even apart from this reciprocal relation. The case is quite different with chemism. Objects chemically biased are what they are expressly by that bias alone. Hence they are the absolute impulse towards integration by and in one another.

§ 201

The product of the chemical process consequently is the **Neutral** object, latent in the two extremes, each on the alert. The notion or concrete universal, by means of the bias of the objects (the particularity), coalesces with the individuality (in the shape of the product), and in that only with itself. In this process too the other syllogisms are equally involved. The place of mean is taken both by individuality as activity, and by the concrete universal, the essence of the strained extremes; which essence reaches definite being in the product.

§ 202

Chemism, as it is a reflectional nexus of objectivity, has presupposed, not merely the bias or non-indifferent nature of the objects, but also their immediate independence. The process of chemism consists in passing to and fro from one form to another; which forms continue to be as external as before. In the neutral product the specific properties, which the extremes bore towards each other, are merged. But although the product is conformable to the notion, the inspiring principle of active differentiation does not exist in it; for it has sunk back to immediacy. The neutral body is therefore capable of disintegration. But the discerning principle, which breaks up the neutral body into biased and strained extremes, and which gives to the indifferent object in general its affinity and animation towards another; that principle, and the process as a separation with tension, falls outside of that first process.

The chemical process does not rise above a conditioned and finite process. The notion as notion is only the heart and core of the process, and does not in this stage come to an existence of its own. In the neutral product the process is extinct, and the existing cause falls outside it.

§ 203

Each of these two processes, the reduction of the biased (not-indifferent) to the neutral, and the differentiation of the indifferent or neutral, goes its own way without hindrance from the other. But that want of inner connection shows that they are finite, by their passage into products in which they are merged and lost. Conversely the process exhibits the nonentity of the presupposed immediacy of the not-indifferent objects. By this negation of immediacy and of externalism in which the notion as object was sunk, it is liberated and invested with independent being in face of that externalism and immediacy. In these circumstances it is the End (Final Cause).

The passage from chemism to the teleological relation is implied in the mutual cancelling of both of the forms of the chemical process. The result thus attained is the liberation of the notion, which in chemism and mechanism was present only in the germ, and not yet evolved. The notion in the shape of the aim or end thus comes into independent existence.

(*c*) *Teleology*

§ 204

In the **End** the notion has entered on free existence and has a being of its own, by means of the negation of immediate objectivity. It is characterized as subjective, seeing that this negation is, in the first place, abstract, and hence at first the relation between it and objectivity still one of contrast. This character of subjectivity, however, compared with the totality of the notion, is one-sided, and that, be it added, for the End itself, in which all specific characters have been put as subordinated and merged. For it therefore even the object, which it presupposes, has only hypothetical (ideal) reality—essentially no-reality. The End, in short, is a contradiction of its self-identity against the negation stated in it, i.e. its antithesis to objectivity, and being so, contains the eliminative or destructive activity which negates the antithesis and renders it identical with itself. This is the realization of the End: in which, while it turns itself into the other of its subjectivity and objectifies itself, thus cancelling the distinction between the two, it has only closed with itself, and retained itself.

The notion of Design or End, while on one hand called redundant, is on another justly described as the rational notion, and contrasted with the abstract universal of understanding. The latter only *subsumes* the particular, and so connects it with itself: but has it not in its own nature. The distinction between the End or *final cause*, and the mere *efficient cause* (which is the cause ordinarily so called), is of supreme importance. Causes, properly so called, belong to the sphere of necessity, blind, and not yet laid bare. The cause therefore appears as passing into its correlative, and losing its primordiality there by sinking into dependency. It is only by implication, or for us, that the cause is in the effect made for the first time a cause, and that it there returns into itself. The End, on the other hand, is expressly stated as containing the specific character in its own self—the effect, namely, which in the purely causal relation is never free from otherness. The End therefore in its efficiency does not pass over, but retains itself, i.e. it carries into effect itself only, and is at the end what it was in the beginning or primordial state. Until it thus retains itself, it is not genuinely primordial. The End then requires to be speculatively apprehended as the notion, which itself in the proper unity and ideality of its characteristics contains the judgement or negation—the antithesis of subjective and objective—and which to an equal extent suspends that antithesis.

By End however we must not at once, nor must we ever merely, think of the form which it has in consciousness as a mode of mere mental representation. By means of the notion of **Inner Design** Kant has resuscitated the Idea in general and particularly the idea of life. Aristotle's definition of life virtually implies inner design, and is thus far in advance of the notion of design in modern Teleology, which had in view finite and outward design only.

Animal wants and appetites are some of the readiest instances of the End. They are the *felt* contradiction, which exists *within* the living subject, and pass into the activity of negating this negation which mere subjectivity still is. The satisfaction of the want or appetite restores the peace between subject and object. The objective thing which, so long as the contradiction exists, i.e. so long as the want is felt, stands on the other side, loses this quasi-independence, by its union with the subject. Those who talk of the permanence and immutability of the finite, as well subjective as objective, may see the reverse illustrated in the operations of every appetite. Appetite is, so to speak, the conviction that the subjective is only a half-truth, no more adequate than the objective. But appetite in the second place carries out its conviction. It brings about the supersession of these finites: it cancels the antithesis between the objective which would be and stay an objective only, and the subjective which in like manner would be and stay a subjective only.

As regards the action of the End, attention may be called to the fact, that in the syllogism, which represents that action, and shows the end closing with itself by the means of realization, the radical feature is the negation of the *termini*. That negation is the one just mentioned both of the immediate subjectivity appearing in the End as such, and of the immediate objectivity as seen in the means and the objects presupposed. This is the same negation as is in operation when the mind leaves the contingent things of the world as well as its own subjectivity and rises to God. It is the 'moment' or factor which (as noticed in the Introduction and § 192) was overlooked and neglected in the analytic form of syllogisms, under which the so-called proofs of the Being of a God presented this elevation.

§ 205

In its primary and immediate aspect the Teleological relation is *external* design, and the notion confronts a presupposed object. The End is consequently finite, and that partly in its content, partly in the circumstance that it has an external condition in the object, which has to be found existing, and which is taken as material for its realization. Its self-determining is to that extent in form only. The unmediatedness of the End has the further result that its particularity or content—which as form-characteristic is the subjectivity of the End—is reflected into self, and so different from the totality of the form, subjectivity in general, the notion. This variety constitutes the finitude of Design within its own nature. The content of the End, in this way, is quite as limited, contingent, and given, as the object is particular and found ready to hand.

Generally speaking, the final cause is taken to mean nothing more than external design. In accordance with this view of it, things are supposed not to carry their vocation in themselves, but merely to be means employed and spent in realizing a purpose which lies outside of them. That may be said to be the point of view taken by Utility, which once played a great part even in the sciences, but of late has fallen into merited disrepute, now that people have begun to see that it failed to give a genuine insight into the nature of things. It is true that finite things as finite ought in justice to be viewed as non-ultimate, and as pointing beyond themselves. This negativity of finite things however is their own dialectic, and in order to ascertain it we must pay attention to their positive content.

Teleological observations on things often proceed from a well-meant wish to display the wisdom of God as it is especially revealed in nature. Now in thus trying to discover final causes for which the things serve as means, we must remember that we are stopping short at the finite, and are liable to fall into trifling reflections: as, for instance, if we not merely studied the vine in respect of its well-known use for man, but proceeded to consider the cork-tree in connection with the corks which are cut from its bark to put into the wine-bottles. Whole books used to be written in this spirit. It is easy to see that they promoted the genuine interest neither of religion nor of science. External design stands immediately in front of the idea: but what thus stands on the threshold often for that reason is least adequate.

§ 206

The teleological relation is a syllogism in which the subjective end coalesces with the objectivity external to it, through a middle term which is the unity of both. This unity is on one hand the *purposive* action, on the other the *Means*, i.e. objectivity made directly subservient to purpose.

The development from End to Idea ensues by three stages, first, Subjective End; second, End in process of accomplishment; and third, End accomplished. First of all we have the Subjective End; and that, as the notion in independent being, is itself the totality of the elementary functions of the notion. The first of these functions is that of self-identical universality, as it were the neutral first water, in which everything is involved, but nothing as yet discriminated. The second of these elements is the particularizing of this universal, by which it acquires a specific content. As this specific content again is realized by the agency of the universal, the latter returns by its means back to itself, and coalesces with itself. Hence too when we set some end before us, we say that we 'conclude' to do something: a phrase which implies that we were, so to speak, open and accessible to this or that determination. Similarly we also at a further step speak of a man 'resolving' to do something, meaning that the agent steps forward out of his self-regarding inwardness and enters into dealings with the environing objectivity. This supplies the step from the merely Subjective End to the purposive action which tends outwards.

§ 207

(1) The first syllogism of the final cause represents the Subjective End. The universal notion is brought to unite with individuality by means of particularity, so that the individual as self-determination acts as judge. That is to say, it not only particularizes or makes into a determinate content the still indeterminate universal, but also explicitly puts an antithesis of subjectivity and objectivity, and at the same time is in its own self a return to itself; for it stamps the subjectivity of the notion, presupposed as against objectivity, with the mark of defect, in comparison with the complete and rounded totality, and thereby at the same time turns outwards.

§ 208

(2) This action which is directed outwards is the individuality, which in the Subjective End is identical with the particularity under which, along with the content, is also comprised the external objectivity. It throws itself in the first place immediately upon the object, which it appropriates to itself as a Means. The notion is this immediate power; for the notion is the self-identical negativity, in which the being of the object is characterized as wholly and merely ideal. The whole Middle Term is this inward power of the

notion, in the shape of an agency, with which the object as Means is 'immediately' united and in obedience to which it stands.

In finite teleology the Middle Term is broken up into two elements external to each other, (*a*) the action and (*b*) the object which serves as Means. The relation of the final cause as power to this object, and the subjugation of the object to it, is immediate (it forms the first premiss in the syllogism) to this extent, that in the teleological notion as the self-existent ideality the object is put as potentially null. This relation, as represented in the first premiss, itself becomes the Middle Term, which at the same time involves the syllogism, that through this relation—in which the action of the End is contained and dominant—the End is coupled with objectivity.

The execution of the End is the mediated mode of realizing the End; but the immediate realization is not less needful. The End lays hold of the object immediately, because it is the power over the object, because in the End particularity, and in particularity objectivity also, is involved. A living being has a body; the soul takes possession of it and without intermediary has objectified itself in it. The human soul has much to do, before it makes its corporeal nature into a means. Man must, as it were, take possession of his body, so that it may be the instrument of his soul.

§ 209

(3) Purposive action, with its Means, is still directed outwards, because the End is also *not* identical with the object, and must consequently first be mediated with it. The Means in its capacity of object stands, in this second premiss, in direct relation to the other extreme of the syllogism, namely, the material or objectivity which is presupposed. This relation is the sphere of chemism and mechanism, which have now become the servants of the Final Cause, where lies their truth and free notion. Thus the Subjective End, which is the power ruling these processes, in which the objective things wear themselves out on one another, contrives to keep itself free from them, and to preserve itself in them. Doing so, it appears as the Cunning of reason.

Reason is as cunning as it is powerful. Cunning may be said to lie in the intermediative action which, while it permits the objects to follow their own bent and act upon one another till they waste away, and does not itself directly interfere in the process, is nevertheless only working out its own aims. With this explanation, Divine Providence may be said to stand to the world and its process in the capacity of absolute cunning. God lets men do as they please with their particular passions and interests; but the result is the accomplishment of—not their plans, but his, and these differ decidedly from the ends primarily sought by those whom he employs.

§ 210

The realized End is thus the overt unity of subjective and objective. It is however essentially characteristic of this unity, that the subjective and objective are neutralized and cancelled only in the point of their one-sidedness, while the objective is subdued and made conformable to the End, as the free notion, and thereby to the power above it. The End maintains itself against and in the objective: for it is no mere one-sided subjective or particular, it is also the concrete universal, the implicit identity of both. This universal, as simply reflected in itself, is the content which remains unchanged through all the three *termini* of the syllogism and their movement.

§ 211

In finite design, however, even the executed End has the same radical rift or flaw as had the Means and the initial End. We have got therefore only a form extraneously impressed on a pre-existing material: and this form, by reason of the limited content of the End, is also a contingent characteristic. The End achieved consequently is only an object, which again becomes a Means or material for other Ends, and so on for ever.

§ 212

But what virtually happens in the realizing of the End is that the one-sided subjectivity and the show of objective independence confronting it are both cancelled. In laying hold of the means, the notion constitutes itself the very implicit essence of the object. In the mechanical and chemical processes the independence of the object has been already dissipated implicitly, and in the course of their movement under the dominion of the End, the show of that independence, the negative which confronts the notion, is got rid of. But in the fact that the End achieved is characterized only as a Means and a material, this object, viz. the teleological, is there and then put as implicitly null, and only 'ideal'. This being so, the antithesis between form and content has also vanished. While the End by the removal and absorption of all form-characteristics coalesces with itself, the form as self-identical is thereby put as the content, so that the notion, which is the action of form, has only itself for content. Through this process, therefore, there is made explicitly manifest what was the notion of design: viz. the implicit unity of subjective and objective is now realized. And this is the Idea.

This finitude of the End consists in the circumstance, that, in the process of realizing it, the material, which is employed as a means, is only externally subsumed under it and made conformable to it. But, as a matter of fact, the object is the notion implicitly: and thus when the notion, in the shape of End, is realized in the object, we have but the manifestation of the inner nature of the object itself. Objectivity is thus, as it were, only a covering under which the notion lies concealed. Within the range of the finite we can never see or experience that the End has been really secured. The consummation of the infinite End, therefore, consists merely in removing the illusion which makes it seem yet unaccomplished. The Good, the absolutely Good, is eternally accomplishing itself in the world: and the result is that it need not wait upon us, but is already by implication, as well as in full actuality, accomplished. This is the illusion under which we live. It alone supplies at the same time the actualizing force on which the interest in the world reposes. In the course of its process the Idea creates that illusion, by setting an antithesis to confront it; and its action consists in getting rid of the illusion which it has created. Only out of this error does the truth arise. In this fact lies the reconciliation with error and with finitude. Error or other-being, when superseded, is still a necessary dynamic element of truth: for truth can only be where it makes itself its own result.

C. THE IDEA

§ 213

The **Idea** is truth in itself and for itself—the absolute unity of the notion and objectivity. Its 'ideal' content is nothing but the notion in its detailed terms: its 'real' content is only the exhibition which the notion gives itself in the form of external existence, while yet, by enclosing this shape in its ideality, it keeps it in its power, and so keeps itself in it.

The definition, which declares the Absolute to be the Idea, is itself absolute. All former definitions come back to this. The Idea is the Truth: for Truth is the correspondence of objectivity with the notion—not of course the correspondence of external things with my conceptions, for these are only *correct* conceptions held by *me*, the individual person. In the idea we have nothing to do with the individual, nor with figurate conceptions, nor with external things. And yet, again, everything actual, in so far as it is true, is the Idea, and has its truth by and in virtue of the Idea alone. Every individual being is some one aspect of the Idea: for which, therefore, yet other actualities are needed, which in their turn appear to have a self-subsistence of their own. It is only in them altogether and in their relation that the notion is realized. The individual by itself does not correspond to its notion. It is this limitation of its existence which constitutes the finitude and the ruin of the individual.

The Idea itself is not to be taken as an idea of something or other, any more than the notion is to be taken as merely a specific notion. The Absolute is the universal and one idea, which, by an act of 'judgement', particularizes itself to the system of specific ideas; which after all are constrained by their nature to come back to the one idea where their truth lies. As issued out of this 'judgement' the Idea is *in the first place* only the one universal *substance*: but its developed and genuine actuality is to be as a *subject* and in that way as mind.

Because it has no *existence* for starting-point and *point d'appui*, the Idea is frequently treated as a mere logical form. Such a view must be abandoned to those theories which ascribe so-called reality and genuine actuality to the existent thing and all the other categories which have not yet penetrated as far as the Idea. It is no less false to imagine the Idea to be mere abstraction. It is abstract certainly, in so far as everything untrue is consumed in it: but in its own self it is essentially concrete, because it is the free notion giving character to itself, and that character, reality. It would be an abstract form, only if the notion, which is its principle, were taken as an abstract unity, and not as the negative return of it into self and as the subjectivity which it really is.

Truth is at first taken to mean that I *know* how something *is*. This is truth, however, only in reference to consciousness; it is formal truth, bare correctness. Truth in the deeper sense consists in the identity between objectivity and the notion. It is in this deeper sense of truth that we speak of a true state, or of a true work of art. These objects are true, if they are as they ought to be, i.e. if their reality corresponds to their notion. When thus viewed, to be untrue means much the same as to be bad. A bad man is an untrue man, a man who does not behave as his notion or his vocation requires. Nothing however can subsist, if it be *wholly* devoid of identity between the notion and reality. Even bad and untrue things have being, in so far as their reality still, somehow, conforms to their notion. Whatever is thoroughly bad or contrary to the notion is for that very reason on the way to ruin. It is by the notion alone that the things in the world have their subsistence; or, as it is expressed in the language of religious conception, things are what they are, only in virtue of the divine and thereby creative thought which dwells within them.

When we hear the Idea spoken of, we need not imagine something far away beyond this mortal sphere. The idea is rather what is completely present: and it is found, however confused and degenerated, in every consciousness. We conceive the world to ourselves as a great totality which is created by God, and so created that in it God has manifested himself to us. We regard the world also as ruled by Divine Providence: implying that the scattered and divided parts of the world are continually brought back, and made conformable, to the unity from which they have issued. The purpose of philosophy has always been the intellectual ascertainment of the Idea; and everything deserving the name of philosophy has constantly been based on the consciousness of an absolute unity where the understanding sees and accepts only separation. It is too late now to ask for proof that the Idea is the truth. The proof of that is contained in the whole deduction and development of thought up to this point. The idea is the result of this course of dialectic. Not that it is to be supposed that the idea is mediate only, i.e. mediated through something else than itself. It is rather its own result, and being so, is no less immediate than mediate. The stages hitherto considered, viz. those of Being and Essence, as well as those of Notion and of Objectivity, are not, when so distinguished, something permanent, resting upon themselves. They have proved to be dialectical; and their only truth is that they are dynamic elements of the idea.

§ 214

The Idea may be described in many ways. It may be called reason (and this is the proper philosophical signification of reason);

subject-object; the unity of the ideal and the real, of the finite and the infinite, of soul and body; the possibility which has its actuality in its own self; that of which the nature can be thought only as existent, etc. All these descriptions apply, because the Idea contains all the relations of understanding, but contains them in their infinite self-return and self-identity.

It is easy work for the understanding to show that everything said of the Idea is self-contradictory. But that can quite as well be retaliated, or rather in the Idea the retaliation is actually made. And this work, which is the work of reason, is certainly not so easy as that of the understanding. Understanding may demonstrate that the Idea is self-contradictory: because the subjective is subjective only and is always confronted by the objective; because being is different from notion and therefore cannot be picked out of it; because the finite is finite only, the exact antithesis of the infinite, and therefore not identical with it; and so on with every term of the description. The reverse of all this however is the doctrine of Logic. Logic shows that the subjective which is to be subjective only, the finite which would be finite only, the infinite which would be infinite only, and so on, have no truth, but contradict themselves, and pass over into their opposites. Hence this transition, and the unity in which the extremes are merged and become factors, each with a merely reflected existence, reveals itself as their truth.

The understanding, which addresses itself to deal with the Idea, commits a double misunderstanding. It takes *first* the extremes of the Idea (be they expressed as they will, so long as they are in their unity), not as they are understood when stamped with this concrete unity, but as if they remained abstractions outside of it. It no less mistakes the relation between them, even when it has been expressly stated. Thus, for example, it overlooks even the nature of the copula in the judgement, which affirms that the individual, or subject, is after all not individual, but universal. But, in the *second* place, the understanding believes *its* 'reflection' —that the self-identical Idea contains its own negative, or contains contradiction—to be an external reflection which does not lie within the Idea itself. But the reflection is really no peculiar cleverness of the understanding. The idea itself is the dialectic which for ever divides and distinguishes the self-identical from the differentiated, the subjective from the objective, the finite from the infinite, soul from body. Only on these terms is it an eternal creation, eternal vitality, and eternal spirit. But while it thus passes or rather translates itself into the abstract understanding, it for ever remains reason. The Idea is the dialectic which again makes this mass of understanding and diversity understand its finite nature and the pseudo-independence in its productions, and which brings the diversity back to unity. Since this double movement is not separate or distinct in time, nor indeed in any other way—otherwise it would be only a repetition of the abstract understanding—the Idea is the eternal vision of itself in the other, notion which in its objectivity *has* carried out *itself*, object which is inward design, essential subjectivity.

The different modes of apprehending the Idea as unity of ideal and real, of finite and infinite, of identity and difference, etc., are more or less formal. They designate some stage of the *specific* notion. Only the notion itself, however, is free and the genuine universal: in the Idea, therefore, the specific character of the notion is only the notion itself—an objectivity, viz. into which it, being the universal, continues itself, and in which it has only its own character, the total character. The Idea is the infinite judgement, of which the terms are severally the independent totality; and in which, as each grows to the fullness of its own nature, it has thereby at the same time passed into the other. None of the other specific notions exhibits this totality complete on both its sides as the notion itself and objectivity.

§ 215

The Idea is essentially a process, because its identity is the absolute and free identity of the notion, only in so far as it is absolute negativity and for that reason dialectical. It is the round of movement, in which the notion, in the capacity of universality which is individuality, gives itself the character of objectivity and of the antithesis thereto; and this externality which has the notion for its substance, finds its way back to subjectivity through its immanent dialectic.

As the idea is (*a*) a process, it follows that such an expression for the Absolute as *unity* of thought and being, of finite and infinite, etc., is false; for unity expresses an abstract and merely quiescent identity. As the Idea is (*b*) subjectivity, it follows that the expression is equally false on another account. That unity of which it speaks expresses a merely virtual or underlying presence of the genuine unity. The infinite would thus seem to be merely *neutralized* by the finite, the subjective by the objective, thought by being. But in the negative unity of the Idea, the infinite overlaps and includes the finite, thought overlaps being, subjectivity overlaps objectivity. The unity of the Idea is thought, infinity, and subjectivity, and is in consequence to be essentially distinguished from the Idea as *substance*, just as this overlapping subjectivity, thought, or infinity is to be distinguished from the one-sided subjectivity, one-sided thought, one-sided infinity to which it descends in judging and defining.

The idea as a process runs through three stages in its development. The first form of the idea is Life: that is, the idea in the form of immediacy. The second form is that of mediation or differentiation; and this is the idea in the form of Knowledge, which appears under the double aspect of the Theoretical and Practical idea. The process of knowledge eventuates in the restoration of the unity enriched by difference. This gives the third form of the idea, the Absolute Idea: which last stage of the logical idea evinces itself to be at the same time the true first, and to have a being due to itself alone.

(*a*) *Life*

§ 216

The *immediate* idea is **Life**. As *soul*, the notion is realized in a body of whose externality the soul is the immediate self-relating universality. But the soul is also its particularization, so that the body expresses no other distinctions than follow from the characterizations of its notion. And finally it is the Individuality of the body as infinite negativity—the dialectic of that bodily objectivity, with its parts lying out of one another, conveying them away from the semblance of independent subsistence back into subjectivity, so that all the members are reciprocally momentary means as well as momentary ends. Thus as life is the initial particularization, so it results in the negative self-asserting unity: in the dialectic of its corporeity it only coalesces with itself. In this way life is essentially something alive, and in point of its immediacy this individual living thing. It is characteristic of finitude in this sphere that, by reason of the immediacy of the idea, body and soul are separable. This constitutes the mortality of the living being. It is only, however, when the living being is dead, that these two sides of the idea are different *ingredients*.

The single members of the body are what they are only by and in relation to their unity. A hand e.g. when hewn off from the body is, as Aristotle has observed, a hand in name only, not in fact. From the point of view of understanding, life is usually spoken of as a mystery, and in general as incomprehensible. By giving it such a name, however, the Understanding only confesses its own finitude and nullity. So far is life from being incomprehensible, that in it the very notion is presented to us, or rather the immediate idea existing as a notion. And having said this, we have indicated the defect of life. Its notion and reality do not thoroughly correspond to each other. The notion of life is the soul, and this notion has the body for its reality. The soul is, as it were, infused into its corporeity; and in that way it is at first sentient only, and not yet freely self-conscious. The process of life consists in getting the better of the immediacy with which it is still beset: and this process, which is itself threefold, results in the idea under the form of judgement, i.e. the idea as Cognition.

§ 217

A living being is a syllogism, of which the very elements are in themselves systems and syllogisms (§§ 198, 201, 207). They are however active syllogisms or processes; and in the subjective unity of the vital agent make only one process. Thus the living being is the process of its coalescence with itself, which runs on through three processes.

§ 218

(1) The first is the process of the living being inside itself. In that process it makes a split on its own self, and reduces its corporeity to its object or its inorganic nature. This corporeity, as an aggregate of correlations, enters in its very nature into difference and opposition of its elements, which mutually become each other's prey, and assimilate one another, and are retained by producing themselves. Yet this action of the several members (organs) is only

the living subject's one act to which their productions revert; so that in these productions nothing is produced except the subject: in other words, the subject only reproduces itself.

The process of the vital subject within its own limits has in Nature the threefold form of Sensibility, Irritability, and Reproduction. As Sensibility, the living being is immediately simple self-relation—it is the soul omnipresent in its body, the outsideness of each member of which to others has for it no truth. As Irritability, the living being appears split up in itself; and as Reproduction, it is perpetually restoring itself from the inner distinction of its members and organs. A vital agent only exists as this continually self-renewing process within its own limits.

§ 219

(2) But the judgement of the notion proceeds, as free, to discharge the objective or bodily nature as an independent totality from itself; and the negative relation of the living thing to itself makes, as immediate individuality, the presupposition of an inorganic nature confronting it. As this negative of the animate is no less a function in the notion of the animate itself, it exists consequently in the latter (which is at the same time a concrete universal) in the shape of a defect or want. The dialectic by which the object, being implicitly null, is merged is the action of the self-assured living thing, which in this process against an inorganic nature thus retains, develops, and objectifies itself.

The living being stands face to face with an inorganic nature, to which it comports itself as a master and which it assimilates to itself. The result of the assimilation is not, as in the chemical process, a neutral product in which the independence of the two confronting sides is merged; but the living being shows itself as large enough to embrace its other which cannot withstand its power. The inorganic nature which is subdued by the vital agent suffers this fate, because it is *virtually* the same as what life is *actually*. Thus in the other the living being only coalesces with itself. But when the soul has fled from the body, the elementary powers of objectivity begin their play. These powers are, as it were, continually on the spring, ready to begin their process in the organic body; and life is the constant battle against them.

§ 220

(3) The living individual, which in its first process comports itself as intrinsically subject and notion, through its second assimilates

its external objectivity and thus puts the character of reality into itself. It is now therefore implicitly a **Kind**, with essential universality of nature. The particularizing of this Kind is the relation of the living subject to another subject of its Kind: and the judgement is the tie of Kind over these individuals thus appointed for each other. This is the Affinity of the Sexes.

§ 221

The process of Kind brings it to a being of its own. Life being no more than the idea immediate, the product of this process breaks up into two sides. On the one hand, the living individual, which was at first presupposed as immediate, is now seen to be mediated and generated. On the other, however, the living individuality, which, on account of its first immediacy, stands in a negative attitude towards universality, sinks in the superior power of the latter.

The living being dies, because it is a contradiction. Implicitly it is the universal or Kind, and yet immediately it exists as an individual only. Death shows the Kind to be the power that rules the immediate individual. For the animal the process of Kind is the highest point of its vitality. But the animal never gets so far in its Kind as to have a being of its own; it succumbs to the power of Kind. In the process of Kind the immediate living being mediates itself with itself, and thus rises above its immediacy, only however to sink back into it again. Life thus runs away, in the first instance, only into the false infinity of the progress *ad infinitum*. The real result, however, of the process of life, in the point of its notion, is to merge and overcome that immediacy with which the idea, in the shape of life, is still beset.

§ 222

In this manner however the idea of life has thrown off not some one particular and immediate 'This', but this first immediacy as a whole. It thus comes to itself, to its truth: it enters upon existence as a free Kind self-subsistent. The death of merely immediate and individual vitality is the 'procession' of spirit.

(*b*) *Cognition in general*

§ 223

The idea exists free for itself, in so far as it has universality for the medium of its existence—as objectivity itself has notional being—

as the idea is its own object. Its subjectivity, thus universalized, is *pure* self-contained distinguishing of the idea—intuition which keeps itself in this identical universality. But, as *specific* distinguishing, it is the further judgement of repelling itself as a totality from itself, and thus, in the first place, presupposing itself as an external universe. There are two judgements, which though implicitly identical are not yet explicitly put as identical.

§ 224

The relation of these two ideas, which implicitly and as life are identical, is thus one of correlation: and it is that correlativity which constitutes the characteristic of finitude in this sphere. It is the relationship of reflection, seeing that the distinguishing of the idea in its own self is only the first judgement—presupposing the other and not yet supposing itself to constitute it. And thus for the subjective idea the objective is the immediate world found ready to hand, or the idea as life is in the phenomenon of individual existence. At the same time, in so far as this judgement is pure distinguishing within its own limits (§ 223), the idea realizes in one both itself and its other. Consequently it is the certitude of the virtual identity between itself and the objective world. Reason comes to the world with an absolute faith in its ability to make the identity actual, and to raise its certitude to truth; and with the instinct of realizing explicitly the nullity of that contrast which it sees to be implicitly null.

§ 225

This process is in general terms **Cognition**. In Cognition in a single act the contrast is virtually superseded, as regards both the one-sidedness of subjectivity and the one-sidedness of objectivity. At first, however, the supersession of the contrast is but implicit. The process as such is in consequence immediately infected with the finitude of this sphere, and splits into the twofold movement of the instinct of reason, presented as two different movements. On the one hand it supersedes the one-sidedness of the Idea's subjectivity by receiving the existing world into itself, into subjective conception and thought; and with this objectivity, which is thus taken to be real and true, for its content it fills up the abstract certitude of itself. On the other hand, it supersedes the one-sidedness of the objective world, which is now, on the contrary, estimated as only a mere semblance, a collection of contingencies and shapes at bottom visionary. It modifies and informs that world by the inward nature of the subjective, which is here taken to be the genuine objective. The former is the instinct of science after Truth, Cognition properly so called—the **Theoretical** action of the idea. The latter is the instinct of the Good to fulfil the same—the **Practical** activity of the idea or Volition.

(α) *Cognition proper*

§ 226

The universal finitude of Cognition, which lies in the one judgement, the presupposition of the contrast (§ 224)—a presupposition in contradiction of which its own act lodges protest—specializes itself more precisely on the face of its own idea. The result of that specialization is that its two elements receive the aspect of being diverse from each other, and, as they are at least complete, they take up the relation of 'reflection', not of 'notion', to one another. The assimilation of the matter, therefore, as a datum, presents itself in the light of a reception of it into categories which at the same time remain external to it, and which meet each other in the same style of diversity. Reason is active here, but it is reason in the shape of understanding. The truth which such Cognition can reach will therefore be only finite: the infinite truth (of the notion) is isolated and made transcendent, an inaccessible goal in a world of its own. Still in its external action cognition stands under the guidance of the notion, and notional principles form the secret clue to its movement.

The finitude of Cognition lies in the presupposition of a world already in existence, and in the consequent view of the knowing subject as a *tabula rasa*. The conception is one attributed to Aristotle; but no man is further than Aristotle from such an outside theory of Cognition. Such a style of Cognition does not recognize in itself the activity of the notion—an activity which it is implicitly, but not consciously. In its own estimation its procedure is passive. Really that procedure is active.

§ 227

Finite Cognition, when it presupposes what is distinguished from it to be something already existing and confronting it—to be the various facts of external nature or of consciousness—has, in the first place, (1) formal identity or the abstraction of universality for the form of its action. Its activity therefore consists in analysing the given concrete object, isolating its differences, and giving them the form of abstract universality. Or it leaves the concrete thing as a ground, and by setting aside the unessential-looking particulars, brings into relief a concrete universal, the Genus, or Force and Law. This is the **Analytical Method**.

People generally speak of the analytical and synthetic methods, as if it depended solely on our choice which we pursued. This is far from the case. It depends on the form of the objects of our investigation, which of the two methods that are derivable from the notion of finite cognition ought to be applied. In the first place, cognition is analytical. Analytical cognition deals with an object which is presented in detachment, and the aim of its action is to trace back to a universal the individual object before it. Thought in such circumstances means no more than an act of abstraction or of formal identity. That is the sense in which thought is understood by Locke and all empiricists. Cognition, it is often said, can never do more than separate the given concrete objects into their abstract elements, and then consider these elements in their isolation. It is, however, at once apparent that this turns things upside down, and that cognition, if its purpose be to take things as they are, thereby falls into contradiction with itself. Thus the chemist e.g. places a piece of flesh in his retort, tortures it in many ways, and then informs us that it consists of nitrogen, carbon, hydrogen, etc. True: but these abstract matters have ceased to be flesh. The same defect occurs in the reasoning of an empirical psychologist when he analyses an action into the various aspects which it presents, and then sticks to these aspects in their separation. The object which is subjected to analysis is treated as a sort of onion from which one coat is peeled off after another.

§ 228

This universality is (2) also a specific universality. In this case the line of activity follows the three 'moments' of the notion, which (as it has not its infinity in finite cognition) is the specific or definite notion of understanding. The reception of the object into the forms of this notion is the **Synthetic Method**.

The movement of the Synthetic method is the reverse of the Analytical method. The latter starts from the individual, and proceeds to the universal; in the former the starting-point is given by the universal (as a definition), from which we proceed by particularizing (in division) to the individual (the theorem). The Synthetic method thus presents itself as the development—the 'moments' of the notion on the object.

§ 229

(*a*) When the object has been in the first instance brought by cognition into the form of the specific notion in general, so that in this way its genus and its universal character or speciality are explicitly stated, we have the **Definition**. The materials and the proof of Definition are procured by means of the Analytical method (§ 227). The specific character however is expected to be a 'mark' only: that is to say it is to be in behoof only of the purely subjective cognition which is external to the object.

Definition involves the three organic elements of the notion: the universal or proximate genus (*genus proximum*), the particular or specific character of the genus (*qualitas specifica*), and the individual, or object defined. The first question that definition suggests, is where it comes from. The general answer to this question is to say, that definitions originate by way of analysis. This will explain how it happens that people quarrel about the correctness of proposed definitions; for here everything depends on what perceptions we started from, and what points of view we had before our eyes in so doing. The richer the object to be defined is, that is, the more numerous are the aspects which it offers to our notice, the more various are the definitions we may frame of it. Thus there are quite a host of definitions of life, of the state, etc. Geometry, on the contrary, dealing with a theme so abstract as space, has an easy task in giving definitions. Again, in respect of the matter or contents of the objects defined, there is no constraining necessity present. We are expected to admit that space exists, that there are plants, animals, etc., nor is it the business of geometry, botany, etc., to demonstrate that the objects in question necessarily are. This very circumstance makes the synthetic method of cognition as little suitable for philosophy as the analytical: for philosophy has above all things to leave no doubt of the necessity of its objects. And yet several attempts have been made to introduce the synthetic method into philosophy. Thus Spinoza, in particular, begins with definitions. He says, for instance, that substance is the *causa sui*. His definitions are unquestionably a storehouse of the most speculative truth, but it takes the shape of dogmatic assertions. The same thing is also true of Schelling.

§ 230

(β) The statement of the second element of the notion, i.e. of the specific character of the universal as particularizing, is given by **Division** in accordance with some external consideration.

Division we are told ought to be complete. That requires a principle or ground of division so constituted that the division based upon it embraces the whole extent of the region designated by the definition in general. But, in division, there is the further requirement that the principle of it must be borrowed from the nature of the object in question. If this condition be satisfied, the division is natural and not merely artificial, that is to say, arbitrary. Thus, in zoology, the ground of division adopted in the classification of the mammalia is mainly afforded by their teeth and claws. That is so far sensible, as the mammals themselves distinguish themselves from one another by these parts of their bodies; back to which therefore the general type of their various classes is to be traced. In every case the genuine division must be controlled by the notion. To that extent a division, in the first instance, has three members: but as particularity exhibits itself as double, the division may go to the extent even of four members. In the sphere of mind trichotomy is predominant, a circumstance which Kant has the credit for bringing into notice.

§ 231

(γ) In the concrete individuality, where the mere unanalysed quality of the definition is regarded as a correlation of elements, the object is a synthetic nexus of distinct characteristics. It is a **Theorem**. Being different, these characteristics possess but a mediated identity. To supply the materials, which form the middle terms, is the office of **Construction**: and the process of mediation itself, from which cognition derives the necessity of that nexus, is the **Demonstration**.

As the difference between the analytical and synthetic methods is commonly stated, it seems entirely optional which of the two we employ. If we assume, to start with, the concrete thing which the synthetic method presents as a result, we can analyse from it as consequences the abstract propositions which formed the presuppositions and the material for the proof. Thus, algebraical definitions of curved lines are theorems in the method of geometry. Similarly even the Pythagorean theorem, if made the definition of a right-angled triangle, might yield to analysis those propositions which geometry had already demonstrated on its behoof. The optionalness of either method is due to both alike starting from an external presupposition. So far as the nature of the notion is concerned, analysis is prior, since it has to raise the given material with its empirical concreteness into the form of general abstractions, which may then be set in the front of the synthetic method as definitions.

That these methods, however indispensable and brilliantly successful in their own province, are unserviceable for philosophical cognition, is self-evident. They have presuppositions; and their style of cognition is that of understanding, proceeding under the canon of formal identity. In Spinoza, who was especially addicted to the use of the geometrical method, we are at once struck by its characteristic formalism. Yet his ideas were speculative in spirit; whereas the system of Wolf, who carried the method out to the height of pedantry, was even in subject-matter a metaphysic of the understanding. The abuses which these methods with their formalism once led to in philosophy and science have in modern times been followed by the abuses of what is called 'Construction'. Kant brought into vogue the phrase that mathematics 'construes' its notions. All that was meant by the phrase was that mathematics has not to do with notions, but with abstract qualities of sense-perceptions. The name 'Construction (*construing*) of notions' has since been given to a sketch or statement of sensible attributes which were picked up from perception, quite guiltless of any influence of the notion, and to the additional formalism of classifying scientific and philosophical objects in a tabular form on some presupposed rubric, but in other respects at the fancy and discretion of the observer. In the background of all this, certainly, there is a dim consciousness of the Idea, of the unity of the notion and objectivity—a consciousness, too, that the idea is concrete. But that play of what is styled 'construing' is far from presenting this unity adequately, a unity which is none other than the notion properly so called: and the sensuous concreteness of perception is as little the concreteness of reason and the idea.

Another point calls for notice. Geometry works with the sensuous but abstract perception of space; and in space it experiences no difficulty in isolating and defining certain simple analytic modes.

To geometry alone therefore belongs in its perfection the synthetic method of finite cognition. In its course, however (and this is the remarkable point), it finally stumbles upon what are termed irrational and incommensurable quantities; and in their case any attempt at further specification drives it beyond the principle of the understanding. This is only one of many instances in terminology, where the title 'rational' is perversely applied to the province of understanding, while we stigmatize as irrational that which shows a beginning and a trace of rationality. Other sciences, removed as they are from the simplicity of space or number, often and necessarily reach a point where understanding permits no further advance: but they get over the difficulty without trouble. They make a break in the strict sequence of their procedure, and assume whatever they require, though it be the reverse of what preceded, from some external quarter—opinion, perception, conception, or any other source. Its inobservancy as to the nature of its methods and their relativity to the subject-matter prevents this finite cognition from seeing that, when it proceeds by definitions and divisions, etc., it is really led on by the necessity of the laws of the notion. For the same reason it cannot see when it has reached its limit; nor, if it have transgressed that limit, does it perceive that it is in a sphere where the categories of understanding, which it still continues rudely to apply, have lost all authority.

§ 232

The necessity which finite cognition produces in the Demonstration is, in the first place, an external necessity, intended for the subjective intelligence alone. But in necessity as such, cognition itself has left behind its presupposition and starting-point, which consisted in accepting its content as given or found. Necessity *qua* necessity is implicitly the self-relating notion. The subjective idea has thus implicitly reached an original and objective determinateness—a something not-given, and for that reason immanent in the subject. It has passed over into the idea of Will.

The necessity which cognition reaches by means of the demonstration is the reverse of what formed its starting-point. In its starting-point cognition had a given and a contingent content; but now, at the close of its movement, it knows its content to be necessary. This necessity is reached by means of subjective agency. Similarly, subjectivity at starting was quite abstract, a bare *tabula rasa*. It now shows itself as a modifying and determining principle. In this way we pass from the idea of cognition to that of will. The passage, as will be apparent on a closer examination, means that the universal, to be truly apprehended, must be apprehended as subjectivity, as a notion self-moving, active, and form-imposing.

(β) *Volition*

§ 233

The subjective idea as original and objective determinateness, and as a simple uniform content, is the **Good**. Its impulse towards self-realization is in its behaviour the reverse of the idea of truth, and rather directed towards moulding the world it finds before it into a shape conformable to its purposed End. This **Volition** has, on the one hand, the certitude of the nothingness of the presupposed object; but, on the other, as finite, it at the same time presupposes the purposed End of the Good to be a mere subjective idea, and the object to be independent.

§ 234

This action of the Will is finite: and its finitude lies in the contradiction that in the inconsistent terms applied to the objective world the End of the Good is just as much not executed as executed, the end in question put as unessential as much as essential, as actual and at the same time as merely possible. This contradiction presents itself to imagination as an endless progress in the actualizing of the Good; which is therefore set up and fixed as a mere 'ought', or goal of perfection. In point of form however this contradiction vanishes when the action supersedes the subjectivity of the purpose, and along with it the objectivity, with the contrast which makes both finite; abolishing subjectivity as a whole and not merely the one-sidedness of this form of it. (For another new subjectivity of the kind, that is, a new generation of the contrast, is not distinct from that which is supposed to be past and gone.) This return into itself is at the same time the content's own 'recollection' that it is the Good and the implicit identity of the two sides—it is a 'recollection' of the presupposition of the theoretical attitude of mind (§ 224) that the objective world is its own truth and substantiality.

While Intelligence merely proposes to take the world as it is, Will takes steps to make the world what it ought to be. Will looks upon the immediate and given present not as solid being, but as mere semblance without reality. It is here that we meet those contradictions which are so bewildering from the standpoint of abstract morality. This position in its 'practical' bearings is the one taken by the philosophy of Kant, and even by that of Fichte. The Good, say these writers, has to be realized: we have to work in order to produce it: and Will is only the Good actualizing itself. If the world then were as it ought to be, the action of Will would be at an end. The Will itself therefore requires that its End should not be realized. In these words, a correct expression is given to the *finitude* of Will. But finitude was not meant to be the ultimate point: and it is the process of Will itself which abolishes finitude and the contradiction it involves. The reconciliation is achieved when Will in its result returns to the presupposition made by cognition. In other words, it consists in the unity of the theoretical and practical idea. Will knows the end to be its own, and Intelligence apprehends the world as the notion actual. This is the right attitude of rational cognition. Nullity and transitoriness constitute only the superficial features and not the real essence of the world. That essence is the notion in *posse* and in *esse*: and thus the world is itself the idea. All unsatisfied endeavour ceases, when we recognize that the final purpose of the world is accomplished no less than ever accomplishing itself. Generally speaking, this is the man's way of looking; while the young imagine that the world is utterly sunk in wickedness, and that the first thing needful is a thorough transformation. The religious mind, on the contrary, views the world as ruled by Divine Providence, and therefore correspondent with what it ought to be. But this harmony between the 'is' and the 'ought to be' is not torpid and rigidly stationary. Good, the final end of the world, has being, only while it constantly produces itself. And the world of spirit and the world of nature continue to have this distinction, that the latter moves only in a recurring cycle, while the former certainly also makes progress.

§ 235

Thus the truth of the Good is laid down as the unity of the theoretical and practical idea in the doctrine that the Good is radically and really achieved, that the objective world is in itself and for itself the Idea, just as it at the same time eternally lays itself down as End, and by action brings about its actuality. This life which has returned to itself from the bias and finitude of cognition, and which by the activity of the notion has become identical with it, is the **Speculative** or **Absolute Idea**.

(*c*) *The Absolute Idea*

§ 236

The Idea, as unity of the Subjective and Objective Idea, is the notion of the Idea—a notion whose object (*Gegenstand*) is the Idea as such, and for which the objective (*Objekt*) is Idea—an Object which embraces all characteristics in its unity. This unity is consequently the absolute and all truth, the Idea which thinks itself—and here at least as a thinking or Logical Idea.

The Absolute Idea is, in the first place, the unity of the theoretical and practical idea, and thus at the same time the unity of the idea of life with the idea of cognition. In cognition we had the idea in a biased, one-sided shape. The process of cognition has issued in the overthrow of this bias and the restoration of that unity, which as unity, and in its immediacy, is in the first instance the Idea of Life. The defect of life lies in its being only the idea implicit or natural: whereas cognition is in an equally one-sided way the merely conscious idea, or the idea for itself. The unity and truth of these two is the Absolute Idea, which is both in itself and for itself. Hitherto *we* have had the idea in development through its various grades as *our* object, but now the idea comes to be its *own object*. This is the νόησις νοήσεως which Aristotle long ago termed the supreme form of the idea.

§ 237

Seeing that there is in it no transition, or presupposition, and in general no specific character other than what is fluid and transparent, the Absolute Idea is for itself the pure form of the notion, which contemplates its contents as its own self. It is its own content, in so far as it ideally distinguishes itself from itself, and the one of the two things distinguished is a self-identity in which however is contained the totality of the form as the system of terms describing its content. This content is the system of Logic. All that is at this stage left as form for the idea is the Method of this content—the specific consciousness of the value and currency of the 'moments' in its development.

To speak of the absolute idea may suggest the conception that we are at length reaching the right thing and the sum of the whole matter. It is certainly possible to indulge in a vast amount of senseless declamation about the idea absolute. But its true content is only the whole system of which we have been hitherto studying the development. It may also be said in this strain that the absolute idea is the universal, but the universal not merely as an abstract form to which the particular content is a stranger, but as the absolute form, into which all the categories, the whole fullness of the content it has given being to, have retired. The absolute idea may in this respect be compared to the old man who utters the same creed as the child, but for whom it is pregnant with the significance of a lifetime. Even if the child understands the truths of religion, he cannot but imagine them to be something outside of which lies the whole of life and the whole of the world. The same may be said to be the case with human life as a whole and the occurrences with which it is fraught. All work is directed only to the aim or end; and when it is attained, people are surprised to find nothing else but just the very thing which they had wished for. The interest lies in the whole movement. When a man traces up the steps of his life, the end may appear to him very restricted: but in it the whole *decursus vitae* is comprehended. So, too, the content of the absolute idea is the whole breadth of ground which has passed under our view up to this point. Last of all comes the discovery that the whole evolution is what constitutes the content and the interest. It is indeed the prerogative of the philosopher to see that everything, which, taken apart, is narrow and restricted, receives its value by its connection with the whole, and by forming an organic element of the idea. Thus it is that we have had the content already, and what we have now is the knowledge that the content is the living development of the idea. This simple retrospect is contained in the *form* of the idea. Each of the stages hitherto reviewed is an image of the absolute, but at first in a limited mode, and thus it is forced onwards to the whole, the evolution of which is what we termed Method.

§ 238

The several steps or stages of the Speculative Method are, first of all, (*a*) the Beginning, which is Being or Immediacy: self-subsistent, for the simple reason that it is the beginning. But looked at from the speculative idea, Being is its self-specializing act, which as the absolute negativity or movement of the notion makes a judgement and puts itself as its own negative. Being, which to the beginning as beginning seems mere abstract affirmation, is thus rather negation, dependency, derivation, and presupposition. But it is the notion of which Being is the negation: and the notion is completely self-identical in its otherness, and is the certainty of itself. Being therefore is the notion implicit, before it has been explicitly put as a notion. This Being therefore, as the still unspecified notion—a notion that is only implicitly or 'immediately' specified—is equally describable as the Universal.

When it means immediate being, the beginning is taken from sensation and perception—the initial stage in the analytical method of finite cognition. When it means universality, it is the beginning of the systematic method. But since the Logical Idea is as much a universal as it is in being—since it is presupposed by the notion as much as it itself immediately *is*, its beginning is a synthetic as well as an analytical beginning.

Philosophical method is analytical as well as synthetic, not indeed in the sense of a bare juxtaposition or mere alternating employment of these two methods of finite cognition, but rather in such a way that it holds them merged in itself. In every one of its movements therefore it displays an attitude at once analytical and synthetic. Philosophical thought proceeds analytically, in so far as it only accepts its object, the Idea, and while allowing it its own way, is only, as it were, an onlooker at its movement and development. To this extent philosophizing is wholly passive. Philosophic thought however is equally synthetic, and evinces itself to be the action of the notion itself. To that end, however, there is required an effort to keep back the incessant impertinence of our own fancies and private opinions.

§ 239

(*b*) The Advance renders explicit the *judgement* implicit in the Idea. The immediate universal, as the notion implicit, is the dialectical force which on its own part deposes its immediacy and universality to the level of a mere stage or 'moment'. Thus is put the negative of the beginning, its specific character: it supposes a correlative, a relation of different terms—the stage of Reflection.

Seeing that the immanent dialectic only states explicitly what was involved in the immediate notion, this advance is Analytical; but seeing that in this notion this distinction was not yet stated, it is equally Synthetic.

In the advance of the idea, the beginning exhibits itself as what it is implicitly. It is seen to be mediated and derivative, and neither to have proper being nor proper immediacy. It is only for the consciousness which is itself immediate, that Nature forms the commencement or immediacy, and that Spirit appears as what is mediated by Nature. The truth is that

Nature is the creation of Spirit, and it is Spirit itself which gives itself a presupposition in Nature.

§ 240

The abstract form of the advance is, in Being, an other and transition into an other; in Essence showing or reflection in the opposite; in Notion, the distinction of individual from universality, which continues itself as such into, and is as an identity with, what is distinguished from it.

§ 241

In the second sphere the primarily implicit notion has come as far as shining, and thus is already the idea in germ. The development of this sphere becomes a regress into the first, just as the development of the first is a transition into the second. It is only by means of this double movement, that the difference first gets its due, when each of the two members distinguished, observed on its own part, completes itself to the totality, and in this way works out its unity with the other. It is only by both merging their one-sidedness on their own part, that their unity is kept from becoming one-sided.

§ 242

The second sphere develops the relation of the different to what it primarily is—to the contradiction in its own nature. That contradiction which is seen in the infinite progress is resolved (*c*) into the end or terminus, where the difference is explicitly stated as what it is in notion. The end is the negative of the first, and as the identity with that, is the negativity of itself. It is consequently the unity in which both of these Firsts, the immediate and the real First, are made constituent stages in thought, merged, and at the same time preserved in the unity. The notion, which from its implicitness thus comes by means of its differentiation and the merging of that differentiation to close with itself, is the realized notion—the notion which contains the relativity or dependence of its special features in its own independence. It is the idea which, as absolutely first (in the method), regards this terminus as merely the disappearance of the show or semblance, which made the beginning appear immediate, and made itself seem a result. It is the knowledge that the idea is the one systematic whole.

§ 243

It thus appears that the method is not an extraneous form, but the soul and notion of the content, from which it is only distinguished, so far as the dynamic elements of the notion even on their own part come in their own specific character to appear as the totality of the notion. This specific character, or the content, leads itself with the form back to the idea; and thus the idea is presented as a systematic totality which is only one idea, of which the several elements are each implicitly the idea, while they equally by the dialectic of the notion produce the simple independence of the idea. The science in this manner concludes by apprehending the notion of itself, as of the pure idea for which the idea is.

§ 244

The Idea which is independent or for itself, when viewed on the point of this unity with itself, is Perception or Intuition, and the percipient Idea is Nature. But as intuition the idea is, through an external 'reflection', invested with the one-sided characteristic of immediacy, or of negation. Enjoying however an absolute liberty, the Idea does not merely pass over into life, or as finite cognition allow life to show in it: in its own absolute truth it resolves to let the 'moment' of its particularity, or of the first characterization and other-being, the immediate idea, as its reflected image, go forth freely as Nature.

We have now returned to the notion of the Idea with which we began. This return to the beginning is also an advance. We began with Being, abstract Being: where we now are we also have the Idea as Being: but this Idea which has Being is Nature.

NOTES AND ILLUSTRATIONS

CHAPTER I

p. 4, § 2. After-thought = Nachdenken, i.e. thought which retraces and reproduces an original, but submerged, thought (cf. Hegel's *Werke*, vi, p. xv): to be distinguished from **Reflection** (cf. *Werke*, i. 174).

p. 6, § 3. On the blending of universal (thought) and individual (sensation) in what is called perception (Wahrnehmen) see *Encycl.* §§ 420, 421.

p. 7, § 3. Cf. Fichte, *Werke*, ii. 454: 'Hence for the common sort of hearers and readers the uncommon intelligibility of certain sermons and lectures and writings, not one word of which is intelligible to the man who thinks for himself—because there is really no intelligence in them. The old woman who frequents the church—for whom by the way I cherish all possible respect—finds a sermon very intelligible and very edifying which contains lots of texts and verses of hymns she knows by rote and can repeat. In the same way readers, who fancy themselves far superior to her, find a work very instructive and clear which tells what they already know, and proofs very stringent which demonstrate what they already believe. The pleasure the reader takes in the writer is a concealed pleasure in himself. What a great man! (he says to himself); it is as if I heard or read myself.'

p. 9, § 6. Cf. Hegel, *Werke*, viii. 17: 'In this conviction (that what is reasonable is actual, and what is actual is reasonable) stands every plain man, as well as the philosopher; and from it philosophy starts in the study both of the spiritual and of the natural universe. . . . The great thing however is, in the show of the temporal and the transient to recognize the substance which is immanent and the eternal which is present. For the work of reason (which is synonymous with the Idea), when in its actuality it simultaneously enters external existence, emerges with an infinite wealth of forms, phenomena and phases, and envelops its kernel with the motley rind with which consciousness is earliest at home—a rind which the notion must penetrate before it can find the inward pulse and feel it still beating even in the outward phases. But the infinite variety of circumstance which is formed in this externality by the light of the essence shining in it—all this infinite material, with its regulations—is not the object of philosophy. . . . To comprehend *what is*, is the task of philosophy: for *what is* is reason. As regards the individual, each, whatever happens, is a son of his time. So too philosophy is its time apprehended in thoughts. It is just as foolish to fancy that a philosophy can overleap its present world as that an individual can overleap his time. If his theory really goes beyond actualities, if it constructs an ideal, a world as it ought to be, then such existence as it has is only in his intentions—a yielding element in which anything you please may be fancy-formed.' Cf. Schelling, *Werke*, iv. 390: 'There are very many things, actions, etc. of which we may judge, after vulgar semblance, that they are unreasonable. All the same we presuppose and assume that everything which is or which happens is reasonable, and that reason is, in one word, the prime matter and the real of all being.'

p. 9, § 6. Actuality (Wirklichkeit) in *Werke*, iv. 178 ff.

p. 10, § 7. Cf. Fichte, *Werke*, ii. 333: 'Man has nothing at all but experience; and everything he comes to he comes to only through experience, through life itself. All his thinking, be it loose or scientific, common or transcendental, starts from experience and has experience ultimately in view. Nothing has unconditional value and significance but life; all other thinking, conception, knowledge has value only in so far as in some way or other it refers to the fact of life, starts from it, and has in view a subsequent return to it.'

p. 11, § 7 (note). Thomas Thomson (1773–1852), Professor of Chemistry at Glasgow, distinguished in the early history of chemistry and allied sciences. The *Annals of Philosophy* appeared from 1813 to 1826. *The Art of Preserving the Hair* was published (anonymously) at London in 1825.

p. 12, § 7 (note). The speech from the throne was read on 3 Feb. 1825.

The shipowners' dinner was on 12 Feb. *The Times* of 14 Feb. gives as Canning's the words 'the just and wise maxims of sound not spurious sophy'.

p. 14, § 10. 'Scholasticus' in the guileless 'freshman', hero of certain *Facetiae* (attributed to the Pythagorean philosopher Hierocles) which used occasionally to form part of the early Greek reading of schoolboys.

K. L. Reinhold (1754–1823) presents in his intellectual history a picture of the development of ideas in his age. At the beginning his *Attempt of a New Theory of the Human Representative Faculty* (1789) is typical of the tendency to give a subjective psychological interpretation of Kant's theory of knowledge. But the period of Reinhold's teaching here referred to is that of the *Contributions to an Easier Survey of the Condition of Philosophy at the Beginning of the Nineteenth Century* (Beiträge, 1801): the tendency which Hegel, who reviewed him in the *Critical Journal of Philosophy* (*Werke*, i. 267 ff.), calls 'philosophizing before philosophy'. A similar spirit is operative in Krug's proposal (in his *Fundamental Philosophy*, 1803) to start with what he called 'philosophical problematics'.

p. 16, § 11. Plato, *Phaedo*, 89d–90e, where Socrates protests against the tendency to confound the defect of a particular piece of reasoning with the incompetence of human reason altogether.

p. 18, § 13. The dictum that the historical succession of philosophical systems is identical with their logical sequence should not be taken too literally and mechanically. Its essential point is simply the theorem that history is not a casual series of unconnected events, the deeds of particular persons, but is an evolution under laws and uniformities: it is this theorem applied to philosophies. But difficulties may easily arise in the application of the general principle: e.g. it will be seen (by comparison of § 86 and § 104) that though Pythagoras precedes Parmenides, and number is a stepping-stone to pure thought, still pure Being comes at an earlier stage than Quantity.

p. 19, § 13. There is a silent reference to what Reinhold professed to make the subject of his teaching at Jena—'philosophy without surnames' (ohne Beinamen), i.e. not a 'critical' philosophy—or to the 'Philosophy which may not bear any man's name' of Beck. As Hegel says, *Werke*, xvi. 138, 'The solicitude and apprehension against being one-sided is only too often part of the weakness which is capable only of many-sided illogical superficiality.'

p. 22, § 16. By 'anthropology' is meant not the anthropology of modern writers, who use the name to denote mainly the history of human culture in its more rudimentary stages, and as exhibited chiefly in material products, but the study of those aspects of psychology which are most closely allied with physiological conditions.

With the power of the intuition of genius to give almost all that logical synthesis can produce, cf. *Werke*, i. 331: 'In this way a grand and pure intuition is able, in the purely architectonic features of its picture, though the interconnection of necessity and the mastery of form does not come forward into visibility, to give expression to the genuine ethical organism —like a building which silently exhibits the spirit of its author in the several features of its mass, without the image of that spirit being set forth anywhere in one united shape. In such a delineation, made by help of notions, it is only a want of technical skill which prevents reason from raising the principle it embraces and pervades into the "ideal" form and becoming aware of it as the Idea. If the intuition only remains true to itself and does not let analytic intellect disconcert it, it will probably—just because it cannot dispense with notions for its expression—behave awkwardly in dealing with them, assume distorted shapes in its passage through consciousness, and be (to the speculative eye) both incoherent and contradictory: but the arrangement of the parts and of the self-modifying characters betray the inward spirit of reason, however invisible. And so far as this appearance of that spirit is regarded as a product and a result, it will as product completely harmonize with the Idea.' Probably Goethe is before Hegel's mind.

p. 23, § 17. The triplicity in unity of thought—its forthgoing ('procession', cf. pp. 282 ff.) and its return, which is yet an abiding in itself (Bei-sich-sein) was first explicitly schematized by Proclus, the consummator of Neo-Platonism. In his *Institutio Theologica* he lays it down that the essential character of all spiritual reality (*ἀσώματον*) is to be *πρὸς ἑαυτὸ ἐπιστρεπτικόν*, i.e. to return upon itself, or to be a unity in and with difference—to be an original and spontaneous principle of movement (c. 15)—or, as in c. 31: *πᾶν τὸ προϊὸν ἀπό τινος κατ' οὐσίαν ἐπιστρέφεται πρὸς ἐκεῖνο ἀφ' οὗ πρόεισιν*. Its movement, therefore, is circular (*κυκλικὴν ἔχει τὴν ἐνέργειαν*) (c. 33): for everything must at the same time remain altogether in the cause, and proceed from it, and revert to it (c. 35). Such an essence is self-subsistent (*αὐθυπόστατον*)—is at once agent (*παράγον*) and patient (*παραγόμενον*). This 'mysticism' (of a trinity which is also unity of motion which is also rest), with its *πρόοδος*, *ἐπιστροφή*, and *μονή*, is taken up, in his own way, by Scotus Erigena (*De Divisione Naturae*) as *processio* (or *divisio*), *reditus*, and *adunatio*. From God 'proceed'—by an *eternal* creation—the creatures, who however are not outside the divine nature; and to God all things created *eternally* return.

CHAPTER II

p. 26, § 19. Truth: as early as *Werke*, i. 82, i.e. 1801, Hegel had come—perhaps influenced by the example of Jacobi—to the conclusion that 'Truth is a word which, in philosophical discourse, deserves to be used only of the certainty of the Eternal and non-empirical Actual.' (And so Spinoza, ii. 310.)

p. 26, § 19. 'The young have been flattered'—e.g. by Fichte, *Werke*, i. 435: 'Hence this science too promises itself few proselytes among men already formed: if it can hope for any at all, it hopes for them rather from the young world, whose inborn force has not yet been ruined in the laxity of the age.'

p. 31, § 20. What Kant actually said (*Kritik der reinen Vernunft: Elementarlehre*, § 16), was 'The *I think* must be able to accompany all my conceptions' (Vorstellungen). Here, as often elsewhere, Hegel seems to quote from memory—with some shortcoming from absolute accuracy.

From this point Fichte's idealism takes its spring, e.g. *Werke*, ii. 505: 'The ground of all certainty, of all consciousness of fact in life, and of all demonstrative knowledge in science, is this: *In* and *with* the single thing we affirm (setzen) (and whatever we affirm is necessarily something single) we also affirm the absolute totality as such. . . Only in so far as we have so affirmed anything, is it certain for us—from the single unit we have comprehended under it away to every single thing in the infinity we shall comprehend under it, from the one individual who has comprehended it, to all individuals who will comprehend it. . . . Without this absolute "positing" of the absolute totality in the individual, we cannot (to employ a phrase of Jacobi's) come to bed and board.

'Obviously therefore you enunciate not the judgement of a single observation, but you embrace and "posit" the sheer infinitude and totality of all possible observations—an infinity which is not at all compounded out of finites, but out of which, conversely, the finites themselves issue, and of which finite things are the mere always-uncompleted analysis. This—

how shall I call it, procedure, positing, or whatever you prefer—this "manifestation" of the absolute totality, I call intellectual vision (Anschauung). I regard it—just because I cannot in any way get beyond intelligence—as immanent in intelligence, and name it so far egoity (Ichheit), not objectivity and not subjectivity, but the absolute identity of the two: an egoity, however, which it was to be hoped would not be taken to mean individuality. There lies in it, what you' (he is addressing Reinhold, who here follows Bardili) 'call a repetibility *ad infinitum*. For me, therefore, the essence of the finite is composed of an immediate vision of the absolutely timeless infinite (with an absolute identity of subjectivity and objectivity), and of a separation of the two latter, and an analysis (continued *ad infinitum*) of the infinite. In that analysis consists the temporal life: and the starting-point of this temporal life is the separation into subject and object, which through the intellectual vision (intuition) are still both held together.'

p. 35, § 22, *the mere fact of conviction*. Cf. *Rechtsphilosophie*, § 140 (*Werke*, viii. 191): 'Finally the mere conviction which holds something to be right is given out as what decides the morality of an action. The good we will to do not yet having any content, the principle of conviction adds the information that the subsumption of an action under the category of good is purely a personal matter. If this be so, the very pretence of an ethical objectivity is utterly lost. A doctrine like this is closely allied with the self-styled philosophy which denies that the true is cognoscible: because for the Will, truth—i.e. the rationality of the Will—lies in the moral laws. Giving out, as such a system does, that the cognition of the true is an empty vanity, far transcending the range of science (which recognizes only appearance), it must, in the matter of conduct, also find its principle in the apparent; whereby moral distinctions are reduced to the peculiar theory of life held by the individual and to his private conviction. At first no doubt the degradation into which philosophy has thus sunk seems an affair of supreme indifference, a mere incident in the futilities of the scholastic world: but the view necessarily makes itself a home in ethics, which is an essential part of philosophy; and it is then in the actual world that the world learns the true meaning of such theories.

'As the view spreads that subjective conviction, and it alone, decides the morality of an action, it follows that the charge of hypocrisy, once so frequent, is now rarely heard. You can only qualify wickedness as hypocrisy on the assumption that certain actions are inherently and actually misdeeds, vices, and crimes, and that the defaulter necessarily is aware of them as such, because he is aware of and recognizes the principles and outward acts of piety and honesty, even in the pretence to which he misapplies them. In other words, it was generally assumed as regards immorality that it is a duty to know the good, and to be aware of its distinction from the bad. In any case it was an absolute injunction which forbade the commission of vicious and criminal acts, and which insisted on such actions being imputed to the agent, so far as he was a man, not a beast. But if the good heart, the good intention, the subjective conviction, are set forth as the true sources of moral worth, then there is no longer any hypocrisy, or immorality at all: for whatever one does, he can always justify it by the reflection on it of good aims and motives; and by the influence of that conviction it is good. There is no longer anything *inherently* vicious or criminal: instead of the frank and free, hardened and unperturbed sinner, comes the person whose mind is completely justified by intention and conviction. My good intention in my act, and my conviction of its goodness, make it good. We speak of judging and estimating an *act*. But on this principle it is only the aim and conviction of the agent—his faith—by which he ought to be judged. And that not in the sense in which Christ requires faith in objective truth, so that for one who has a bad faith, i.e. a conviction bad in its content, the judgement to be pronounced must be bad, i.e. conformable to this bad content. But faith here means only fidelity to conviction. Has the man (we ask) in acting kept true to his conviction? It is formal subjective conviction on which alone the obligation of duty is made to depend.

'A principle like this, where conviction is expressly made something subjective, cannot but suggest the thought of possible error, with the further implied presupposition of an absolutely-existing law. But the law is no agent: it is only the actual being who acts; and in the aforesaid principle the only question in estimating human actions is how far he has received the law into his conviction. If, therefore, it is not the actions which are to be estimated and generally measured by that law, it is impossible to see what the law is for, and what end it can serve. Such a law is degraded to a mere outside letter, in fact an empty word; which is only made a law, i.e. invested with obligatory force, by my conviction.

'Such a law may claim its authority from God or the State: it may even have the authority of tens of centuries during which it served as the bond that gave men, with all their deed and destiny, subsistence and coherence. And these are authorities in which are condensed the convictions of countless individuals. And for me to set against that the authority of my single conviction—for as my subjective conviction its sole validity is authority—that self-conceit, monstrous as it at first seems, is, in virtue of the principle that subjective conviction is to be the rule, pronounced to be no self-conceit at all.

'Even if reason and conscience—which shallow science and bad sophistry can never altogether expel—admit, with a noble illogicality, that error is possible, still by describing crime and wickedness as only an error we minimize the fault. For to err is human: Who has not been mistaken on one point or another, whether he had fresh or pickled cabbage for dinner, and about innumerable things more or less important? But the difference of more or less importance disappears if everything turns on the subjectivity of conviction and on persistency in it. But the said noble illogicality which admits error to be possible, when it comes round to say that a wrong conviction is only an error, really only falls into a further illogicality—the illogicality of dishonesty. One time conviction is made the basis of morality and of man's supreme value, and is thus pronounced the supreme and holy. Another time all we have to do with is an error: my conviction is something trivial and casual, strictly speaking something outside, that may turn out this way or that. And, really, my being convinced *is* something supremely trivial: if I cannot *know* truth, it is indifferent how I think; and all that is left to my thinking is that empty good—a mere abstraction of generalization.

'It follows further that, on this principle of justification by conviction, logic requires me, in dealing with the way others act against my action, to admit that, so far as they in their belief and conviction hold my actions to be crimes, they are quite in the right. On such logic not merely do I gain nothing, I am even deposed from the post of liberty and honour into a situation of slavery and dishonour. Justice—which in the abstract is mine as well as theirs—I feel only as a foreign subjective conviction, and in the execution of justice I fancy myself to be only treated by an external force.'

p. 36, § 23. Selbstdenken—to think and not merely to read or listen is the recurrent cry of Fichte (e.g. *Werke*, ii. 329). According to the editors of *Werke*, xv. 582, the reference here is to Schleiermacher and to his *Monologues*. Really it is to the Romantic principle in general, especially F. Schlegel.

p. 36, § 23. Cf. Fichte, *Werke*, ii. 404: 'Philosophy (Wissenschaftslehre), besides (for the reason above noted that it has no auxiliary, no vehicle of the intuition at all, except the intuition itself), elevates the human mind higher than any geometry can. It gives the mind not only attentiveness, dexterity, stability, but at the same time absolute independence, forcing it to be alone with itself, and to live and manage by itself. Compared with it, every other mental operation is infinitely easy; and to one who has been exercised in it nothing comes hard. Besides, as it prosecutes all objects of human lore to the centre, it accustoms the eye to hit the proper point at first glance in everything presented to it, and to prosecute it undeviatingly. For such a practical philosopher therefore there can be nothing dark, complicated, and confused, if only he is acquainted with the object of discussion. It comes always easiest to him to construct everything afresh and *ab initio*, because he carries within him plans for every scientific edifice. He finds his way easily, therefore, in any complicated structure. Add to this the security and confidence of glance which he has acquired in philosophy—the guide which conducts in all *raisonnement*, and the imperturbability with which his eye meets every divergence from the accustomed path and every paradox. It would be quite different with all human concerns, if men could only resolve to believe their eyes. At present they inquire at their neighbours and at antiquity what they really see, and by this distrust in themselves errors are eternalized. Against this distrust the possessor of philosophy is for ever protected. In a word, by philosophy the mind of man comes to itself, and from henceforth rests on itself without foreign aid, and is completely master of itself, as the dancer of his feet, or the boxer of his hands.'

p. 36, § 23. Aristotle, *Metaph.* i. 2, 19 (cf. *Eth.* x. 7). See also *Werke*, xiv. 280 ff.

p. 37, § 24. Schelling's expression, 'petrified intelligence'. The reference is to some verses of Schelling in *Werke*, iv. 546 (first published in *Zeitschrift für speculative Physik*, 1800). We have no reason to stand in awe of the world, he says, which is a tame and quiet beast.

> Steckt zwar ein Riesengeist darinnen,
> Ist aber versteinert mit allen Sinnen;
> In todten und lebendigen Dingen
> Thut nach Bewußtseyn mächtig ringen.

In human shape he at length awakes from the iron sleep, from the long dream: but as man he feels himself a stranger and exile; he would fain return to great Nature; he fears what surrounds him and imagines spectres, not knowing he might say of Nature to himself:

> Ich bin der Gott, den sie im Busen hegt,
> Der Geist, der sich in allem bewegt:
> Vom frühsten Ringen dunkler Kräfte
> Bis zum Erguß der ersten Lebenssäfte,
> . . . .
> Herauf zu des Gedankens Jugendkraft
> Wodurch Natur verjüngt sich wieder schafft,
> Ist eine Kraft, ein Wechselspiel und Weben,
> Ein Trieb und Drang nach immer höherm Leben.

Cf. Oken, *Naturphilosophie*, § 2913: 'A natural body is a thought of the primal act, turned rigid and crystallized—a word of God.'

Phrases of like import are not infrequent in Schelling's works (about 1800–1), e.g. *Werke*, 1. Abth. iii. 341: 'The dead and unconscious products of nature are only unsuccessful attempts to "reflect" itself; so-called dead nature is in all cases an immature intelligence (unreife Intelligenz)', or, iv. 77, 'Nature itself is an intelligence, as it were, turned to rigidity (erstarrte), with all its sensations and perceptions'; and ii. 226 (*Ideen zu einer Philosophie der Natur*, 1797), 'Hence nature is only intelligence turned into the rigidity of being; its qualities are sensations extinguished to being; bodies are its perceptions, so to speak, killed.'

A close approach to the phrase quoted is found in the words of another of the 'Romantic' philosophers: 'Nature is a petrified magic-city (versteinerte Zauberstadt)', (Novalis, *Schriften*, ii. 149.)

p. 38, § 24. Cf. Fichte to Jacobi: (Jacobi's *Briefwechsel*, ii. 208) 'My absolute Ego is obviously not the individual: that explanation comes from injured snobs and peevish philosophers, seeking to impute to me the disgraceful doctrine of practical egoism. But the *individual must be deduced from the absolute ego*. To that task my philosophy will proceed in the "Natural Law". A finite being—it may be deductively shown—can only think itself as a sense-being in a sphere of sense-beings, on one part of which (that which has no power of origination) it has causality, while with the other part (to which it attributes a subjectivity like its own) it stands in reciprocal relations. In such circumstances it is called an individual, and the conditions of individuality are called rights. As surely as it affirms its individuality, so surely does it affirm such a sphere—the two conceptions indeed are convertible. So long as we look upon ourselves as individuals—and we always so regard ourselves in life, though not in philosophy and abstract imagination—we stand on what I call the "practical" point of view in our reflections (while to the standpoint of the absolute ego I give the name "speculative"). From the former point of view there exists for us a world independent of us—a world we can only modify; while the pure ego (which even on this altitude does not altogether disappear from us) is put outside us and called God. How else could we get the properties we ascribe to God and deny to ourselves, did we not after all find them within us, and only refuse them to ourselves in a certain respect, i.e. as individuals? When this "practical" point of view predominates in our reflections, realism is supreme: when speculation itself deduces and recognizes that standpoint, there results a complete reconciliation between philosophy and common sense as premised in my system.

'For what good, then, is the speculative standpoint and the whole of philosophy therewith, if it be not for life? Had humanity not tasted of this forbidden fruit, it might dispense with all philosophy. But in humanity there is a wish implanted to behold that region lying beyond the individual; and to behold it not merely in a reflected light but face to face. The first who raised a question about God's existence broke through the barriers, he shook humanity in its main foundation pillars, and threw it out of joint into an intestine strife which is not yet settled, and which can only be settled by advancing boldly to that supreme point from which the speculative and the practical appear to be at one. We began to philosophize from pride of heart, and thus lost our innocence: we beheld our nakedness, and ever since we philosophize from the need of our redemption.'

p. 40, § 24. Physics and Philosophy of Nature: cf. *Werke*, vii. 1, p. 18: 'The Philosophy of Nature takes up the material, prepared for it by physics out of experience, at the point to which physics has brought it, and again transforms it, without basing it ultimately on the authority of experience. Physics therefore must work into the hands of philosophy, so that the latter may translate into a true comprehension (Begriff) the abstract universal transmitted to it, showing how it issues from that comprehension as an intrinsically necessary whole. The philosophic way of putting the facts is no mere whim once in a way, by way of change, to walk on the head, after walking a long while on the legs, or once in a way to see our everyday face besmeared with paint. No; it is because the method of physics does not satisfy the comprehension that we have to go on further.'

p. 40, § 24. The distinction of ordinary and speculative Logic is partly like that made by Fichte (i. 68) between Logic and Wissenschaftslehre. 'The former', says Fichte, 'is conditioned and determined by the latter.' Logic deals only with form; epistemology with import as well.

p. 42, § 24. The Mosaic legend of the Fall; cf. similar interpretations in Kant: *Religion innerhalb der Grenzen der bloßen Vernunft*, 1. Stück; and Schelling, *Werke*, i. (1. Abth.) 34.

CHAPTER III

p. 48, § 28. Fichte—to emphasize the experiential truth of his system—says (*Werke*, ii. 331): 'There was a philosophy which professed to be able to expand by mere *inference* the range thus indicated for philosophy. According to it, thinking was—not, as we have described it, the analysis of what was given and the recombining of it in other forms, but at the same time—a production and creation of something quite new. In this system the philosopher found himself in the exclusive possession of certain pieces of knowledge which the vulgar understanding had to do without. In it the philosopher could reason out for himself a God and an immortality and talk himself into the conclusion that he was wise and good.'

Wolf's definition of philosophy is 'the Science of the possible in so far as it can be'; and the possible = the non-contradictory.

p. 50, § 29. The oriental sage corresponds (cf. Hegel, *Werke*, xii. 229) to the writer known as Dionysius the Areopagite (*De Mystica Theologia*, and *De Divinis Nominibus*). The same problem as to the relation of the Infinite (God) to the Finite (world) is discussed in Jewish speculation (by Saadia, Mamuni, etc.) as the question of the divine names—a dogma founded on the thirteen names (or attributes) applied to God in Exodus 34: 6. (Cf. D. Kaufmann, *Geschichte der Attributenlehre*.) The same spirit has led to the list of ninety-nine 'excellect names' of Allah in Islam, a list which tradition derives from Muhammad.

p. 51, § 31. Cf. *Werke*, ii. 47 ff.: 'The nature of the judgement or proposition—involving as it does a distinction of subject and predicate—is destroyed by the "speculative" proposition. This conflict of the propositional form with the unity of comprehension which destroys it is like the antagonism in rhythm between metre and accent. The rhythm results from the floating "mean" and unification of the two. Hence even in the "philosophical" proposition the identity of subject and predicate is not meant to annihilate their difference (expressed by the propositional form): their unity is meant to issue as a *harmony*. The propositional form lets appear the definite shade or accent pointing to a distinction in its fulfilment: whereas in the predicate giving expression to the substance, and the subject itself falling into the universal, we have the unity in which that accent is heard no more. Thus in the proposition "God is Being" the predicate is Being; it represents the substance in which the subject is dissolved away. Being is here meant not to be predicate but essence: and in that way God seems to cease to be what he is—by his place in the proposition—viz. the permanent subject. The mind—far from getting further forward in the passage from subject to predicate—feels itself rather checked, through the loss of the subject, and thrown back, from a sense of its loss, to the thought of the subject. Or, since the predicate itself is enunciated as a subject (as Being or as Essence) which exhausts the nature of the subject, it again comes face to face with the subject even in the predicate. Thought thus loses its solid objective ground which it had on the subject: yet at the same time in the predicate it is thrown back upon it, and instead of getting to rest in itself it returns upon the subject of the content. To this unusual check and arrest are in the main due the complaints as to the unintelligibility of philosophical works—supposing the individual to possess any other conditions of education needed for understanding them.'

p. 52, § 32. On the relation of dogmatism and scepticism see the introduction to Kant's *Criticism of Pure Reason*, and compare Caird's *Critical Philosophy of I. Kant*, vol. i, chap. i.

p. 53, § 33. The subdivision of 'theoretical' philosophy or metaphysics into the four branches, Ontology, Cosmology, Psychology (rational and empirical), and Natural Theology, is more or less common to the whole Wolfian school. Wolf's special addition to the preceding scholastic systems is found in the conception of a general Cosmology. Metaphysics precedes physics, and the departments of practical philosophy. In front of all stands logic or rational philosophy. Empirical psychology belongs properly to physics, but reasons of practical convenience put it elsewhere.

p. 54, § 34. The question of the 'Seat of the Soul' is well known in the writings of Lotze (e.g. *Metaphysic*, § 291).

Absolute actuosity. The *Notio Dei* according to Thomas Aquinas, as well as the dogmatics of post-Reformation times, is *actus purus* (or *actus purissimus*). For God *nihil potentialitatis habet*. Cf. *Werke*, xii. 228: 'Aristotle especially has conceived God under the abstract category of activity. Pure activity is knowledge (Wissen)—in the scholastic age, *actus purus*—but in order to be put as activity, it must be put in its "moments". For knowledge we require another thing which is known: and which, when knowledge knows it, is thereby appropriated. It is implied in this that God—the eternal and self-subsistent—eternally begets himself as his Son—distinguishes himself from himself. But what he thus distinguishes from himself, has not the shape of an otherness: but what is distinguished is *ipso facto* identical with what it is parted from. God is spirit: no darkness, no colouring or mixture enters this pure light. The relationship of father and son is taken from organic life and used metaphorically—the natural relation is only pictorial and hence does not quite correspond to what is to be expressed. We say, God eternally begets his Son, God distinguishes himself from himself: and thus we begin from God, saying he does this, and in the other he creates is utterly with himself (the form of Love): but we must be well aware that God is this *whole action itself*. God is the beginning; he does this: but equally is he only the end, the totality: and as such totality he is spirit. God as merely the Father is not yet the true (it is the Jewish religion where he is thus without the Son): he is rather beginning and end: he is his presupposition, makes himself a presupposition (this is only another form of distinguishing): he is the eternal process.'

Nicolaus Cusanus speaks of God (*De docta Ignorantia*, ii. 1) as *infinita actualitas, quae est actu omnis essendi possibilitas*. The term 'actuosity' seems doubtful.

p. 57, § 36. *Sensus eminentior*. Theology distinguishes three modes in which the human intelligence can attain a knowledge of God. By the *via causalitatis* it argues that God is; by the *via negationis* what he is not; by the *via eminentiae* it gets a glimpse of the relation in which he stands to us. It regards God i.e. as the cause of the finite universe; but as God is infinite, all that is predicated of him must be taken as merely approximative (*sensu eminentiori*) and there is left a vast remainder which can only be filled up with negations (Durandus de S. Porciano on the *Sentent*. i. 3. 1). The *sensus eminentior* is the subject of Spinoza's strictures, *Ep*. 6 (56 in *Opp*. ii. 202): while Leibniz adopts it in the preface to *Théodicée*, 'Les perfections de Dieu sont celles de nos âmes, mais il les possède sans bornes: il est un océan, dont nous n'avons reçu que les gouttes; il y a en nous quelque puissance, quelque connaissance, quelque bonté; mais elles sont toutes entières en Dieu.'

The *via causalitatis* infers, e.g. from the existence of morality and intelligence here, a Being whose will finds expression therein: the *via eminentiae* infers that that will is good, and that intelligence wise in the highest measure, and the *via negationis* sets aside in the conception of God all the limitations and conditions to which human intelligence and will are subject.

CHAPTER IV

p. 63, § 38. The verses (forming part of the advice which Mephistopheles, personating Faust, gives to the recently arrived pupil) stand in the original in a different order: beginning „Dann hat er die Theile in seiner Hand", etc. The meaning of these and the two preceding lines is somewhat as follows, in versification even laxer than Goethe's:

If you want to describe life and gather its meaning,
To drive out its spirit must be your beginning,
Then though fast in your hand lie the parts one by one
The spirit that linked them, alas! is gone.
And 'Nature's Laboratory' is only a name
That the chemist bestows on't to hide his own shame.

One may compare *Wilhelm Meisters Wanderjahre*, iii. 3, where it is remarked, in reference to some anatomical exercises: 'You will learn ere long that building up is more instructive than tearing down, combining more than separating, animating the dead more than killing again what was killed already. . . . Combining means more than separating: reconstructing more than onlooking.' The first part of *Faust* appeared 1808: the *Wanderjahre*, 1828–9.

p. 64, § 39. The article on the 'Relation of scepticism to philosophy, an exposition of its various modifications, and comparison of the latest with the ancient'—in form a review of G. E. Schulze's *Criticism of Theoretical Philosophy*—was republished in vol. xvi of Hegel's *Werke* (vol. i of the *Vermischte Schriften*).

p. 68, § 42. In an earlier review of Kant's work (*Werke*, i. 83) on Glauben und Wissen (an article in Schelling and Hegel's *Journal*) Hegel attaches more weight to a factor in the critical theory of knowledge, here neglected. Kant, he says, has—within the limits allowed by his psychological terms of thought—'put (in an excellent way) the *a priori* of sensibility into the original identity and multiplicity, and that as transcendental imagination in the "higher power" of an immersion of unity in multiplicity: while Understanding (Verstand) he makes to consist in the elevation to universality of this *a priori* synthetic unity of sensibility—whereby this identity is invested with a comparative antithesis to the sensibility: and Reason (Vernunft) is presented as a still higher power over the preceding comparative antithesis, without however this universality and infinity being allowed to go beyond the stereotyped formal pure infinity. This genuinely rational construction, by which, though the bad name "faculties" is left, there is in truth presented a single identity of them all, is transformed by Jacobi into a series of faculties, *resting* one upon another.'

p. 69, § 42. Fichte: cf. *Werke*, i. 420: 'I have said before, and say it here again, that my system is no other than the Kantian. That means: it contains the same view of facts, but in its method is quite independent of the Kantian exposition. . . . Kant, up to now, is a closed book.' i. 442. There are two ways of critical idealism. 'Either' (as Fichte) 'it actually deduces from the fundamental laws of intelligence that system of necessary modes of action, and with it, at the same time, the objective conceptions thus arising, and thus lets the whole compass of our conceptions gradually arise under the eyes of the reader or hearer; or' (like Kant and his unprogressive disciples) 'it gets hold of these laws from anywhere and anyhow, as they are immediately applied to objects, therefore on their lowest grade (on this grade they are called *categories*), and then asseverates that it is by these that objects are determined and arranged.' And i. 478: 'I know that the categories which Kant laid down are in no way *proved* by him to be conditions of self-consciousness, but only said to be so: I know that space and time, and what in the original consciousness is inseparable from them and fills them both, are still less deduced as such conditions, for of them it is not even said expressly—as of the categories—that they are so, but only inferentially. But I believe quite as surely that I know that Kant had the thought of such a system: that everything he actually propounds are fragments and results of this system; and that his statements have meaning and coherence only on this presupposition.' Cf. viii. 362.

p. 70, § 42. Transcendental unity of self-consciousness. Kant's *Kritik der reinen Vernunft*, § 16: 'The *I think* must be able to accompany all my ideas.... This idea is an act of spontaneity.... I name it pure apperception . . . or original apperception . . . because it is that self-consciousness which can be accompanied by none further. The unity of it I also call the transcendental unity of self-consciousness, in order to denote the possibility of cognition *a priori* from it.'

p. 72, § 44. *Caput mortuum*: a term of the Alchemists to denote the non-volatile precipitate left in the retort after the spirit had been extracted: the fixed or dead remains, *quando spiritus animam sursum vexit*.

p. 73, § 45. Reason and Understanding. In the Wolfian school (e.g. in Baumgarten's *Metaphysik*, § 468) the term intellect (Verstand) is used of the general faculty of higher cognition, while *ratio* (Vernunft) specially denotes the power of seeing distinctly the connections of things. So Wolf (*Vernünftige Gedanken von Gott*, etc. § 277) defines Verstand as 'the faculty of distinctly representing the possible', and Vernunft (§ 368) as 'the faculty of seeing into the connection of truths'. It is on this use of *Reason* as the faculty of inference that Kant's use of the term is founded: though it soon widely departs from its origin. For upon the 'formal' use of reason as the faculty of syllogizing, Kant superinduces a transcendental use as a 'faculty of *principles*', while the understanding is only 'a faculty of *rules*'. 'Reason', in other words, 'itself begets conceptions', and 'maxims, which it borrows neither from the senses nor from the understanding'. (*Kritik d. r. Vern.*, *Dialektik*, Einleit. ii. A.) And the essential aim of Reason is to give unity to the various cognitions of understanding. While the unity given by understanding is 'unity of a possible experience', that sought by reason is the discovery of an unconditioned which will complete the unity of the former (*Dial.* Einleit. iv), or of 'the totality of the conditions to a given conditioned' (*Dial.* vii.).

It is this distinction of the terms which is dominant in Fichte and Hegel, where Verstand is the more practical intellect which seeks definite and restricted results and knowledges, while Vernunft is a deeper and higher power which aims at completeness. In Goethe's more reflective prose we see illustrations of this usage: e.g. *Wilh. Meisters Wanderjahre*, i, it is said to be the object of the 'reasonable' man 'das Entgegengesetzte zu überschauen und in Uebereinstimmung zu bringen': or Bk. ii, reasonable men when they have devised something verständig to get this or that difficulty out of the way, etc. Goethe, in his *Sprüche in Prosa* (896), *Werke*, iii. 281, says 'Reason has for its province the thing in process (das Werdende), understanding the thing completed (das Gewordene): the former does not trouble itself about the purpose, the latter asks not whence. Reason takes delight in developing; understanding wishes to keep everything as it is, so as to use it.' (Similarly in *Eckermann's Convers.* 13 Feb. 1829. Cf. Oken, Naturphilosophie, § 2914. Verstand ist Microcosmus, Vernunft Macrocosmus.

Kant's use of the term Reason, coupled with his special view of Practical Reason and his use of the term Faith (Glaube), leads on to the terminology of Jacobi. In earlier writings Jacobi had insisted on the contrast between the superior authority of feeling and faith (which are in touch with truth) and the mechanical method of intelligence and reasoning (Verstand and Vernunft). At a later period however he changed and fixed the nomenclature of his distinction. What he had first called Glaube he latterly called Vernunft, which is in brief a 'sense for the supersensible'—an intuition giving higher and complete or total knowledge, an immediate apprehension of the real and the true. As contrasted with this reasonable faith or feeling, he regards Verstand as a mere faculty of inference or derivative knowledge, referring one thing to another by the rule of identity.

This distinction, which is substantially reproduced by Coleridge (though with certain clauses that show traces of Schellingian influence), has connections—like so much else in Jacobi—with the usage of Schopenhauer. 'Nobody', says Jacobi, 'has ever spoken of an animal Vernunft: a mere animal Verstand however we all know and speak of' (Jacobi's *Werke*, iii. 8). Schopenhauer repeats and enforces the remark. All animals possess, says Schopenhauer, the power of apprehending causality, of cognizing objects: a power of immediate and intuitive knowledge of real things: this is Verstand. But Vernunft, which is peculiar to man, is the cognition of *truth* (not of reality): it is an abstract judgement with a sufficient reason (*Welt als W.* i. § 6).

One is tempted to connect the modern distinction with an older one which goes back in its origin to Plato and Aristotle, but takes form in the Neo-Platonist School, and enters the Latin world through Boethius. *Consol. Phil.* iv. 6: *Igitur uti est ad intellectum ratiocinatio, ad id quod est id quod gignitur, ad aeternitatem tempus*, and in v. 4 there is a full distinction of *sensus*, *imaginatio*, *ratio*, and *intelligentia* in ascending order. *Ratio* is the discursive knowledge of the idea (*universali consideratione perpendit*); *intelligentia* apprehends it at once, and as a simple *forma* (*pura mentis acie contuetur*); (cf. Stob. *Ecl.* 1. 49. 23–4; Porphyr. *Sentent.* 15). Reasoning belongs to the human species, just as intelligence to the divine alone. Yet it is assumed—in an attempt to explain divine foreknowledge and defend freedom—that man may in some measure place himself on the divine standpoint (v. 5).

This contrast between a higher mental faculty (*mens*) and a lower (*ratio*) which even Aquinas adopts from the interpretation of Aristotle (*Summa Theol.* i. 79, 9) is the favourite weapon in the hands of mysticism. After the example of Dionysius Areop. Nicolaus of Cusa, Reuchlin, and other thinkers of the Renaissance depreciate mere discursive thought and logical reasoning. It is the inner *mens*—like a simple ray of light—penetrating by an immediate and indivisible act to the divine—which gives us access to the supreme science. This *simplex intelligentia*—superior to imagination or reasoning—as Gerson says, *Consis. de Th.* 10, is sometimes named *mens*, sometimes *spiritus*, the light of intelligence, the shadow of the angelic intellect, the divine light. From Scotus Erigena to Nicolaus of Cusa one tradition is handed down: it is taken up by men like Everard Digby (in his *Theoria Analytica*) and the group of Cambridge Platonists and by Spinoza in the seventeenth century, and it reappears, profoundly modified, in the German idealism between 1790 and 1820.

p. 78, § 48. *Science of Logic*; Hegel's large work on the subject, published between 1812 and 1816. The discussions on the Antinomies belong chiefly to the first part of it.

p. 80, § 50. 'Natural Theology', here to be taken in a narrower sense than on p. 56, where it is equivalent to Rational Theology in general. Here it means 'Physico-theology'—the argument from design in nature.

p. 83, § 50. Spinoza—defining God as 'the union of thought with extension'. This is not verbally accurate; for according to *Ethica*, i. pr. 11, God, or the substance, consists of infinite attributes, each of which expresses the eternal and infinite essence. But Spinoza mentions of 'attributes' only two: *Ethica*, ii. pr. 1, Thought is an attribute of God; pr. 2, Extension is an attribute of God. And he adds, *Ethica*, i. pr. 10, Schol. 'All the attributes substance has were always in it together, nor can one be produced by another.' And in *Ethica*, ii. 7, Sch. it is said: 'Thinking substance and extended substance is one and the same substance which is comprehended now under this, now under that attribute.'

p. 87, § 54. 'Practical in the true sense of the word.' Cf. Kant, *Werke*, Ros. and Sch. i. 581: 'A great misunderstanding, exerting an injurious influence on scientific methods, prevails with regard to what should be considered "practical" in such sense as to justify its place in practical philosophy. Diplomacy and finance, rules of economy no less than rules of social intercourse, precepts of health and dietetic of the soul no less than the body, have been classed as practical philosophy on the mere ground that they all contain a collection of practical propositions. But although such practical propositions differ in mode of statement from the theoretical propositions which have for import the possibility of things and the exposition of their nature, they have the same content. "Practical", properly so called, are only those propositions which relate to *Liberty* under laws. All others whatever are nothing but the theory of what pertains to the *nature* of things—only that theory is brought to bear on the way in which the things may be produced by us in conformity with a principle; i.e. the possibility of the things is presented as the result of a voluntary action which itself too may be counted among physical causes.' And Kant, *Werke*, iv. 10. 'Hence a sum of practical precepts given by philosophy does not form a special part of it (co-ordinate with the theoretical) merely because they are practical. Practical they might be, even though their principle were wholly derived from the theoretical knowledge of nature—as *technico-practical* rules. They are practical in the true sense, when and because their principle is not borrowed from the nature-conception (which is always sensuously conditioned) and rests therefore on the supersensible, which the conception of liberty alone makes knowable by formal laws. They are therefore ethico-practical, i.e. not merely *precepts and rules* with this or that intention, but laws without antecedent reference to ends and intentions.'

p. 87, § 54. Eudaemonism. But there is Eudaemonism and Eudaemonism; as cf. Hegel, *Werke*, i. 8. 'The time had come when the infinite longing away beyond the body and the world had reconciled itself with the reality of existence. Yet the reality which the soul was reconciled to—the objective which the subjectivity recognized—was actually only empirical existence, common world and actuality. . . . And though the reconciliation was in its heart and ground sure and fast, it still needed an objective form for this ground: the very necessity of nature made the blind certitude of immersion in the reality of empirical existence seek to provide itself with a justification and a good conscience. This reconciliation for consciousness was found in the Happiness-doctrine: the fixed point it started from being the empirical subject, and what it was reconciled to, the vulgar actuality, wherein it might now confide, and to which it might surrender itself without sin. The profound coarseness and utter vulgarity, which is at the basis of this happiness-doctrine, has its only elevation in its striving after justification and a good conscience, which however can get no further than the objectivity of mere intellectualism.

'The dogmatism of eudaemonism and of popular philosophy (Aufklärung) therefore did not consist in the fact that it made happiness and enjoyment the supreme good. For if Happiness be comprehended as an *Idea*, it ceases to be something empirical and casual—as also to be anything sensuous. In the supreme existence, reasonable act (Thun) and supreme enjoyment are one. So long as supreme blessedness is supreme *Idea* it matters not whether we try to apprehend the supreme existence on the side of its ideality—which as isolated may be first called reasonable act—or on the side of its reality—which as isolated may be first called enjoyment and feeling. For reasonable act and supreme enjoyment, ideality and reality are both alike in it and identical. Every philosophy has only one problem—to construe supreme blessedness as supreme Idea. So long as it is by reason that supreme enjoyment is ascertained, the distinguishability of the two at once disappears: for this comprehension and the infinity which is dominant in act, and the reality and finitude which is dominant in enjoyment, are taken up into one another. The controversy with happiness becomes a meaningless chatter, when happiness is known as the blessed enjoyment of the eternal intuition. But what was called eudaemonism meant—it must be said—an empirical happiness, an enjoyment of sensation, not the eternal intuition and blessedness.'

p. 88, § 55. Schiller. *Ueber die aesthetische Erziehung des Menschen* (1795), Letter 18. 'Through beauty the sensuous man is led to form and to thought; through beauty the intellectual man is led back to matter and restored to the sense-world. Beauty combines two states which are opposed to one another.' Letter 25. 'We need not then have any difficulty about finding a way from sensuous dependence to moral liberty, after beauty has given a case where liberty can completely coexist with dependence, and where man in order to show himself an intelligence need not make his escape from matter. If—as the fact of beauty teaches—man is free even in association with the senses, and if—as the conception necessarily involves—liberty is something absolute and supersensible, there can no longer be any question how he comes to elevate himself from limitations to the absolute: for in beauty this has already come to pass.' Cf. *Ueber Anmuth und Würde* (1793). 'It is in a beautiful soul, then, that sense and reason, duty and inclination harmonize; and grace is their expression in the appearance. Only in the service of a beautiful soul can nature at the same time possess liberty.' (See Bosanquet's *History of Aesthetic.*)

p. 90, § 60. The quotation in the note comes from § 87 of the *Kritik der Urtheilskraft* (*Werke*, ed. Ros. and Sch. iv. 357).

p. 94, § 60. Fichte, *Werke*, i. 279. 'The principle of life and consciousness, the ground of its possibility, is (as has been shown) certainly contained in the Ego: yet by this means there arises no actual life, no empirical life in time—and another life is for us utterly unthinkable. If such an actual life is to be possible, there is still needed for that a special impulse (Anstoß) striking the Ego from the Non-ego. According to my system, therefore, the ultimate ground of all actuality for the Ego is an original action and reaction between the Ego and something outside it, of which all that can be said is that it must be completely opposed to the Ego. In this reciprocal action nothing is brought into the Ego, nothing foreign imported; everything that is developed from it *ad infinitum* is developed from it solely according to its own laws. The Ego is merely put in motion by that opposite, so as to act; and without such a first mover it would never have acted; and, as its existence consists merely in action, it would not even have existed. But the source of motion has no further attributes than to set in motion, to be an opposing force which as such is only felt.

'My philosophy therefore is realistic. It shows that the consciousness of finite natures cannot at all be explained, unless we assume a force existing independently of them, and completely opposed to them—on which as regards their empirical existence they are dependent. But it asserts nothing further than such an opposed force, which is merely *felt*, but not *cognized*, by finite beings. All possible specifications of this force or non-ego, which may present themselves *ad infinitum* in our consciousness, my system engages to deduce from the specifying faculty of the Ego.

'That the finite mind must necessarily assume outside it something absolute (a Ding-an-sich), and yet must on the other hand acknowledge that this something only exists for the mind (is a necessary noumenon): this is the circle which may be infinitely expanded, but from which the finite mind can never issue.' Cf. Fichte's *Werke*, i. 248, ii. 478.

CHAPTER V

p. 95, § 62. F. H. Jacobi (*Werke*, v. 82) in his *Woldemar* (a romance contained in a series of letters, first published *as a whole* in 1781) writes: 'The philosophical understanding (Verstand) is jealous of everything unique, everything immediately certain which makes itself true, without proofs, solely by its existence. It persecutes this faith of reason even into our inmost consciousness, where it tries to make us distrust the feeling of our identity and personality.' 'What is absolutely and intrinsically true', he adds (v. 122), 'is not got by way of reasoning and comparison: both our immediate consciousness (Wissen)—I am—and our conscience (Gewissen) are the work of a secret something in which heart, understanding, and sense combine.' 'Notions (Begriffe), far from embalming the living, really turn it into a corpse' (v. 380).

Cf. Fichte's words (*Werke*, ii. 255), Aus dem Gewissen allein stammt die Wahrheit, etc.

p. 96, § 62. The Letters on the doctrine of Spinoza, published in 1785, were reissued in 1789 with eight supplements.

'A science', says Jacobi in his latest utterance (*Werke*, iv. pref. xxx), 'is only a systematic register of cognitions mutually referring to one another—the first and last point in the series is wanting.'

p. 96, § 62. Lalande's dictum is referred to by Fries (*Populäre Vorlesungen über Sternkunde*, 1813) quoted by Jacobi in his *Werke*, ii. 55. What Lalande has actually written in the preface to his work on astronomy is that the science as he understands it has no relation to natural theology—in other words, that he is not writing a Bridgewater treatise.

p. 97, § 63. Jacobi, *Werke*, ii. 222. 'For my part, I regard the principle of reason as all one with the principle of life.' And ii. 343: 'Evidently reason is the true and proper life of our nature.' It is in virtue of our inner tendency and instinct towards the eternal (Richtung und Trieb auf das Ewige)—of our sense for the supersensible—that we, human beings, really subsist (iv. 6. 152). And this Organ der Vernehmung des Uebersinnlichen is Reason (iii. 203, etc.).

The language of Jacobi fluctuates, not merely in words, but in the intensity of his intuitionalism. Thus, e.g. iii. 32: 'The reason man has is no faculty giving the science of the true, but only a presage' (Ahndung des Wahren). 'The belief in a God', he says, at one time (iii. 206), 'is as natural to man as his upright position': but that belief is, he says elsewhere, only 'an inborn devotion (Andacht) before an unknown God.' Thus, if we have an immediate awareness (Wissen) of God, this is not knowledge or science (Wissenschaft). Such intuition of reason is described (ii. 9) as 'the faculty of *presupposing* the intrinsically (an sich) true, good, and beautiful, with full confidence in the objective validity of the presupposition'. But that object we are let see only in feeling (ii. 61). 'Our philosophy', he says (iii. 6), 'starts from feeling—of course an objective and pure feeling.'

p. 97, § 63. Jacobi (*Werke*, iv. a, p. 211): 'Through faith (Glaube) we know that we have a body.' Such immediate knowledge of our own activity—'the feeling of I am, I act' (iii. 411)—the sense of 'absolute self-activity' or freedom (of which the 'possibility cannot be cognized', because logically a contradiction) is what Jacobi calls Anschauung (Intuition). He distinguishes a sensuous and a rational intuition (iii. 59).

p. 98, § 63. Jacobi expressly disclaims identification of his Glaube with the faith of Christian doctrine (*Werke*, iv. a, p. 210). In defence he quotes from Hume, *Inquiry* v, and from Reid, passages to illustrate his usage of the term 'belief'—by the distinction between which and faith certain ambiguities are no doubt avoided.

p. 102, § 66. Kant had said '*Concepts without intuitions are empty*.' It is an exaggeration of this half-truth (the other half is *Intuitions without concepts are blind*) that is the basis of these statements of Jacobi (and of Schopenhauer)—a view of which the following passage from Schelling (*Werke*, ii. 125) is representative. 'Concepts (Begriffe) are only silhouettes of reality. They are projected by a serviceable faculty, the understanding, which only comes into action when reality is already on the scene—which only comprehends, conceives, retains what it required a creative faculty to produce. . . . The mere concept is a word without meaning. . . . All reality that can attach to it is lent to it merely by the intuition (Anschauung) which preceded it. . . . Nothing is real for us except what is *immediately* given us, without any mediation by concepts, without our feeling at liberty. But nothing reaches us immediately except through intuition.' He adds, however, 'Intuition is due to the activity of mind (Geist): it demands a disengaged sense (freier Sinn) and an intellectual organ (geistiges Organ).'

p. 105, § 71. Cicero: *De Natura Deorum*, i. 43 (ii. 10–12), *De quo autem omnium natura consentit, id verum esse necesse est*; cf. Seneca, *Epist.* cxvii. 6. The principle is common to Stoics and Epicureans: it is the maxim of Catholic truth *Quod semper, quod ubique, quod ab omnibus creditum est*—

equivalent to Aristotle's ὃ πᾶσι δοκεῖ, τοῦτ' εἶναί φαμεν. But as Aristotle remarks (*An. Post.* i. 31) τὸ καθόλου καὶ ἐπὶ πᾶσιν ἀδύνατον αἰσθάνεσθαι.

Jacobi: *Werke*, vi. 145. 'The general opinion about what is true and good must have an authority equal to reason.'

p. 107, § 72. Cf. *Encyclop.* § 400: 'That the heart and the feeling is not the form by which anything is justified as religious, moral, true, and just, and that an appeal to heart and feeling either means nothing or means something bad, should hardly need enforcing. Can any experience be more trite than that hearts and feelings are also bad, evil, godless, mean, etc.? Ay, that the heart is the source of such feelings only, is directly said in the words: Out of the heart proceed evil thoughts, etc. In times when the heart and the sentiment are, by scientific theology and philosophy, made the criterion of goodness, religion, and morality, it is necessary to recall these trivial experiences.'

CHAPTER VI

p. 114, § 80. Goethe; the reference is to *Werke*, ii. 268 (Natur und Kunst):

> Wer Großes will, muß sich zusammenraffen:
> In der Beschränkung zeigt sich erst der Meister,
> Und das Gesetz nur kann uns Freiheit geben.

Such 'limitation' of aim and work is a frequent lesson in *Wilhelm Meisters Wanderjahre*, e.g. i. ch. 4. 'Many-sidedness prepares, properly speaking, only the element in which the one-sided can act. . . . The best thing is to restrict oneself to a handiwork.' And i. ch. 12: 'To be acquainted with and to exercise one thing rightly gives higher training than mere tolerableness (halfness) in a hundred sorts of things.' And ii. ch. 12: 'Your general training and all establishments for the purpose are fool's farces.'

p. 116, § 81. Cf. Fichte, *Werke*, ii. 37. 'Yet it is not *we* who analyse: but knowledge analyses itself, and can do so, because in all its being it is a *for-self* (Für-sich)', etc.

p. 117, § 81. Plato, the inventor of Dialectic. Sometimes (on the authority of Aristotle, as reported by Diog. Laert. ix. 25), Zeno of Elea gets this title; but Hegel refers to such statements as Diog. Laert. iii. 56 τρίτον δὲ Πλάτων προσέθηκε τὸν διαλεκτικὸν λόγον, καὶ ἐτελεσιούργησε τὴν φιλοσοφίαν.

Protagoras. But it is rather in the dialogue *Meno*, pp. 81–97, that Plato exhibits this view of knowledge. Cf. *Phaedo*, 72 e, and *Phaedrus*, 245.

Parmenides; especially see Plat. *Parmen.* pp. 142, 166; cf. Hegel, *Werke*, xiv. 204.

With Aristotle dialectic is set in contrast to apodeictic, and treated as (in the modern sense) a quasi-inductive process (Ar. *Top.* Lib. viii.): with the Stoics, dialectic is the name of the half-rhetorical logic which they, rather than Aristotle, handed on to the schoolmen of the Middle Ages.

p. 118, § 81. The physical elements are fire, air, earth, and water. Earthquakes, storms, etc., are examples of the 'meteorological process'. Cf. *Encyclop*. §§ 281–9.

p. 119, § 82. Dialectic; cf. *Werke*, v. 326 ff.

p. 121, § 82. Mysticism; cf. Mill's *Logic*, bk. v, ch. 3, § 4: 'Mysticism is neither more nor less than ascribing objective existence to the subjective creations of the mind's own faculties, to mere ideas of the intellect; and believing that by watching and contemplating these ideas of its own making, it can read in them what takes place in the world without.' Mill thus takes it as equivalent to an ontological mythology—probably a rare use of the term.

CHAPTER VII

p. 123, § 85. The Absolute. The term, in something like its modern usage, is at least as old as Nicolaus Cusanus. God, according to him, is the *absoluta omnium quidditas* (*Apol*. 406), the *esse absolutum*, or *ipsum esse in existentibus* (*De ludo Globi*, ii. 161 a), the *unum absolutum*, the *vis absoluta* or *possibilitas absoluta*, or *valor absolutus*: *absoluta vita*, *absoluta ratio: absoluta essendi forma*. On this term and its companion *infinitus* he rings perpetual changes. But its distinct employment to denote the 'metaphysical God' is much more modern. In Kant, e.g. the 'Unconditioned' (Das Unbedingte) is the metaphysical, corresponding to the religious, conception of deity; and the same is the case with Fichte, who however often makes use of the adjective 'absolute'. It is with Schelling that the term is naturalized in philosophy: it already appears in his works of 1793 and 1795: and from him apparently it finds its way into Fichte's *Darstellung der Wissenschaftslehre* of 1801 (*Werke*, ii. 13) 'The absolute is neither knowing nor being; nor is it identity, nor is it indifference of the two; but it is throughout merely and solely the absolute.'

The term comes into English philosophical language through Coleridge and later borrowers from the German. See Ferrier's *Institutes of Metaphysic*, Prop. xx, and Mill's *Examination of Hamilton*, chap. iv.

p. 125, § 86. Cf. Schelling, iii. 372: I = I expresses the identity between the 'I', in so far as it is the producing, and the 'I' as the produced; the original synthetical and yet identical proposition: the *cogito = sum* of Schelling.

Definition of God as *Ens realissimum*, e.g. Meier's *Baumgartens Metaphysic*, § 605.

Jacobi, *Werke*, iv. 6, thus describes Spinoza's God.

As to the beginning cf. Fichte, *Werke*, ii. 14 (speaking of 'absolute knowing'): 'It is not a knowing of something, nor is it a knowing of nothing (so that it would be a knowing of somewhat, but this somewhat be nothing): it is not even a knowing of itself, for it is no knowledge at all *of*, nor is it *a* knowing (quantitatively and in relation), but it is (the) knowing (absolutely qualitatively). It is no act, no event, or that somewhat is in knowing; but it is just the knowing, in which alone all acts and all events, which are there set down, can be set down.'

History of Philosophy; cf. Hegel, *Werke*, i. 165. 'If the Absolute, like its phenomenon Reason, be (as it is) eternally one and the same, then each reason, which has turned itself upon and cognized itself, has produced a true philosophy and solved the problem which, like its solution, is at all times the same. The reason, which cognizes itself, has in philosophy to do only with itself: hence in itself too lies its whole work and its activity; and as regards the inward essence of philosophy there are neither predecessors nor successors.

'Just as little, as of constant improvements, can there be talk of "peculiar views" of philosophy.... The true peculiarity of a philosophy is the interesting individuality, in which reason has organized itself a form from the materials of a particular age; in it the particular speculative reason finds spirit of its spirit, flesh of its flesh; it beholds itself in it as one and the same, as another living being. Each philosophy is perfect in itself, and possesses totality, like a work of genuine art. As little as the works of Apelles and Sophocles, if Raphael and Shakespeare had known them, could have seemed to them mere preliminary exercises for themselves, but as cognate spiritual powers; so little can reason in its own earlier formations perceive only useful preparatory exercises.' Cf. Schelling, iv. 401.

p. 126, § 86. Parmenides (fr. 2.[3] D–K): of the two ways of investigation the first is that *it is*, and that not-to-be is not.

ἡ μὲν ὅπως ἔστιν τε καὶ ὡς οὐκ ἔστι μὴ εἶναι.

p. 127, § 87. The Buddhists. Cf. Hegel, *Werke*, xi. 387. Modern histories of Buddhism insist upon the purely ethico-religious character of the teaching. Writers like von Hartmann (*Religionsphilosophie*, p. 320) on the contrary hold that Buddhism carried out the esoteric theory of Brahmanism to the consequence that the abstract one is nothing. According to Vassilief, *Le Bouddhisme*, pp. 318 ff., one of the Buddhist metaphysical schools, the Madhyamikas, founded by Nāgārjuna 400 years after Buddha, taught that All is Void. Such metaphysics were probably reactions of the underlying Brahmanist idea.

But generally Buddhism (as was not unnatural sixty years ago) is hardly taken here in its characteristic historical features.

p. 131, § 88. Aristotle, *Phys.* i. 8 (191[a]26): 'Those philosophers who first sought the truth and the real substance of things got on a false track, like inexperienced travellers who fail to discover the way, and declared that nothing can either come into being or disappear, because it is necessary that what comes into being should come into being either from what is or from what is not, and that it is from both of these impossible: for what is does not become (it already is), and nothing would become from what is not.'

(5) is an addition of ed. 3 (1830); cf. *Werke*, xvii. 181.

p. 132, § 88. The view of Heraclitus here taken is founded on the interpretation given by Plato (in the *Theaetetus*, 152; *Cratylus*, 401) and by Aristotle, of a fundamental doctrine of the Ephesian—which however is expressed in the fragments by the name of the ever-living fire. The other phrase (Ar. *Met*. i. 4) is used by Aristotle to describe the position, not of Heraclitus, but of Leucippus and Democritus. Cf. Plutarch, *adv. Colotem*, 4. 2 *Δημόκριτος διορίζεται μὴ μᾶλλον τὸ δὲν ἢ τὸ μηδὲν εἶναι*; cf. Simplic. in Ar. *Phys*. 28. 12 Diels.

p. 133, § 89. Daseyn: Determinate being. Cf. Schelling, i. 209. 'Being (Seyn) expresses the absolute, Determinate being (Daseyn) a conditional, "positing": Actuality, one conditioned in a definite sort by a definite condition. The single phenomenon in the whole system of the world has *actuality*; the world of phenomena in general has Daseyn; but the absolutely posited, the Ego, *is*. *I am* is all the Ego can say of itself.'

p. 135, § 91. Being-by-self: An-sich-seyn.

Spinoza, *Epist*. 50, *figura non aliud quam determinatio et determinatio negatio est*.

p. 136, § 92. Grenze (limit or boundary) and Schranke (barrier or check) are distinguished in *Werke*, iii. 128–139 (see Stirling's *Secret of Hegel*, i. 377 ff.). Cf. Kant's remark, *Krit. d. r. Vernunft*, p. 795, that Hume only einschränkt our intellect, ohne ihn zu begrenzen.

p. 136, § 92. Plato, *Timaeus*, 35a–b (formation of the world-soul): 'From the individual and ever-identical essence (*οὐσία*) and the divisible which is corporeal, he compounded a third intermediate species of essence. . . . And taking these, being three, he compounded them all into one form (*ἰδέα*), adjusting perforce the unmixable nature of the other and the same, and mingling them all with the essence, and making of three one again, he again distributed this total into as many portions as were fitting, but each of them mingled out of the same and the other and the essence.'

p. 138, § 94. Philosophy. Cf. Schelling, *Werke*, ii. 377. 'A various experience has taught me that for most men the greatest obstacle to the understanding and vital apprehension of philosophy is their invincible opinion that its object is to be sought at an infinite distance. The consequence is, that while they should fix their eye on what is present (das Gegenwärtige), every effort of their mind is called out to get hold of an object which is not in question through the whole inquiry.' 'The aim of the sublimest science can only be to show the actuality—in the strictest sense the actuality, the presence, the vital existence (Daseyn)—of a God in the whole of things and in each one. . . . Here we deal no longer with an extra-natural or supernatural thing, but with the immediately near, the alone-actual to which we ourselves also belong, and in which we are.'

p. 140, § 95. Plato's *Philebus*, ch. xii–xxiii (pp. 23–38): cf. *Werke*, xiv. 214 ff.: 'The absolute is therefore what in one unity is finite and infinite.'

Idealism of Philosophy: cf. Schelling, ii. 67. 'Every philosophy therefore is and remains Idealism; and it is only under itself that it embraces realism and idealism; only that the former Idealism should not be confused with the latter, which is of a merely relative kind.'

Hegel, *Werke*, iii. 163. 'The proposition that the finite is "ideal" constitutes Idealism. In nothing else consists the Idealism of philosophy than in recognizing that the finite has no genuine being. . . .The contrast of idealistic and realistic philosophy is therefore of no importance. A philosophy that attributed to finite existences as such a genuine ultimate absolute being would not deserve the name philosophy. . . . By "ideal" is meant existing as a representation in consciousness: whatever is in a mental concept, idea, or imagination is "ideal": "ideal" is just another word for "in imagination"—something not merely distinct from the real, but essentially not real. The mind indeed is the great idealist: in the sensation, representation, thought of the mind the fact has not what is called *real* existence; in the simplicity of the Ego such external being is only suppressed, existing *for me*, and "ideally" in me. This subjective idealism refers only to the representational form, by which an import is mine.'

p. 141, § 96. The distinction of nature and mind as real and ideal is especially Schelling's: see e.g. his *Einleitung*, etc., iii. 272. 'If it is the problem of Transcendental Philosophy to subordinate the real to the ideal, it is on the contrary the problem of the philosophy of nature to explain the ideal from the real.'

p. 144, § 98. Newton: see Scholium at the end of the *Principia*, and cf. *Optics*, iii. qu. 28.

Modern Atomism, besides the conception of particles or molecules, has that of mathematical centres of force.

Kant, *Werke*, v. 379 (ed. Rosenk.). 'The general principle of the *dynamic* of material nature is that all reality in the objects of the external senses must be regarded as moving force: whereby accordingly so-called solid or absolute impenetrability is banished from natural science as a meaningless concept, and repellent force put in its stead; whereas true and immediate attraction is defended against all the subtleties of a self-misconceiving metaphysic and declared to be a fundamental force necessary for the very possibility of the concept of matter.'

p. 144, § 98. Abraham Gotthelf Kästner (1719–1800), professor forty-four years at Göttingen, enjoyed in the latter half of the eighteenth century a considerable repute, both in literature and in mathematical science. Some of his epigrams are still quoted.

p. 149, § 102. The two 'moments' of number, Unity and Sum (Anzahl), may be compared with the Greek distinction between one and *ἀριθμός* (cf. Arist. *Phys*. iv. 12 *ἐλάχιστος ἀριθμὸς ἡ δυάς*). According to Rosenkranz (*Leben Hegels*) the classification of arithmetical operations often engaged

Hegel's research. Note the relation in Greek between λογικόν and λογιστικόν. Cf. Kant's view of the 'synthesis' in arithmetic.

p. 151, § 103. Intensive magnitude. Cf. Kant, *Kritik der reinen Vernunft*, p. 207, on Anticipation of Perception (Wahrnehmung), and p. 414, in application to the question of the soul's persistence.

p. 153, § 104. Not Aristotle, but rather Simplicius on the *Physics* of Aristotle, 141. 5 Diels: giving Zeno's argument against the alleged composition of the line from a series of points. What you can say of one supposed small real unit, you can say of a smaller, and so on *ad infinitum*. (Cf. Burnet's *Early Greek Philosophy*, p. 329.)

p. 153, § 104. The distinction between imagination and intellect made by Spinoza in *Ep*. xii (*olim* xxix) in *Opp*. ed. Land vol. ii. 40 ff. is analogous to that already noted (p. 311) between *ratio* and *intellegentia*, and is concerned, as by Boethius, with the distinction which Plato, *Timaeus* 37, draws between eternity (αἰών) and time.

The infinite (*Eth*. i. prop. 8. Schol. 1) is the 'absolute affirmation of a certain nature's existence', as opposed to finitude which is really *ex parte negatio*. 'The problem has always been held extremely difficult, if not inextricable, because people did not distinguish between what is concluded to be infinite by its own nature and the force of its definition, and what has no ends, not in virtue of its essence, but in virtue of its cause. It was difficult also because they did not distinguish between what is called infinite because it has no ends, and that whose parts (though we may have a maximum of it) we cannot equate or explicate by any number. Lastly because they did not distinguish between what we can only understand (*intelligere*), but not imagine, and what we can also imagine.'

To illustrate his meaning, Spinoza calls attention to the distinction of substance from mode, of eternity from duration. We can 'explicate' the existence only of modes by duration: that of substance, 'by eternity, i.e. by an infinite fruition of existence or being' (*per aeternitatem, hoc est infinitam existendi, sive, invita latinitate, essendi fruitionem*). The attempt therefore to show that extended *substance* is composed of parts is an illusion—which arises because we look at quantity 'abstractly or superficially, as we have it in imagination by means of the senses'. So looking at it, as we are liable to do, a quantity will be found divisible, finite, composed of parts and manifold. But if we look at it as it really is—as a Substance—as it is in the intellect alone (which is a work of difficulty), it will be found infinite, indivisible, and unique. 'It is only therefore when we abstract duration and quantity from substance, that we use time to determine duration and measure to determine quantity, so as to be able to imagine them. Eternity and substance, on the other hand, are no objects of imagination but only of intellect; and to try to explicate them by such notions as measure, time, and number—which are only modes of thinking or rather of imagining—is no better than to fall into imaginative raving.' 'Nor will even the modes of Substance ever be rightly understood, should they be confounded with this sort of *entia rationis*' (i.e. *modi cogitandi* subserving the easier retention, explication, and *imagination* of things *understood*) 'or aids to imagination. For when we do so, we separate them from substance, and from the mode in which they flow from eternity, without which they cannot be properly understood.' (Cf. Hegel's *Werke*, i. 63.)

p. 154, § 104. The verses from Albr. von Haller come from his poem on Eternity (1736). Hegel seems to quote from an edition before 1776, when the fourth line was added in the stanza as it thus finally stood:

> Ich häufe ungeheure Zahlen,
> Gebürge Millionen auf,
> Ich welze Zeit auf Zeit und Welt auf Welten hin,
> Und wenn ich auf der March des endlichen nun bin,
> Und von der fürchterlichen Höhe
> Mit Schwindeln wieder nach dir sehe,
> Ist alle Macht der Zahl, vermehrt mit tausend Malen,
> Noch nicht ein Theil von dir.
> Ich tilge sie, und du liegst ganz vor mir.

Kant, *Kritik d. r. Vernunft*, p. 641. 'Even Eternity, however *eerily* sublime may be its description by Haller', etc.

p. 154, § 104. Pythagoras in order of time probably comes between Anaximenes (of Ionia) and Xenophanes (of Elea). But the mathematical and metaphysical doctrines attributed to the Pythagorean are known to us only in the form in which they are represented in Plato and Aristotle, i.e. in a later stage of development. The Platonists (cf. Arist. *Met.* i. 6; xi. 1. 12; xii. 1. 7; cf. Plat. *Rep.* 510 d) treated mathematical fact as mid-way between 'sensibles' and 'ideas'; and Aristotle himself places mathematics as a science between physical and metaphysical (theological) philosophy.

The tradition (referred to p. 155) about Pythagoras is given by Iamblichus, *Vita Pyth.* §§ 115 ff.: it forms part of the later Neo-Pythagorean legend, which entered literature in the first centuries of the Christian era.

p. 157, § 107. Hebrew hymns: e.g. Psalms 74 and 104, Proverbs 8, and Job 38. *Vetus verbum est*, says Leibniz (ed. Erdmann, p. 162), *Deum omnia pondere, mensura, numero, fecisse*.

p. 159, § 108. The antinomy of measure. These logical puzzles are the so-called fallacy of Sorites (a different thing from the chain-syllogism of the logic-books)—cf. Cic. *Acad.* ii. 92; *De Divin.* ii. 11—and the φαλακρός; cf. Horace, *Epist.* ii. 1. 45.

CHAPTER VIII

p. 165, § 113. Self-relation—(sich) auf sich beziehen.

p. 167, § 115. The 'laws of thought' is the magniloquent title given in the Formal Logic since Kant's day to the principles or maxims (*principia*,

Grundsätze) which Kant himself described as 'general and formal criteria of truth'. They include the so-called principle of contradiction, with its developments, the principle of identity and excluded middle: to which, with a desire for completeness, eclectic logicians have added the Leibnizian principle of the reason. Hegel has probably an eye to Krug and Fries in some of his remarks. The three laws may be compared and contrasted with the three principles, homogeneity, specification, and continuity of forms, in Kant's *Kritik d. r. Vern.* p. 686.

p. 169, § 117. Leibniz, *Nouveaux Essais*, Liv. ii. ch. 27, § 3 (ed. Erdmann, p. 273: cf. fourth Letter to Clarke). *Il n'y a point deux individus indiscernables. Un gentilhomme d'esprit de mes amis, en parlant avec moi en présence de Madame l'Electrice dans le jardin de Herrenhausen, crut qu'il trouverait bien deux feuilles entièrement semblables. Madame l'Electrice l'en défia, et il courut longtems en vain pour en chercher.*

The principle of individuation or indiscernibility is: 'If two individuals were perfectly alike and equal and, in a word, indistinguishable by themselves, there would be no principle of individuation': (Leibniz, ed. Erdm. p. 277) *Poser deux choses indiscernables est poser la même chose sous deux noms* (p. 756). *Principium individuationis idem est quod absolutae specificationis quâ res ita sit determinata, ut ab aliis omnibus distingui possit.*

p. 173, § 119. Polarity. Schelling, ii. 489. 'The law of Polarity is a universal law of nature'; cf. ii. 459: 'It is a first principle of a philosophic theory of nature to have a view (in the whole of nature) on polarity and dualism.' But he adds (476), 'It is time to define more accurately the concept of polarity.' So Oken, *Naturphilosophie*: § 76: 'A force consisting of two principles is called Polarity.' § 77: 'Polarity is the first force which makes its appearance in the world.' § 81: 'The original movement is a result of the original polarity.'

p. 174, § 119. Cf. Fichte, ii. 53. 'To everything but this the logically trained thinker can rise. He is on his guard against contradiction. But, in that case, how about the possibility of the maxim of his own logic that we can think no contradiction? In some way he must have got hold of contradiction and thought it, or he could make no communications about it. Had such people only once regularly asked themselves how they came to think the *merely* possible or contingent (the not-necessary), and how they actually do so! Evidently they here leap through a not-being, not-thinking, etc., into the utterly unmediated, self-initiating, free—into beënt non-being—in short, the above contradiction, as it was laid down. With consistent thinkers the result of this incapacity is nothing but the utter abolition of freedom—the most absolute fatalism and Spinozism.'

p. 177, § 121. Leibniz (ed. Erdmann, p. 515). 'The principle of *la raison déterminante* is that nothing ever occurs without there being a cause for it, or at least a determinant reason, i.e. something which may serve to render a reason *a priori* why that is existent rather than in any other way. This great principle holds good in all events.' Cf. p. 707. 'The principle of "sufficient reason" is that in virtue of which we consider that no fact could be found true or consistent, no enunciation truthful, without there being a sufficient reason why it is so and not otherwise. . . . When a truth is necessary, we can find the reason of it by analysis, resolving it into simpler ideas and truths, until we come to primitive ideas. . . . But the sufficient reason ought also to be found in contingent truths or truths of fact, i.e. in the series of things spread through the universe of creatures, or the resolution into particular reasons might go into a limitless detail: . . . and as all this detail embraces only other antecedent, or more detailed contingencies, . . . the sufficient or final (*dernière*) reason must be outside the succession or series of this detail of contingencies, however infinite it might be. And it is thus that the final reason of things must be in a "necessary substance", in which the detail of the changes exists only *eminenter*, as in the source—and it is what we call God.' (*Monadology*, §§ 32–8.)

Hence the supremacy of final causes. Thus *Opp.* ed. Erdmann, p. 678: *Ita fit ut efficientes causae pendeant a finalibus, et spiritualia sint natura priora materialibus*. Accordingly he urges, p. 155, that final cause has not merely a moral and religious value in ethics and theology, but is useful even in physics for the detection of deep-laid truths. Cf. p. 106: *C'est sanctifier la Philosophie que de faire couler ses ruisseaux de la fontaine des attributs de Dieu. Bien loin d'exclure les causes finales et la considération d'un être agissant avec sagesse, c'est de là qu'il faut tout déduire en Physique*. Cf. also *Principes de la Nature* (Leibn. ed. Erdm. p. 716): 'It is surprising that by the sole consideration of efficient causes or of matter, we could not render a reason for those laws of movement discovered in our time. *Il y faut recourir aux causes finales*.'

p. 178, § 121. Socrates. The antithesis between Socrates and the Sophists belongs in the main to the Platonic dialogues—not to the historical Socrates. It is the literary form in which the philosophy of Plato works out its development through the criticism of contemporary opinions and doctrines. And even in Plato's writings the antagonism is very unlike what later interpretations have made out of it.

p. 180, § 124. Thing by itself (thing in itself): the Ding=an=sich.

p. 183, § 126. Cf. *Encycl.* § 334 (*Werke*, viii. 1, p. 411). 'In empirical chemistry the chief object is the *particularity* of the matters and products, which are grouped by superficial abstract features which make impossible any system in the special detail. In these lists, metals, oxygen, hydrogen, etc.—metalloids, sulphur, phosphorus—appear side by side as *simple* chemical bodies on the same level. The great physical variety of these bodies must of itself create a prepossession against such co-ordination; and their chemical origin, the process from which they issue, is clearly no less various. But in an equally chaotic way, more abstract and more real processes are put on the same level. If all this is to get scientific form, every product ought to be determined according to the grade of the concrete and completely developed process from which it essentially issues, and which gives it its peculiar significance; and for the purpose it is not less essential to distinguish grades in abstractness or reality of the process. Animal and vegetable substances in any case belong to a quite other order: so little can their nature be understood from the chemical process, that they are rather destroyed in it, and only the way of their death is apprehended. These substances, however, ought above all to serve to counteract the metaphysic predominant in chemistry as in physics—the ideas or rather wild fancies of the *unalterability of matters* under all circumstances, as well as the categories of the *composition* and the *consistence* of bodies from such matters. We see it generally admitted that chemical matters lose in combination the *properties* which they show in separation: and yet we find the idea prevailing that they are the same things *without* the properties as they are *with* them—so that as things *with* these properties they are not results of the process.' Cf. *Werke*, vii. a. 372: 'Air does not consist of oxygen and nitrogen: but these are the forms under which air is put,' cf. ibid., 403.

p. 188, § 131. Fichte's *Sonnenklarer Bericht* appeared in 1810.

p. 193, § 136. Herder's *Gott: Gespräche über Spinoza's System*, 1787, 2nd ed. 1800. 'God is, in the highest and unique sense of the word, Force, i.e. the primal force of all forces, the soul of all souls' (p. 63). 'All that we call matter, therefore, is more or less animate: it is a realm of efficient forces. One force predominates: otherwise there were no *one*, no whole' (p. 207). 'The supreme being (Daseyn) could give its creatures nothing higher than being. (*Theophron.*) But, my friend, being and being, however simple in the concept, are in their estate very different; and what do you suppose, Philolaus, marks its grades and differences? (*Phil.*) Nothing but forces. In God himself we found no higher conception; but all his forces were only one. The supreme force could not be other than supreme goodness and wisdom, ever-living, ever-active. (*Theoph.*) Now you yourself see, Philolaus, that the supreme, or rather the All (for God is not a supreme unit in a scale of beings like himself), could not reveal himself otherwise than in the universe as active. In him nothing could slumber, and what he expressed was himself. He is before everything, and everything subsists in him: the whole world an expression, an appearance of his ever-living, ever-acting forces' (p. 200).

'It was the mistake of Spinoza', says Herder, 'to be unduly influenced by the Cartesian phraseology. Had he chosen the conception of force and effect, everything would have gone easier, and his system become much more distinct and coherent. Had he developed the conception of power, and the conception of matter, he must in conformity with his system necessarily have come to the conception of forces, which work as well in matter as in organs of thinking: he would in that case have regarded power and thought as forces, i.e. as one.' (Cf. H. Spencer, 'Force, the Ultimate of Ultimates', *First Princ.*, p. 169.)

According to Rosenkranz (*Leben Hegels*, p. 223) there exists in manuscript a criticism by Hegel on the second edition of Herder's *God.* Herder's Dialogue belongs to the controversy aroused by Jacobi's letters on Spinoza.

p. 195, § 136. Newton. Leibniz charges him with the view that 'God needs from time to time *remonter sa montre*, otherwise it would cease going: that his machine requires to be cleaned (*décrasser*) by extraordinary aid' (ed. Erdm., p. 746).

p. 197, § 140. The verses quoted occur in Goethe's *Werke*, ii. 376, under the heading Allerdings. Originally the first four lines appeared in Haller's poem *Die menschlichen Tugenden*, thus:

Ins Innre der Natur dringt kein erschaffner Geist:
Zu glücklich, wenn sie noch die äußre Schale weist!

(To nature's heart there penetrates no mere created mind:
Too happy if she but display the outside of her rind.)

[Hegel—reading weißt for weist—takes the second line as:

Too happy, if he can but know the outside of her rind.]

Goethe's attack upon a vulgar misuse of the lines belongs to his dispute with the scientists. His verses appeared in 1820 as *Heiteres Reimstück* at the end of Heft 3 *zur Morphologie*—of which the closing section is entitled *Freundlicher Zuruf* (*Werke*, xxvii. 161)—as follows:

„Ins Innre der Natur,"
O du Philister! —
Dringt kein erschaffner Geist."
. . . .
„Glückselig! wem sie nur
Die äußre Schale weis't."
Das hör' ich sechzig Jahre wiederholen,
Ich fluche drauf, aber verstohlen:
Sage mir tausend tausendmale:
Alles giebt sie reichlich und gern;
Natur hat weder Kern
Noch Schale,
Alles sti sie mit einem Male.

[The last seven lines may be thus paraphrased in continuation:

I swear—of course but to myself—as rings within my ears
That same old warning o'er and o'er again for sixty years,
And thus a thousand times I answer in my mind—
With gladsome and ungrudging hand metes nature from her store:
She keeps not back the core,
Nor separates the rind,
But all in each both rind and core has evermore combined.]

p. 198, § 140. Plato and Aristotle: cf. Plato, *Phaedrus*, 247 a (φθόνος γὰρ ἔξω θείου χοροῦ ἵσταται); *Timaeus*, 29 e; and Aristotle, *Metaph.* i. 2. 22.

p. 199, § 140. Goethe: *Sämmtl. Werke*, iii. 203 (*Maxime und Reflexionen*). Gegen große Vorzüge eines Andern giebt es kein Rettungsmittel als die Liebe. Cf. Schiller to Goethe, 2 July 1796. 'How vividly I have felt on this occasion . . . that against surpassing merit nothing but Love gives liberty' (daß es dem Vortrefflichen gegenüber keine Freiheit giebt als die Liebe).

'Pragmatic'. This word, denoting a meddlesome busybody in older English and sometimes made a vague term of abuse, has been in the present century used in English as it is here employed in German.

According to Polybius, ix. 2. 5, the πραγματικὸς τρόπος τῆς ἱστορίας is that which has a directly utilitarian aim. So Kant, *Foundation of Metaph. of Ethic* (*Werke*, viii. 41, note): 'A history is pragmatically composed when it renders prudent, i.e. instructs the world how it may secure its advantage better or at least as well as the ages preceding.' Schelling (v. 308) quotes in illustration of pragmatic history-writing the words of Faust to Wagner (Goethe, xi. 26):

Was ihr den Geist der Zeiten heißt,
Das ist im Grund der Herren eigner Geist,
In dem die Zeiten sich bespiegeln.

Cf. also Hegel, *Werke*, ix. 8. 'A second kind of reflectional history is the pragmatic. When we have to do with the past and are engaged with a distant world, the mind sees rising before it a present, which it has from its own action as a reward for its trouble. The events are different; but their central and universal fact, their structural plan is identical. This abolishes the past and makes the event present. Pragmatic reflections, however abstract they be, are thus in reality the present, and vivify the tales of the past with the life of today. Here too a word should specially be given to the moralizing and the moral instructions to be gained through history—for which it was often studied. . . . Rulers, statesmen, nations, are especially bidden learn from the experience of history. But what experience and history teach is that nations and governments never have learned anything from history, or acted upon teaching which could have been drawn from it.'

Cf. Froude: *Divorce of Catherine*, p. 2. 'The student (of history) looks for an explanation (of political conduct) in elements which he thinks he understands—in pride, ambition, fear, avarice, jealousy, or sensuality.'

p. 200, § 141. Cf. Goethe, xxiii. 298. 'What is the outside of an organic nature but the ever-varied phenomenon of the inside? This outside, this surface is so exactly adapted to a varied, complex, delicate, inward structure that it thus itself becomes an inside: both aspects, the outside and the inside, standing in most direct correlation alike in the quietest existence and in the most violent movement.'

p. 202, § 143. Kant, *Kritik der reinen Vernunft*, 2nd ed., p. 266.

p. 209, § 147. Schelling, *Werke*, v. 290 (cf. iii. 603). 'There are three periods of history, that of nature, of destiny, and of providence. These three ideas express the same identity, but in a different way. Destiny too is providence, but recognized in the real, as providence is also destiny, but beheld (angeschaut) in the ideal.'

p. 214, § 151. On the relation between Spinoza and Leibniz cf. Hegel, *Werke*, iv. 187–93. It would be a mistake, however, to represent Leibniz as mainly engaged in a work of conscious antagonism to Spinoza.

p. 216, § 153. Jacobi. Jacobi (like Schopenhauer) insists specially on the distinction between grounds (Gründe), which are formal, logical, and verbal, and causes (Ursachen), which carry us into reality and life and nature. To transform the mere *Because* into the *cause* we must (he says) pass from logic and the analytical understanding to experience and the inner life. Instead of the timelessness of simultaneity which characterizes the logical relation of ground and consequent, the nexus of cause and effect introduces the element of time—thereby acquiring reality (Jacobi, *Werke*, iii. 452). The conception of Cause—meaningless as a mere category of abstract thought—gets reality as a factor in experience, ein Erfahrungsbegriff, and is immediately given to us in the consciousness of our own causality (Jacobi, *Werke*, iv. 145–58). Cf. Kant, *Kritik der reinen Vern.*, p. 116.

p. 220, § 158. The *Amor intellectualis Dei* (Spinoza, *Eth.* v. 32) is described as a consequence of the third grade of cognition, viz. the *scientia intuitiva* which 'proceeds from an adequate idea of the formal essence of certain attributes of God to the adequate cognition of the essence of things' (ii. 40, Schol. 2). From it arises (v. 27) the highest possible *acquiescentia mentis*, in which the mind contemplates all things *sub specie aeternitatis* (v. 29), knows itself to be in God, and sees itself and all things in their divine essence. 'But this intellectual love of mind towards God is part of the infinite love wherewith God loves himself' (v. 36). 'From these things we clearly understand in what our salvation or blessedness or liberty consists: to wit, in the constant and eternal love towards God, or in the love of God towards men' (Schol. to v. 36).

CHAPTER IX

p. 224, § 161. Evolution and development in the stricter sense in which these terms were originally used in the seventeenth and eighteenth centuries imply a theory of preformation, according to which the growth of an organic being is simply a process of enlarging and filling out a miniature organism, actual but invisible, because too inconspicuous. Such was the doctrine adopted by Leibniz (*Considérations sur le principe de vie*; *Système nouveau de la Nature*; etc.). According to it development is no real generation of new parts, but only an augmentation into bulk and visibility of parts already outlined. This doctrine of preformation (as opposed to epigenesis) is carried out by Charles Bonnet, who in his *Considérations sur les corps organisés* (1762) propounds the further hypothesis that the 'germs' from which living beings proceed contain, enclosed one within another, the germs of all creatures yet to be. This is the hypothesis of *Emboîtement*. 'The system which regards generations as mere educts', says Kant (*Kritik der Urtheilskraft*, § 80; *Werke*, iv. 318), 'is called that of *individual* preformation or the evolution theory: the system which regards them as products is called Epigenesis—which might also be called the theory of *generic* preformation, considering that the productive powers of the generants follow the inherent tendencies belonging to the family characteristics, and that the specific form is therefore a "virtual" preformation. In this way the opposing theory of individual preformation might be better called the involution theory, or theory of Einschachtelung (*Emboîtement*)'. Cf. Leibniz (*Werke*, Erdmann, 715). 'As animals generally are not entirely born at conception or *generation*, no more do they entirely perish at what we call *death*; for it is reasonable that what does not commence naturally, does not finish either in the order of nature. Thus quitting their mask or their rags, they only return to a subtler theatre, where however they can be as sensible and well regulated as in the greater. . . . Thus not only the souls, but even the animals are neither generable nor perishable: they are only developed, enveloped, reclothed, unclothed—transformed. The souls never altogether quit their body, and do not pass from one body into another body which is entirely new to them. There is therefore no metempsychosis, but there is metamorphosis. The animals change, take, and quit only parts: which takes place little by little and by small imperceptible parcels, but continually, in nutrition: and takes place suddenly, notably but rarely, at conception, or at death, which make them gain or lose much all at once.'

The theory of *Emboîtement* or *Enveloppement*, according to Bonnet (*Considérations*, etc., ch. 1), is that 'the germs of all the organized bodies of one species were enclosed (*renfermés*) one in another, and have been developed successively'. So according to Haller (*Physiology*, Tome vii, § 2) 'it is evident that in plants the mother-plant contains the germs of several generations; and there is therefore no inherent improbability in the view that *tous les enfans, excepté un, fussent renfermés dans l'ovaire de la première Fille d'Eve*'. Cf. Weismann's *Continuity of the Germ-Plasma*. Yet Bonnet (*Contemplation de la Nature*, part vii, ch. 9, note 2), says, 'The germs are not enclosed like boxes or cases one in another, but a germ forms part of another germ, as a grain forms part of the plant in which it is developed.'

p. 228, § 163. Rousseau, *Contrat social*, liv. ii, ch. 3.

p. 230, § 165. The 'adequate' idea is a sub-species of the 'distinct'. When an idea does not merely distinguish a thing from others (when it is *clear*), or in addition represent the characteristic marks belonging to the object so distinguished (when it is *distinct*), but also brings out the farther characteristics of these characteristics, the idea is *adequate*. Thus adequate is a sort of second power of distinct. (Cf. Baumeister's *Instit. Philos. Ration.* 1765, §§ 64–94.) Hegel's description rather agrees with the 'complete idea' 'by which I put before my mind singly marks sufficient to discern the thing represented from all other things in every case, state, and time' (Baumeister, ibid. § 88). But cf. Leibniz, ed. Erdm., p. 79: *notitia adaequata*.

p. 231, § 166. Cf. Baumeister, *Instit. Phil. Rat.* § 185: *Judicium est idearum conjunctio vel separatio*.

p. 232, § 166. *Punctum saliens*: the *punctum sanguineum saliens* of Harvey (*de Generat. Animal. exercit.* 17), or first appearance of the heart: the *στιγμὴ αἱματίνη* in the egg, of which Aristotle (*Hist. Anim.* vi. 3) says *τοῦτο τὸ σημεῖον πηδᾷ καὶ κινεῖται ὥσπερ ἔμψυχον*.

p. 233, § 169. Cf. Whately, *Logic* (Bk. ii, ch. 1, § 2), 'Of these terms that which is spoken of is called the *subject*; that which is said of it, the *predicate*.'

p. 235, § 171. Kant, *Kritik der reinen Vernunft* (p. 95, 2nd ed.), § 9.

p. 236, § 172. Cf. Jevons, *Principles of Science*, ch. 3, on 'limited identities' and 'negative propositions'.

p. 240, § 175. Ear-lobes. The remark is due to Blumenbach: cf. Hegel's *Werke*, v. 285.

p. 242, § 177. Colours, i.e. painters' colours; cf. *Werke*, vii. 1. 314 (lecture-note). 'Painters are not such fools as to be Newtonians: they have red, yellow, and blue, and out of these they make their other colours.'

p. 245, § 181. For the genetic classification of judgements and syllogisms and the passage from the former to the latter compare especially Lotze's *Logic*, Book i. And for the comprehensive exhibition of the systematic process of judgement and inference see B. Bosanquet's *Logic, or the Morphology of Knowledge*. The passage from Hegel's *Werke*, v. 139, quoted at the head of that work is parallel to the sentence in p. 318, 'The interest, therefore,' etc.

p. 249, § 186. The letters I P U, of course, stand for Individual, Particular, and Universal.

p. 250, § 187. Fourth figure. This so-called Galenian figure was differentiated from the first figure by the separation of the five moods, which (after Arist. *An. pr.* i. 7. and ii. 1) Theophrastus and the later pupils, down at least to Boethius, had subjoined to the four recognized types of perfect syllogism. But its Galenian origin is more than doubtful.

p. 253, § 190. Cf. Mill's *Logic*, Bk. ii, ch. 3. 'In every syllogism considered as an argument to prove the conclusion there is a *petitio principii*.'

Hegel's Induction is that strictly so called or complete induction, the argument from the sum of actual experiences—that *per enumerationem simplicem*, and *διὰ πάντων*. Of course except by accident or by artificial arrangement such completeness is impossible *in rerum natura*.

p. 254, § 190. The 'philosophy of Nature' referred to here is probably that of Oken and the Schellingians; but later critics (e.g. Riehl,

Philosoph. Criticismus, iii. 120) have accused Hegel himself of even greater enormities in this department.

p. 255, § 192. *Elementarlehre*: Theory of the Elements, called by Hamilton (*Lectures on Logic*, i. 65) Stoicheiology as opposed to methodology. Cf. the Port Royal Logic. Kant's *Kritik* observes the same division of the subject.

p. 258, § 193. Anselm, *Proslogium*, c. 2. In the *Monologium* Anselm expounds the usual argument from conditioned to unconditioned (*Est igitur unum aliquid, quod solum maxime et summe omnium est*; *per quod est quidquid est bonum vel magnum, et omnino quidquid aliquid est. Monol.* c. 3). But in the *Proslogium* he seeks an argument *quod nullo ad se probandum quam se solo indigeret*—i.e. from the conception of (God as) the highest and greatest that can be (*aliquid quo nihil majus cogitari potest*) he infers its being (*sic ergo vere* EST *aliquid quo majus cogitari non potest, ut nec cogitari possit non esse*). The absolute would not be absolute if the idea of it did not *ipso facto* imply existence.

Gaunilo of Marmoutier in the *Liber pro insipiente* made the objection that the fact of such argument being needed showed that idea and reality were prima facie different. And in fact the argument of Anselm deals with an Absolute which is object rather than subject, thought rather than thinker; in human consciousness realized, but not essentially self-affirming—implicit (an=sich) only, as said on pp. 257, 259. And Anselm admits, c. 15: *Domine, non solum es, quo majus cogitari nequit, sed es quiddam majus quam cogitari potest* (transcending our thought).

p. 259, line 9. This sentence has been transposed in the translation. In the original it occurs after the quotation from the Latin on p. 258.

p. 260, § 194. Leibniz: for a brief account of the Monads see Caird's *Crit. Philosophy of I. Kant*, i. 86–95.

A monad is the simple substance or indivisible unity corresponding to a body. It is as simple what the world is as a multiplicity: it 'represents', i.e. concentrates into unity, the variety of phenomena: is the expression of the material in the immaterial, of the compound in the simple, of the extended outward in the inward. Its unity and its representative capacity go together (cf. Lotze, *Mikrokosmus*). It is the 'present which is full of the future and laden with the past' (ed. Erdm., p. 197); the point which is all-embracing, the totality of the universe. And yet there are monads—in the plural.

p. 260, § 194. Fichte, *Werke*, i. 430. 'Every thorough-going dogmatic philosopher is necessarily a fatalist.'

p. 263, § 195. Cf. *Encyclop.* § 463. 'This supreme inwardizing of ideation (Vorstellung) is the supreme self-divestment of intelligence, reducing itself to the mere being, the general space of mere names and meaningless words. The ego, which is this abstract being, is, because subjectivity, at the same time the power over the different names, the empty link which fixes in itself series of them and keeps them in fixed order.'

Contemporaneously with Hegel, Herbart turned psychology in the line of a 'statics and dynamics of the mind'. See (besides earlier suggestions) his *De Attentionis mensura causisque primariis* (1822) and his *Ueber die Möglichkeit und Nothwendigkeit, Mathematik auf Psychologie anzuwenden* (1822).

p. 265, § 198. *Civil* society: distinguished as the social and economic organization of the *bourgeoisie*, with their particularist-universal aims, from the true universal unity of *citoyens* in the state or ethico-political organism.

p. 268, § 204. Inner design: see Kant's *Kritik der Urtheilskraft*, § 62.

Aristotle, *De Anima*, ii. 4 ($415^{b}15$) φανερὸν δ' ὡς καὶ οὗ ἕνεκα ἡ ψυχὴ αἰτία; ii. 1 ζωὴν λέγομεν τὴν δι' αὑτοῦ τροφήν τε καὶ αὔξησιν καὶ φθίσιν.

p. 271, § 206. Neutral first water, cf. *Encyclop.* § 284, 'without independent individuality, without rigidity and intrinsic determination, a thorough-going equilibrium'. Cf. *Werke*, vii. 6. 168. 'Water is absolute neutrality, not like salt, an individualized neutrality; and hence it was at an early date called the mother of everything particular.' 'As the neutral it is the solvent of acids and alkalis.' Cf. Oken's *Lehrbuch der Naturphilosophie*, §§ 294 and 432.

p. 271, § 206. Conclude = beschließen: Resolve = entschließen. Cf. Chr. Sigwart, *Kleine Schriften*, ii. 115 ff.

p. 280, § 216. Aristotle, *De Anim. Generat.* i. ($726^{b}24$) ἡ χεὶρ ἄνευ ψυχικῆς δυνάμεως οὐκ ἔστι χεὶρ ἀλλὰ μόνον ὁμώνυμον.

Arist. *Metaph.* vii. 6 ($1045^{b}11$) οἱ δὲ (λέγουσι) σύνθεσιν ἢ σύνδεσμον ψυχῆς σώματι τὸ ζῆν.

p. 281, § 218. Sensibility, etc. This triplicity (as partly distinguished by Haller after Glisson) of the functions of organic life is largely worked out in Schelling, ii. 491.

p. 281, § 219. Cf. Schelling, ii. 540. As walking is a constantly prevented falling, so life is a constantly prevented extinction of the vital process.

p. 286, § 229. Spinoza (*Eth.* i. def. 1) defines *causa sui* as *id cujus essentia involvit existentiam*, and (in def. 3) defines *substantia* as *id quod in se est et per se concipitur*.

Schelling: e.g. *Darstellung meines Systems der Philosophie* (1801), (*Werke*, iv. 114): 'I call reason the absolute reason, or reason, in so far as it is thought as total indifference of subjective and objective.'

p. 287, § 230. 'Mammals distinguish themselves': unterscheiden, instead of scheiden: cf. *Werke*, ii. 181. 'The distinctive marks of animals, e.g., are taken from the claws and teeth: for in fact it is not merely cognition which by this means distinguishes one animal from another: but the animal thereby separates itself off: by these weapons it keeps itself to itself and separate from the universal.' Cf. *Werke*, vii. a. 651 ff. (*Encycl.* § 370) where reference is made to Cuvier, *Recherches sur les ossements fossiles des quadrupèdes* (1812), etc.

p. 287, § 230. Kant, *Kritik der Urtheilskraft*: Einleitung, § 9 (note),

(*Werke*, ed. Ros. iv. 39); see Caird's *Critical Philosophy of I. Kant*, Book i. ch. 5; also Hegel's *Werke*, ii. 3.

p. 288, § 231. An example of Wolf's pedantry is given in Hegel, *Werke*, v. 307, from Wolf's *Rudiments of Architecture*, Theorem viii. 'A window must be broad enough for two persons to recline comfortably in it, side by side. *Proof.* It is customary to recline with another person on the window to look about. But as the architect ought to satisfy the main views of the owner (§ 1) he must make the window broad enough for two persons to recline comfortably side by side.'

'Construction': cf. *Werke*, ii. 38. 'Instead of its own internal life and spontaneous movement, such a simple mode (as subject, object, cause, substance, etc.) has expression given to it by perception (here = sense-consciousness) on some superficial analogy: and this external and empty application of the formula is called "Construction". The procedure shares the qualities of all such formalism. How stupid-headed must be the man, who could not in a quarter of an hour master the theory of asthenic, sthenic, and indirectly asthenic diseases' (this is pointed at Schelling's *Werke*, iii. 236) 'and the three corresponding curative methods, and who, when, no long time since, such instruction was sufficient, could not in this short period be transformed from a mere practitioner into a "scientific" physician? The formalism of *Naturphilosophie* may teach e.g. that understanding is electricity, or that the animal is nitrogen, or even that it is *like* the South or the North, or that it represents it—as baldly as is here expressed or with greater elaboration in terminology. At such teachings the inexperienced may fall into a rapture of admiration, may reverence the profound genius it implies—may take delight in the sprightliness of language which instead of the abstract *concept* gives the more pleasing *perceptual* image, and may congratulate itself on feeling its soul akin to such splendid achievement. The trick of such a wisdom is as soon learnt as it is easy to practice; its repetition, when it grows familiar, becomes as intolerable as the repetition of juggling once detected. The instrument of this monotonous formalism is not harder to manipulate than a painter's palette with two colours on it, say red and green, the former to dye the surface if a historic piece, the latter if a landscape is asked for.'

Kant (*Werke*, iii. 36) in the 'Prolegomena to every future Metaphysic', § 7, says: 'We find, however, it is the peculiarity of mathematical science that it must first exhibit its concept in a percept, and do so *a priori*—hence in a pure percept. This observation with regard to the nature of mathematics gives a hint as to the first and supreme condition of its possibility: it must be based on some pure percept in which it can exhibit all its concepts *in concreto* and yet *a priori*, or, as it is called, *construe* them.'

The phrase, and the emphasis on the doctrine that 'perception must be taken as an auxiliary in mathematics', belong specially to the second edition of the *Kritik*, e.g. Pref. xii. To learn the properties of the isosceles triangle the mathematical student must 'produce [by "construction"] what he himself thought into it and exhibited *a priori* according to concepts'.

'Construction, in general', says Schelling (*Werke*, v. 252: cf. iv. 407), 'is the exhibition of the universal and particular in unity'—'absolute unity of the ideal and the real.' v. 225. Darstellung in intellektueller Anschauung ist philosophische Construktion.

p. 290, § 234. 'Recollection' = Erinnerung: i.e. the return from differentiation and externality to simplicity and inwardness: distinguished from Gedächtniß = memory (specially of words).

p. 292, § 236. Cf. Schelling, *Werke*, iv. 405. 'Every particular object is in its absoluteness the Idea; and accordingly the Idea is also the absolute object (Gegenstand) itself—as the absolutely ideal also the absolutely real.'

p. 292, § 236. Aristotle, *Metaphys*. xi. 9 (1074^b33) *αὑτὸν ἄρα νοεῖ* (*ὁ νοῦς = θεός*), *εἴπερ ἐστὶ τὸ κράτιστον, καὶ ἔστιν ἡ νόησις νοήσεως νόησις*. Cf. Arist. *Metaph*. xi. 7.

p. 294, § 239. 'Supposes a correlative' = ist für Eines. On Seyn-für-Eines cf. *Werke*, iii. 168. Das Ideëlle ist nothwendig für-Eines, aber es ist nicht für ein Anderes: das Eine für welches es ist, ist nur es selbst. . . . God is therefore for-self (to himself) in so far as he himself is that which is for him.

p. 296, § 244. The percipient idea (anschauende Idee), of course both object and subject of intuition, is opposed to the Idea (as logical) in the element of *Thought*: but still as *Idea* and not—to use Kant's phrase (*Kritik der r. Vern*. § 26)—as *natura materialiter spectata*.

what he himself thought into it and exhibited *a priori* according to concepts.

'Construction, in general', says Schelling (*Werke*, v. 252: cf. iv. 407), is the exhibition of the universal and particular in unity or absolute unity of the ideal and the real (v. 225: Darstellung in intellektueller Anschauung ist philosophische Construktion).

p. 200, § 234. 'Recollection' = Erinnerung: i.e. the return from differentiation and externality to simplicity and inwardness: distinguished from Gedächtnis = memory (specially of words).

p. 202, § 236. Cf. Schelling, *Werke*, iv. 405. 'Every particular object is in its absoluteness the Idea; and accordingly the Idea is also the absolute object (Gegenstand) itself—as the absolutely ideal also the absolutely real.'

p. 202, § 236. Aristotle, *Metaph.* xi. 9 (1074b 34) αὑτὸν ἄρα νοεῖ (ὁ νοῦς = θεός), εἴπερ ἐστὶ τὸ κράτιστον, καὶ ἔστιν ἡ νόησις νοήσεως νόησις. Cf. Arist. *Metaph.* xi. 7.

p. 204, § 240. 'Supposes a correlative' = ist für Eines. Du Seiende ist cf. *Werke*, iii. 168: Das Seiende ist aufgehoben für-Eines, aber es ist nicht für ein Anderes: das Eine ist nur für es selbst . . . God is therefore for-self (to himself) in so far as he himself is that which is for him.

p. 206, § 244. The percipient Idea (anschauende Idee), of course both object and subject of intuition, is opposed to the Idea (as logical) in the element of *Thought*; but still as *Idea* and not—to use Kant's phrase (*Kritik der r. Vern.* § 76)—as *natura materialiter spectata*.

INDEX